PARTISAN CANONS

PARTISAN CANONS

EDITED BY ANNA BRZYSKI

Duke University Press
Durham and London
2007

Printed in the United States of America on
acid-free paper ∞ Designed by Amy Ruth Buchanan
Typeset in Bembo by Tseng Information Systems, Inc.

Library of Congress Cataloging-in-Publication Data
Partisan canons / edited by Anna Brzyski.
p. cm.
Includes bibliographical references and index.
ISBN-13: 978-0-8223-4085-0 (cloth : alk. paper)
ISBN-13: 978-0-8223-4106-2 (pbk. : alk. paper)
1. Canon (Art). 2. Art—Historiography.
I. Brzyski, Anna, 1969–
N72.5.P37 2007
701'.18—dc22 2007005226

CONTENTS

Introduction: Canons and Art History

ANNA BRZYSKI

Since the 1980s the canon has been the subject of ongoing discussions and debates, which have generally relied on a particularly narrow and referential understanding of what the canon is and how it functions. The canon, defined as a body of works traditionally considered to be the most significant and therefore the most worthy of study, has been consistently identified, for better or for worse, by critics and defenders alike as an expression of a universalized or universal standard of quality. Even when the possibility of multiple canons specific to a subfield, culture, or genre has been acknowledged, the idea persists that some of those structures, in particular the Western canon, occupy a uniquely privileged position, regulating, in effect, the entire system of cultural appraisal.

Up to this point, the majority of critiques of the canonical paradigm have relied on the concept of canonicity to describe general dynamics of privilege and status negotiation in a particular cultural field, such as literature or art.[1] Those critiques have provided important theoretical frameworks for understanding how the canon affects the production of meaning as well as the economic and symbolic values assigned to cultural objects. Through them we have learned much about the canon's function as a mechanism of oppression, a guardian of privilege, a vehicle of exclusion, and a structure for class, gender, and racial interests. Many of these critiques have also explored the canon's relationship to capitalism as an economic, social, and cultural system, and in particular to the function of art markets, by aligning the canon's function and logic with the concept of commodity fetishism and the mechanisms of cultural hegemony.[2]

The critiques of canonicity have become as commonplace in art history as they are in other disciplines.[3] In fact the literature has become so abundant that it is hardly an outrageous assertion to argue that there is near consensus on key issues. It is more than curious, therefore, that despite the extensive nature of the critiques of canonicity and their wide acceptance, mainstream art history continues to embrace canonical logic in its day to day operations, research, presentation of scholarship, pedagogy, and curatorial practice. This paradox exists in part because scholars no longer consider the canon to be the obstacle it once was perceived to be. After all, the argument goes, the canon no longer appears to impose serious limits on our practice. We are free to pursue diverse, extra-canonical subject areas, and we encourage our students to do likewise. Not only is there no penalty for shunning the canon, often there is a premium attached to doing so. Moreover, what used to be considered noncanonical art is now routinely incorporated into survey courses and the job prospects for candidates working on non-Western subjects have never been better. Given both the ubiquity of the canonical works and authors and the equally ubiquitous disavowals of the canon's prestige, it is not surprising that an important art historian such as Hal Foster would conclude in a recent article, "For better or worse, all my figures are men and all my texts are canonical, but the men do not look so triumphant in retrospect and today the canon appears less a barricade to storm than a ruin to pick through."[4]

It may be true that the idea of the canon has been tarnished and no longer commands the authority it once held, but the announcement of the canon's demise seems premature. No matter what we profess, as teachers, curators, and researchers we make qualitative distinctions, constantly identifying some works and artists as more significant than others. We may no longer regard the canon as the ultimate arbiter of cultural value, but we continue to embrace its logic. In most universities and colleges, survey courses still consist mainly of great masters, although the word "genius" has been banned from our lexicon. While it would seem that many art historians would like to distance themselves from the survey textbook's litany of canonical artists, those "greats" still receive the greatest bulk of scholarly interest, as any survey of recent art historic bibliography will readily demonstrate. Likewise, museums clearly understand the economic advantages of blockbuster exhibitions drawing on the canonical standards. Although they certainly embark on noncanonical projects, they also provide us with a steady diet of Impressionist and Post-Impressionist shows because they know what will garner most attention and, in the end, attract the largest crowds.

Given the persistence of the canon in art historical and museological practice, the problem for those who seek to unhinge its primacy may no longer be a question of analyzing how the canon expresses power in social relationships across generically conceived fields of "art" and "culture," but rather how it does so in specific situations and under particular conditions. To that end and in their various ways, the contributors to this volume are concerned with what can be called the mechanics of the canonical system: how and where canons are formed, by whom, and why, how they function under particular circumstances, how they are maintained, and why they may undergo change. Until now, such questions have been largely ignored by general critiques of canonicity, in part because scholars have tended to accept the canon as an unproblematic given and describe it in exclusively negative terms.

Does, however, the definition of the canon as "a body of literary works traditionally regarded as the most important, significant, and worthy of study"[5] exhaust the meanings of the canon as a conceptual structure? This anthology is based on the thesis that the rhetorical insistence on the singularity of the canon, an insistence that can be found in equal measure in critiques and defenses of the canon, obscures a structural and functional condition that not only allows for, but actually requires multiplicity. To a large extent, the confusion results from a failure to distinguish between the structure and its contents, a distinction that is key to understanding the functional persistence of canonical structures. The case studies in this anthology present compelling evidence for the existence of multiple, historically situated canonical formations, that is, of different canons, produced at different times and in different geographic locations by individuals, groups, and institutions pursuing at times very different agendas. On the level of function, those canonical formations are discursive structures that organize information within a particular field according to a hierarchic order, which engenders cultural meanings, confers and withholds value, and ultimately participates in production of knowledge. Each subdivision of the cultural field creates the potential for formation of a new canon. Every subfield, in so far as it relates to a specific culture, period, and/or genre, requires its own organization and hierarchy in order to convert information into usable knowledge and create a historic understanding of a particular tradition. Consequently, if we assume that the canon of art creates an understanding of art as a historic continuum, we must also assume that the canon of Chinese art does the same work for the field of Chinese art history, with the canon of Polish nineteenth-century painting doing the same for the field of Polish art history, the canon of Impressionism doing the same for the field of French art history, and so forth. Our ignorance of the specific content of any one of these parallel canonical formations (our inability to identify the most important works within the particular canonical set) should not prevent us from accepting in principle that such canons exist and that someone (an expert somewhere) can, in fact, identify their contents.

The production of local canons specific to a particular subfield does not involve the importation of the canon's contents, but rather redeployment of the canon's structural framework and logic. From this functional perspective, canonical formations are initially empty structures; that is, they are empty before being put to a specific application. As such, they are available to agents who may occupy entirely opposed positions: they may be used by those who represent established power structures and are invested in maintaining the status quo, but they are also available to those who occupy oppositional or fringe positions and seek to challenge the established hierarchy, presumably for their own advantage or the advantage of whatever agenda they seek to promote. When two or more ideologically opposed agents claim ownership of the same cultural territory, different, contending interpretations of historic tradition and therefore different, contending canons may arise. The fascinating case of the Taiwanese and mainland Chinese art canons explored by Jane Ju in the anthology is a vivid example of such a situation. In other cases, a canon can become a point of dispute when at stake is a question of who gets to define the cultural identity of a particular group. This phenomenon is explored in Julie McGee's essay, which deals with the ongoing struggle over who has the right to produce the art history of South Africa and of what this history should consist.

In those instances when a field of study is defined by those disenfranchised within the dominant tradition, formation of a canon may become an effective strategy of resistance and empowerment. Henry Louis Gates Jr. recognized this reality when he observed about the *Norton Anthology of African American Literature*, "Once our anthology is published, no one will ever again be able to use unavailability of black texts as an excuse not to teach our literature. A well marked anthology functions in the academy to create a tradition, as well as define and preserve it."[6] He also explicitly addressed the issue of the canon, noting its necessary contingency at the site of production. "I am not unaware of the politics and ironies of canon formation," he wrote. "The canon that we define will be 'our' canon, one possible set of selections among several possible sets of selections." Yet he also concluded, "Our task will be to bring together the 'essential' texts of the canon, the 'crucial central authors,' those whom we feel to be indispensable to an understanding of a shape, and shaping, of the tradition. A canon is often represented as the 'essence' of the tradition, indeed, as the marrow of tradition: the connection between the texts of the canon is meant to reveal the tradition's inherent, or veiled, logic, its internal rationale."[7]

Gates's clear recognition of the contingency of "his" canon, and his insistence, which he explicitly acknowledges as a political act, that there is a unique African American literary tradition and that, therefore, there must be a canon of African American literature, which defines that tradition for internal and external consumption, illustrates both the potentially subversive power of the canon and its ubiquity. As soon as a tradition is postulated, or to put it in a different way, as soon as we engage in the production of history of a particular cultural phenomenon, we create a potential for the canon. The canon is simply a function of thinking in terms of traditions and historic narratives.

Since its inception in the nineteenth century as a university-based discipline, art history has been structurally committed to the idea of tradition. In fact, it is the only fully fledged academic discipline within the humanities dedicated exclusively to the history of a particular cultural form. Although the adjacent fields of musicology and literary studies certainly produce a steady stream of studies dealing with the history of music and literature, those studies have never coalesced into autonomous "historic" fields. Unlike art history, which early on claimed autonomy, they occupy positions closely adjacent to criticism and practice. In art history, the existence of field specific canons does not necessarily undermine the function of the canon as such. If anything, it entrenches and extends the logic of the canonic system. The canon of Chinese art may coexist with the canon of Impressionism and the canon of Polish nineteenth-century painting, but there can only be one of each. Each canon is predicated on a claim to absolute authority. In each case, the canon identifies those works that define a particular tradition (in a particular way) and that are therefore considered to be the most significant and worthy of study by those embracing that particular conception of the tradition.

The entire system, however, has a fixed point of reference. When the canon appears unaccompanied by a specific modifier (as in the canon of "Chinese" art) it actually refers to the Western cultural tradition. That tradition initially created the practices upon which all canonical distinctions are based and has been exporting and extending them across new territories. In the eighteenth century, Europe defined fine art as the pinnacle of hierarchy that ranked cultural artifacts on a developmental scale from the barbaric to the civilized. Its own cultural tradition, which not only produced fine art, but continued to refine it, was automatically distinguished from other cultural traditions that either failed to produce a similar artistic heritage or that stopped developing, according to the European perspective, at a particular stage. As a result, the material culture of the West, enshrined by the designation "art," became the domain of art history, while the material culture of the rest of the world, classed under the rubric "artifact," was relegated to the domain of ethnography and later anthropology, from which it did not emerge until well into the twentieth century.

Although non-Western art has been since then incorporated into the domain of art history, we are still experiencing the consequences of the initial segregation. The Western art canon continues to function as an implicit measure of all things, by defining the mainstream of the category "art." It identifies the most significant works, locates the most important areas of study for art history as a unified field of study, and, in effect, engenders a hierarchy among the various subfields. Those subfields belonging to the Western cultural sphere and sharing canonical members in common with the dominant canon (for instance, the Impressionist canon) gain comparative advantage over those that do not (the Polish art canon). Those located outside the West (the Chinese art canon, for instance) have a more ambivalent position. In principle, they are different but equal; in reality and in practice they are treated by us as less interesting and less significant than our own cultural tradition and our own canon. Because this attitude exceeds national boundaries, the term nationalism does seem appropriate here. At the same time, its scope suggests the existence of a broader but analogous category, not necessarily limited to the West, namely of culturalism.

Numerous questions arise when we expand the definition and terrain of canonicity. For example, is it possible for a canonical ranking to emerge without active agency or for an agent (be it collective or individual) not to have an agenda or a specific purpose when creating a particular hierarchy? Is it possible for a listing, which identifies the most significant artists and works of art, to be neutral in character, or do we have to assume that any such ordering entails evaluation and therefore necessarily embodies and promotes particular political, cultural, or aesthetic values and beliefs? And, if, in fact, all canonical rankings are bound to be partisan, how should we deal with that reality? Is it productive to disavow the canon as an inherently oppressive structure when we daily embrace its logic and participate in its production and maintenance? These questions point to an overarching question that art historians have hardly begun to consider: Can we practice traditional art history without canonical formations and therefore without value judgments and qualitative distinctions? If not, what options are open to us as we contemplate art practice in an increasingly heterogeneous and decentered field of knowledge and discourse?

We can not begin addressing these questions unless we consider the function of canons, in particular their role in the definition of what counts as art. That definition, predicated on a historic understanding of art, identifies an artwork as a privileged text, ontologically distinct from and by implication superior to all other cultural artifacts, meaningful on its own terms and as part of a great historic unfolding.[8] If we reconsider canons from the functional perspective—as conceptual structures implicated in the production of qualitative distinctions and therefore in the definition of art as a historic tradition—then we must conclude that canons are not only still in evidence but are being continually produced and reinforced through our daily practice. I would like to propose that they can not be avoided in the context of conventional or classical art history, which since its inception has been engaged in the project of evaluation.[9]

The canon creates a reciprocal and symbiotic relationship between significance and scholarship. The significance of the canonical work makes it irresistible as a subject of discourse, and the production of discourse confirms the work's canonical status. Since our understanding of art is predicated on the idea of historic tradition, any effort to distinguish between major and minor figures and works within an implicit or explicit account of historic development has to invoke, reproduce, or produce a canon. That is why the narratives of classical art history may present themselves as value neutral, but they are always and necessarily implicated on a metaphoric level in transactions that determine perception and ultimately evaluation.[10]

Collectively, the evidence presented here demonstrates that the language of the canon obscures the historic existence of multiple, temporally and geographically situated canonical formations. The overlaps and continuities, as well as the persistence of the core canon, as discussed by James Elkins, Robert Jensen, and James Cutting, which can be linked to a shared historic consciousness of the Western artistic tradition and to specific historic origins of art history as a discipline, are in many instances as revealing as the discontinuities, disagreements, and local variations explored by other contributors, in particular Paul Duro, Linda Stone-Ferrier, and Jane Ju. The gender, racial, and ethnic biases inscribed within and naturalized by canonical structures, examined by Marcia Brennan, Despina Stratigakos, and Julie McGee, are no less important from this perspective. Similarly significant, the issue of artists' agency—their participation in the production of canons and their strategic usage of canonical concepts for self-validation—is explored in Duro's essay, my own, and that of Monica Kjellman-Chapin.

In rare instances, the origins of a particular canonical formation are quite apparent and can be traced to a single text, a well-defined body of texts, or an event, such as an exhibition. Several essays in the anthology focus on such precise foundational moments. Jenny Anger discusses one of the most influential books in the early history and historiography of European modernism, Julius Meier-Graefe's *Entwickelungsgeschichte der modernen Kunst*, and Barbara Jaffee examines an equally significant work for American art history, Helen Gardner's *Art through the Ages*. Most often, however, a visible point of origin can not be easily found, or, I would argue, it has not been looked for, and perhaps it is not as significant as the process of the canon's development and modification.

The case studies also reveal a diversity of factors affecting the production and maintenance of canons. In many instances canonical hierarchies emerge as a result of market forces (Jensen, Monica Kjellman-Chapin, Brzyski, Cutting), but they are just as frequently implicated in the discourses of nationalism (Ju, McGee, Brzyski), gender (Anger, Stratigakos, Brennan, Jaffee), and race (Jaffee, McGee), in negotiations of power positions among artists within a particular art world (Stratigakos, Brzyski, Jensen, Duro), and in dynamics of art history as an academic discipline (Elkins, Anger, Brennan, Jaffee, Stone-Ferrier). In most cases, production of specific canons occurs within a complex matrix of social, political, cultural, institutional, and discursive transactions that prevent unambiguous identification of a single factor as the sole or even the most important determinant. Similarly, while some canons emerge as a result of diffuse collective endeavors, others have clearly identifiable authorship. Yet all canons are created and revised under particular historic circumstances, and they are shaped by conditions present on a local or a regional level. They are affected by external events and pressures, and are formulated in response to deeply held yet seldom articulated beliefs grounded in particular value systems. They are market driven, but they extend beyond the economic sphere to encompass markets of ideas. Finally, they may be affected by such pragmatic considerations as access to works, availability of reproductions, publishing interests and exigencies, physical and linguistic availability of documents and research materials, and so forth.

If we acknowledge historicity and location of particular canons are we inevitably heading for relativism? Can art history as currently conceived survive such interrogation? In this context, and throughout this book, "value" is used neither as a conceptual abstraction nor as a term based exclusively on an analysis of purely economic relations. It indicates a negotiated perception of significance related to individual or collective use (status, exchange potential, or utility), as well as economic, ideological, emotional, or discursive location of particular phenomena. Value, or rather perception of value, is, therefore, affected by external conditions, such as the character of a given market, physical location, or cultural context, as well as subjective, irrational, and non-optimal factors, such as ideological and emotional investments, imperfect information, different levels of skill, and other nonlinear and chaotic features affecting individual and institutional behavior.[11]

Steven Connor has argued that we approach the world, in all its varied aspects, from an inherently evaluating perspective—always identifying what is better and what is worse, and consequently what has value for us (individually and collectively) and what does not. Our evaluative activity extends from the most basic considerations of food and shelter to complex social and cultural interactions. Within art history, the inscription of particular artists, phenomena, and works into art discourse constitutes such an evaluative activity. The act of naming and therefore of rendering visible particular individuals and works as key to particular historic moments confers value by recognizing significance. Conversely, the failure to identify an artist or an entire context of art production as worthy of attention has significant implications for their perception and (e)valuation.

Connor argues that the "imperative to value," our inherently evaluative approach, extends to the values themselves. Once made, an evaluation becomes subject to appraisal.[12] This constant reassessment, which both drives and is a function of historic processes, gives all values and value judgments their contingency. The reflexive character of the "imperative to value" dictates that all value systems—and therefore all canons, since all canons function as evaluative systems—must be subject to scrutiny and evaluation. It does not mean, however, that all canons, understood as specific historic phenomena, carry equal weight. Specific historic and cultural conditions have allowed some canons, for instance the canon of Western art, to occupy a dominant position vis-à-vis other canonical formations.

Canons emerge when value judgments made by a particular individual or a group begin to affect to a significant degree the general perception of the historic significance of particular works or artists within a particular field. How does this consensus develop? We tend to assume that canonical works set up evaluative criteria that determine quality. While that certainly has been one of their functions, they have been also used, and perhaps with greater consequences, to police the borders of conceptual categories. Those borders are determined by actual exposure, not just theoretical definition. In art history that exposure is visual as well as verbal; we come to understand what art is (and by extension what Chinese or Polish art is), how it functions, and what it means by being exposed repeatedly and often peripherally to images of normative examples, that is, type members that define a particular conceptual category. We encounter those normative examples, the canonical works of art, in popular culture, through education, and in professional practice. Since they are the most often cited and reproduced, our familiarity with them is repeatedly reinforced by verbal assertions of their superior significance and by visual markers.[13]

It is clear that this acculturation into the canonical system has been an integral part of education in the West, and that it has encompassed not just the members of the art world, but also the general public. We may not know exactly why particular works are canonical, but we have been assured repeatedly through various forms of didactic and visual exposure that they *are*. As James Cutting explains in his essay, repeated exposure to particular stimuli, such as images, is not without consequence. It shapes our preferences and ultimately affects our perception of their significance. Since this phenomenon, called *mere exposure*, affects all members of a society exposed to particular images—including art historians and artists—it suggests that the stability of the canon may need more complex explanations than the ones we tend to offer and which fall back either on the assertion of the inherent superiority of the canonical works or on the persistence of particular power structures and interests.

Hal Foster's earlier cited statement concerning the canon's demise is particularly relevant in this context because it occurs in an essay that addresses a key concept in the discussion of cultural exposure, namely the archive.[14] For Foster, citing Foucault, the archive is "'the system that governs the appearance of statements,' that structures the particular expressions of a particular period. In this sense an archive is neither affirmative nor critical per se; it simply supplies the terms of discourse."[15] Contrary to Foster's interpretation, however, Foucault's original definition of the archive establishes an unambiguous, if metaphorically veiled, link between the function of the archive and the processes of preservation, ranking, and evaluation. In *The Archaeology of Knowledge*, Foucault writes,

> The archive is first the law of what can be said, the system that governs the appearance of statements as unique events. But the archive is also

> that which determines that all things said do not accumulate endlessly in an amorphous mass, nor that they inscribe in an unbroken linearity, nor do they disappear at the mercy of chance external accidents; but they are grouped together in distinct figures, composed together in accordance with multiple relations, maintained or blurred in accordance with specific regularities; that which determines that they do not withdraw at the same pace in time, but shine, as it were, like stars, some that seem close to us shining brightly from a far off, while others that are in fact close to us are already growing pale.[16]

Although Foucault does not invoke the canon, he does suggest that archives of disciplinary knowledge produce and maintain hierarchies, since they preserve what is already deemed valuable and worthy of preservation (and therefore study). Within that project, the principle of organization and classification that enables retrieval is of paramount importance. For Foucault, the concept of the archive is as antithetical to random accumulation, which results in an "amorphous" and, therefore, unintelligible mass, as it is to a strictly temporal, "linear" arrangement that gives all statements equal weight. The archive produces knowledge by inscribing its contents within the bounds of a hierarchical taxonomy that brings statements together into meaningful categories, relates those categories to one another within an overarching system, and, most significantly for us, determines the relative visibility (and hierarchy) of statements according to "specific regularities," or criteria of value.[17] Although, at first glance, the star metaphor seems to suggest that the contents of the archive vary with respect to inherent value—that some statements simply are "brighter" than others—Foucault does not, in fact, make that claim. Rather, he specifies that it is the archive itself that ultimately "determines" relative "visibility" by preventing its contents from "withdraw[ing] at the same pace in time." In other words, far from being "neither affirmative nor critical," the archive ensures that certain statements remain visible—irrespective of their distance from the present—while others rapidly disappear from view.

Foucault's analysis has profound implications for art history as it enters the digital age. Since its inception as discursive practice, our discipline has relied on visual archives aspiring to what Donald Preziosi has termed a panoptic gaze over their subject.[18] In the nineteenth century, the rapid development of reproduction technologies along with the commercial availability of standalone engraved reproductions, later of photographic ones, and of illustrated art books enabled the creation and rapid multiplication of reference collections at various sites of production of cultural knowledge. Preziosi's argument focuses on the university-based image archive and its end users, art historians. However, it is worth noting that by the 1890s visual reference collections of varying sizes were being formed throughout Europe and America and that they were not exclusive to the newly professionalized discipline of art history. Whether owned by private individuals or located in public places, such as libraries, schools, art academies, or museums, they functioned to disseminate and consolidate knowledge and played a key role in shaping the perception of value and visual recognition of canonical works among those able to enjoy access to "proper" education (fig. I.1).

The present day university image collections and pedagogic practices, in particular survey courses, which still define a shared core knowledge—information both visual and textual that defines knowledge necessary for membership in a particular discipline—are not just related to art history's panoptic project, but also to general expectations concerning cultural literacy that go back to those nineteenth-century roots.[19] Not surprisingly, those expectations vary radically from place to place. For example, one would be hard pressed to find any images of Polish art in an average university image collection in the United States, but in Poland they form the core holdings of art history programs at universities and art schools. The pedagogical visual archives may aspire philosophically to a panoptic condition, but in reality they respond to local conditions and demands. While in the West the archives all tend to cover the core of the Western art canon, outside its limited scope the holdings reflect local interests, needs, and expectations. Moreover, their scope and depth is often mitigated by pragmatic and budgetary considerations—the costs of image production, manpower, housing, and so forth—and availability of good quality reproductions from which slides or digital images can be made.

It is worth pausing for a moment at the last factor, which so far has not registered in discussions of the archive, the canon, or art history. In the United States as elsewhere, the images we use in teaching are most often made from published reproductions. What gets published and what gets illustrated in those publications reflect not only the state of research, but also prior exposure of the books' authors to particular images, ownership and location of particular works, and the cost of reproduction, as well as the perception of value and relevance of particular objects by the artists, the academic community, the publishers, and the public. As teachers, we routinely order new images when teaching specialized courses. What happens, however, when we lack an image to illustrate a particular point? Most often we simply substitute or go in another direction. We may order the missing image later, but what

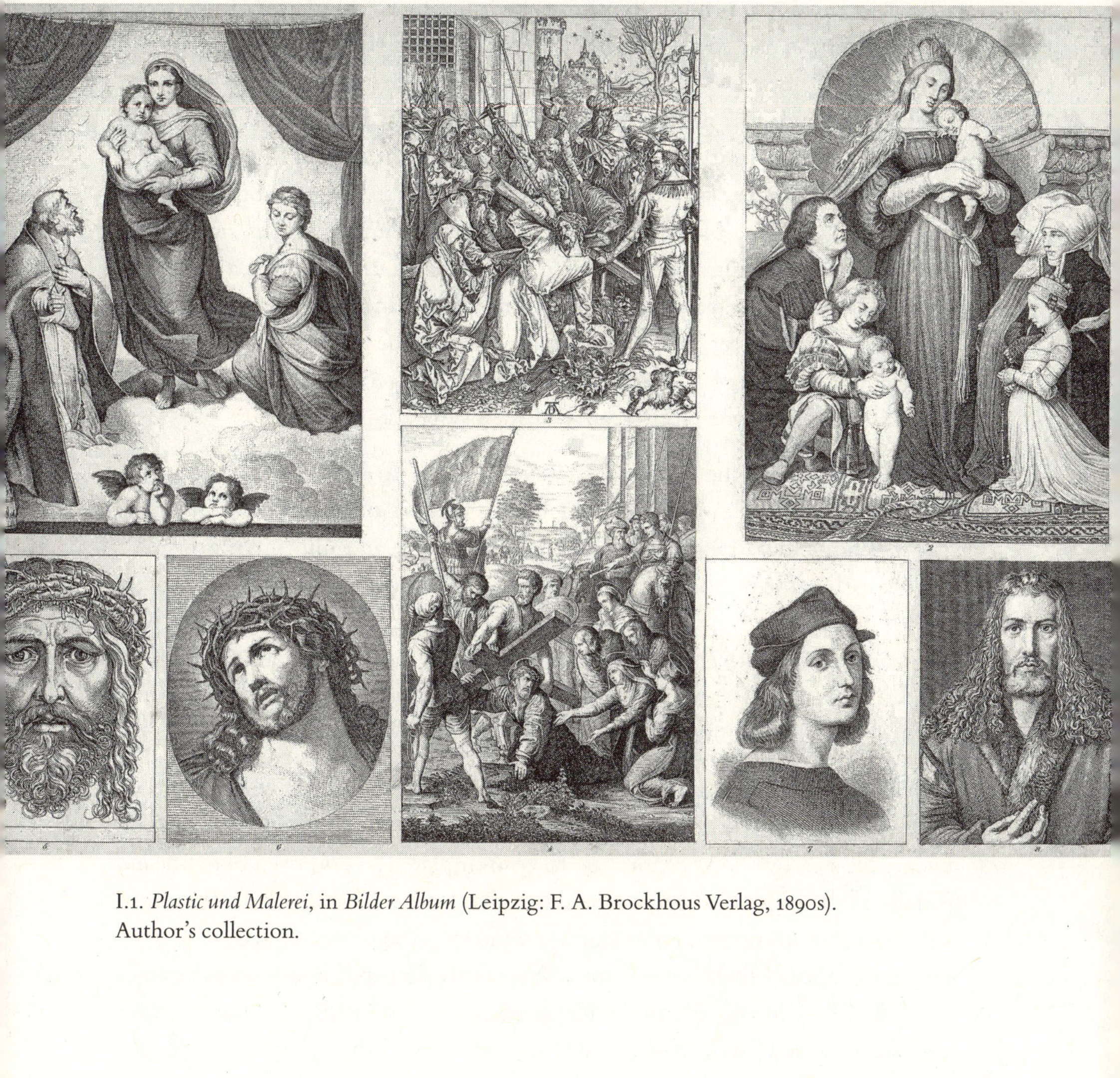

I.1. *Plastic und Malerei*, in *Bilder Album* (Leipzig: F. A. Brockhous Verlag, 1890s). Author's collection.

if a reproduction can not be found or perhaps does not yet exist? This may not be a problem encountered by those teaching in the mainstream fields of art history, but it is one often facing those working in so-called peripheral areas. The missing reproductions limit the functional boundaries of what gets discussed in the classroom and what does not, what the students are exposed to and what they are not, what constitutes "necessary knowledge" and what does not, and what future artists see as part of their tradition and what they do not. Since our students are our future colleagues and artists, the unintended consequences of the lack of mere exposure are worth considering. It is, after all, not just an issue of seeing but of perceiving something—as significant, innovative, important, great, valuable, and so forth; it is not just a matter of reproduction, but of (re)production of knowledge and production of value.

Will we fare better in the digital age? Discussing digital libraries, rather than image archives of the near future, Robert Nelson noted in 1997 both the great potential and the likely reality of such systems.

> Conceptually, the wired library would seem to be the metaphoric rhizome that Gilles Deleuze and Felix Guattari once predicted, a space without hierarchy or state control, spreading and multiplying organically like the rhizome and creating diverse chains of relationships, unfettered by externally imposed order or structure. Indeed, the terms Web and Internet are rhizomic metaphors. But human agency is not likely to disappear. Someone will still write the data programs and organize the modes of reference.[20]

Nelson's pragmatic assessment, made almost ten years ago, when the digital technology was still very much in its infancy, seems prophetic today as events outside our control force us to contemplate the potential benefits and pitfalls of the digital image archives. In 2003, Kodak Corporation announced that owing to diminishing demand it would stop the production of slide projectors in 2004.[21] In January 2006, Nikon revealed that it would no longer produce film cameras for the consumer market. The reality is that whether we like it or not, slides are on the way out. Given the current rate of improvements in digital technology it is inevitable that art history will make the transition from the analogue to the digital mode in the near future. In many places, that transition is already well under way.

One of the most significant developments within the digital revolution has been the launch in the fall of 2004 of the ARTstor database funded and operated by a subsidiary of the Andrew W. Mellon Foundation. By its projected completion in 2006, ARTstor expected to include over 500,000 images, surpassing the vast majority of existing slide collections and all current resident digital collections. At the core of the ARTstor, the database's administrators have identified a "survey collection" of 4,000 images. According to the database website, this collection of works

> has been defined on the basis of an "overlap concordance" based on 13 standard [U.S.] art history survey texts, some consulted in multiple editions. It is intended to include at least one image of every art object or monument reproduced in at least two of these standard survey texts. It thus represents an experiment in defining empirically a "consensus collection" supporting widespread teaching needs, but one that does not yoke the teacher or student to any one particular text, pedagogical approach, or "canon."[22]

Let us pause for a moment to consider whether or not the "consensus collection" nested within the ARTstor archive functions in effect, if not by intention, as a canon?

The inevitability of the digital shift makes it likely that despite considerable cost, ARTstor will emerge in the near future as the discipline's standard. The sheer size of the database, the quality of the reproduced images, the built-in flexibility, and the ability to form collaborations with major institutions and image providers, combined with nonprofit status and protection against copyright infringement virtually guarantees that ARTstor will become our shared superarchive. It is also inevitable, despite claims to the contrary, that the survey collection nestled within the database, yet spotlighted by its separation and manageable size, will in effect function as the discipline's supercanon. Moreover, if ARTstor's vision comes to pass, this "consensus"-based supercanon will have an unprecedented impact on the perception of art and art's history in the United States, and perhaps globally, for years to come.[23] Ironically, if ARTstor achieves the market penetration it aspires to, we may find ourselves living in a world of an unprecedented global standardization of knowledge—in a world where the canon will have for the first time a concrete referential reality that, one could argue, it never quite had before.

No doubt ARTstor's core survey collection will be modified over time. It may become much more inclusive and varied, but as long as it is maintained as a separate and specifically labeled entity, it will determine which "stars" shine brightest in the vast reaches of the archival universe. True to the traditional function of archives, the entire collection of 500,000 images will not contain all extant and available images, but only those judged worthy of inclusion. Though enormous, the collection is in fact quite limited in scope when one considers the world's total production of art, architecture, design, and artifacts. Its content will be determined by the availability of reproductions, the stated interests and needs of the primary subscribers-consumers, the location of the main institutional collaborators, and the knowledge and interests of the human agents controlling the archive's content and its organization. Assuming that the cultural logic of globalism will apply here as it does elsewhere, the archive will inevitably reflect by virtue of its location and affiliation *our*, that is, Western, interests and perceptions, and perhaps even more narrowly those that are Anglo-American. It is very likely that this will be especially true with regard to art historically peripheral and non-Western subject areas.

ARTstor is not the only image database, but it is currently the largest and best funded such project. It is also most closely affiliated with the power centers of the contemporary art world and art history. The conclusions we can draw at this point concerning the long-term impact of ARTstor and other image databases on art history are necessarily provisional owing to the fast pace of change, but they do indicate certain trends. The exponential increase in the size of our archival universe, made possible by new, ever improving technologies, will increase the need for efficient road maps—search engines, subject and category indices, separate image collections, and so forth—that will allow us to navigate and ultimately to order the chaos of visual information into usable art historic knowledge. The information and image databases incorporate, as a matter of course, such structures into their architecture. We rarely pause to consider the assumptions behind these navigational aids, which determine designation of key words, categories, browsable subject areas, or collections. Our perception of their impact on our ability to find something is most often vague, if it registers at all. As the size of the archive increases, it is likely that currently available technologies that allow for automatic identification of user preferences and that give search engines the ability to quickly and efficiently point users in the "right direction" will play an increasing role. But such custom tailored encounters, whether externally imposed or self-fashioned through users' own identification of their preferences, are not without consequences. They narrow the scope of encounters, tend to reproduce knowledge, as suggested by Allison Pearlman, maintain parochialism, and reinforce cultural myopia.[24]

In the digital age, value is produced by ordering vast amounts of data into usable information. The digital age canon is a ghost of the digital archive—the shared core of knowledge deemed essential for all "properly educated" art historians, artists, and other members of the art public. It still determines valuation, but it does so from the wings rather than the main stage. It is a product of ongoing negotiation between pragmatic need, traditions, majority perceptions, and perception shifts. Its existence as an organizing structure is neither "good" nor "bad" in and of itself, though certainly it can be seen as either depending on one's assumptions and position. I have no doubt that it will be welcomed by instructors teaching survey courses, who have to contend with massive teaching loads, hundreds of students, and a lack of resources. I also have no doubt that it will be criticized by those of us who see it as a reflection of a particular, limited, and limiting perception of art's history. That the survey collection is an incarnation of the canon—a new form of the old structure—is equally apparent.

I am very skeptical of claims that assume that it is possible to practice art history without producing or relying on canons of historic significance. Those canons emerge as soon as we identify particular "key works" and "turning points." Assuming that art history in its various operations can not avoid evaluation and therefore escape the logic of the canon, what are the options open to us? In *Metaphors We Live By*, George Lakoff and Mark Johnson have argued that our cognitive systems are structured through systems of conceptual metaphors that are built into our language on the most basic level.[25] Experimental studies conducted since the publication of their book in 1980 have established that we rely on cross-domain references to understand complex concepts and to overcome conceptual dissonance. We use the familiar ideas to establish understanding of the more abstract and unfamiliar ones. These metaphorical mappings are culturally specific and highlight certain features of a concept while downplaying and hiding others.[26] Lakoff and Johnson have argued that by developing new metaphors, which focus on different aspects of given phenomena, we can fundamentally change our perception and understanding. Since understanding shapes our attitudes and guides our actions, by developing and adopting new metaphors we can gain new insights that may lead us to modifying our approaches and ultimately to produce very different outcomes from the ones we have been getting under the old metaphoric regime.[27]

Canonical formations are key components of the metaphoric regime of classical art history. The classical paradigm of art history, which has been in place since art history's emergence as a distinct form of art discourse, is based on a set of four interrelated assumptions. First, the concept of art is not synonymous with the entire spectrum of production that potentially can be or is identified as art at any historic moment. Second, art is by definition a historic phenomenon, a cultural tradition, and the history of that tradition can be studied, interpreted, and ultimately conveyed through art historic statements (textual, verbal, and/or visual). Third, art history does not deal with the entire spectrum of art practice but only with *its historically significant* aspects. Fourth, and finally, art's history is not affected by art historic discourse. Art's history is, in other words, external and independent of art historic commentary. It is therefore empirically available for art historic narration, analysis, and interpretation. I would further suggest that even if epistemological validity of art historic interpretation is questioned within the logic of the classical paradigm, the autonomy of art history as a discourse is never the subject of doubt and neither is the a priori assumption of the historic significance of the evidence under investigation.[28]

The canons of significant works and artists—those works and artists identified as "great" under the old definition, and as necessary knowledge under the new—allow classical art history to chart art's history as a coherent and meaningful tradition, a narrative sequence of key works, turning points, responses, resistances, and achievements that together form the history of art. Within the narrative logic of the classical paradigm, the works that either contribute to or exemplify the general or the local developments in art's history (and therefore can be located within the narrative structure) are granted historic significance; those that do not are marginalized or never included in the account.[29] Classical art history is therefore narrative not just in its form and format, but also in its fundamental assumptions. It is structured by an understanding (metaphoric in character) of history as a narrative. Art's history is not just conveyed in a narrative form; it *is* a narrative. Because the classical paradigm of art history is currently dominant, the metaphoric character of its conception of art's history is not readily apparent. However, if we assume that classical art history is one of many possible ways of practicing art history, there is nothing to prevent us from considering the production of art historic discourse under an alternative metaphoric regime.

What would happen if we changed our point of reference, replacing the metaphor *art's history is a narrative* with the metaphor *art's history is a synchronic and diachronic mapping system*? [30] One could immediately raise an objection that by doing so one is simply substituting one arbitrary frame of reference for another. That is certainly true. The map analogy is a simple metaphor and should be approached with caution. But it is equally true that the narrative analogy is metaphoric in character and as such is also necessarily limiting. It organizes the historic record in a particular manner and imposes on it a very specific set of values and expectations. In this context, I do not claim for the mapping metaphor an absolute status as a singular "true" interpretation, but rather I find it useful for switching gears and approaching the practice of art history from a different perspective.[31] I must also make clear that when I refer to a mapping, I am not calling up an image of a traditional two-dimensional map. I have two points of reference: the information mapping used increasingly in the sciences and the social sciences to analyze complex data sets; and the uses of similar techniques and technologies by artists working on visualization of complex structures, such as the Internet, or engaging in mapping of their own cultural geographies.[32]

What are the advantages of visual mapping? The most important is that maps and diagrammatic representations are neither linear nor inherently hierarchical, even though they can be "read" or, to borrow Preziosi's term, "reckoned with" in such a way that what results is a linear, hierarchical, or narrative account.[33] Also, although a traditional map has a static presence, the ideal digital mapping system is a dynamic representation and as such can be used to explore a nonequilibrium history—a perception of the past that does not assume a singular resolution or complete knowledge, but rather insists on a dynamic and partial view of culture predicated on the constancy of multilateral change, transition, flux, negotiation, renegotiation, accommodation, and interaction on the level of historic record as well as its interpretation.[34]

Any map or a diagram is also by definition coded; it functions with an awareness, heightened by the conventions of visual coding, of the distance between the representation and that which is represented. The territory in my example is the entire cultural environment, including the discursive (and art historic), institutional, economic, and cultural matrix, rather than art practice itself. As with traditional maps, we can strip a particular layer to reveal art practice on its own, but in such "taking away" there would always be an acknowledgment that this presentation represents a mode of interpretation rather than a singular epistemological reality that takes priority over any other. Within consideration of art practice, the territorial approach allows not only for consideration of historically significant features (and shifts in their designation), in other words, the topographic landmarks established by canons, but of the entire spectrum of art production, including those regions that have been until now ignored as insignificant. The East Art Map project coordinated by the Slovenian art group IRWIN and dedicated to (re)construction of the last fifty years of the history of visual arts in Eastern Europe is clearly predicated on the keen awareness of this principle, which is articulated in the group's slogan "History is not given. It has to be constructed."

Even if those regions of the map are left unexplored and therefore uncharted, their visibility as blank spaces may lead to future charting and at the very least may prompt awareness that the major landmarks, which tend to attract our attention, do not account for the entire territory, and, moreover, that their identity as landmarks depends on their location within the total field of cultural production. Ultimately those landmarks tell us little about the vast stretches of the terra incognita, which extends synchronically and diachronically across the plane of the present and into the geological strata of the past.

Maps have another advantage over narratives. They can incorporate the practice of art history as part of the mapped terrain. That is not true of classical art historic narratives. Within the logic of the narrative, the task of the art historian is to tell the story of what happened. There is an a priori presumption that the narrative account attempts to recover epistemological "truth" (even when this is disavowed) and that it reflects the historical coherence of art as tradition. There is also an implicit assumption of the total separation between the narrator and the narrative, the art historian and the subject of his inquiry. In the case of the map metaphor there is neither an assumption of art's coherence nor of such separation. Art historic interpretation becomes part of the mapped terrain. By rendering art practice and art history into objects of historiographic, or, to stay with our mapping metaphor, cartographic and geological analysis, we may ultimately throw into question not just the dogma of the autonomy of art, but also that of art history, revealing functional interdependencies between the two domains.

As a result, the canon is not excluded, but is contextualized. It can be recognized as an ordering system based on specific assumptions and arising from specific interests, and its impact can be examined on the level of art discourse and art markets, as well as art practice. If the problem of the art canon were simply an internal matter of art historic procedures, one could agree that after more than two decades of criticism the canon's authority within the academic sphere would have been undermined to such an extent that no further discussion would be necessary. But the canon or rather canons are never just a matter of discourse and, more to the point, they are never neutral or inconsequential. They determine not only what is good, significant, or valuable at a particular time and in a particular place, but also what is not. Because of that we simply cannot afford to critique the canon in the abstract, to deal only with issues of canonicity, and to imply the possibility of canon-less art history, while neglecting historical evidence of the production and persistence of particular canons and canonical formations.

This volume lays the groundwork for a different approach to the canon problematic. It is conceived as a map and a site of discourse rather than as a coherent argument. That definition presumes not only tension and a multiplicity of perspectives, but also a fundamental lack of agreement. If there were an agreement on the issue of the canon, there would be no need for discussion and no need for this volume. On the structural level the anthology is organized around two poles: my introduction and the coda written by Terry Smith. Both texts are primarily theoretical position statements, bookends that establish the frame of reference for the essays comprising the anthology. They are based on different assumptions and cover different terrain; they are not in agreement, but in dialogue. The authors of the essays contained between the introduction and the coda do not necessarily agree with my conclusions or those of Smith. Neither do they embrace a single perspective on the issue; they differ in focus, assumptions, and conclusions. Individual authors' understanding of the geo-temporal "location" of the canon(s) spans the spectrum from the local art worlds considered in a particular historic moment to the entirety of post-Renaissance Western cultural tradition. All the essays are, however, case studies. They function as concrete points of reference and checks on theoretical models. They may verify certain claims and at the same time create a possibility for the existence of evidence that may refute them. Ultimately, the anthology is meant to engage the reader in the dialogue, to allow for active reading and critical participation, and to encourage further work on the subject rather than suggest closure.

What are the potential consequences of our effort to identify multiple canonical formations, to historicize the production of art canons and canonical values? Since the canonical paradigm is predicated on its claim to a transcendent status, its rhetorical structure does not permit admission of its historical location, much less the possibility of its being produced by specific individuals pursuing specific agendas. However, once art history begins addressing the specific circumstances of canons' production, examining various and variously situated players, publications, and institutions involved and exploring their relationships to each other and to the external as well as internal factors and conditions, we will have to adjust our approaches to doing art history. This will require reconsidering some of our most fundamental assumptions concerning the status and the impact of our own professional practice. In total, this book is not an argument for the expansion of the canon, for the inclusion of hitherto ignored phenomena, for the repositioning within the canonical hierarchy of those artists and works traditionally relegated to the periphery, or for the demotion of revered canonical masters and masterpieces. It is a call for the acknowledgment of the inevitable persistence of canonical formations and of the potential variability of outcomes. If we acknowledge these things we will be better positioned to consider not only the heterogeneity, incommensurability, and resistance to systemic classification of art practices past and present, but also the local and global impact of art history (as a discipline and as a tool) on the reception and the practice of art.

Notes

1 For discussion of the concept of canonicity, see Sheffy, "The Concept of Canonicity in Polysystem Theory."

2 For a background to that discussion see Horkheimer, *Critical Theory*, in particular the essays "Traditional and Critical Theory," 188–243, and "Art and Mass Culture," 273–90; and Adorno, *The Culture Industry*.

3 For examples of recent contributions within art history, see Perry and Cunningham, *Academies, Museums, and Canons of Art*, with contributions by the editors, Emma Barker, Linda Walsh, and Anabel Thomas; Pollock, *Differencing the Canon*, which examines the issue from a feminist perspective; Mansfield, *Art History and Its Institutions*, which includes a section on the canon with contributions by David Carrier, Christopher B. Steiner, Ivan Gaskel, Marc Gotlieb, Gabriel P. Weisberg, Claire Farago, and Mary G. Morton, 113–28; and Zimmermann, *The Art Historian*, which admittedly does not include a separate section on the canon, but does address the canon problematic throughout its contents from the perspective of the disciplinary practice of art history.

4 Foster, "Archives of Modern Art," 81; the sentence also appears in Foster's essay "Dialectics of Seeing," in Holly and Moxey, *Art History, Aesthetics, Visual Studies*, 215. The two essays are slightly modified versions of the same text; they have the same contents, present the same conclusions, and offer the same examples. The minor differences reflect the specifics of the Clark conference, rather than any major shifts in Foster's thinking.

5 Definition of the word "canon" from the *English Oxford Dictionary*, 2nd ed., on-line version, accessed January 10, 2006.

6 Gates, *Loose Canons*, 31.

7 Ibid., 32.

8 Preziosi, *Rethinking Art History*, especially chap. 2. For further discussion of the origins of an autonomous conception of art, see Belting, *Likeness and Presence* and *The Invisible Masterpiece*; Shiner, *The Invention of Art*; Holly and Moxey, *Art History, Aesthetics, and Visual Studies*, 105–21; and Kristeller's somewhat older, but still relevant essay, "The Modern System of the Arts."

9 I use the term "classical" in order to identify a particular tradition within art historic discourse, one that has functioned as the standard mode for the production of art histories and the perception of art's history. See the *Oxford English Dictionary*, 2nd ed., on-line ed. for the definition of "classical" as "standard." This exercise in framing is not meant to produce an indictment of classical art history but to suggest a need for an analytic critique of its premises and, ultimately, to create a space for the possibility of art history that is not classical in its assumption. The possibility of such art historic practice

does not negate the contribution of classical art history or suggest its "end," either as a mode of discourse or a function of the historic record. The classical paradigm is further defined and discussed later in this essay.

10 On the rhetorical logic of the narrative form, in particular its tendency to *narrativize*, namely to produce accounts in which historic narration is presented as an objective report of historic facts, see Hyden White, *The Content of the Form*, 1–25.

11 For a comprehensive survey of the standard understanding and usage of the term "value" in art history, see Nelson and Shiff, *Critical Terms for Art History*, 419–34.

12 Connor, *Theory and Cultural Value*, 3. Barbara Herrnstein Smith presents a similar argument for the inevitability of evaluation and the cultural contingency of value in her "Contingencies of Value," 5–39, but unlike Connor she does not extend the imperative to value to the values themselves. Also, her analysis of contingency is presented in reference to an individual subject, rather than a historic cultural matrix.

13 See Cutting, *Impressionism and Its Canon*, 21–40.

14 See Preziosi, *Rethinking Art History*, 54–79; and Preziosi, *Brain of the Earth's Body*; also, Haxthausen, *The Two Art Histories*, 52–59.

15 Foster, "Archives of Modern Art," 81.

16 Foucault, *The Archaeology of Knowledge and the Discourse on Language*, 129.

17 Foucault pursues in much more detail the link between knowledge and taxonomy in *The Order of Things*.

18 Preziosi, *Rethinking Art History*, 54–79.

19 The university level art survey course is, as far as I am able to ascertain, an American phenomenon. The general surveys are not taught at European universities, except for when they are needed by exchange students from the United States. In Europe, the knowledge one would obtain from such a survey is imparted much earlier, over the course of primary and secondary education, and is simply assumed for those entering art history or studio programs. This is as much a reflection of differences between American and European education systems as it is of radically different expectations concerning middle-class cultural literacy.

20 Nelson, "The Map of Art History," 33. On agency in the production of disciplinary archives, see also Derrida's *Archive Fever*.

21 "Kodak Confirms Plans to Stop Making Slide Projectors" posted at *http://www.kodak.com/US/en/digital/av/slideProjectors/stop_slideProjectors.shtml*, site accessed on August 23, 2004.

22 "Art History Survey Collection," ARTstor database test website, *http://www.artstor.org/index.htm*, accessed August 14, 2004.

23 The progressive fee structure, which aims to make the database available to all secondary institutions regardless of their size and budget—a laudable feature distinguishing ARTstor from the commercial databases—will make it exceedingly affordable for community colleges; plans are already underway for extending access to K-12 schools and public libraries. ARTstor is also extending its outreach internationally. It is currently available to non-profit institutions in Canada, Australia, New Zealand, and the United Kingdom.

24 See Pearlman, "Landscapes in a Clustered World," 41–43.

25 Lakoff and Johnson, *Metaphors We Live By*.

26 See also Preziosi, *Rethinking Art History*, 19, 37–38.

27 I am using the term "metaphor" not as a literary or art historic concept, but as one developed within cognitive linguistics and neuroscience. As such "metaphor" refers to a set of mental processes relative to the understanding and organization of information, that is, cognition, rather than to a literary form embedded within a particular set of textual traditions and conventions. For work in empirical psychological research on metaphor, see the journals *Metaphor and Symbolic Activity* and *Cognitive Linguistics*; see also Gibbs, *The Poetics of Mind*, and Ortony, *Metaphor and Thought*. In art discourse, the use of the term "metaphor" largely depends on its usage and understanding within the field of literary studies. For an example of how "metaphor" is used in reference to visual representation, see Kristine Stiles's entry on performance in Nelson and Shiff, *Critical Terms for Art History*, 75–97. The term "metaphor" does not have a separate entry in the book, thus confirming its ultimately literary origins. Art historians and art critics tend to prefer alternative terms to cover similar conceptual ground. See Stafford's use of "analogy" in *Visual Analogy*, W. J. T. Mitchell's use of "image-text" in *Picture Theory*, and Owens's use of "allegory" in "The Allegorical Impulse."

28 Classical art history's assumption that art has a history and that this history is external to and independent of art historic discourse aligns it with other classical paradigms, in particular those in physics and economics that assume that phenomena are empirically available for observation and that the results of observation *are not* affected by the act of observing or by the production of analysis. The self-consciousness concerning art history's status as a discourse, which emerged in the wake of poststructuralism, does not pose a fundamental challenge to those classical assumptions since it only questions the epistemological status of the interpretation (history), without questioning its impact on or relationship to the visual and historic evidence. However, since production of art history is here identified as a discursive practice, it may be productive to differentiate this type of art historic discourse as neoclassical.

29 According to this reasoning, modern art is not a particular form of art practice, one among many synchronic types of production; it is the only historically significant form of art practice, synonymous with art itself, for the modern period. The art of the modern period is modern art; forms of art practice that are not modern or are insufficiently modern cease to be historically relevant since they can not be accommodated, except as a negative foil, within the historic narrative.

30 The potential usefulness of a map metaphor has been suggested earlier by Nelson in "The Map of Art History." Here the term "art practice" defines the entire spectrum of professional behaviors, including, but not limited to, the making of works. The term "art" implies focus on a single outcome of art practice, namely the production of the art object. I am indebted to Robert Jensen for this key distinction.

31 Such a metaphoric reorientation is one of the most often used, yet largely unacknowledged ways in which new paradigms and critical perspectives are introduced. In science, one of the most often cited examples of the metaphoric shift is that from the Newtonian universe as a "clock" to the post-Einsteinian universe as a "game of dice." For a recent example in art history, see Belting's shifting of the metaphor for the museum from a "frame" to a "stage" in *Art History after Modernism*, 96–111.

32 For a discussion of mapping and visualization strategies in the analysis of complex

data and new media, see Frieling, *Mapping and Text*. See also Goldman, Papson, and Kersey, *Landscapes of Capital*; and IRWIN's East Art Map project (http://www.nskstate.com/irwin/works-projects/eastartmap.php; http://www.eastartmap.org/; and IRWIN, *East Art Map*).

33 Preziosi, *Rethinking Art History*, 50.

34 My definition of nonlinearity and nonequilibrium is based on terms used by De Landa in *A Thousand Years of Nonlinear History*. This "quantum" perception of history does not argue against the possibility of historic interpretation or treat historic interpretation as a purely rhetorical field. It does, however, embrace multiple perspectives, incorporates the uncertainty principle, which focuses on probability rather than certainty, and recognizes the impact of historic constructions on the historic record.

1

Measuring Canons: Reflections on Innovation and the Nineteenth-century Canon of European Art

ROBERT JENSEN

The Canon and Its Discontents

A truism: intellectual disciplines are dominated by acts of convention. Or, as Hayden White once put it, "Every discipline, I suppose, is, as Nietzsche saw most clearly, constituted by what it *forbids* its practitioners to do."[1] This is no more or less true of art history. However, other disciplines, especially those outside the humanities, are better prepared by intellectual tradition to consider challenges to those conventions, to accept paradigm shifts where sufficient evidence makes opposition no longer feasible. Because the sciences especially employ the procedural model of hypothesis and verification, scientists (and many "hard" social scientists) have reasonably objective means to distinguish between personal values and tastes and what might be legitimate, if opposing, contributions to a field of inquiry.

Art historians, however, generally share in the recent humanist distrust of scientific methods and of the positivism they typically express. They assume that in culture all hypotheses or general statements are so ruled by contingency as to be ultimately unverifiable. Nowhere is this habit of mind more evident than in their general avoidance of quantitative methods, which proceed from evidence to interpretation. Faced with an approach fundamentally at odds with the normative procedures and assumptions of the discipline, their response has been either to marginalize the work (let sociologists and economists do it so long as it does not touch on issues perceived as core to the discipline) or to ignore it.

Art historians, of course, must generalize; however, they rarely pursue those generalizations in a systematic and ultimately verifiable way. The modus operandi in recent years has been to apply a theory or theories to a particular object of study, without seeking to examine the validity of the theory or theories in light of the evidence obtained. Rather, art historians often accept only such evidence as conforms to the assumptions upon which the applied theories are based. In this way, theories get treated as empirically valid findings rather than as descriptive models. Evidence contradictory to the hypothesis prima facie is either ignored or otherwise suppressed. Similarly, art historical interpretations, once established, are often treated as if they constituted factual knowledge. These parallel habits—the suspicion of generalization, the theorization that predetermines evidence, and the unexamined persistence of received interpretations—have been expressed so often in recent art history that it is now all too rare to find art historians generalizing about what they can factually demonstrate, but all too common to find them generalizing about what they believe. When, for example, art historians write about the "commodification of art" are they in fact submitting Marx's idea of commodity fetishism to serious critique or are they simply finding confirmation of Marx's perception in the material under study?[2]

Nowhere are conventional beliefs and procedures more in evidence than in the discussion of canons. It is a subject as sensitive as a toothache, because the question of canons touches upon the biggest concerns the discipline now faces. Matters of race, gender, geographical location and cultural traditions, and so on are reshaping not only the objective field the discipline is working on, but also the attitudes and methods used to interpret the rapidly expanding arena of inquiry that some continue to call art and others "visual culture."

It is unfortunate, then, that art historians have tended to make of canons straw men, safeguarding outworn traditions, girded by privilege and by the force of capital, which are mechanisms of exclusion favoring the few at the expense of the many. Curiously joined to this oppressive view of canons is a long-standing conviction held by many art historians that canons are in fact highly mutable cultural institutions, matters of taste and changing fashions, and therefore subject to continual change and revision, truly made out of straw rather than oppressive marble.[3] This alternating view of hegemony and instability arises from the discipline's insistence on approaching canons exclusively from the vantage of qualitative judgments. In the world of endlessly shifting perspective and uncertain standards of evidence, canons might naturally appear to be both impervious and gaseous.

It should be obvious, however, that individuals do not generate canons; whatever else they are, canons represent forms of consensus built up over time. In such cases, quantitative analysis is uniquely suited to understanding the collective perceptions of a discipline, where individual judgments are necessarily subordinate to what a discipline in toto holds to be most important.

In measuring canons, therefore, we should not be looking for "intrinsic qualities" possessed by an art object or for the "genius" possessed by the artist. The association of canons with quality is a monumental blind alley. Nothing cultural in the world possesses intrinsic value. Values must always be collectively conferred. Duchamp, for example, taught us that even beauty might not be an important criterion when judging the value of a work of art. This was a truly revolutionary perception. However, we should also understand that the revolution that is the ready-made lay dormant for almost half a century, until the problems it posed were taken up by artists during the 1960s. Before 1958, Duchamp was barely a participant in the modern canon and his 1912 *Nude Descending a Staircase, No. 2* was a far more likely candidate for serious art historical discussion than his 1917 *Fountain*. Since the 1960s, no twentieth-century artwork has been the object of more serious discussion, both art historical and philosophical, than the *Fountain*. Not only does the *Fountain* demonstrate how objects can acquire meaning and indeed fundamental importance over time, it also shows us a better way of thinking about "genius" as something other than a code word for someone who possesses an absolute and transcendent originality (another deeply problematic word). As the best literature on the artist argues, Duchamp recombined ideas and attitudes already widely circulating in early twentieth-century European culture and articulated them in a radically new way. Following Duchamp, let us strip "genius" of its connotation as a purveyor of ineffable and incommensurable values. Making art (and its makers) is neither more ineffable nor more incommensurable than other kinds of intellectual labor (and laborers). If we can measure the value of other forms of intellectual labor, which we can, then we can measure the values attached to art. The problem is not whether art can be measured, but in finding the best, most appropriate measures.

Approaching canons quantitatively, we should not look for their origins or measure their impact through the influence of a particular critic, curator, dealer, or art historian (or even government). Ernst Gombrich and Clement Greenberg, to take notable examples referred to elsewhere in this volume, did not make the reputations of Leonardo and Pollock respectively. At best, what they wrote enhanced those reputations and provided a clearer sense of the bases on which they rested. When we criticize these authors, therefore, what is at stake is not the artist's reputation but the specific arguments Gombrich and Greenberg made regarding how that reputation is to be viewed. We may, therefore, dismiss the analyses of Gombrich's and Greenberg's respective canons, as has often been done, for being too inflexible, too deterministic, and too teleological. However, we should be chary of confusing their arguments about a canon with the canon itself, especially if we hope to get closer to understanding the mechanisms of canon formation.

Undoubtedly, critics, art historians, and curators have played and will continue to play significant roles in explaining, refining, and transmitting canons. Yet why should we assume that art history's professionals are the most important players in the formation of canons and that artists are but the material with which they play? In all other intellectual disciplines, we would have no problem accepting the axiom that the discipline's practitioners define their fields. We would not say that historians of science made Isaac Newton canonical. Who would question that leading innovators in science, technology, medicine, philosophy, jurisprudence, and so on are all regarded as such first by the respective professionals in those fields? The greatness of their respective innovations has been and will continue to be measured by how and how much they altered the disciplines in which they worked. Professional art history has rarely been so generous to artists and less so today than ever before.

Innovation

In his sadly neglected 1962 book *The Shape of Time*, George Kubler argued that it was precisely through the pattern of innovation and its dispersion that art and science most resembled each other. For Kubler, "The value of any rapprochement between the history of art and the history of science is the display of common traits of invention, change, and obsolescence that the material works of artists and scientists both share in time."[4] A great work of art, in Kubler's sense, is very much like a new idea in physics. It arises from a complex stew of cultural material, including not only major scientific or artistic discoveries that precede the innovation, but also, among other elements, the contributions of lesser ideas and individuals. Kubler also argued that no matter how canonical an artist or a work of art may be, revolutions in art, like revolutions in science, are never the work of an isolated individual. However, within these collaborative environments, individual figures clearly play decisive roles.

For most art historians innovation is usually a word of only small compass, used to describe the specific achievements of a given artist or work of art, whereas originality is used to refer to a general, if widely contested, model of artistic creativity.[5] Among economists, the reverse holds true. They invest originality, or what they would term invention, with little significance, while attaching enormous importance to innovation. For economists, what makes an invention significant is its use. An idea not applied is essentially worthless. To innovate, according to *Webster's*, is "to introduce new methods, devices, etc."[6] Innovation means putting into practice a new idea, method, or technological discovery. Originality is a backward-looking concept, pointing toward an imaginary moment of origin and a single producer; innovation as a concept looks both forward and backward, embracing both novelty and tradition.[7]

Artistic innovation must, however, be distinguished from either scientific or technological innovation in that art history is replete with examples of conscious reversals, in which artists have returned to older methods and styles as the source for new ideas. This does not mean that the achievements of any given era are permanently lost (although the craft skills necessary to achieve them may not be continuously available to subsequent generations of artists). If innovations are forward-looking, they are not directed toward some predetermined goal (as Greenberg argued). One might find a series of solutions to an artistic problem without any sense of a final endpoint. Indeed, one might easily value an early contribution to this set as much or more than that of the latest contributor. This is because no solution to a problem can ever be absolutely authoritative, resolving a question for all time. No one now believes the world is flat, but not even Picasso could forestall what was possible within the vocabulary of Cubism. Witness Juan Gris's subsequent contributions to Cubism. However, Picasso's stature is greater than Gris's because his work had the greater impact. The greater the resonance of an innovation the more important the contribution made by the particular artist or artwork.[8] At the same time, innovation is not about absolute novelty (that is, originality), but the successful reorganization of ideas and practices already available.

We should also be careful to disentangle innovation from aesthetics; certainly innovations in art are most often formal, but again, as Duchamp demonstrated, form is only one of many possible criteria, not the exclusive one. Concepts, politics, identity, and pioneering techniques are among the many other factors that might lead to the identification of importance in a particular artist or work of art.

Artists' innovations have the power to reshape retrospectively art history's perception of past art. One could point as an example to the undoing by artists of Greenberg's influence on both contemporary art and art history, when, during the 1960s and 1970s artists refashioned what was possible in art. In the process, they rendered Greenberg's formalism and his endgame of pure abstraction irrelevant. New work may also endow past art with new relevance. As it has often been observed, there were numerous scholars in the first half of the twentieth century who wrote, like Meyer Schapiro, about both medieval and modern art. The freedom from representational illusionism in modern art provided the context for the wholesale reexamination of pre-Renaissance art in the West.

However, there are limits to the alteration of the canon once it is in place. Since the establishment of art history as an intellectual discipline during the nineteenth century, rediscoveries in art, in which forgotten "old master" artists become canonical, have become increasingly rare.[9] Even among twentieth-century artists, we have seen little shifting in the relative reputations of artists working before 1970; we have also witnessed a general hardening of the reputations of artists who made their most significant contributions between 1970 and 1990. In addition, it just does not happen that an artist, having achieved the canon, may be subsequently removed from it. The labors of past art history are, as far as we can tell from all of the evidence currently available, irreversible. This does not preclude new works from being added to a canon; far from it, canons are continually expanding when they represent living traditions.

Counting the Canonical

I have made a number of claims about innovation's role in the formation of artistic canons, based on models offered by science and economics. The validity of this analysis I have supported with a handful of examples. I now want to reverse my approach by first establishing what and who belong to the canon under investigation—for this essay, nineteenth-century European art—and only then offering preliminary explanations for some of what may be discovered in these findings, and thus pointing the way to avenues for future research. The methods I used in measuring the nineteenth-century canon are simple and easily duplicated, while the results are readily verifiable. Much of what this work tells us the profession in a sense already knows. Yet, there is often considerable difference between what one knows intuitively and what one can demonstrate empirically. It is here that the clarity brought by quantitative work may have the largest benefit to scholarship. I am convinced, in any case, that any method has value if it allows one to examine old problems in new ways, can be duplicated and improved by others, and especially if it raises new questions.

Following the work of the economist David Galenson, I have found that the most convenient way to determine what is currently canonical in the visual arts is by conducting a textbook illustration survey. By using this simple quantitative method, it is possible to discover who are the most reproduced artists and what are the most frequently reproduced works of art. This method is similar to citation studies used in the social sciences to determine the most influential work within a discipline. Because art historians use textbooks to introduce students both to the material and to the methods of the discipline, these texts represent the consensus view of what has been considered important in the art surveyed. Art history survey textbooks have steadily evolved in scope and manner of presentation during the last seventy-five years as the body of art historical literature has continued to mature and new methods and subjects have appeared. Rarely has this expansion altered what art history considers the most important artists, although it has considerably refined what are considered the most important works of art.

To take but one influential example, in comparing the first edition with the latest edition (the twelfth) of *Gardner's Art through the Ages*, what is most striking is the difference in scale between the two.[10] The first edition has far fewer illustrations and the physical size of the volume is much smaller. For example, the number of paintings, prints, and drawings belonging to European art from the fifteenth century through the end of the seventeenth totaled 64 in the first edition. In the most recent edition, there are 138, or over twice as many. Yet, the relative number of images per canonical artist has remained roughly constant. For another essay, I selected 14 frequently reproduced old master painters, whose work I then ranked by number of illustrations overall and by which works have been most frequently reproduced in modern survey textbooks.[11] I compared these same 14 painters to those reproduced in the first edition of *Art through the Ages*. Of these, only Caravaggio and Robert Campin were not illustrated in 1926. Raphael had 3 reproductions in the first edition and 5 in the latest edition; Rembrandt had 4 illustrations in 1926 and 5 today; and so on. The only painter to have fewer reproductions today than in 1926 was Holbein, who once had 3 images in *Art through the Ages* and now has only one. What this means is that about half of the new reproductions in the twelfth edition were used to expand the number of artists represented in the book. Otherwise, since 1926 there have been few changes in the relative importance of the most canonical painters vis-à-vis the lesser canonical painters. In fact, the most significant difference between the first edition and the latest edition lies in the relatively low proportion of illustrations of now canonical paintings in the first edition. That three-fourths of a century of art history labor has altered the principal representatives of the canon so little is impressive testimony to the general stability of art history's view regarding which artists are most important. This example, however, also illustrates how art history has refined much more precisely the specific contributions of the respective artists and incorporated the contributions of many other artists overlooked in 1926.

It is worth adding that while in the United States survey textbooks have become dominant pedagogical tools, at no time have such texts been the exclusive province of American art history. British authors have written a number of the texts used most often in the United States; furthermore, the textbooks used in many other Western countries are comparable to those used in American colleges and universities.[12] Individually, textbooks portray personal, corporate, and national biases, but when they are examined collectively these biases become less pronounced, above all by that which is held to be most canonical.[13] Divergent opinions appear in connection with lesser art and artists, where nationality, individual scholarly perspective, access to reproductions, and other such contingent factors have greater influence over the selection process.

To get as diverse a data set as possible, therefore, I chose textbooks by German, Italian, French, English, and American authors published roughly over the last four decades. My university library yielded thirty-six texts that included significant surveys of nineteenth-century European art.[14] My first purpose was to discover the most frequently reproduced artists in these textbooks. A quick survey of nine survey textbooks in my personal collection established the most often illustrated artists. Important, but noncanonical artists, such as William Bouguereau or Léon Gérôme, are never represented by more than a single image in the survey texts and are not present in even half of them. However, because I wanted to compare the absolutely canonical with the merely important, I made a somewhat arbitrary selection of some well-known artists whose work is to be found occasionally, but not consistently, in the textbooks. On their own the artists in the bottom third of my sample might not have garnered enough reproductions to warrant their inclusion.[15]

The artists in the last two columns of table 1.1 have between one-fourteenth and one-fifteenth fewer illustrations in the sample survey books than do the artists at the top of the first column. What this means is that one textbook author might choose to reproduce a Rossetti but not a Burne-Jones, whereas another author might sacrifice both in favor of a Millais. For the bottom twenty artists in table 1.1, only one textbook, Rudolf Zeitler's 1966 German-language survey, gives as many as three illustrations to any artist. Not surprisingly the two artists with three illustrations are German: Adolf Menzel and Arnold Böcklin. This clearly indicates that the farther removed one gets from the core of the canon, the more uncertain the specific contributions of an artist or an

Table 1.1. Artists ranked according to total number of illustrations in 36 European and American textbooks from approximately the last 40 years that include surveys of 19th century European art.* A "t" denotes a shared position in the ranking.

Rank	Artist	Ills.	Rank	Artist	Ills.	Rank	Artist	Ills.
1	Goya	157	18	Constable	69	35	Rousseau	23
2	Monet	152	19	Friedrich	63	36	Morisot	22
3	Cézanne	144	20	Munch	59	37	Runge	21
3t	Manet	144	21	Whistler	52	38	Puvis	20
5	van Gogh	130	21t	Corot	52	38t	Caillebotte	20
6	Delacroix	124	23	Lautrec	51	40	Millais	19
7	David	122	24	Millet	49	41	Rossetti	18
8	Degas	114	25	Cassatt	48	42	Bonheur	17
9	Ingres	106	26	Canova	46	42t	Sisley	17
10	Gauguin	105	27	Ensor	40	44	Gérôme	16
11	Courbet	102	28	Blake	39	45	Böcklin	15
12	Rodin	100	29	Pissarro	38	46	Sargent	13
13	Daumier	88	30	Menzel	37	46t	Brown	13
14	Turner	83	31	Gros	28	48	Couture	11
15	Renoir	78	32	Moreau	27	49	Bouguereau	10
16	Géricault	77	33	Girodet	25	49t	Meissonier	10
17	Seurat	73	34	Rude	24			

*See the appendix for books included in the survey.

artwork become and the more dependent a selection is on local factors, such as the nationality of the author or publication.

Only the presence of Jean-Baptiste Camille Corot and Edvard Munch among the highly ranked artists surveyed in table 1.1 might surprise specialists regarding nineteenth-century art. (The taste for Corot and the relative importance attached to his art may seem to have faded in recent decades, while art historians specializing in the nineteenth century might regard Munch's career as having begun so late in the century as to belong only tangentially to the field.) That just under two-thirds of the artists in this table are French is no surprise. Yet, even if these findings might be predicted, it is still worth asking whether they might nonetheless be arbitrary. To test their validity I sought corroboration through other measurements.

Another way of establishing an artist's importance is to measure the quantity of literature devoted to that artist. This approach not only reveals scholarly interest in the artist, but also the public's interest, which helps feed the scholarly demand (and of course feeds off the self-same scholarly activity). To obtain the rankings in table 1.2, I used the electronic catalogue of the Getty Research Institute, arguably among the finest art libraries in the world, especially for post-medieval Western art, which, in addition, has a very large acquisition budget. To simplify the data collection, I chose to use only the Library of Congress's artist subject-heading listings as my search filter in the electronic browser.[16] Searching the Getty catalogue for each artist under his or her respective subject heading yielded the total number of titles in the library. These totals are listed next to the artists' names in table 1.2.

I also wanted to see how constant the scholarly interest in a particular artist has been. Using the time-limiting filter in the Getty catalogue, I re-searched the Getty holdings for citations for each artist published since 1990. The second column to the right of the artist's name in table 1.2 indicates the total number of monographs in the Getty library published on each artist since 1990. A comparison of the two columns provides clear indications of whether or not recent interest in an artist is consistent with scholarly interest over a much longer period. Furthermore, a comparison of the number of recent monographs to the total number in the Getty library provides some measure of the growth of interest in an artist.

A look at the rankings between tables 1.1 and 1.2 demonstrates that overall an artist's position either near the top or near the bottom of the rankings remains extremely consistent. Among the top twenty-five in table 1.1 only Caspar David Friedrich and Mary Cassatt lose their places in table 1.2 (in favor of Camille Pissarro and James Ensor). Artists ranked in the last third of table 1.1 are very likely to have few monographs devoted to them. Incidentally, Corot, who I suspected was fading in historical importance, actually has retained sufficient academic and public interest to appear at about the same rank in citations since 1990 as he does overall in the Getty's holdings. Most artists place within five positions in the rankings in both tables. Goya, Cézanne, and van Gogh, notably, are among the top four in both tables.

Some artists, however, do change position between the two tables more dramatically. Auguste Renoir, for example, ranks higher in overall monographs, eleventh, than he does in the number of textbook illustrations, fifteenth, while Claude Monet has almost twice as many illustrations as Renoir in the textbook illustration study, yet ranks below Renoir in the total number of monographs in the Getty collections. This appears to be evidence of the force that public popularity exerts on publishers, curators, and writers to

Table 1.2. Artists ranked according to the total number of citations found through a subject heading search of the library catalogue of the Getty Research Institute, Los Angeles (July 2004). A "t" denotes a shared position in the ranking.

Rank	Artist	Total citations	Citations since 1990	Rank	Artist	Total citations	Citations since 1990
1	van Gogh	383	58	27	Millet	51	4
2	Goya	261	38	28	Menzel	49	6
3	Cézanne	231	28	29	Rossetti	48	6
4	Gauguin	221	21	30	Friedrich	40	9
5	Lautrec	175	16	31	Moreau	33	6
6	Degas	159	14	31t	Böcklin	33	2
7	Turner	155	7	33	Morisot	32	6
8	Munch	154	13	34	Millais	31	1
9	Rodin	151	14	34t	Sargent	31	5
10	Delacroix	147	14	36	Cassatt	30	4
11	Renoir	142	11	37	Sisley	25	2
12	Monet	131	24	38	Runge	24	1
13	Daumier	130	6	39	Puvis de Chavannes	22	0
14	Manet	127	12				
15	Ensor	108	9	40	Hunt, H.	18	1
15t	Ingres	108	11	41	Gérôme	17	3
17	Courbet	107	10	41t	Rousseau	17	0
18	Blake	102	9	43	Meissonier	16	0
19	Whistler	99	7	44	Delaroche	13	1
20	Corot	94	7	45	Girodet	10	2
21	Constable	79	4	46	Bonheur	9	0
22	Canova	76	9	46t	Bouguereau	9	0
23	Seurat	62	13	46t	Caillebotte	9	3
24	David	59	4	49	Rude	7	0
25	Pissarro	54	3	50	Couture	5	0
26	Géricault	53	5				

satisfy public demand. Renoir, we may safely assume, has been more popular with the general public than has Monet—at least until recently. Since 1990, Monet has surpassed Renoir in the number of monographs devoted to the respective artists. Edouard Manet's importance to the development of art, which is unquestioned by scholars, is reflected in his ranking in table 1.1. However, Manet slips in the ranking to fourteenth in overall citations and eleventh in citations since 1990, suggesting that the artist is less popular with the general public, whereas Paul Gauguin, clearly a popular favorite, effectively takes Manet's place in table 1.2.

The disjunction between the professional art historical perception of an artist's contribution to nineteenth-century art and the popular appreciation (or lack thereof) of that same artist appears clearly to stand behind the most striking anomalies between the two rankings. For example, Baron Gros's paintings are routinely included among textbook illustrations (he is ranked thirty-first in table 1.1), but the artist does not rank in the top fifty in monographs as per table 1.2, a difference of nineteen. Jacques-Louis David makes a slightly less dramatic slip of seventeen spots from table 1.1 to 1.2. Conversely, a few artists are valued dramatically more in monographs than in textbook illustrations, most notably Henri Toulouse-Lautrec. He ranks twenty-third in the total number of illustrations (51) but in the Getty monograph survey, he ranks fifth overall (with 175 citations). Notable, but less dramatic upward swings are represented by Edvard Munch and James Ensor, both of whom appear twelve levels higher in the monograph survey than they do in the textbook illustration study.

We can conclude, then, that the canonical artists derived from the textbook study are consistent overall with the number of monographs devoted respectively to these artists. The discrepancies that do occur between frequency of illustration and the number of monographs are most likely to be explained by the difference between a scholarly view of artistic importance and the popularity of some artists' work among nonprofessional audiences.

In addition to ranking the artists, I wanted to establish the most frequently reproduced works by the artists in my sample. Table 1.3 lists fifty-two works overall, which represents all the works made by the artists in my sample that appeared in at least nine separate textbooks, or one-fourth of the total number of books surveyed. Before going on, let me emphasize that table 1.3 is not an absolute ranking of the most frequently reproduced works of nineteenth-century European art. A number of the works that appear near the bottom of table 1.3 would lose their place if more canonical images by artists outside my sample were included. An example would be Jean-Baptiste Carpeaux's

Table 1.3. Fifty-two nineteenth-century paintings, prints, and sculptures ranked according to the number of times each work was illustrated in thirty-six textbooks. A "t" denotes a shared position in the ranking.

Rank	Artist	Title	#
1	Géricault	*Raft of the Medusa*	29
2	Goya	*Third of May, 1808*	27
2t	Seurat	*La Grande Jatte*	27
4	Manet	*Olympia*	26
4t	David	*Oath of the Horatii*	26
6	Constable	*The Hay Wain*	22
6t	Delacroix	*Death of Sardanapalus*	22
6t	Manet	*Déjeuner sur l'herbe*	22
9	Courbet	*Burial at Ornans*	21
9t	David	*Death of Marat*	21
9t	Manet	*Bar at the Folies-Bergère*	21
12	Courbet	*Studio of the Painter*	20
12t	Delacroix	*Liberty Leading the People*	20
12t	Monet	*Rouen Cathedral* (all versions)	20
15	Rude	*La Marseillaise*	19
16	Rodin	*Gates of Hell*	18
16t	Turner	*Rain, Steam and Speed*	18
18	Munch	*The Scream*	17
19	Goya	*Family of Charles IV*	16
19t	Monet	*Impression: Sunrise*	16
19t	Renoir	*Moulin de la Galette*	16
22	Daumier	*Third Class Carriage*	15
22t	Delacroix	*Massacres at Chios*	15
22t	Millet	*The Gleaners*	15
22t	Rodin	*Burghers of Calais*	15
22t	van Gogh	*Night Café*	15
22t	van Gogh	*Starry Night*	15
28	Daumier	*Rue Transnonain*	14
29t	Gauguin	*Vision after the Sermon*	14
29t	Gros	*Pesthouse at Jaffa*	14
31	Courbet	*The Stonebreakers*	13
31t	Goya	*The Sleep of Reason Produces Monsters*	13
31t	Manet	*Emile Zola*	13
34	David	*Napoleon Crossing Alps*	12
34t	Delacroix	*Women of Algiers*	12
34t	Gauguin	*Where Do We Come From? . . .*	12

Table 1.3. *Continued*

Rank	Artist	Title	#
34t	Rodin	*Balzac*	12
34t	Seurat	*Bathers at Asnières*	12
39	Caillebotte	*Paris Street: Rainy Day*	11
39t	Canova	*Paolina Borghese as Venus*	11
39t	Rodin	*The Thinker*	11
42	Cézanne	*Large Bathers* (Phil.)	10
42t	Degas	*14 year old dancer*	10
42t	Ensor	*Entry of Christ into Brussels*	10
42t	Monet	*Women in Garden*	10
42t	Renoir	*The Boating Party*	10
42t	Rossetti	*Annunciation*	10
42t	Whistler	*Falling Rocket*	10
49	Gauguin	*The Specter Watches Over Her*	9
49t	Goya	*Saturn Devouring Children*	9
49t	Ingres	*Large Odalisque* (Louvre)	9
49t	Turner	*Slave Ship*	9

The Dance (1868), which was designed for the Paris Opera, a work that appears frequently enough to eclipse many of the works ranked at the bottom of table 1.3. Indeed, it is an interesting and almost unexplored fact that there are a number of nineteenth-century artists who each made a canonical work, yet would not be in the canon save for that one work.[17] Only a few of the thirty-six textbooks in my sample illustrated works by Carpeaux other than *The Dance*. In a similar vein, Paul Sérusier's *The Talisman* is the artist's only contribution to art history in any of the textbooks I surveyed. Among the artists in my sample, the contributions of François Rude and Gustave Caillebotte are similarly restricted, with Rude limited almost exclusively to *La Marseillaise* on the Arc de Triomphe and with Caillebotte's *Paris Street: Rainy Day* representing over half of the artist's paintings surveyed.

What else do we learn from ranking the most frequently reproduced works of art? There is a fundamental difference between the authors of the works of art at the top of table 1.3 compared to the ranking of artists in tables 1.1 and 1.2. Géricault, ranked sixteenth in table 1.1, painted the most frequently reproduced painting of the nineteenth century. Seurat, ranked seventeenth in table 1.1, painted the second most reproduced work. Monet, Cézanne, van

Table 1.4. The frequency with which three survey textbooks on nineteenth-century art illustrated paintings ranked in table 3.

Author	Overall percentage of 50 highest ranked works reproduced	Percentage of pre-1865 works reproduced (28 total)	Percentage excluding Impressionists + Rodin (39 total)
Chu	94	96	97
Eisenman	76	93	89
Rosenblum and Janson	76	78	84

Gogh, Degas, and Gauguin—all ranked well above Géricault and Seurat in table 1.1—are absent from the top of the rankings in table 1.3. With the exception of Seurat's *Sunday Afternoon on the Island of La Grand Jatte* and Manet's *Bar at the Folies-Bergère*, the top twelve most frequently reproduced works were painted before 1870. Despite having 152 illustrations overall, Monet's first painting to appear in table 1.3 is *Impressionism: Sunrise*, which is tied at nineteenth. Cézanne, with 144 illustrations overall, manages to get only one work, the *Large Bathers* in the Philadelphia Museum of Art, reproduced as many as ten times, behind both Caillebotte and Rude, represented respectively by twenty and nineteen illustrations overall. What this means is that if an author is going to choose a Rude it will be *La Marseillaise*, but if the same author chooses a Cézanne (or rather, Cézannes) a good number of works seemingly will suit. What explains this differing treatment?

To place in sharper focus the question of unequal attention given to specific works by canonical artists, I compared the general textbook canon of important nineteenth-century works of art against what specialists on the nineteenth century regard as the important art and artists of that century. I chose three leading English-language textbooks devoted exclusively to nineteenth-century European art (all three include American art under this rubric, but exclude representatives from virtually all other non-European countries). The authors, Petra ten-Doesschate Chu, Stephen Eisenman (and five co-contributors), and Robert Rosenblum and H. W. Janson, are all preeminent specialists in the field. Table 1.4 indicates the percentage of the ranked works of art in table 1.3 that appears in each of these textbooks.[18] The most recent text, by Chu, is the most canonical at 94 percent. The books by Eisenman and Rosenblum and Janson have the same percentage of canonical works, 76.

However, if we tabulate only the works created prior to 1865 that are illustrated, we discover Eisenman's text to be only slightly less canonical (at 93 percent) than Chu's (at 96 percent). While the text by Rosenblum and Janson shows little change when restricted to works produced prior to 1865, if we perform the tabulation a third time, this time excluding only works by the Impressionists (and Rodin), then the percentage of canonical images in Rosenblum's and Janson's text rises to 84.

It says something about the academic textbook market that the book by Rosenblum and Janson, published two decades ago, is the least canonical of the three.[19] Market pressures apparently have led the most recent books to be the most canonical, even when, as in Chu's case, the author also illustrates the work of many noncanonical artists. These percentages, however, are more interesting in that they conform so strongly to the biases found in tables 1.1–1.3. All three textbooks have little disagreement about who are the major artists and what are the major works of art in Europe in the first half of the nineteenth century. In fact, the two artists represented with the most illustrations in these three survey textbooks for the nineteenth-century are Goya (46) and David (45). Among the top twenty-five ranked artists in table 1.1 only four artists fail to have at least three illustrations per text: Renoir (Eisenman illustrates only two), Whistler (with two illustrations in each text), Millet (with only two illustrations in Eisenman), and Cassatt (Chu gives her only two illustrations and Rosenblum and Janson only one).[20] Among the bottom twenty-five in the rankings the situation is reversed. Only Ensor (ranked twenty-seventh) is represented in all three texts by at least three illustrations. More telling still is the fact that even a text such as Rosenblum's and Janson's, which seems consciously intent on being anti-canonical, gives no more than one reproduction to an otherwise noncanonical artist. Chu and Eisenman are no different in this regard.

Given the predominantly French flavor of the rankings in table 1.1, one might expect the recent revisionist histories to make significant room for non-French artists and to explore extensively national traditions outside France. However, this has hardly been the case, especially for art made in the first half of the century. Table 1.5 compares the frequency of illustrations for the top twenty artists in the textbooks on the nineteenth century to the overall frequency listed in table 1.1. In such a small sample, individual authors can strongly affect the rankings. It is perhaps even more notable, then, that the emphasis on French art is retained in the textbooks on the nineteenth century. There are, of course, some adjustments between the two rankings. In the survey texts on the nineteenth century, Cassatt ranks among the top twenty,

Table 1.5. A comparison of top twenty rankings between recent survey textbooks on the nineteenth century and the top twenty most illustrated artists in general textbook studies. A "t" denotes a shared position in the ranking.

Recent Surveys of 19th c. Art			General Textbook Surveys*		
Rank	Artist	#	Rank	Artist	#
1	Goya	46	1	Monet	134
2	David	32	2	Manet	120
3	Cézanne	27	3	Cézanne	117
3t	van Gogh	27	3t	Goya	111
5	Courbet	26	5	Delacroix	106
6	Manet	24	6	van Gogh	103
7	Gauguin	23	7	Degas	99
7t	Ingres	23	8	David	90
9	Seurat	21	9	Ingres	83
10	Rodin	20	10	Gauguin	82
11	Cassatt	19	11	Rodin	80
12	Delacroix	18	12	Courbet	76
12t	Géricault	18	13	Daumier	73
12t	Monet	18	14	Renoir	68
15	Daumier	15	14t	Turner	68
15t	Degas	15	16	Géricault	59
15t	Turner	15	17	Constable	56
18	Constable	13	18	Seurat	52
19	Girodet	12	18t	Friedrich	52
20	Lautrec	11	20	Munch	49
20t	Menzel	11			

*Since these same recent nineteenth-century survey textbooks were used in compiling table 1, the illustrations from these volumes were subtracted from the total number of illustrations listed here.

whereas Renoir drops out. However, it is also the case that Girodet-Trioson is added to the survey textbooks on the nineteenth century whereas Friedrich fails to place among the top twenty. Finally, Toulouse-Lautrec and Menzel share the twentieth position in the textbooks on the nineteenth century, but at the expense of Edvard Munch.

If the textbooks on the nineteenth century preserve the primacy of French art, within the French tradition they reshuffle the rankings. Generally, the leading artists working in the second half of the century as ranked in table 1.1 get proportionately fewer reproductions in the survey textbooks on the nineteenth century than do the artists working in the first half of the century. The Impressionists, excepting Cassatt, all slip significantly. The Post-Impressionists consistently rank higher than the Impressionists, but both groups rank below both Goya and David. Van Gogh and Cézanne tie for third with only twenty-seven reproductions each (compared to first-ranked Goya's forty-six); Gauguin ties for seventh with twenty-three, and Monet ties for twelfth with only eighteen. How are we first to account for the denigration of the Impressionists exhibited by the textbooks on the nineteenth century compared with the general surveys, and second, what are we to make of the preponderance of illustrations for the canonical artists in the first half of the century, which we also observed in table 1.3, compared to the second?

Interpreting the Evidence

Let me suggest several possible explanations for how the contemporary art historical canon might reflect historical developments that originally structured this canon. The most obvious explanation for the differing treatment of canonical artists who were at work before and after 1850 is the inherent artificiality of the time limits entailed in these texts on the nineteenth century, which has the effect of subtly altering the respective presentations of the canon. All of the texts articulate how artists such as Goya and David responded to and redefined traditions of representation stretching well back into the eighteenth century and even into the seventeenth, and they demonstrate the relevance of their innovations for later nineteenth-century artists. The innovations of artists whose contributions come after 1880, however, were mostly felt during the twentieth century. If these texts had embraced a "long nineteenth century" to include art up to 1914, then they would have necessarily to account for the resonances of Cézanne or Gauguin on subsequent generations of artists. Of the three survey textbooks on the nineteenth century, Eisenman's most fully articulates this point.

Another explanation would be that this quantitative data indirectly reflects basic changes that occurred in the market structure within which the respective artists made their work. As the royal court painter, Goya, for example, was clearly Spain's most important artist. Today's textbooks regard Goya as the only Spanish artist of real significance since Velázquez. Similarly, David, as Napoleon's chief artist-spokesperson, is centrally important to any discussion of French art under the empire. Why is it, however, that other early nineteenth-century French artists, such as Delacroix and Géricault, who worked in a much richer artistic milieu than Goya, enjoy similarly unchallengeable positions in the canon? One conclusion would be that because the salon system in which they exhibited was a monopoly the most important French art and artists of the day would invariably be recognized as such within the salon system. There are no domestic rivals to the French canon in the first half of the nineteenth century. Consequently, the only way a Géricault might be displaced from the canon would be through the highly unlikely event that today's art historians decide that the most representative and influential art made in post-Napoleonic Europe occurred outside France.

Since such an occurrence is neither likely nor very useful to consider, we should attend rather to how these relative percentages illustrate the power and efficiency of the salon monopoly. It is within this monopoly that the French canonical artists emerged during the first half of the century. It is also likely that the monopoly enabled Paris to assume its central position in the European constellation of art-producing cities, a position it would enjoy for over a century.

Also related to the change in market structures is the transformation of the objects and practices made under these new conditions. After 1865, and more especially, after the first Impressionist exhibition in 1874, the salon's control over the production of important art collapsed, leaving artists to vie for their reputations through rival exhibition societies and commercial gallery shows. One important victim was the salon masterwork. It is still the case that some artists continued to aspire to salon-style *machines*, such as Georges Seurat with his *Sunday Afternoon on the Island of La Grand Jatte*, and achieved canonical status accordingly. Generally, however, during the last quarter of the nineteenth century many subsequently canonical artists ceased to invest a single work with comparable effort and ambition. They did not always have the opportunity, as Seurat did at the last Impressionist exhibition in 1886, to show their work so advantageously, before such a large audience in such an important venue. Dealer showrooms and small exhibition societies favored the display of a body of work, a collection, rather than the single masterwork.

Even Seurat briefly explored the possibilities of the serial image as a substitute for the masterwork during the enormously competitive and fruitful year of 1888, in his series of landscape paintings that created a composite view of the fishing village Port-en-Bassin. The renewed vitality of the Salon des Indépendants after 1900, as well as the addition of the Salon d'Automne in 1903, seems to have stimulated the resurgence in the production of salon-style, large-scale masterworks in Paris. Many of the canonical works from the early twentieth century are considerably larger than those made a generation earlier.[21]

Art history has been sensitive to these changes in market conditions, without necessarily realizing either their proper causes or their real effects. Table 1.3 illustrates how a body of work could effectively substitute for a masterwork in this very different market environment. I inserted into the table Monet's series of paintings of Rouen Cathedral without distinguishing between the paintings in the series; instead, I simply counted them as a single work. Collectively, the different versions of *Rouen Cathedral* reproduced outnumber the total illustrations given to Monet's most often illustrated individual painting, the work that gave the movement its name, *Impression: Sunrise*. This collective art historical judgment regarding the significance of Monet's series paintings is a good example of the unexpected yields produced by quantitative analyses.

Paul Cézanne's *oeuvre* offers an even more striking example of how a body of work, rather than individual works, could become enormously influential. Although table 1.1 indicates that Cézanne was among the most important nineteenth-century artists by number of illustrations, the artist has only one painting in table 1.3, ranking low on the list. Cézanne, who long desired to achieve recognition at what he called "Bouguereau's Salon," used the financial independence he gained late in life to embark on a series of salon-style masterworks, but significantly, unlike Seurat, he would never manage to complete them to his own satisfaction. We should not be surprised, therefore, that it is the *Large Bathers* in Philadelphia that is the single painting by Cézanne to be ranked in table 1.3. That it did not rank as high as other masterworks, such as Géricault's *The Raft of the Medusa* or Seurat's *La Grand Jatte*, is because there is no scholarly consensus that this painting best articulates Cézanne's contribution to late nineteenth-century art. However, it is important that the *Large Bathers* is a very late painting. The preponderance of images by Cézanne come from his mid-to-late career, which is to say that art history regards the later Cézanne as the most important.

While I may have explained why very few artists made absolutely canonical works during the second half of the century I have not yet accounted for why the total number of illustrations given to a canonical artist such as Monet is smaller than the total number given to Delacroix in the texts on the nineteenth century. Another effect of the transformation of the market structure from the salon system and what I have elsewhere termed the salons system was the acceleration of innovation, driven by competition in the market place. Whereas before the 1870s artists established their reputations in France by conforming to or rebelling against the tastes of the salon juries, late in the century, groups of artists, exhibiting in their own "salons," primarily competed against each other. It is a characteristic of economic activity that competition encourages creativity and reinforces pluralism. The end of the nineteenth century is characterized by an extraordinary diversity of styles, and even hugely important artists, such as van Gogh, had to make space not only for their avant-gardist rivals, but for the academicians, realists, fellow travelers, and so on that made up this fecund period in the history of modern art. This would account at least in part for why van Gogh overwhelms all other nineteenth-century artists in the number of monographs cited in table 1.2, yet ranks only fifth in the number of illustrations listed in table 1.1. Similarly, although van Gogh has two paintings among the top fifty-two in table 1.3, there is much less of a sense that his contribution to contemporary painting need be summarized through one or two canonical masterworks. Other paintings might do as well.

Returning to table 1.2, an interesting question is posed by the fact that among the artists in the bottom third of the rankings, only two, François Rude and Gustave Caillebotte, made works ranked among the top fifty-two listed in table 1.3. For the rest of the artists in the lowest third in table 1.2, when their works are illustrated at all it is usually by only one example and rarely is it the same work. One possible explanation for this is that the farther removed one gets from the core of the canon, the more uncertain the specific contributions of an artist or a work of art become; or, conversely, the more uncertain an artist's specific contributions are, the less canonical the artist. Important, but not widely influential artists, such as Berthe Morisot, although frequently illustrated in the textbooks, are represented by a great variety of works. No one painting by Morisot is reproduced more than twice among the twenty-two illustrations found in the thirty-six textbooks. Not only did Morisot fail to produce a masterwork even in the sense of Caillebotte's *Paris Street: Rainy Day*, but also no work by Morisot enjoyed a specific importance either on the occasion of its first exhibition or in the subsequent receptions of her work. In contrast, Caillebotte is never represented in any of the textbooks by works he painted after 1879. Although the reproduced paintings by

Morisot are concentrated in the 1870s (the most important years of the group identity of the Impressionists with whom she exhibited), illustrated works also date from the late 1860s as well as the late 1880s and early 1890s.

As women artists in a male-dominated canon, Rosa Bonheur and Mary Cassatt fared better than Morisot did in the sense of having made signature work. These are often reproduced in the textbooks, and they reflect well-defined moments in the respective artist's career. Although Bonheur (seventeen) had fewer illustrations overall than Morisot (twenty-two), twelve of Bonheur's reproductions were devoted to just two paintings, *Ploughing in the Nivernais Region* (1849), in the Musée d'Orsay, and the *Horse Fair* (1855), in the Metropolitan Museum. Bonheur was twenty-seven and thirty-three respectively when she painted these works. Cassatt had significantly more illustrations than did Morisot and Bonheur, but her most frequently reproduced work, the comparatively late painting *The Boating Party* (1894), in the National Gallery, Washington, appears in just six textbooks. She was fifty at the time. However, Cassatt is also frequently represented by the series of prints she made during the early 1890s (again, while she was in her late forties). Taken as a single work of art they would rank near the middle of the fifty-two most illustrated works listed in table 1.3.

Here then is a fundamental distinction we can make between artists. Concerning lesser or noncanonical artists we value no one period of their careers over any other, precisely because their specific innovations are so undefined. However, concerning major artists, we discover a pronounced tendency to ascribe their most important work to well-defined moments in their careers. Knowing that Cézanne produced his most important work late and that Bonheur made her contribution early, one might then begin to anticipate different modes of creative behavior and new explanations for the successes (and failures) of each artist based on these career profiles. We have new ground through which to generalize about artists' careers and creative behavior.

It was in thinking about the productive life cycles of artists that David Galenson made the surprising and important discovery that the major modern artists he has studied fall into two distinct camps. On the one hand are those artists who exhibited early maturity (like Seurat, who finished *La Grande Jatte* at the age of twenty-seven) and on the other hand are those who matured later (like Cézanne, whose most often reproduced works were painted after 1885, or when the artist was at least forty-six years old). To explain this difference, Galenson developed the hypothesis that within the continuum of creative behavior exist two radically opposed types. At one pole are the conceptual innovators. These are the early developing artists, whose primarily intellectual, non-craft-based, creative behavior made it possible for them to make early, and often the most radical, innovations. At the other pole are the late maturing artists whom Galenson has termed experimental innovators, in keeping with the slow and continuous development of their art. These artists proceed with much uncertainty and struggle to develop their ideas in close dialogue with their respective mediums.

Conceptual artists, by virtue of their predisposition toward planning, are better equipped to produce the ambitious, large-scaled masterwork and are more likely to derive their ideas from earlier art, self-consciously remaking the work of famous predecessors. Being driven by ideas, they are quick to adapt to changing environments. Experimental artists are quite the reverse; their art develops from perceptual observation and refinement, grounded in the craft skills of their respective disciplines. They labor, often with great difficulty (as Cézanne did) to acquire mastery over their means of expression and are consequently less adaptable to changes around them.

Working from Galenson's hypothesis, we see that the artists who first benefited from the collapse of the salon hegemony were almost all experimental painters and sculptors. For most of them, their work continued to mature and grow in significance even after they had reached mid-career. Would such artists as Monet, Cézanne, Rodin, and Cassatt have been able to compete in the conceptually dominated arena of the old salon? Although there is much work still to be done on questions like these, the ability to type an artist through a general model of creative behavior has many potential interpretive uses. It casts new, comparative light, for example, on the similarities in practices between a Rodin and a Cézanne, and their procedural distance from a Gauguin.

Conclusion

Economists know that markets reward innovation. Insofar as a market economy has been an integral part of Western society since at least the late Middle Ages, its effect has been to put a fundamental emphasis on artistic innovation in Western art. Consequently, the close linkage between market behavior and success or failure in the production of important art offers many fruitful areas for future study. The canon of nineteenth-century art is the canon of great innovators, regardless of the market environment in or the aesthetic expectations with which these innovators may have worked. Yet we also value the careers of canonical artists in significantly different ways, which in turn can be used to raise new questions about often very familiar subjects.

Recognizing that artistic importance derives from artistic innovation may have the further beneficial effect of sharpening the ways in which art history approaches canons. In a discipline that tends to be dismissive of its introductory textbooks and treats canons as if they were alien creatures feeding off the body of art, we can hardly expect survey textbooks to be better than most of them currently are. If one doesn't understand why canons exist and what their relationships are to art history, then it is obviously going to be difficult to describe how artworks and artists make their contributions. It is, however, through just such texts that the profession of art history reaches its widest audience and therefore for which it ought to feel the greatest sense of responsibility.

Appendix: Textbook Survey Sources

Adams, Laurie Schneider. *Art across Time*. Boston: McGraw-Hill College, 1999.

Annoscia, Enrico, et al. *Art: A World History*. New York: DK Publishing, 1998.

Argan, Guilio C. *Die Kunst des 20: Jahrhunderts*. Berlin: Propyläen Verlag, 1977.

Bocola, Sandro. *The Art of Modernism*. Munich: Prestel, 1999.

Brettell, Richard R. *Modern Art 1851–1929*. Oxford: Oxford University Press, 1999.

Chu, Petra ten-Doesschate. *Nineteenth-Century European Art*. New York: Harry N. Abrams, 2003.

Cole, Bruce, and Adelheid Gealt. *Art of the Western World*. New York: Summit Books, 1989.

Craske, Matthew. *Art in Europe 1700–1830*. Oxford: Oxford University Press, 1997.

Eisenman, Stephen, ed. *Nineteenth-Century Art*. London: Thames and Hudson, 2002.

Fleming, William. *Art and Ideas*. 8th ed. Fort Worth: Holt, Rinehart and Winston, 1990.

Frontisi, Claude, ed. *Histoire visuelle de l'art*. Paris: Larousse, 2001.

Gauthier, Maximilien. *Tout l'art du monde*. Vol. 3. Paris: Larousse, 1966.

Gebhardt, Volker. *The History of Art*. Hauppauge, N.Y.: Barron's, 1997.

Gombrich, Ernst. *The Story of Art*. 16th ed. Englewood Cliffs, N.J.: Prentice-Hall, 1995.

Gowing, Lawrence, ed. *A History of Art*. Rev. ed. Abingdon, Oxfordshire: Andromeda, 1995.

Hamilton, George Heard. *19th and 20th Century Art*. New York: Harry N. Abrams, 1970.

———. *Painting and Sculpture in Europe 1880–1940*. New Haven, Conn.: Yale University Press, 1993.

Hartt, Frederick. *Art*. 4th ed. New York: Harry N. Abrams, 1993.

Hollingsworth, Mary. *L'Arte nella Storia dell'Uomo*. Florence: Giunti, 1989.

Honour, Hugh, and John Fleming. *The Visual Arts: A History*. 6th ed. Upper Saddle River, N.J.: Prentice-Hall, 2002.

Huyghe, René, ed. *L'Art et l'homme*. Paris: Larousse, 1961.

Janson, H. W. *History of Art*. 6th ed. New York: Harry N. Abrams, 2001.

Johnson, Paul. *Art: A New History*. New York: HarperCollins, 2003.

Kemp, Martin, ed. *The Oxford History of Western Art*. Oxford: Oxford University Press, 2000.

Kleiner, Fred S., Christin J. Mamiya, and Richard G. Tansey. *Gardner's "Art through the Ages."* 11th ed. Fort Worth: Harcourt College Publishers, 2001.
Lucie-Smith, Edward. *Art and Civilization.* New York: Harry N. Abrams, 1993.
Novotny, Fritz. *Painting and Sculpture in Europe 1780–1880.* Harmondsworth: Penguin, 1960.
Penck, Stefanie, ed. *Prestel Atlas Bildende Kunst.* Munich: Prestel, 2002.
Raynal, Maurice. *The Nineteenth Century.* Geneva: Skira, 1951.
Read, Herbert. *The Styles of European Art.* New York: Harry N. Abrams, 1965.
Reynolds, Donald Martin. *Nineteenth-century Art.* Cambridge: Cambridge University Press, 1985.
Rosenblum, Robert, and H. W. Janson. *Art of the Nineteenth Century.* London: Thames and Hudson, 1984.
Sayre, Henry M. *World of Art.* 2nd ed. Englewood Cliffs, N.J.: Prentice-Hall, 1997.
Silver, Larry. *Art in History.* Englewood Cliffs, N.J.: Prentice-Hall, 1993.
Stokstad, Marilyn. *Art History.* Rev. ed. New York: Harry N. Abrams, 1999.
Terrarikum, Valerio, ed. *Lezioni di Storia dell'Arte.* Vol. 3. Milan: Skira, 2003.
Thullier, Jacques. *History of Art.* Paris: Flammarion, 2003.
Wilkins, David G., Bernard Schultz, and Katheryn M. Linduff. *Art Past, Art Present.* 2nd ed. New York: Harry N. Abrams, 1994.
Zeitler, Rudolf. *Die Kunst des 19: Jahrhunderts.* Berlin: Propyläen Verlag, 1966.

Notes

1 I would like to thank David Galenson for the many conversations that inform this text and without whose work I would never have thought to write it. Regarding the quotation, see Hayden White, "The Fiction of Factual Representation," 27.

2 It is not just theoretical constructs such as "commodification" that are rarely examined in light of historical evidence. There are also seemingly empirical historical constructs, such as Harrison White's and Cynthia White's famous description of the "dealer-critic system," that are constantly reiterated without serious interrogation. Yet the Whites' thesis that art dealers in late nineteenth-century France were able to provide artists with support comparable to the patronage of Renaissance princes and that they were able to establish artists' careers are patently wrong, if one but reflects on the historical record. The Whites' 1965 book, *Canvases and Careers* was reprinted in 1993 and remains in print today. It has been cited as an authoritative text, often without comment, by, among others, the following authors: Clark, *The Painting of Modern Life*, 260; House, *Monet*, 234 n. 25; Mainardi, "Editor's Statement," 7; Green, "Circuits of Production, Circuits of Consumption," 29, 33 n. 6; Fitzgerald, *Making Modernism*, 7; Ward, *Pissarro, Neo-Impressionism, and the Spaces of the Avant-Garde*, 4; Cottington, *Cubism in the Shadow of War*, 37; O'Brian, *Ruthless Hedonism*, 12, 41–42, 105; Rubin, *Impressionism*, 331, 440; and Nord, *Impressionists and Politics*, 71, 118. Galenson and I have written a systematic rebuttal of the Whites' thesis; see Galenson and Jensen, "Careers and Canvases" for a working version of the rebuttal. A more condensed version of our essay is scheduled to be published in 2007 in *Van Gogh Studies*.

3 Haskell has been particularly influential on the mutability of canons. He described im-

portant historical rediscoveries of long-overlooked masters as evidence that tastes are subject to radical change. See especially his *Rediscoveries in Art*.

4 Kubler, *The Shape of Time*, 10.

5 It is also the case that even the most respected art historians often use originality interchangeably with innovation, without realizing that these terms may be used to articulate quite different concepts. See, for example, Richard Shiff's essay on originality in Nelson and Shiff, *Critical Terms for Art History*, 1st ed., 103–15. Shiff quite correctly discusses the tradition of locating originality within the individual creator, but he then goes on to conflate originality with innovation, as when he writes about artists "acting on their desire for originality and self-expression as they created one modernist innovation after another, or at least what passed for innovation" (109). Shiff assumes here that a creator solely determines an innovation. Shiff is hardly alone in using these terms without careful distinction. Another recent example may be found in Herbert, "Impressionism, Originality, and Laissez-faire."

6 *Webster's New World Dictionary of the American Language*. College ed. (New York: World Publishing Co., 1959).

7 As Krauss argued in her often-cited essay "The Originality of the Avant-Garde," in *The Originality of the Avant-Garde and Other Modernist Myths*, originality belonged more to art history than to artistic practice: "[The] discourse of originality serves much wider interests—and is thus fueled by more diverse institutions—than the restricted circle of professional art-making. The theme of originality, encompassing as it does the notions of authenticity, originals, and origins, is the shared discursive practice of the museum, the historian, and the maker of art. And throughout the nineteenth century all of these institutions were concerted, together, to find the mark, the warrant, the certification of the original" (161). However, Krauss also argues that avant-garde practice could essentially be reduced to the thirst for originality: the ambition to make "a literal origin, a beginning from ground zero, a birth" (157). Since the desire to establish originals clearly predates the rise of the avant-gardes, it is difficult to test Krauss's thesis that some causal relationship exists between the avant-garde art practices she described in her essay and this particular form of market behavior. Also, we should be careful to distinguish between what artists claimed to do and what they actually did, which is to say that none of them actually did begin at "ground zero."

8 I have learned to use resonance from de Duve's work on Duchamp. See especially de Duve, *Pictorial Nominalism*.

9 Kubler noted that "The discovery of hitherto unknown painters of the stature of Rembrandt or Goya is far less likely than our suddenly becoming aware of the excellence of many craftsmen whose work has only lately come to be accepted as art" and that in the process art history reveals "unfamiliar types of artistic effort, each with its own biographical roster" (*The Shape of Time*, 123).

10 Kleiner and Mamiya, *Gardner's "Art through the Ages"*; and Gardner, *Art through the Ages*, 1st ed.

11 Jensen, "Anticipating Artistic Behavior." The painters were, in order of frequency of reproductions: Raphael, Titian, Rembrandt, Velázquez, Caravaggio, Leonardo, van Eyck, Masaccio, Vermeer, Michelangelo, Giorgione, Hals, Holbein, and Campin.

12 Using the Library of Congress electronic catalogue (November 2004), I searched its

holdings of survey textbooks catalogued under its most common call number: N5300. I organized these findings by decade and by the nationality and/or location of publication. An English writer published the first art history survey text in the 1820s. The Library of Congress possesses no surveys in any language published during the 1830s; it has three dating from the 1840s (English, German, and American), one each from the 1850s and 1860s, four from the 1870s, including two French texts, five from the 1880s, and three from the 1890s. The explosion in such books, if the holdings of the Library of Congress are to be our guide, occurred during the first decade of the twentieth century, with thirteen. Thereafter the lowest number of new survey texts published per decade (as opposed to republication) occurred during the 1970s, with nine. The greatest number, not surprisingly considering the postwar expansion of higher education, belonged to the 1960s, with twenty-seven. Overall, authors writing in English contributed sixty-six such texts to the library's holdings, in German thirty-eight; in French thirty; in Italian fifteen; in Spanish fourteen; in Swedish five; in Portuguese four; and in Dutch three.

13 That differences do occur, for example, between American and French evaluations of what is important in contemporary art is just the sort of historically concrete material that can be usefully compared in order to understand both art cultures better. On this example, see Galenson, "The New York School versus the School of Paris."

14 I actually consulted thirty-nine textbooks in conjunction with table 1. However, I counted them as thirty-six texts because Argan and Zeitler, Brettell and Craske, and Hamilton and Novotny each belong to two-volume series surveying the entire nineteenth century. See the appendix for the complete references.

15 While it would be possible to create a precise ranking of nineteenth-century artists from 1 through 50, the data collection involved becomes much more complex. Every illustrated artist would have to be counted in the sample of thirty-six textbooks. Such a ranking, while interesting in itself, would not further illuminate the arguments advanced below.

16 Anyone familiar with the Library of Congress subject-heading listings knows that they are not all inclusive. For any given artist, other subject headings might be offered, broken down into such categories as exhibitions, criticism, and so forth. Monographs might appear here that the bibliographers failed to include under the general subject heading. Thus, the numbers I used in table 1.2 are a relative measure of interest in each artist compared to the rest, not an absolute number of monographs devoted to that artist in the Getty collections.

17 Galenson has observed this phenomenon, what he calls "one hit wonders." See his study *Old Masters and Young Geniuses*.

18 These titles were also included in my general sample. See the appendix for the complete references.

19 Other survey texts of the nineteenth century published since Rosenblum's and Janson's text share similar resistances to building their narratives around canonical art. See Eitner, *An Outline of 19th-Century Art*; and Boime, *A Social History of Modern Art*.

20 Among the three texts on the nineteenth century only Eisenman's gave Monet as few as three illustrations, yet his text also gives the most illustrations of the three to Cézanne (thirteen), van Gogh (fourteen), and Gauguin (twelve). In other words, Eisenman's text

tends to devalue the popular Impressionists (excepting Cassatt) in favor of the leading Post-Impressionists. These sorts of editorial aberrations, however, are mitigated when one looks at survey textbooks on the nineteenth century overall.

21 Compare, for example, the sizes of such major entries to the salons of 1905 and 1906 as Matisse's *Le Bonheur de vivre*, 174 × 238 cm (5 feet 8½ inches × 7 feet 9¾ inches), and Derain's *The Age of Gold*, 176 × 189 cm (5 feet 9¼ inches × 6 feet 2⅜ inches), with canonical paintings from the 1880s such as Gauguin's *Vision after the Sermon*, 73 × 92 cm (28¾ × 36¼ inches), and van Gogh's *Starry Night*, 73 × 93 cm (28¾ × 36½ inches).

2

Canon and Globalization in Art History

JAMES ELKINS

What does it mean to say that art history is or is not a global enterprise? This question, which I think is the most important one that currently faces the discipline—more pressing, for example, than theoretically driven questions such as the future of postcolonial theory, the limits of identity politics, or the assumptions behind institutional critique—is difficult to frame with accuracy.[1] The philosophic and pedagogic issues are entangled with assumptions about disciplinarity and Westernness that are nearly impossible to state clearly. My purpose in this essay is something simpler than the adjudication of terms, and certainly simpler than the philosophic framing of questions. I aim only to gather information on three subjects that are amenable to quantitative research, and a fourth that almost is. With this accumulation of figures and graphs I hope to demonstrate that some working assumptions that currently structure the discussion about world art history might in fact be false.

In particular, and in regard to the present collection of essays, I want to suggest that the recent proliferation of scholarship on canons risks obscuring the continuing existence and worldwide influence of a relatively unreconstructed canon that I will call, echoing E. H. Gombrich, the "story of art." (That story, roughly speaking, follows the familiar trajectory of periods, artists, and works that leads from Egypt through Greece and Rome to the Renaissance and modernism in western Europe and North America.)[2] It is salutary to study canons in specific regions and countries and in different historical settings. What concerns me is that such scholarship can be understood to be solving, or even to have solved, the influence of the standard "story of art." It is optimistic, I think, to look at the enormous variety of canons that have been and continue to be employed and conclude that art history is composed of many local practices. Canons are historically relative to their contexts, but that does not mean that shifting attention to local canons and away from the canon embedded in the "story of art" (from here on, I will omit the scare quotes, with the understanding that they are always implied) will automatically or naturally produce a more local art history, less beholden to what used to be called "dead white males." It is not that canons are not developed in relation to local contexts: it is that the story of art exerts a strong influence on the discipline that may not be meliorated by turning scholarly attention to local contexts. I am not claiming that the story of art and its attendant canon are somehow transhistorical, or that the attendant canon is possessed of a greater historical permanence than any other canon, but I would say that the canon of the story of art is far more deeply entangled in what it means to write or study art history irrespective of specific location than it might seem now that canons of all sorts are open for examination. One way to think about the insidiousness of the canon implied by the standard story of art is to gather statistics about art historical practices worldwide in order to learn more about the constitution of art history and its potential independence from western European and North American narrative and conceptual models.

Here, then, are the three quantitative subjects I have in mind, and the one qualitative subject. First, it can be asked how art history departments are distributed worldwide. It would be of interest to know if there are more art history departments in western Europe, for example, than in South America (to compare two regions with approximately the same number of countries).

Second, it is possible to survey art historical publications worldwide to see which regions and countries produce the most. Art historical *production* could then be correlated with art history as a discipline in universities, and both of those could be compared to the populations of the regions in question. I take it that the general answers to these first two questions will not be surprising, but I want to set them out here with actual statistics because it can seem as though art historical practices throughout the world are effectively unencompassable, and that property can be taken in turn as evidence that the practices are heterogeneous and local. The evidence of art history's homogeneity and European and North American focus leads me to the question of the place occupied by the standard canon.

Third, then, it can be asked whether art historians worldwide study mainly the art of western Europe and North America. Within this question are two others: Do art historians study mainly the best-known figures and periods—the canon of the story of art—or is the new scholarship effectively redistributing the interests of the field in the direction of lesser-known artists?

And is art history focused principally on European and North American artists (those, for example, in the canon of the story of art), or is it expanding outward to encompass world art?

A fourth subject cannot be studied quantitatively, but it is crucial for any assessment of the discipline: Does art history have identifiable methodological interests? Is it focused on iconography more than on semiotics, on style analysis less than on formal analysis? Interpretive proclivities can't be measured, but there are ways to deliberately misuse databases to arrive at approximate results.

These four subjects all go to an underlying question, which I cannot answer here—in fact, I can barely open the issue.[3] Are there emerging non-Western art histories? Or is the world's art being studied mainly by using interpretive methods, protocols of argument and evidence, and styles of writing developed predominately in Germany, France, England, and the United States?[4] It can be argued that the very fact that it is not easy to find the kind of information that this volume presents is already evidence that art history is not global. The information is difficult to come by partly because relatively few scholars are interested in comparing cultures and canons, and partly because the relevant databases are themselves Western projects, as I will suggest. Non-Western publications, and especially ephemeral ones, are not consistently represented in the principal art historical indices and databases. Hence the information I present in this essay is partial and partly uncontrolled for error: my only excuse is that it is necessary to begin—otherwise there will be no way to step outside the self-portrait of Western art history.

How Is Art History Distributed Worldwide?

One way to measure the presence of art history in different parts of the world is to look at the number of universities that have departments of art history. There is no definitive list, and even if there were, the results would be blurred by the existence of art schools and art academies, which often have art historians on staff, although it can be impossible to determine which have degrees in art history and which are artists or critics. A country may have one or more universities that have departments of art history, and as many universities or colleges that offer a few courses in art history in other departments, so that there is no clear cut-off point. In Colombia, for instance, Andrés Gratán of the Pontifica Universidad Javeriana in Bogotá informs me that there are six other universities in Bogotá that have art history courses, and also two in Cali, two in Medellín, and one each in Santa Marta, Cartagena, and Bucaramanga.[5] That list only includes a couple of art academies, and most of the universities do not have art history departments; instead, they have departments of communication or design with art historians on staff. It would be necessary to visit the schools in order to determine how many of the instructors are trained in art history. Smaller countries and regions may not have art history departments, but they will sometimes have full-time art historians teaching in other departments. This kind of data is not at all impossible to gather, but so far no compilation exists.[6]

The University College Cork, Ireland, has assembled a database of more than eight hundred institutions worldwide that have art history departments.[7] The list is larger than any Internet source because it combines the largest sources, and it is almost five times the size of the World of Learning database.[8] Institutions included in the University College Cork database must have art history departments, which helps clarify the collection of information. Given that criterion there are indications that the list is nearly complete. Art historians from Finland, Jordan, Singapore, Germany, and Denmark have written to the database giving definitive lists of institutions in their countries, and their lists have corresponded well with the database.[9] So on that admittedly insecure ground I can draw some tentative conclusions about how widespread art history is as a named discipline within universities.[10]

The approximate number of institutions with departments of art history in Ireland and the United Kingdom is 97. The number for continental Europe, including Turkey (which has 10 universities with art history departments), is 193. (The data are summarized in fig. 2.1.) Eastern Europe and southeastern Europe have relatively few institutions with art history departments: the database registers 2 in Slovakia (one, the Slovak Academy of Sciences, is internationally active), 2 in Romania, and 2 in Bulgaria.

The number of departments of art history in universities in the United States and Canada is 226, so it appears there is more art history being taught in Europe than in the United States—with the caveat that smaller colleges in the United States are likely to incorporate art departments, so that what would in Europe be art colleges and academies are counted disproportionately. (There are over three thousand universities and colleges in the United States and Canada; less than one-tenth of them have departments of art history.) For South America and Central America the number of art history departments is forty-eight, although the numbers are low because of the sporadic web presence of institutions. The actual number might be more on the order of

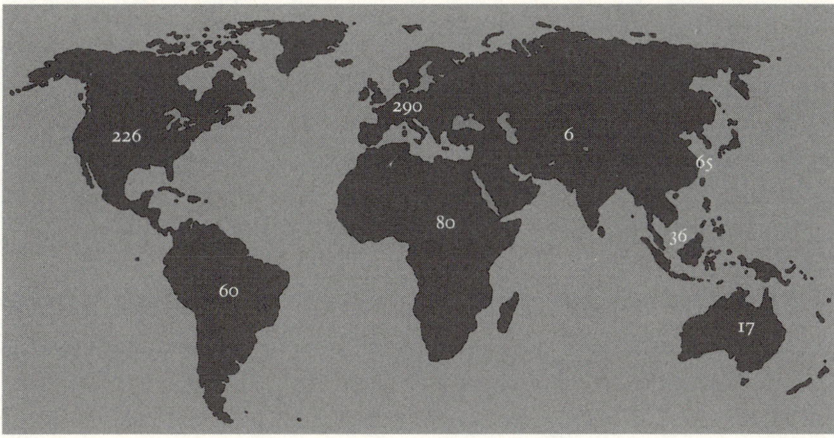

2.1. The world map showing the number of art history departments in each geographic region.

sixty. For Africa the database has seventy-nine institutions, a number that is raised by a recent poll undertaken by the University of Maryland, which gives addresses for sub-Saharan countries, but lowered by the very uneven web presence of African institutions. I was amazed to discover that the Ahmadu Bello University in Nigeria, the country's largest with thirty-two thousand students, had no official web page as of November 2006. The database shows seventeen universities with art history departments in Australia and New Zealand; sixty-five in China, Japan, and Korea; thirty-six in southeast Asia excluding Australia; and another half-dozen in central Asia (Tajikistan, Turkmenistan, Uzbekistan, Kazakhstan, Kyrgyzstan, Iran, Iraq, and Pakistan), where the low numbers partly reflect the Islamic tradition and partly the influence of the Soviet system, which placed art academies and art history outside of universities.

This survey is incomplete in the ways I have mentioned, and also in that it has no entries for countries that I assume may have universities with art history departments, such as Belarus, Moldova, and Andorra in Europe; or Guinea, Liberia, Togo, Burundi, the Democratic Republic of the Congo, and Somalia in Africa. But it is a fairly accurate and reasonably exhaustive poll, and the conclusion it suggests is that as a discipline and as a unit within universities, art history is very much a North American and western European phenomenon.

What Parts of the World Produce the Most Art Historical Writing?

The initial problem with assessing the worldwide production of art history is that databases are biased toward Western sources. WorldCat, a standard source in Europe and North America, is a reflection of the purchases made by libraries in the United States. The RLIN is somewhat better in that respect, since it has spearheaded the acquisition of "CJK" data—Chinese, Japanese, and Korean.

The situation is similar among specialized art history databases. Art Abstracts (formerly the Art Index), for example, is overtly Western. In July 2004, a search of Art Abstracts for essays written in the United States yielded 318,089 entries. Similar searches for essays written in France, Germany, and the United Kingdom yielded, respectively, the following numbers: 46,923; 22,855; and 131,193. But the reason that Art Abstracts lists 764 essays published in Ireland is that it indexes *Circa*, the Irish art magazine; likewise, Art Abstracts registers 93 essays published in Denmark because it includes the *Scandinavian Journal of Design History*. Many other countries yield no results whatsoever: Art Abstracts has nothing published in South Africa, Brazil, Argentina, Chile, Norway, Poland, Russia, or China. The other principal database that is specialized in art history, the Bibliography of the History of Art, is configured so that it is impossible to search for essays published in different countries.[11] The BHA can, however, be searched for the languages of the essays it indexes, and the results show a sharp drop-off after English, Italian, German, French, Spanish, and Dutch.[12]

Outside of these, and Art Bibliographies Modern, there are apparently no digital indices of art historical publications in any language.[13] To get an idea of how much might be missing from Western databases, it is possible to sample the numbers of art periodicals in different countries. The bar graph, fig. 2.2, shows the number of Chinese journals indexed by the major Western databases (the three left-hand bars) compared with the number listed by the two principal commercial distributors that sell bulk subscriptions to libraries (the two right-hand bars). East View Information Services (second bar from the right) offers libraries a package of academically inclined Chinese journals in "fine art and art theory": it is a good assumption that the journals in East View's list are all potentially relevant to art history.[14] The *Catalogue of Chinese Newspapers and Periodicals* (right-hand bar) offers a broader and less academic subject category of "art," some of which are how-to-paint magazines, art therapy journals, and children's art magazines. Still, the disparity is a serious one, and it points to the Western bias of sources such as Art Abstracts.[15]

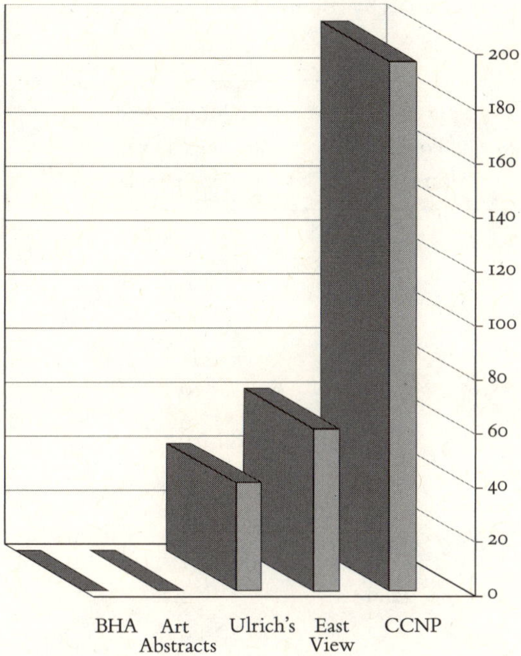

2.2. The number of Chinese periodicals catalogued by major Western bibliographic databases (BHA, Art Abstracts, Ulrich's) versus those listed by two principal commercial distributors (East View Information Services and the *Catalogue of Chinese Newspapers and Periodicals*).

It seems likely, given this data, that more is missing from Western databases when it comes to Asian countries than is missing from the databases' listings of Western countries.

A somewhat more dependable way to judge the worldwide production of art historical texts is to count refereed art journals. The periodical database Ulrich's, now available online, is more internationally inclined than Art Abstracts or the Bibliography of the History of Art. According to Ulrich's, many countries do not have refereed art journals, and countries with refereed journals are almost exclusively in western Europe and North America. Table 2.1 gives figures for a sampling of countries, correlated with population (in millions); the right-hand column gives the number of refereed art journals per one hundred thousand people. The highest ratio of refereed art journals to general population is in the Netherlands, New Zealand, Denmark, and Belgium. The United States has less than half as many journals per capita as these four countries. This kind of data could be used to talk about which countries are most invested in art—although more work would have to be done to determine the significance of the figures.

The Ulrich's database captures many refereed art journals that are not pertinent to art history, but it may be considered proportionately representative because it includes most of the major art historical serials.[16] I take it that

Table 2.1. The number of refereed art journals by country based on a survey of Ulrich's bibliographic database.

Country	No. of refereed art journals	Population (in millions)	No. of refereed art journals per 100,000 people
Algeria	0	32	0
Argentina	0	37	0
Australia	17	19	90
Austria	3	8	38
Belgium	10	10	100
Bolivia	0	8	0
Brazil	3	176	2
Bulgaria	0	8	0
Canada	12	31	39
Chile	1	15	7
China	3	1289	0.2
Colombia	1	42	2
Costa Rica	0	4	0
Cyprus	0	0.7	0
Czech Republic	0	10	0
Denmark	6	5	120
Ecuador	0	12	0
Egypt	0	72	0
Estonia	0	1	0
Finland	0	5	0
France	7	60	12
Germany	16	83	19
Greece	1	11	9
Guatemala	0	11	0
Hungary	3	10	30
India	1	1069	0.1
Ireland	3	4	75
Israel	2	6	33
Italy	8	57	14
Japan	2	128	2
Jordan	0	7	0
Kenya	0	31	0
Latvia	0	2	0
Lithuania	0	4	0
Mexico	2	105	2

Table 2.1. *Continued*

Country	No. of refereed art journals	Population (in millions)	No. of refereed art journals per 100,000 people
Netherlands	35	16	218
New Zealand	5	4	125
Nicaragua	0	5	0
Nigeria	0	134	0
Norway	1	4	20
Pakistan	0	149	0
Paraguay	0	5	0
Peru	0	26	0
Poland	7	39	17
Portugal	0	10	0
Romania	2	22	9
Russia	0	146	0
Slovakia	0	5	0
South Africa	4	44	9
South Korea	0	47	0
Spain	5	40	12
Sweden	4	9	11
Switzerland	3	7	42
Taiwan	1	22	5
Tunisia	0	10	0
Uganda	0	24	0
Ukraine	1	50	2
United Kingdom	45	59	75
United States	123	292	40
Uruguay	1	3	30

Ulrich's lists are more capacious by a factor of two or three than they need to be to delineate just the history of art; and they are also immeasurably biased toward Europe and toward English-language publications. Nevertheless Ulrich's is an international standard, and it has no relevant competition on other languages.

Ulrich's data can be presented in several forms. Table 2.1 gives the numbers by country. Dividing the world into regions also yields interesting results. If Europe is divided east of Germany and Austria, so that the eastern portion contains Greece, Bulgaria, Romania, Hungary, the Czech Republic, Poland, and the Baltic states, but not Italy or Austria, then the division captures a steep gradient on either side of the line. To the west of the line there are 143 refereed journals, which is 43 percent of the worldwide total. To the east of the line there are only 16, which is 5 percent of the total.[17] If refereed journals are gathered according to continents, the results are even more stark than on the map of art history departments worldwide (see fig. 2.1)—indeed, the small numbers in some continents would not even show up on the map. Europe (considered as a whole) has 159 refereed art journals, which is 48 percent—nearly half—of the world total. North America has 135 refereed journals, which is 40 percent. The entire remainder of the world has only 12 percent: only 8 in Central and South America, only 4 in Africa, 8 in all of Asia, and 22 in Australia and Oceania. (That's 2 percent, 1 percent, 2 percent, and 7 percent respectively.) These numbers fall off much more rapidly outside of Europe and North America than the numbers of art history departments. I conclude that the production of art historical texts is strongly constrained to North America and western Europe (with "western" interpreted in the way I have suggested), and it seems likely that the production of art historical essays per capita is even more strongly constrained to a region that might be described as northwestern Europe: the United Kingdom, Denmark, the Netherlands, and Belgium.

Do Art Historians Study Mainly the Art of Europe and North America?

In asking about canons in the history of art, it is also helpful to ask about canons formed *by* the history of art. The artists who were of most interest to critics in nineteenth-century France, for example, are studied by twenty-first-century art historians, but they—the contemporary art historians—also study artists who were for various reasons not prominent in the nineteenth century. In other words: what we study is a canon, even if—perhaps especially if—what we study are other people's canons. (Canons, in other words, can be considered as objects or artists or movements of interest, but they can also be considered as texts about those objects or artists or movements; both can be enumerated.)

The canon hasn't been a question in art history as it has in English, comparative literature, classics, and philosophy, principally because the first-year survey in art history, which typically presents a version of the story of art, usually includes several thousand artists—as many as will fit in a one-year course.[18] Textbooks such as Marilyn Stokstad's *Art History* are massive (typically on the order of six pounds) because they try to avoid making choices in favor of the most wide-ranging possible treatment of the world's art.[19] That luxury isn't available in subjects such as English, where there are limits to the number of novels and poems that can be read in a year. It can appear, then, as if the history of art has no canon of indispensable masterpieces, and even as if it has avoided the problem altogether. But art historians' research habits prove otherwise.

Michael Rinehart, the editor-in-chief of the Bibliography of the History of Art, showed me a printout he had made of all the subject categories listed by the BHA from 1972 to 1987.[20] The most frequently cited artists were no surprise; table 2.2 gives the top fifty, in order of popularity. Inevitably in lists like this, one looks for one's favorites. I was disappointed that David didn't make the list (he was number fifty-one) and amused by the odd bedfellows the list generates (Dalí, at number sixty-two, is just above Malevich, at number sixty-three).

I transcribed the first several hundred names, and then when that got tedious I began counting the number of citations each artist received, noting how many artists had been cited forty-four times, forty-three times, and so on. Eventually even that became impossible, and I had to estimate the number of artists who had been cited ten or fewer times. I have put some of the data in table 2.3, which shows the top thirty entries and the drop in numbers after the fiftieth entry.[21] I thought at first that if I were to plot the number of citations against the number of artists, I would get a smooth sloping curve, from the most studied to the least studied. But then, going over the numbers, I found an uneven slide from art history's most popular artist (Picasso) to the approximately ten thousand artists who are lost in the oblivion of single citations. And sure enough, by graphing on log-log paper, which condenses the axes, a pattern emerges (see fig. 2.3).

The graph plots the number of citations (on the horizontal axis) against the number of artists who got that number of citations.[22] Picasso is at the far bottom-right: he has 757 citations, and he is the only artist who was cited

Table 2.2. The fifty most cited artists in the *BHA* database, 1972–1987, with the number of citations for each.

Rank	Artist	No. of citations	Rank	Artist	No. of citations
1	Picasso	757	26	Poussin	202
2	Dürer	616	27	Ingres	201
3	Rubens	600	28	Manet	200
4	Michelangelo	537	29	Blake	199
5	Leonardo	526	30	Giorgione	191
6	Raphael	460	31	Velázquez	181
7	Rembrandt	442	32	Piranesi	180
8	Titian	418	33	Friedrich	177
9	Goya	391	34	Bosch	163
10	Palladio	377	35	Rodin	162
11	Van Gogh	283	36	Duchamp	161
12	Turner	270	37	Brughel the Elder	160
13	Cézanne	267	38	Ernst	159
14	Brunelleschi	243	39	Degas	156
15	Klee	240	40	Munch	155
16	Matisse	224	41	Cranach	154
17	Bernini	220	42	Watteau	152
18	Alberti	218	43	Monet	151
19	Courbet	215	44	Viollet-le-Duc	151
20	Le Corbusier	214	45	Gauguin	147
21	Schinkel	213	46	Donatello	145
22	Caravaggio	211	47	Van Eyck	145
23	Delacroix	209	48	Tiepolo	144
24	Kandinsky	205	49	Constable	141
25	Giotto	203	50	Lotto	141

Table 2.3. The number of artists who are cited a particular number of times in the BHA database, 1972–1987.

No. of citations	No. of artists	No. of citations	No. of artists
1	ca. 10,000	22	28
2	ca. 5,000	23	26
3	ca. 1,400	24	21
4	1,105	25	29
5	715	26	15
6	494	27	16
7	390	28	14
8	312	29	9
9	234	30	12
10	208		
11	152	50	5
12	118	51	4
13	82	52	4
14	77	53	3
15	64	54	3
16	47	55	1
17	55	56	5
18	57	57	5
19	35	58	5
20	34	59	2
21	30	60	4

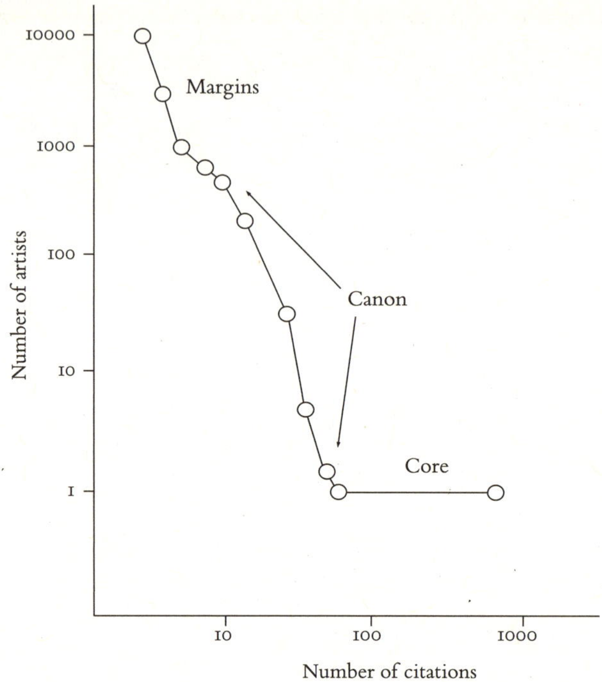

2.3. A log-log graph of the art canon based on the survey of artist citations in *BHA* 1972–87.

that number of times (number 1 on the vertical axis). All of the artists I list in table 2.2 are along that bottom horizontal line: Dürer has 616 citations, and no one else has, so he is on the same horizontal line. Then the graph in fig. 2.3 begins to move slowly upward. Five artists have 57 citations each, but eleven artists have 38 citations each; and finally, at the top-left, somewhere around ten thousand artists were cited once each; that portion reflects the data given in table 2.3.

The graph is not a smooth curve or a line. It has three distinct portions. I call the lowest horizontal line and its little curving tail the core. The artists in this portion are those who garnered the most attention from art historians indexed in the BHA in the period 1972–1987. The top third is the margins: the endless stream of artists who attracted one, two, or three articles each. That leaves the middle third, which is the bread and butter of art history. Along with the core it is, I think, nothing more or less than the canon of the story of art, as it is reflected—strongly—in the best available database.

In a book called *Why Are Our Pictures Puzzles? On the Modern Origins of Pictorial Complexity*, I argued—using statistics from the Wilson Index, another principal database for art history—that the discipline is growing in two directions.[23] Art historians write on a small group of artists, generating *intensive* scholarship on just a few names and works; and we also spread ourselves over time and space, writing *extensively* on ever-more obscure artists. The intensive scholarship shows up here as the core, and the extensive scholarship appears as the margins. It is still an open question as to which part of art history is growing faster.

The moral is simple: as of 1987, art history, as it appears in the BHA, did indeed have a canon, and it was irredeemably Eurocentric, obstinately focused on modernism and premodernism and entirely fixated on painting (with a bit of architecture and virtually no sculpture). Given that the only years for which this kind of data is available are 1972–87, it is worth appending a few remarks on the growth of the discipline. If art history has grown by an order of magnitude since then, these data will no longer be valid, and it might in fact be the case that art history has become effectively multicultural. A quick way to assess the discipline's growth is to look at the number of articles published on selected subjects over a longer time span, and for that a convenient starting place is the inception of the Art Index, which began in 1929. (It is now called the Art Index Retrospective, covering 1929–84; Art Abstracts covers 1985 to the present.) Fig. 2.4 gives sample results. The top wavy line is the number of articles on Picasso in each five-year period; the middle wavy line is the same for Michelangelo; and the bottom wavy line represents articles on Cambodian art.[24] (That is: a modern artist, a Renaissance artist, and a non-Western subject.) The smoother, black lines are regressions—mathematical extrapolations.[25] They show that the growth of writing on Picasso and Michelangelo, at least, is leveling off. That may indicate that the discipline of art history as a whole is not growing as fast as it did in the first half of the twentieth century, or that scholarship has turned in directions that are not reflected in this data—although I suspect that if the latter were true, even unexpected and innovative approaches to Michelangelo, say, would appear in the indices under "Michelangelo." The abrupt rise in essays on Cambodian art suggests that non-Western art may be a growth industry: much more data would have to be collected, but it would be easy to do. (My apples-and-oranges comparison here is a reflection of the paucity of indexed research on individual Cambodian monuments and artists. To get a statistically supportable quantity of data, I had to choose the country's art as a whole for my criterion.)

It appears that interest in non-Western subjects is growing rapidly, but the total number of articles on such subjects is low enough that it may not have upset the general trend in regard to Western art. I would suggest that

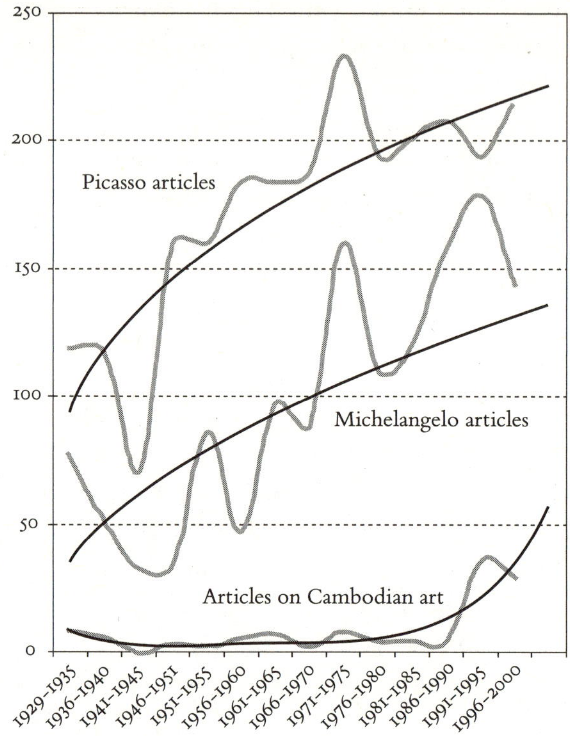

2.4. The growth of the discipline indicated by the number of articles on Picasso, Michelangelo, and art in Cambodia published from 1929 to 2000, based on a survey of the Art Index Retrospective and the Art Abstracts databases.

the results of a larger-scale examination would be that the discipline has not changed by an order of magnitude since 1987, and that the canon of the story of art is still very much with us.

Does Art History Have Identifiable Methodological Interests?

Named theories, such as psychoanalysis and semiotics, are on the rise in art history. Fig. 2.5, compiled from keyword searches of the Bibliography of the History of Art, shows this unequivocally: this is bad news for those who hoped that theory was on the way out. The average of these increases is nearly exponential. Even subjects such as "the gaze," which is sometimes said to be recherché, are rapidly becoming more central to the discipline. Because these data come from keyword searches, they reflect articles whose authors, or edi-

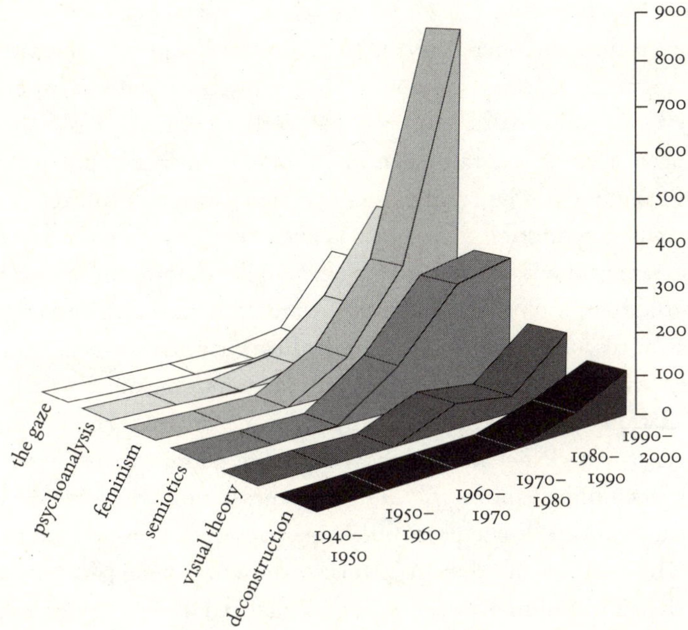

2.5. Theory in art history, 1940–2000, based on a keyword search of the *Bibliography of the History of Art*.

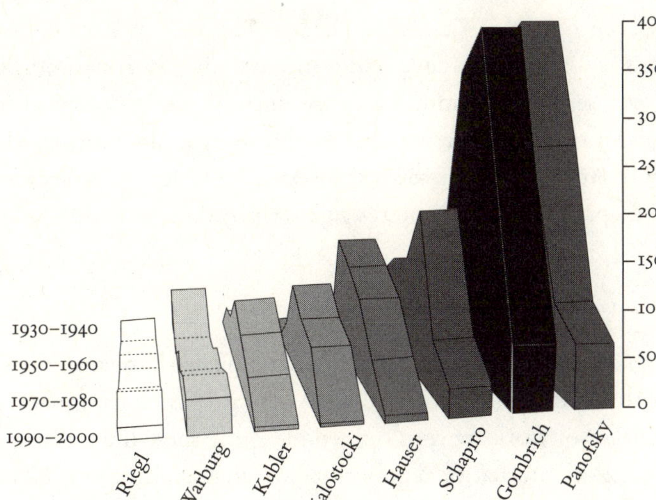

2.6. The rise and fall of an older art history, 1930–2000, based on the frequency of the citation of selected writers according to the results of a keyword search of the *Bibliography of the History of Art*.

tors, took "psychoanalysis," for example, as one of the essay's principal subjects. Hence these numbers may be biased toward papers on methodology or historiography. The figures would presumably be somewhat different for essays that *use* psychoanalysis, for example, without naming it as such. Hence this graph is a more accurate measure of interest in methodology than in the use of methods. (The latter is immeasurable, although full-text searches might trawl for symptoms of a psychoanalytic bent.)

At the same time it is possible to observe that what might be regarded as older methodological models and theories are declining: citations of scholars such as Panofsky and Gombrich all peaked over twenty years ago and have been decreasing since (fig. 2.6). At the front I have put the much smaller numbers of citations of Alois Riegl and Aby Warburg, both of whom were cited in the 1930s (as was Panofsky) and show slight but definite increases in the last twenty years (unlike Panofsky).[26] In light of these numbers the revived interest in Riegl and Warburg appears minor, perhaps out of proportion to its influence. The selection of other art historians shows a general pattern: citations were at their maximum between 1960 and 1980 and have been decreasing, in some cases precipitously.[27]

In this way, art history's methodological interests can also be quantified, suggesting that the current wave of interest in theories such as psychoanalysis and semiotics, which together comprise what is still called Theory with a capital "T," is growing at a tremendous rate. This does not, of course, show that art history is not also developing interests in other methods, but it is relevant because it demonstrates a consistency of methodological interests. A next step for this kind of research would be to search art historical writing in, say, South America, for these same interests, in order to determine if some interpretive approaches are limited by geography.

Some Conclusions

The data that I have presented here in such a pitilessly quantitative fashion can be helpful in dispelling notions about the discipline's nature and growth. A large amount of work remains to be done along these lines. A useful study has been done on international publishing in science, and it suggests lines for future research. Scientists collaborate more often than scholars in the humanities, but there is so far no study of art historical collaboration. The authors of the study of international scientific publication found that North American scientists collaborate least often. They also discovered that Latin America has the largest growth rate in publications; that since 1994 Europe has been producing more scientific papers than North America, but that North America produces more papers per capita; and that scientific work is increasing most slowly in eastern Europe.[28] Those are the kinds of statistics that would help us to understand what is happening to art history as it slowly, problematically, becomes disseminated throughout the world.

At the beginning of the twenty-first century it is clear even without statistics that art history is fundamentally regional, in the sense that it is produced and consumed principally in western Europe, and Canada and the United States, and that it focuses mainly on a small subset of Western artists. Each country and region, in my experience, focuses on its own artists and movements, and those interests mean that art history is divided, to some degree, into regional practices. But—to continue my thoughts at the beginning about the canon in the story of art and its often underestimated influence—art history's regional differences are *variations* on a basic model, which appears, as closely as the figures allow us to say, to be built on the artists, artworks, and periods of western Europe and North America.

Once more data has been collected—and it is my hope that a large organization such as the Getty might find this sort of project worthwhile—then more interesting questions can be asked. In the end we might be able to make some headway on the most important questions: Is art history becoming global, in the sense that Western interests and interpretive methods are becoming hegemonic? Or are we heading toward a more pluralist future, in which art history comprises importantly different senses of what art is important and what methods are best to address it? These data, at least, make me pessimistic about the possibility of a genuinely multicultural, polymorphous art history. It appears that art history is spreading throughout the world in the same way capitalism is: as a more-or-less uniform doctrine and practice, ideologically centered on its points of origin.

Notes

1 For more on global art history, see Elkins, "Review" (of David Summers); the review, along with a roundtable conversation and contributions by forty scholars, is in Elkins, ed., *Is Art History Global?*.

2 Much of this essay continues on from my own *Stories of Art*, which is a response to Gombrich's *Story of Art*. The "story of art" I mention here is defined in more detail in *Stories of Art*.

3 It is discussed, with examples, in Elkins, *Stories of Art*.

4 See, for example, the essay by McGee in this volume; and Elkins, "Review" (of David Summers).

5 Personal communication, May 2004.

6 Here are some further examples. The Universidad de Puerto Rico has at least one full-time modernist art historian (Margerita Fernandez), and the most prominent art school, the Escuela de Artes Plásticas, has another (Haydee Benedas); neither one teaches in a department of art history. In Thailand, at least three institutions employ art historians: the Prince of Songkla University, the Silpakorn University, and Bangkok University. In each case there is one full-time art historian; two of them teach in departments that cover studio art. In addition to these sorts of problems, information is sometimes unexpectedly difficult to come by. The Georgian S. Rustaveli State Institute of Theater and Film in Tbilisi, Georgia may have that country's only full-time art historians, but the institute's promotional material is unclear, and again a visit would be necessary. The situation is similar with Pakistan's only university that might offer art history, the Pashto Academy in Peshawar.

7 This database is proprietary and unpublished; it was developed under my direction, beginning in January 2004. For further information, see www.imagehistory.org.

8 The database was assembled from the worldwide list at www.unites.uqam.ca/AHWA/Departments/. It was augmented by smaller sites such as www.chart.ac.uk/vlib/departments.html; the European University Association's www.eua.be/eua/jsp/en/client/members_directory_select.jsp; www.portalkunstgeschichte.de/forschung_lehre/institute_deutschland/; the U.S. list of colleges at www.mit.edu:8001/people/cdemello/univ.html; and the commercial database World of Learning, which was searched for "history of art," "art history," "Kunstgeschichte," and "histoire de l'art" (the latter two were controls, since the database is uniform in English). The World of Learning database includes a large number of museums, which are excluded from the Cork database because they are nonteaching institutions.

9 The correspondence occurred in March-June 2004; the version of the database I am reporting on here is from July 2004.

10 So far the list consists mainly of universities and colleges, and not yet art schools and academies; and so these numbers should be considered proportionally and not in absolute terms. The database could be expanded by searching for "art history" in American art schools (via the All Art Schools site, www.allartschools.com/find/results.php?searchterm=%22art+history%22&submit=Search) and by incorporating world art schools through Art Schools.com (www.artschools.com/world/).

11 This is unfortunate especially because the BHA indexes 4,360 journals as of 2002, while Art Abstracts indexes on the order of 300 journals.

12 This search cannot be done by end-users. Nancy Spiegel, the art reference librarian at the University of Chicago's Regenstein Library, found the following data (these are averaged for 1999, 2000, and 2001): English-language articles 11,683; Italian, 4,700; German, 4,157; French, 4,135; Spanish, 1,559; Dutch, 1,035; Czech, 286; Polish, 231; and Catalan, 149. The other thirty-two languages indexed had less than 149 entries on average. The next few languages, in descending order of the number of articles, are Greek, Norwegian, Hungarian, Slovak, Serbo-Croatian (written in Cyrillic script), Bulgarian, Serbo-Croatian (written in Roman script), Slovene, Swedish, Portuguese, Icelandic,

Japanese, Latin, Finnish, Galician, Basque, Esperanto, Hebrew, and Chinese. I take it that the poor showing of Japanese and Chinese (in the list along with Latin!) is more evidence of the Western slant of the database.

13 For this information I thank Nancy Spiegel; Yuan Zhou, a Chinese reference librarian; June Farris, a Slavic reference librarian; and Eizaburo Okuizumi, a Japanese studies librarian—all at the University of Chicago.

14 This is estimated; East View's subscription package F69, which covers "fine art and art theory," is a service that culls articles on a short list of subjects (calligraphy, art theory, painting, and so on) from a list of hundreds of journals. Hence the number of journals represented is variable. The humanities and social sciences list is available at http://online.eastview.com/resources/html/caj-edu.htm. East View's number in fig. 2.2 (sixty) is an estimate arrived at by doubling the number of journals on that list (twenty-six) that have "Art" in their translated titles. These include *World Art*, *Oriental Art*, *Journal of the Nanjing Arts Institute*, *Guangdong Arts*, *Theory and Criticism of Literature and Art*, *Literature and Art Studies*, and *Literature and Art Criticism*, and at least another thirty journals are relevant to art history and criticism. I thank Tammy Byrne for information on East View.

15 *Catalogue of Chinese Newspapers and Periodicals, 2002–2003*, category no. 12, *yìshù* [art], 120–25.

A similar study could be made of Japanese periodicals. A starting point would be the *Guide to the Gordon W. Prange Magazine Collection, University of Maryland Libraries*, 1525–59, which lists several hundred periodicals collected between 1945 and 1949.

16 For example, for Ireland it lists *Crossings*, the *Geological Curator*, and the *Irish Arts Review*: the first two are not relevant, and the third is to some degree a glossy magazine. For France the entries are *Anka*, *Cahiers de l'Iroise*, *Dix-huitième siècle*, *Gazette des Beaux-Arts*, *Histoire de l'art*, *Museum internacional* (the Spanish edition, published in France), and *Revue du Louvre et des Musées de France*. The first 16 of the 123 entries for the United States is a typical mixture of irrelevant and central publications: *African Arts*, *American Art*, *American Art Journal*, *American Indian Art Magazine*, *American Institute for Conservation of Historic and Artistic Works*, *American Journal of Art Therapy*, *American Romanian Academy of Arts and Sciences*, *Animation Journal*, *Archives of Asian Art*, *Ars Orientalis*, *Art Bulletin*, *Art Business News*, *Art Criticism*, *Art Documentation*, *Art Education*, and *Art Journal*.

17 It is sometimes said by German and Austrian scholars that the sum total of German-language publications on art history is the same as English-language publications, and it is certainly the case that English-speaking scholars tend to ignore the German literature. However, the database indicates that German-language scholarship in art history does not compare in quantity with English-language scholarship, because even without counting North America, countries in which German is spoken have fifty institutions and the United Kingdom and Ireland have roughly double that.

18 There is no reliable information on how many countries use first-year world art textbooks in their college curricula. The phenomenon is most definitely *not* an American one (see my *Stories of Art* for examples of Indian, Egyptian, German, Russian, Chinese, and Japanese textbooks), but it is not clear when and where such surveys have become general practice.

19 Stokstad et al., *Art History*.

20 Given what I have said about the Western slant of the BHA, these data have to be taken with some consideration for how they might appear if there were other databases available—but since there aren't, I present them as they are. I thank Michael Rinehart for providing the material, and John Onians for providing the setting—the Second Clark Conference, on global art history—which made me think of analyzing the data in this way. Technically the data here comes from the predecessor of the Bibliography of the History of Art, called the RAA (Répertoire d'Art et d'Archéologie).

21 The limits of accuracy vary depending on the portion of the sample. There are three principal sources of error: (1) several names are repeated because of slight differences in spelling; (2) after the number of citations per artist sank beneath ten, I began estimating by using an average number of citations per page of printout (the error is approximately 5 percent); and (3) I only saw the first volume out of three volumes of printouts. Vol. 1 ended with the artists cited three times still unfinished; so the estimates for the artists cited three, two, and one time each are extrapolations from the number of pages in vol. 1 (the error is approximately 25 percent). Rinehart, who read an earlier version of this essay, made the following pertinent observations: "I suppose an underlying question is whether the source is a reliable indicator. The statistics must sometimes be skewed by brief flurries of publication around centenaries, conferences, exhibitions, etc. A 2-page article and a 300-page book carry equal weight in the data, as does a publication that sinks unnoticed vs. one that has a major impact. Still, over a long period it presumably evens out" (personal communication, 2000).

22 Note that the graph is on a log-log scale. That was necessary because the "tails" of the graph would stretch too far to allow them to appear in a single graphic—evidence of the enormous interest in just a few artists (on the one hand) and of the equally huge interest in previously unstudied or understudied artists (on the other).

23 Elkins, *Why Are Our Pictures Puzzles?*, 20, with thanks to Alison Dickey.

24 The Art Index Retrospective search was done for "features" on Picasso, Michelangelo, and "Cambodia." The five-year period 1981–85 is averaged, since it spans the two databases. The Art Abstracts search was done for the same terms, but as "subjects," and with the searches limited to "articles." That was to make the lines match as much as possible. The data here fits well with searches done on Art Bibliographies Modern, using "title" searches and limiting to "journal articles."

25 The top two are power series, with the equations $y = 93.911x^{0.3176}$ (Picasso) and $y = 35.351x^{0.4966}$ (Michelangelo). The bottom smooth curve is a fourth-order polynomial extrapolation. R squared values are on the order of 0.7.

26 These data are not from the Bibliography of the History of Art, but from the larger Arts and Humanities Citation Index, which includes many journals in the humanities. The BHA data follow this but the numbers are smaller and therefore less statistically reliable. At the same time, the includes some very dubious figures: Barthes, for instance, is cited three times in the 1930s, once for his *Camera Obscura*. (Those references are because of mistakes in the originals, or in the process of digitizing.)

27 Others show different patterns; citations of Damisch peaked between 1970 and 1980 and are also in decline, but not as steeply. References to Henri Focillon were always low in the Arts and Humanities Citation Index, peaking between 1980 and 1990. The Bibliography of the History of Art can also be used for this purpose, but it does not

have the longer time range that is necessary to reveal these patterns. In the BHA, citations of Benjamin are constant in the period 1970–2000, and so are citations of Barthes, although those run fully ten times lower than citations of Benjamin. Citations of Lacan have increased to a modest level in the last twenty years. Because BHA numbers are lower than AHCI numbers, they are less statistically reliable.

28 Gálvez et al., "Scientific Publication Trends and the Developing World."

3

Mere Exposure, Reproduction, and the Impressionist Canon

JAMES CUTTING

Every act of writing or curatorial practice, whenever it gets to the point of naming a name, is participating in a certain level of canon formation, no matter what the intent of its author, no matter whether it represents a challenge to the status quo or a confirmation of it.

—Russell Ferguson, "Can We Still Use the Canon?"

It has been said that canons are the "legitimating backbone of cultural and political identity."[1] They are also the bread and butter of what is taught in the humanities, and in art they are what the general public flocks to see. Art museums and art historians feature canonical images. They reproduce them in great quantity such that these images are now seen in greater numbers, and by greater proportions, of people than ever before. Blockbuster exhibits guarantee continuing links among particular images, publicity, and capital—both cultural and otherwise.

But what exactly are the contents of a given canon? How do we determine which works are canonical? And how did they attain that status? In an attempt to answer these questions, I will focus on the canon of French Impressionism and argue that canons are cultural constructs created, in part, through repeated reproduction and exposure. That is, following the epigraph of Russell Ferguson, the curator at the Museum of Contemporary Art in Los Angeles, I claim that art historians have been complicitous in the formation and maintenance of the Impressionist canon, and that over decades their wares have fed a sustaining public whose opinions, along with those of art historians themselves, have crystallized and now drag heavily against systematic change.[2]

There are several reasons for choosing French Impressionism as a case study. First, it is a relatively recent, well-documented, and well-defined art phenomenon. These facts make it easier to outline its formation, maintenance, and structure. Second, it is sufficiently old that virtually the entire corpus of works is known and accounted for. The artists collectively identified as the Impressionists have been dead for about a century, and about 35 percent of their work is currently owned by museums.[3] The remainder is in private hands, but as I will demonstrate no canonical images come from those holdings.

Third, and perhaps the most significant reason for this study, is that French Impressionism was extraordinarily popular across the twentieth century and continues to be so today.[4] The Impressionist images bequeathed to the State of France were gathered into the Louvre by the mid-1930s and then sent to the Musée du Jeu de Paume in 1947.[5] There, overcrowding soon became a problem. From the 1960s through the mid-1980s the Musée du Jeu de Paume was the most heavily trafficked museum per square meter in the world. Significantly, many of those visitors were from the United States. In 1986, the contents were then moved to the Musée d'Orsay, which was instantly one of the most visited museums in the world, receiving over four million people annually.[6] To be sure, there are also well-known and frequently seen collections of French Impressionist paintings elsewhere in Europe and, in particular, in the United States. In addition, French Impressionist paintings often commanded the highest sale prices at art auctions throughout the twentieth century, and over the course of the 1980s and 1990s they were featured in some of the largest and best-attended exhibitions.[7] Moreover, French Impressionism's high public profile, popularity, and importance for the history of modern art generated, over the course of the twentieth century, a thick texture of literature on the artists and their *oeuvres* that I will draw upon.

Finally, Impressionism is deeply embedded in contemporary American popular culture. Consider two sources of supporting evidence. First, in his 1987 book, *Cultural Literacy: What Every American Needs to Know*, Edward Hirsch lists thirty-one artists across all of time that he thought U.S. citizens should know. Five are Impressionists.[8] Hirsch's volume, however odd it may appear, can be interpreted as an early and politically charged salvo in the "culture for dummies" offensive. His "requirement" for Americans to learn about Impressionism was surely motivated by its historic visibility in the United States. Many of its most avid collectors were American, and those collectors tended to give works to American museums. Indeed, five of the seven museums with the largest, most diverse Impressionist collections are in the United States—the Metropolitan Museum of Art in New York, the National Gallery of Art in Washington, the Philadelphia Museum of Art, the Art Institute of Chicago, and the Museum of Fine Arts in Boston. The works within their galleries—along with those in the Musée d'Orsay and the National Gallery of

Art in London—are icons of modernism and are deeply embedded in Western visual culture.[9] They even appear on towels, scarves, coasters, t-shirts, refrigerator magnets, and textbook covers.

Consider a second source—Impressionism as displayed within contemporary U.S. mail-order catalogues. Among the hundreds of catalogues my household received in 2003, many had images of rooms with furniture, lamps, and rugs for sale, but they also showed books on shelves, coffee tables, and desks. These books were not for sale, but were included gratuitously to create a particular ambience in each room, populating it with appropriate tokens of concretely identifiable social aspirations. The presence of such books is not accidental. They are almost always about food, travel, or art—three aspects of conspicuous American consumption. The books on single artists are the most interesting. After taking care to exclude duplicate images, I focused on seventeen catalogues. In those, I found books on just nineteen different painters, excluding a few from the mid- and late twentieth century. Van Gogh was the most common—six different catalogues had different images of books with the title *Van Gogh* on their covers or spines; Cézanne was second with five; next were Picasso (four), Rembrandt (four), Leonardo (three), Michelangelo (three), Mondrian (two), and Sargent (two). Artists singly featured were Breugel, Cassatt, Duchamp, Gauguin, Goya, Monet, Renoir, Seurat, Toulouse-Lautrec, Velázquez, Vermeer, and Whistler. French Impressionists (four) and artists associated with broader late-nineteenth- and early-twentieth-century French art (eight more) dominated in these portrayals of upscale American domesticity. Anecdotal as it may be, such a survey clearly demonstrates that certain high art *is* part of popular culture. It is linked to the commerce of goods catering to upwardly mobile, middle-class tastes, where demand for high quality is met and reinforced through association with canonical art.

Mere Exposure, Preference, and Value

"Mere exposure" is a key term in psychology, my own field of research. Robert Zajonc discovered the phenomenon in the late 1960s. Among other things, he demonstrated that the more times a nonsense word like *dilikli* was repeated, the more likely a listener would later think it meant something good rather than bad. Since then, laboratory studies with many kinds of materials—unfamiliar graphic characters, nonsense geometric constructions, photographs of unfamiliar people, as well as melodies and musical passages—have confirmed the validity of the mere exposure effect.[10] The basic finding is that, other things being equal, we tend to like things we have seen before, indeed we tend to value them more.[11] My own research has shown that this also holds true for art. Repeated exposure to particular images creates and reinforces preferences.

I conducted a set of experiments on the effects of mere exposure to paintings and pastels. I presented pairs of French Impressionist images to undergraduates (only 17 percent of whom had previously taken an art history course), older adults (graduate students and faculty in Cornell University's Department of Psychology), and children ages six to ten.[12] I chose images widely, but they were generally by Paul Cézanne, Edgar Degas, Edouard Manet, Claude Monet, Camille Pissarro, Pierre-Auguste Renoir, and Alfred Sisley.[13] I selected sixty-six pairs of paintings. The images in each pair were by the same artist, produced roughly in the same year, and fell within the same genre—portrait, group portrait, landscape, cityscape, seascape, still life, nude. Some images are part of the Impressionist canon, as I will discuss later, but most are seldom reproduced and are familiar only to the specialist.

Because I was interested in mere exposure, I needed a gauge for how likely and often individuals might have seen each image before. The one I chose was indirect, but I think compelling: I counted every occurrence of each of the 132 images in all of the books that Cornell University owns.[14] I found these images in almost a thousand different books, published between 1901 and 2002, mostly in English and French, some in German, and a few in Italian, Dutch, Spanish, Danish, and Japanese. Results of those tallies ranged from two reproductions (one of which was always from a *catalogue raisonné*) to almost three hundred (an image included in over a quarter of the books). I do not presume that any of my subjects spent time thumbing through the art books in Cornell's libraries, but I do assume that the relative reproduction frequency of images well approximates the relative likelihood of their having been seen before.

I asked observers to indicate their preference between the two images. The result, consistent with the mere exposure thesis, was that individuals preferred the more frequently reproduced image in each pair about 60 percent of the time. Moreover, the greater the discrepancy in relative frequency of reproduction, the more likely viewers were to prefer the more reproduced image.[15] Few participants in this study recognized particular paintings, and recognition was unrelated to preferences. This latter result was not a surprise. The effects of mere exposure are not a rational response to one's surroundings. Research has shown that we often cannot express the reasons for what we like, but all evidence here points to the fact that we prefer what we have likely seen before and seen more often.[16]

There is, of course, the thorny issue of quality. One might claim that paintings that are reproduced more often are "better" paintings and that people respond to quality in art. This latter idea, associated with Kantian aesthetics, was occasionally embraced by modernist art history, but it is not likely to be true.[17] In another experiment I presented the same images to students in my undergraduate course on perception. I randomly interspersed them among the slides in my PowerPoint presentations on various scientific topics. I presented them as non sequiturs for a few seconds, each without comment. Four times, across two dozen lectures, I showed my class the images that were less frequently reproduced in each pair. I presented the more frequently reproduced images only once. At the end of the semester, I performed the same experiment with this class and found that I had reversed preferences. The students now slightly preferred the images that they had seen more often in class.[18]

Which Images Are in the Impressionist Canon?

Let me offer a thesis contrary to that of Walter Benjamin in his "The Work of Art in the Age of Mechanical Reproduction." Canonical images—the images that hold the greatest prestige and that are considered to be the most significant, and therefore most valued by experts and the public alike—are those images that have been reproduced the most often. That is, the aura of art in the age of reproduction does not wither but, as Michael Camille also pointed out, is reinforced.[19] To determine which images are canonical for French Impressionism, I consulted a second sample, which included all books on Impressionism in the Cornell University libraries—a total of nearly one hundred publications covering the breadth of the twentieth century. "As Harry Abrams once said . . . about such publications, nobody reads the text anyway; it's all about the . . . reproductions."[20] Prompted by the epigraph of Russell Ferguson, I tabulated all images by title and by artist.[21] But first, how many French Impressionist paintings are there?

If one counts images in *catalogues raisonnés* of Cézanne, Degas, Manet, Monet, Pissarro, Renoir, and Sisley, the answer is about 9,000. If one includes others—Frédéric Bazille, Gustave Caillebotte, Mary Cassatt, Eva Gonzalès, Armand Guillaumin, and Berthe Morisot—the answer is closer to 12,000.[22] How many of these 12,000 appeared in the books included in my sample? The answer is just over 2,500. More interestingly, about 1,400 images appeared only once, about 975 appeared between two and nine times, and only 138 appeared ten times or more. Fig. 3.1, which presents these data in a graphic

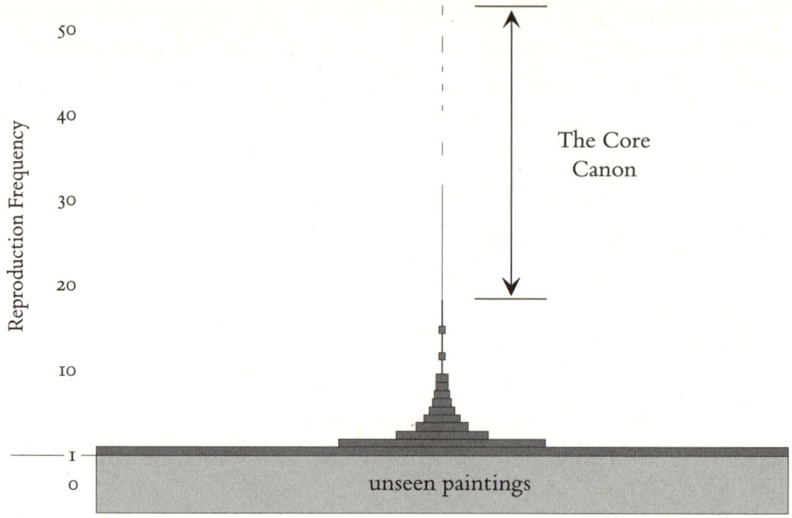

3.1. A graphical depiction of all of the images of Impressionism by their frequency of appearance in ninety-five books, a veritable iceberg.

form, reveals a veritable iceberg of Impressionism. It has a vast number of unreproduced images at the bottom, floating beneath the surface of visibility. The uppermost spire represents the most frequently reproduced images—the core canon of Impressionism. Notice that it is miniscule in proportion to the entire Impressionist corpus. The spire also demonstrates the extreme consensus with which scholars reproduce images to tell the story of Impressionism. For the purpose of further analysis, I will define the core canon of French Impressionism as the fifty most frequently reproduced images.[23]

Who Originally Owned the Core Canon?

The bulk of the core canon was owned by a *very* small number of people. The most important of these was Gustave Caillebotte, whose story has been told many times.[24] Inheriting his father's wealth, Caillebotte was a millionaire and a painter at the age of twenty-eight. He was invited by Renoir and by Henri Rouart to join the second Impressionist exhibition. He participated in, organized, and bankrolled it and four others. More importantly here, he also bought his friends' paintings. In 1894 Caillebotte died suddenly of a stroke, and he left his collection to the French state. His only condition was that the collection should be exhibited intact. Haggling went on for years, taxing Renoir, the executor of Caillebotte's will. Eventually thirty-nine artworks were accepted, plus two of Caillebotte's own paintings donated by the family. This part of his collection was installed in the Musée du Luxembourg in Paris in 1897. Strikingly, Caillebotte owned eight images now in the core canon, all in the Musée d'Orsay—Degas's *Femmes à la terrasse d'un café, le soir* (1877), Manet's *Le balcon* (1869), Monet's *Régates à Argenteuil* (1872) and *La gare Saint-Lazare* (1877), Pissarro's *Toits rouges* (1877) and *Printemps à Pontoise, potager et arbres en fleurs* (1879), and Renoir's *Bal au Moulin de la Galette* (1876) and *Balançoire* (1876).

Only one other collector comes close to Caillebotte, the financier Isaac de Camondo. Camondo was a leading banker in fin de siècle France and a quiet member of an important Turkish-immigrant family. He began buying Impressionist works in 1893 and collected them until his death in 1911. By his will, its endowment, and his considerable political clout, his collection went straight to the Louvre.[25] Camondo owned six core canon images, all now in the Orsay—Cézanne's *La maison du pendu* (1873), Degas's *Absinthe* (1876) and *Repasseuses* (1884), Manet's *Le fifre* (1866), the most popular of Monet's *Cathédrales de Rouen* series (1891; Camondo owned four), and the most popular of Sisley's *L'Inondation à Port-Marly* series (1876; he owned two).[26]

In England two collectors and benefactors promoted Impressionism. The first was Hugh Lane, an Irishman and a successful London art dealer. In 1908 he established the Municipal Gallery of Modern Art in Dublin, now known as the Hugh Lane Gallery. Lane had a small but remarkably important Impressionist collection. He died on board the *Lusitania* in 1915, and by his official will his collection was given to the National Gallery of Art. But in an unwitnessed codicil Lane stated that the paintings should go to the new gallery in Dublin. The court did not honor the amendment and the paintings went to London. Years of furor and negotiation followed. Finally, an agreement was reached in 1959 and, at least ostensibly, the works are now shared between the two museums. Three images owned by Lane are in the core canon—Manet's *La musique aux Tuileries* (1862), Renoir's *Les parapluies* (1881–86), and Morisot's *Eté* (1879)—but several more are not far behind.[27]

The other English patron was Samuel Courtauld, the silk magnate. He is important here for two reasons. First, impressed by Lane's collection, he established a fund for the National Gallery and the Tate to purchase modern works, and he oversaw that fund. Between 1923 and 1926, the Courtauld Fund purchased ten Impressionist paintings and other more recent works. Second, he also established his own museum in what is now the Courtauld Institute. After the death of his wife in 1931 he gave his paintings, the lease to his house, and an endowment to the University of London.[28] Combining those works of art purchased through his fund and those from his private collection, Courtauld accounts for three images in the core canon—Manet's *Le bar aux Folies-Bergère* (1881, Courtauld Institute), Renoir's *La loge* (1874, Courtauld Institute), and Monet's *La plage à Trouville* (1870, National Gallery, London).

Finally, the Havemeyers were the most important U.S. benefactors of Impressionism—with bequests to the Metropolitan Museum of Art and, through their children, to other museums. In particular, Louisine Elder Havemeyer was active in the women's suffrage movement, a close friend of Mary Cassatt, and intensely interested in Impressionism. The Havemeyers owned over 150 Impressionist works, and more than 60 went to the Met. Three of the paintings owned by the Havemeyers are in the core canon—Monet's *La Grenouillère* (1869, Metropolitan), Manet's *En bateau* (1874, Metropolitan), and his *Le chemin de fer* (1873, National Gallery of Art, Washington).[29]

So few hands controlled so much of the French Impressionist canon. Five collectors—Gustave Caillebotte, Isaac de Camondo, Hugh Lane, Samuel Courtauld, and Louisine Havemeyer—account for almost half of it. Other collectors who left important bequests to various museums—Etienne Moreau-Nélaton (mostly in 1906) to the State of France; the Palmers to the Art Institute of Chicago (1922); Antonin Personnaz to the Louvre (1937); Paul Gachet *fils* to the Louvre (through the 1950s); the Tysons to the Philadelphia Museum of Art (1956); and Chester Dale (1963), Paul Mellon (1970–1999), and Ailsa Mellon Bruce (1970) to the National Gallery in Washington—together account for only three images in the core canon. These are Manet's *Le déjeuner sur l'herbe* (1863, Moreau-Nélaton bequest to the French state), Cézanne's pastiche, *Une moderne Olympia* (1872, Gachet bequest to the Louvre), and Renoir's *Les grandes baigneuses* (1887, Tyson bequest to the Philadelphia Museum of Art). Most of these donations generally came later than those discussed earlier. In the case of Moreau-Nélaton's bequest, it languished for thirty years neither in the Luxembourg nor in the Louvre, and in the case of the Palmers' bequest, it simply achieved less publicity.[30] Moreover, as one can see in fig. 3.2, the accrual of canonical images in museums peaked early, in the decades of the 1910s and 1920s. As Impressionism became accepted, even mainstream, fewer of the images given to museums would achieve canonical status.

Who Sold the Core Canon?

Dealers handled fewer than half of these core images. This contrasts with the larger corpus of twelve thousand images, where nearly two-thirds were controlled at one time or another by sixteen different dealers.[31] Accounting for

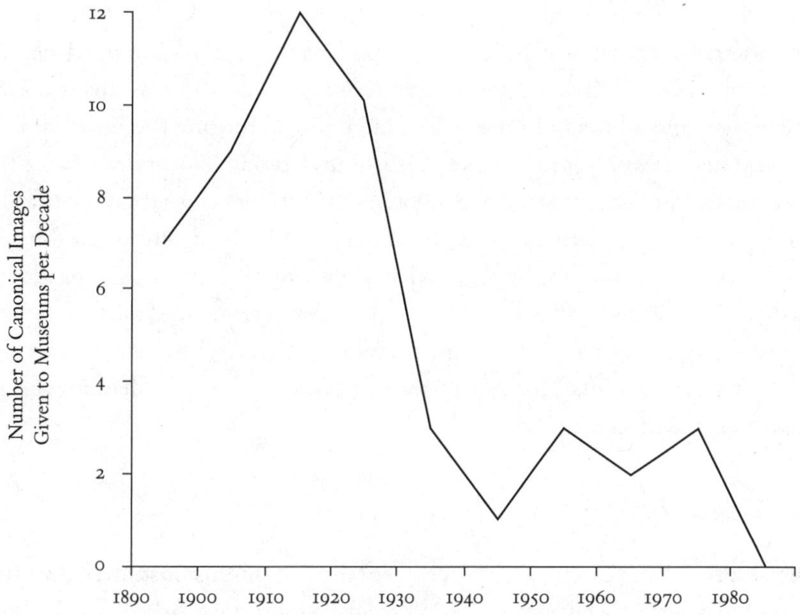

3.2. A graphical depiction of the museum acquisitions by decade of what would later be the fifty Impressionist images in the core canon.

half of the core canon images are friends who bought directly from the artists (such as Caillebotte and Paul Gachet *père*), the families of the artists (such as Marc Bazille, a nephew of Frédéric, for *Atelier de l'artiste, rue Condamine* [1869] and *Réunion de famille* [1867]; the De Gas family for *La famille Bellelli* [1858–61], which was held back from the fourth Degas estate sale; and the Pontillon family of Morisot's sister for *Le berceau* [1872]), and the families of friends (such as the Dihau family, featuring the oboist in Degas's *Orchestre à l'Opéra* [1870–71]). A few others were direct museum purchases (Degas's *Portraits dans un bureau, Nouvelle-Orléans* [1873, Musée des Beaux-Arts, Pau]), or gifts by subscription (for example, that of Manet's *Olympia*, which was led by Monet and John Singer Sargent to support Manet's widow and to keep the painting from going to the United States).

Thus, after one omits those paintings not handled by dealers, only half remain. Despite this, one-third of these fifty images—or two-thirds of those remaining—were handled by Paul Durand-Ruel. From 1871 until his death in 1922 Durand-Ruel made his living by selling both the works of Impressionists and the more acceptable Salon painters. For sales of works now in the core canon, the next most important dealers were the Galeries Bernheim-

Jeune, Paul Rosenberg, Georges Petit, Ambrose Vollard, and Wildenstein in that order, but the sum of these five is only half the total of Durand-Ruel.[32]

Perhaps Durand-Ruel had extraordinary taste, guiding his buyers to the best images and allowing him to play a huge role in forging the Impressionist canon. This is possible, but not likely. Without denying his importance for the dissemination of Impressionism,[33] there is little evidence that he specifically controlled which paintings would be canonical. Yes, he dealt with a third of these fifty images, but he also dealt with one-third of *all* the images produced by the Impressionist artists. Over a period of fifty years he sold more than four thousand paintings by thirteen Impressionist artists. By this account he was an enormously successful salesman for Impressionism, but he had no special impact on its core canon.

Who Publicized the Core Canon?

The Impressionist canon grew incrementally. Beginning just after the turn into the twentieth century, scholars began to reproduce images in the core canon in their books. In order to determine the history of the Impressionist canon's reproduction, I analyzed a third sample of ninety-five books published in French, English, and German between 1901 and 1949 that reproduced any Impressionist images at all.[34] On average, each book introduced one or two new images that would later become canonical. But two books clearly stand out—Charles Borgmeyer's *The Master Impressionists* (1913), an otherwise minor work that introduced nine new canonical images, all from the Caillebotte and Camondo legacies; and John Rewald's *The History of Impressionism* (1946), which introduced ten. Moreover, Rewald's perspicacity extended beyond the presentation of new images. He also republished two dozen core images that appeared in earlier books. This means that he published two-thirds of the core canon. Before him even Borgmeyer had published only one-third. Shown in fig. 3.3 are the numbers of now core canon images that appeared in all ninety-five books. Notice the pattern—a gradual coalescence of agreement about what is in the canon across the twentieth century, and Rewald led the way. His accomplishment was not eclipsed in a single volume for thirty-five years.[35] Clearly, Rewald played an extraordinary role in shaping the canon. What he published, several generations of art historians who followed also published. Indeed, no Impressionist scholar of the last half-century could ignore what Rewald presented.

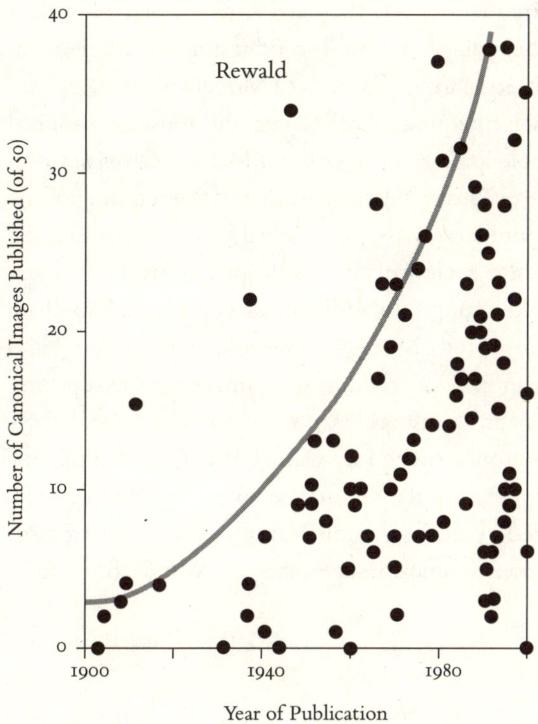

3.3. A scatter plot of ninety-five books on Impressionism published between 1901 and 2001, and the number of images they included that are now in the core canon.

Has the Core Canon Changed?

Over the course of the twentieth century the discipline of art history may have changed as much or more than any other. It began the twentieth century with biographies and connoisseurship, it ended it with sophisticated social histories and theoretically driven analyses. Did the reproduction of canonical images change as well? No, or at least very little. Analyses of my databases show that 85 percent of the images that were in the core canon in the books published in the first half of the century are still there today. Thus one could argue that even though the arguments are relatively fresh in the field of art history, the images are not.

To be sure, some images are published a bit less often. Renoir's *Bal au Moulin de la Galette* was by far and away the most reproduced Impressionist image in the first half of the twentieth century. It is now merely among the top four. And Degas's *Etoile, danseuse sur la scène* (1876–78, also from the Caillebotte bequest) was once among the top dozen images, but has subsequently fallen out of the top fifty. Furthermore, many other images are now published more often. For example, those of Bazille, Caillebotte, Cassatt, Gonzalès, and

Morisot now appear more frequently, but they are largely not in the core canon. But consider two other images whose reproduction has burgeoned. Since it was given to the Musée Marmottan in 1957 Monet's *Impression, soliel levant* (1873, Donop de Monchy bequest) has become the most reproduced Impressionist image, even outstripping in this context Manet's *Olympia* (1863) and his *Déjeuner sur l'herbe* (1863). This is in large part due to the retelling of the semi-apocryphal tale—first popularized by John Rewald—of this image, the art critic Louis Leroy, his derisive review of the first Impressionist exhibition, and his supposed naming of the group.[36] In addition, as a centennial purchase for the Metropolitan Museum in 1967 Monet's *Terrasse à Sainte-Adresse* (1867) has also leapt into the core canon. Nonetheless, such images are exceptions. The Impressionist canon, perhaps like all others, is relatively fossilized. Scholars continue to display images once owned by Caillebotte, Camondo, Lane, Courtauld, and the Havemeyers, and they continue to follow Rewald. The art promoter least encumbered by this hegemonic uniformity, showing most often and most consistently noncanonical images, is Sister Wendy Beckett.[37]

Why Reproduction Matters

Let me return to mere exposure. There is another group that plays an important role in maintaining the canon—the general public, the "audience" of art. Members of the public may acquire knowledge about the canon through overt study of individual paintings, but more broadly and more importantly they are influenced by mere exposure. All other things being equal, the more often they see or hear something—so long as this is distributed across time, rather than massed in a small amount of time—the more they will tend to like it. This mostly unconscious exposure shapes their preferences and, as noted by Patricia Mainardi, this "audience exerts a profound influence on the kind of art history we produce."[38]

Equally importantly, scholars are no different from the public in the effects of mere exposure. From childhood through college and throughout adulthood, we are all exposed to hundreds of thousands of images. Some are representations of art; others, as during a museum visit, are the artworks themselves. We do not remember each occurrence of each image, or where we saw it. We often will not even recognize the image if we see it again, but its trace can influence our future assessments. These are not overt cognitive responses on our part. They are not directly related to the formal part of our education, but they are very much a part of our general and higher education. The effects of mere exposure are quite automatic and independent of what we pay attention to in our day to day activities. They accrue simply as the result of being a member of a culture, of experiencing cultural artifacts. If all other things are equal, the more often canonical images are published, the more likely everyone—the public as well as scholars—tends to like them. Walter Benjamin suggested that "reproduction of art changes the reaction of the masses toward art."[39] Indeed, I would argue that it has effects far beyond, and in a direction opposite of, those he considered.

Notes

I thank Claudia Lazzaro for many discussions over the years on the topic of canons and Anna Brzyski for her unrelenting eye for editorial detail, her unsurpassed enthusiasm, and her patience with my own professional deformities. This chapter is based, in part, on my monograph *Impressionism and Its Canon*.

1 Pollock, *Differencing the Canon*, 3.

2 This argument bears some resemblance to ideas in the sociology of art (see, for example, J. Wolff, *The Social Production of Art*), except that it applies not simply to the production of individual images, but to the relationships among all images in the canon as a whole. This approach is also very much against the zeitgeist of work within Impressionist scholarship, which generally regards the corpus of canonical images as given and not shaped by their own efforts, or those of collectors, curators, and chance. Among the hundred books on Impressionism that I have surveyed, few authors mention what governed their choice of images. Howard, in his *Encyclopedia of Impressionism*, comes closest to what I present here: "The works reproduced in this book are among the best known and best loved paintings . . . in the world and our appetite for them is boundless. . . . These familiar images have kept their power to enthrall. . . . They are kept before our eyes by a flood of advertising campaigns" (6).

3 The basis of this assertion comes first from the number of images by a given artist in museums at the time of that artist's *catalogues raisonnés*, the number being given in those volumes. This number is then modified by the amount of time that has passed since their publication. The modification is based on the fact that both Cézanne and Manet have had two *catalogues raisonnés*. With two, one can look at the accession rates into museums between those publications. These relative rates are essentially the same for these two painters and, although different painters are differentially popular, the rates can be applied to the thirteen Impressionists considered here—Bazille, Caillebotte, Cassatt, Cézanne, Degas, Gonzalès, Guillaumin, Manet, Monet, Morisot, Pissarro, Renoir, and Sisley—and extrapolated to 2005.

4 Herbert, in his essay "Impressionism, Originality, and Laissez-faire," in his *From Millet to Léger*, 91–97, expands on the many reasons why Impressionism embedded itself in popular culture.

5 The Jeu de Paume was technically a part of the Louvre and not a separate museum, although it is four hundred meters down the Rue du Rivoli. Part of the rationale for this was that the will of Isaac de Camondo, whom I will discuss later, insisted that his

paintings be hung in the Louvre. See, for example, Bazin, *Impressionist Paintings in the Louvre*.

6 For the volume of visitors to the Jeu de Paume and the Orsay, see Schneider, *Creating the Musée d'Orsay*, 12, 106.

7 On Impressionist art sales, see *The Art Newspaper* 9, no. 100 (February 2000): 61, which reported that six of the twelve most expensive paintings sold at auction in 1999 were Impressionist works—three Cézannes, two Monets, and a Degas. The "Art Market" column in *The Art Newspaper* 9, no. 106 (September 2001): 70 also commented on the skyrocketing sales prices of Impressionist art over the 1990s. In addition, among the four most expensive paintings ever sold (through 2002) was a Cézanne and a Renoir. Even more striking is the tally of artists with the most works sold at auction for over one million dollars through 2001: the first is Picasso with 272, but the next five are Impressionists—Monet (218), Renoir (196), Degas (100), Cézanne (80), and Pissarro (74). See Ash, *The Top 10 of Everything*. On art exhibitions, see *The Art Newspaper* 11, no. 111 (February 2001): 20, which reported that 2000 was the first year since 1994 that there wasn't an Impressionist exhibit in the top ten most frequented exhibitions worldwide. In 1999 there were three in the top ten, and in 1998 there were two. See also, Mainardi, "Repetition and Novelty," on the force of Impressionism in museums; and see Tinterow, "Blockbuster, Art History, and the Public."

8 Hirsch, *Cultural Literacy*. In his appendix, which he compiled with the collaborators Joseph Kett and James Trefil, he included Cassatt, Cézanne, Degas, Manet, and Renoir, plus Gauguin (who also exhibited at four of the Impressionist exhibitions). He did not include Monet.

9 The Philadelphia Museum of Art and the National Gallery in London each have just under one hundred Impressionist paintings and pastels. The Musée Marmottan in Paris and the Barnes Foundation in Merion, Pennsylvania, have more than this, but these collections are not diversified. The Marmottan has almost one hundred Monets but few paintings by other Impressionists, and the Barnes more than sixty Cézannes and more than forty Renoirs, but again few by others.

10 Zajonc, "Attitudinal Effects of Mere Exposure." The very many studies on the phenomenon in its first two decades were then summarized by Bornstein, "Exposure and Affect." For recent results with music, see Szpunar, Schellenberg, and Plinar, "Liking and Memory for Musical Stimuli as a Function of Exposure."

11 Two additional points should be made. First, for mere exposure to affect positively the evaluation of a given item it should be initially perceived as at least neutral. Unpleasant items typically become more unpleasant with exposure. Second, mere exposure works best either when one does not pay much attention to each presentation, or when the intervals between presentations are relatively long. Otherwise, overexposure and boredom can result.

12 These studies are reported in detail in Cutting, "Gustave Caillebotte, French Impressionism, and Mere Exposure."

13 I recognize that strictly speaking Manet was not an Impressionist, and that arguments against the inclusion of Cézanne can be made as well. Nonetheless, both are very much a part of the Impressionist story.

14 Cornell University is a major research institution and its libraries hold more than six

million volumes. Its fine arts collection is extremely extensive, and it is likely to hold all of the major works within any artistic subdiscipline.

15 For example, images that were up to 40 percent more frequent than their mates were preferred 57 percent of the time, those that were about twice as frequent were preferred 60 percent of the time, and those that were about four times as frequent were preferred 63 percent of the time.

16 See, for example, Nisbett and Ross, *Human Inference*. Note also that children did not show the adult preference pattern. To be sure, they enjoy art and have strong preferences, but those do not match rates of reproduction. Children have simply not lived long enough in Western culture to benefit from the effects of mere exposure to art.

17 For statements outside art history concerning the perception of quality in art, see, for example, Kant, *Critique of Judgment*; Pirsig, *Zen and the Art of Motorcycle Maintenance*; and Feynman, *"Surely You're Joking, Mr. Feynman."* For statements within art history, see, for example, Rosenberg, *On Quality in Art*; and Woodford, *Looking at Pictures*. For counters to the notion of artistic quality, see Bal and Bryson, "Semiotics and Art History"; Cheetham, *Kant, Art, and Art History*; and Moxey, *The Practice of Theory*.

18 Viewers preferred the less frequently published images 52 percent of the time. In previous studies the same images in the same pairs were preferred 40 percent of the time. The difference was statistically highly reliable.

19 Camille, "Rethinking the Canon."

20 Mainardi, "Repetition and Novelty," 83–84.

21 A somewhat similar analysis was done by Galenson, *Painting Outside the Lines*. Galenson, in part of his study, analyzes all of the images that appear in general art history textbooks dealing with his topic. However, most of his work deals with market forces on the sales of images by 125 modern painters and inferences that might be made about creativity. Robert Jenson's essay in this volume follows in this tradition.

22 The exact number of Impressionist images is not known, in part, because Renoir's *catalogue raisonné* is unfinished. Nonetheless, these totals are based on tallies from the other *catalogues* and an estimate for Renoir based on his productivity in a comparable period to that of Cézanne, Degas, and Monet. The basis for claiming that these seven painters were the "major" Impressionists comes from the tally of thirty books on Impressionism published throughout the twentieth century. Works by these seven artists were included in at least twenty-nine of them. Only Cézanne and Sisley were missing from one each. In comparison, works by Bazille appeared in nineteen, Caillebotte in fourteen, Cassatt in twenty-one, and Morisot in twenty-five.

23 A cutoff of 50 is completely arbitrary, but the same general patterns as those reported here recur at 25, 100, or even 350 images.

24 For histories, see Bérhaut, *Gustave Caillebotte*; Marrinan, "Caillebotte as Professional Painter"; Nord, *Impressionists and Politics*; and Varnedoe, *Gustave Caillebotte*.

25 On Camondo, see Migeon, Jamot, Vitry, and Dreyfus, *La Collection Isaac de Camondo au Musée du Louvre*. Camondo was also a friend of Georges Clemenceau, and his bequest made Degas, Monet, and Renoir the only living artists ever to have works in the Louvre.

26 The full title of the particular Rouen Cathedral image is *La cathédrale de Rouen, le portail et la tour Saint-Romain, plein soleil, harmonie bleue et or*.

27 On Lane, see *http://www.hughlane.ie/about/hugh.shtml*. Since 1979 Manet's *Portrait d'Eva Gonzalès* (1870), Morisot's *Eté* (1979), and Renoir's *Les parapluies* (1881–86) have been in Dublin, but Degas's *Bain de mer: Petite fille peignée par sa bonne* (1868–69) and Manet's *La musique aux Tuileries* (1862) have stayed in London.

28 For data on the Courtauld fund, see the website of the National Gallery of Art in London: *http://www.nationalgallery.uk.org*. On the Courtauld Institute, see Murdock, *The Courtauld Gallery at Somerset House*. Also, the collections of the National Gallery and the Tate were shuffled in 1996, with all Impressionist images going the National Gallery, the Tate afterward being reserved for British works. The images owned by Courtauld that just missed the list of the fifty most reproduced images include Degas's *Mlle La La au cirque Fernando* (1879, National Gallery London) and Manet's *La serveuse de Bocks* (1878–79, National Gallery London).

29 On Louisine Havemeyer, see Frelinghuysen, Tinterow, Stein, Wold, and Meech, *Splendid Legacy*.

30 The most reproduced image of the Palmers' bequest is Monet's *Au bords de l'eau, Bennecourt* (1868, Art Institute of Chicago); that of Personnaz is the most popular of Monet's several *Pont d'Argenteuil* (1874, Musée d'Orsay); that of Dale is Morisot's *Dans la salle à manger* (1886, National Gallery, Washington); that of Mellon is Manet's *La prune* (1877, National Gallery, Washington); and that of Mellon Bruce is Renoir's *Le pont neuf* (1872, National Gallery, Washington). But again, none of these is in the most frequent fifty. Two earlier bequests to the French state with core canon images were those of Marc Bazille, Frédéric's nephew, in 1904 (*Atelier de l'artiste, rue Condamine*, 1869, and *Réunion de famille*, 1867), and Etienne Moreau-Nélaton in 1906 (for Manet's *Le déjeuner sur l'herbe*, 1863).

31 This analysis is based on the study of the *catalogues raisonnés* of the Impressionist painters. In addition, see White and White, *Canvases and Careers* for an account of the role of dealers in the changing art world of the mid- to late nineteenth century.

32 Again, the calculations are based on going through the *catalogues raisonnés* of each artist, or museum catalogues, checking for provenance.

33 See Assouline, *Grâces lui soient rendues*.

34 The list was compiled largely based on an appendix in Rewald, *The History of Impressionism*.

35 That book was Kelder's *The Great Book of French Impressionism*.

36 The story of Louis Leroy's naming of Impressionism stems from a widely cited account that Monet gave in an interview in 1900. For an important revisiting of this account, see Roos, *Early Impressionism and the French State, 1866–1874*.

37 See Beckett and Wright, *The Story of Painting*; and Beckett, *Sister Wendy's 1,000 Masterpieces*.

38 Mainardi, "Repetition and Novelty," 81.

39 Benjamin, "The Work of Art in the Age of Mechanical Reproduction," 234.

4

Imitation and Authority: The Creation of the Academic Canon in French Art, 1648–1870

PAUL DURO

Until the middle of the nineteenth century, the role of imitation in French academic circles was never in doubt. Emulation of the example of past art was deemed to confer on artists both the knowledge required to produce a painting and the aesthetic vocabulary necessary for the construction of a significant pictorial statement, thereby bonding together theory and practice into a whole that dominated, or so it seemed to many, the entire field of art making. As a result, emulation of canonical art was not only the keystone of the academic system of the arts, but also the single most important element of artistic association. The desire not merely to make a painting but to make it within an aesthetic framework that was immediately recognizable to all comers conferred on the practice of imitation the status of a dogma and the authority of an ideology.

None of this was new. When the Académie royale de peinture et de sculpture opened its doors in Paris in 1648, its first priority was to differentiate the artistic practices of its members from those of its rivals, especially the artists of the Maîtrise—the guild of master painters and sculptors—whose familial structure and artisanal procedures had, according to the account professed by the new Academy's supporters, actively undermined the dignity of painting and compromised its claim to be counted among the liberal arts. *Fine* artists, so the Academy's argument went, were subjected to a demeaning identification with their craft-based cousins whose artistic practices categorically removed them from the membership of a learned profession.[1] In contrast, the Academy represented itself as the embodiment of a theory of painting that based its claim to importance on renewing the link with the art of past centuries and of antiquity. According to the Academy, art making had previously been a question of routine, and it placed the blame squarely on the guild for ignoring the creative or intellectual aspects of art making. It accused the artists of the Maîtrise of being mere color grinders and hewers of stone engaged in perpetuating a cycle of repetition by copying from pattern books in which, one account emanating from the Academy indignantly tells us, "art" was nowhere to be found.[2]

When, in 1669, the Academy's *amateur honoraire*, André Félibien, published his apologia for the pretensions to superiority of the still-young Academy in *Conférences de l'académie royale de peinture et de sculpture pendant l'année 1667*, he did so precisely with these categorical distinctions in mind. In Félibien's account, paintings are ranked according to criteria that were still familiar to the critics of the nineteenth century.[3] Essentially the hierarchy is designed to privilege history painting above all other genres. The ability to represent life, above all human life and the lives of the gods, is the preeminent skill a painter must possess. Félibien—who had devoted his eighth *Entretien* to Poussin,[4] is clearly taking aim at the practitioners of the lower genres—principally the Academy's rivals, the artists of the Maîtrise. While the imputation was unjustified, the association of the guild with "inferior" painting was certainly an effective form of attack, especially since some of the Academy's founding members (such as the Le Nain brothers) were not history painters in the commonly accepted sense of the term and needed to be protected from accusations of anti-intellectualism.[5] But perhaps more importantly, Félibien established once and for all the scale of values that are attached to the hierarchy of the genres and consequently the shaping of the academic canon.

> He who paints landscapes perfectly is above the painter who only paints fruit, flowers, and seashells. He who paints living animals is more estimable that the painter who only paints things that are lifeless and without movement. And since mankind is the most perfect of God's works on Earth, it is certain that he who makes himself the imitator of God in painting the human figure is much more estimable than all the others. . . . A painter who paints only portraits has not achieved the highest perfection and cannot pretend to those honours that the most erudite receive. For that one must move from one figure to the representation of several together; one must depict history and fable and represent great deeds like historians, or charming subjects like poets; and climbing ever higher, one must in allegorical compositions know how to cover under the veil of fable the virtues of great men, and the most exalted mysteries. We call a painter great who can perform such tasks well.[6]

Thus an artist who paints "fruit, flowers, and seashells" must necessarily occupy the lowest rung of the hierarchy, since his representation is confined to the simple copying of lifeless things (significantly, still life is called *nature morte*—dead nature—in French). Above still life comes landscape, followed by "living animals;" next comes portraiture, since it depicts human beings—"the most perfect of God's works on Earth." But the artist cannot rest here; while it is noble to depict the human figure, especially in groups (where the potential for the representation of dramatic action becomes possible), the ambitious artist must represent ancient history and fable—"great deeds like historians, or charming subjects like poets." "Climbing ever higher," the artists reaches the uppermost rung of the hierarchy, the domain of allegory, which contains the means to express "the most exalted mysteries" of existence. But while Félibien's account undoubtedly seeks to separate significant (history) painting from inconsequential (genre) painting, the paramount from the subordinate, it did not discriminate between paintings on aesthetic grounds. While "good" and "bad" may well be implied in Félibien's judgments—as in "we call a painter great who can perform such tasks well"—the canon was founded on other, ostensibly firmer grounds—those of doctrinal authority.

We get a sense of what this authority was if we compare it to the original *kanon*—the list of books of the Judeo-Christian Bible. The comparison is significant, for both seek to establish a list of legitimate works. The key word here is authority, since it requires that a recognized group—in these cases the early theologians of Christianity and the officers of the Academy—be both competent and empowered to pronounce on a given text's legitimacy. In such a system, certain works were considered more significant than others. Thus the canon aspires to pronounce on the value of its works, reserving legitimacy for those that were considered doctrinally sound and exclusion for those that were not.[7] Yet more importantly, canonical authority was linked with institutional authority. In the case of the Academy, it sought to associate the authority it garnered as a royal institution with its self-ratifying authority to pronounce on the legitimacy of the canon, thereby welding into an indissoluble whole the question of aesthetic preference and institutional power.

But while comparison between the biblical and academic canons may illuminate the importance of terms such as legitimacy, authority, orthodoxy, and so on to our understanding of the canon, our task is to reconstruct the historical circumstances under which the academic canon was produced and *reproduced*, in other words, to examine its production, dissemination, reception, pedagogical structure, and theoretical underpinnings.[8] If history painting was central to the production of the canon (that is, regard for a body of work, opinions, and theories intimately associated with the aims, values, and aspirations of the Academy), then, as a genre, history painting may be seen as both the cause and the result of the academicization of art practice in France. Under these conditions, the "academic" canon is less a standard of excellence or a repository of values and more of a central focus around which the aspirations of a group of artists from diverse backgrounds and genres were drawn into a new form of professional association—that of the Academy itself.

However, it is no simple matter to establish the parameters of what constituted the canon in the first place. While certain artists, such as Raphael or Poussin, were always part of the canon, others, such as Rubens, were not. This suggests that far from being objective, or based on a strict meritocracy (qualities the early Academy worked hard to promote), the Academy's judgments were inherently doctrinal. In other words there is an inexpungable ideological bias to canon production that colors the entire enterprise. Canon formation was not a discreet process, but one imbricated in the social structure of the fine art economy—a visual manifesto of what significant painting stood for. Thus an overwhelmingly ideological complexion colors our understanding of the canon, since it cannot be separated from the institution (the Academy) that gave it meaning.

The canon, then, was a result of a deliberate shaping of the aims, aspirations, and goals of the Academy into a visual ideology. That this shaping was conscious is evidenced in countless examples of strategic positioning throughout the Academy's history. In this way the *conférences* of 1667 are both a record of the Academy's intellectual pretensions (and thus a slap in the face for the supposedly anti-intellectual guild) and an attempt to create a bond between the Academy and those it held to be the defenders of the faith (of the seven *conférences*, two are devoted to Raphael, and two to Poussin).[9] What we are witnessing here is the construction of an ideological formation—a social grouping in which like-minded practitioners defined and shaped their common beliefs into a visual language, both by promoting individual works whose inclusions were held to be necessary and by legislating against those considered unsuitable and/or inferior. And since these judgments were made within the context of academic debate, the result (at least in theory), was that the Academy's needs, and not those of individual artists, were paramount in organizing the visual knowledge that constituted canonical art production.

While the importance of intellectual production for the success of canon formation and legitimizing academic art practice cannot be overestimated (indeed, excepting the obvious importance of royal protection, what the

Academy *said* it was doing may be the single most important factor in its triumph over the guild), something else was required to ensure that its ideology be not only central to academic art production but also remain central into the foreseeable future. That something was art education.[10] Henri Testelin, the Academy's secretary in the years after its foundation, related the compelling reasons for identifying training as the Academy's privileged defense against the guild's aggression (the guild was attempting to block the registration of the Academy's title of association, its *lettres patentes*):

> The Academy . . . informed of the circumstances, debated its response to this incident: to advance, to promote, to bring to perfection the public exercises of the new school easily won out over any other strategy with men as passionate as they were for the glory of their art and the success of this establishment. *They regarded success in this field as the most natural and sure way of meriting more and more the support of the throne and the suffrage of persons of authority truly animated by a love for the public good* [my emphasis].[11]

The intention could not be clearer. By putting pedagogy at the center of its theoretical and practical activity the Academy could control not only the discourse on art but also the way its visual ideology was communicated to the next generation, thereby bringing together canon formation and canon maintenance under the same, unified, pedagogical enterprise.

Training, both inside the Academy and in the Academy-oriented teaching studios, focused on canonical works to the exclusion of all others.[12] In this respect, the works of Raphael and Poussin, as well as the universally admired sculptures of antiquity, were crucial in forming taste. Anticipating the yet-more-intransigent nineteenth century, the sculptor Gerard van Opstal argued in 1667 with respect to the *Laocoön* (fig. 4.1): "Through study of this statue one could learn to correct even the faults that are ordinarily found in nature, because in it everything appears in a state of perfection. . . . In sum, this statue is so accomplished that everyone agrees that it is from this model that the Rome School, which has produced so many great artists, has drawn, as if from a very pure spring, most of its fine understanding."[13] A mere twenty years after the foundation of the Paris Academy artists were advocating a restricted and prescriptive canon of significant works to guide the student. This suggests that, along with the predictable reification of academic values occasioned by the passage of time, the Academy as it were embraced restriction as a quality of association. That this happened institutionally is beyond doubt, but it is significant to see its parallel in the active limitation of emulative models effected through canon control.

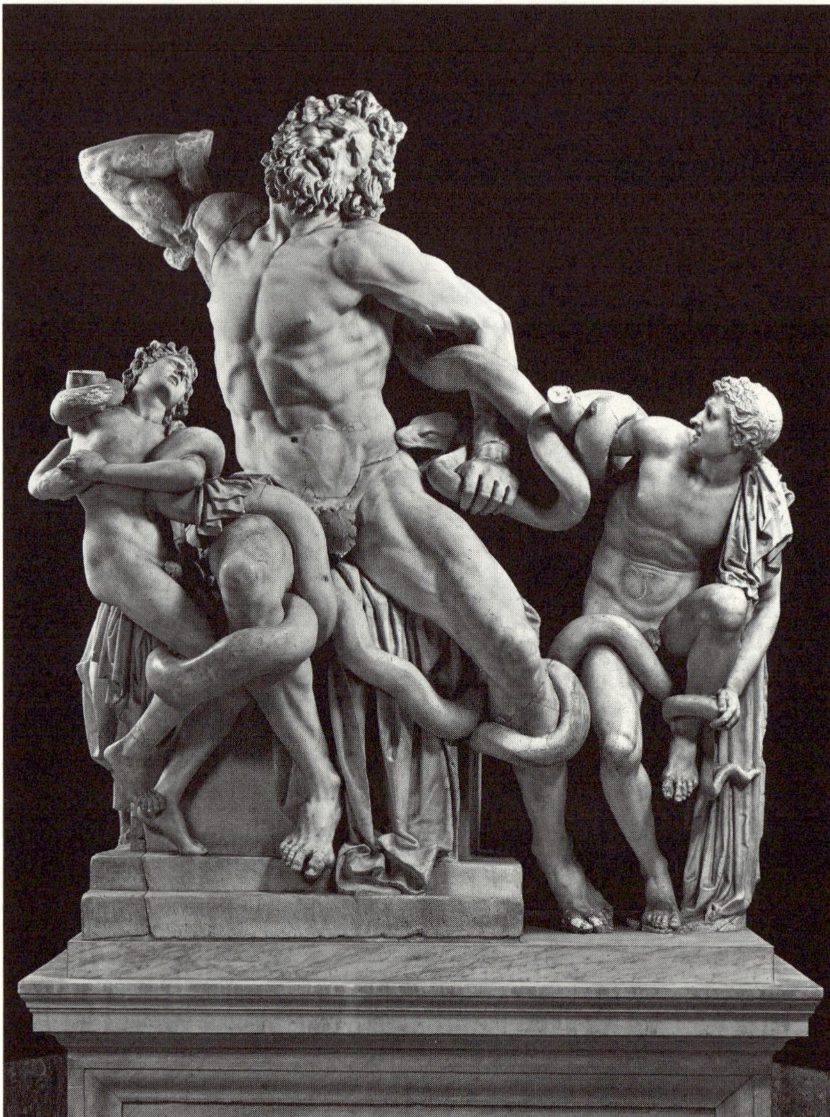

4.1. Hagesandros, Polydoros, and Athenodoros, *Laocoön*, 2nd century BCE–1st century CE, marble, Vatican Museum, Rome. Photo: Scala/Art Resource, New York.

Van Opstal's remarks did not go unchallenged. In 1672 Philippe de Champaigne argued that imitation of the canon meant an *active* selection, not slavish imitation, and certainly not uncritical acceptance. Indeed, Champaigne complained that students who "limit themselves to copying servilely and directly the particular manner of [one] original, holding it up as the only goal and model they need to consult," would thereby undermine their own creative potential:

> This inclination [to copy] may be excused in the young student who is still under the wing of his master, and it is so natural for the beginner that we should not seek to forbid it completely; but that which entirely prevents the attainment of wisdom in our art is, as I have often remarked, that advanced students who show promise suddenly limit themselves to an infatuation with copying and the making of exact copies in the manner of a particular artist, thus subjecting their genius to one style, instead of which they should be taking whatever is the most beautiful from every style and making, like bees, their own honey, that is, a beauty that is their own.[14]

But the Academy's hands were tied. Given its role as the institutional expression of such values (which, of course, it was largely responsible for professing), its ability to negotiate a position between outright acceptance of canonical works and a more liberated, critical interrogation of their qualities was all but impossible.

By the nineteenth century, the hitherto unified process of canon formation and canon maintenance gave way to canon preservation; that is, to the ossifying of a formerly dynamic process into a defensive strategy tending to stasis.[15] Jean-Auguste-Dominique Ingres expresses the idea most trenchantly: "Is there anything left to discover in the arts? . . . [No], nothing essential remains to be found after Phidias or Raphael, but there is always something to do, even now, to maintain the cult of truth and to perpetuate the tradition of the beautiful."[16] Whether this reluctance to develop the canon reflected an age more intent on arresting a slide into aesthetic relativism than seeking out a more ecumenical approach to the art of the past, or whether the distinction was thought unimportant, it resulted in a renewed emphasis on the imitation of past art as a means of situating current practice within timeless norms. As the Academy's *Dictionnaire de l'Académie des Beaux-Arts* argued: "Analysis of the procedures of a master seems the most instructive way to attain a personal style. To struggle with such difficulties, even when they are not crowned with complete success, is not a pointless exercise. . . . Moreover, such a struggle has the inestimable advantage of preventing one's taste from going astray. On the contrary, it forms taste, directs it, and allows one to discover secrets that a simple examination would not be enough to reveal."[17]

All in all this treats the whole question of canonicity and imitation as if it were self-evidently unproblematic—merely a matter of training artists to reproduce (whether literally or emulatively) models drawn from the corpus. Not everyone was so sure. As the critic Thoré-Bürger observed in 1844: "When one takes a walk through the old Louvre, with a little understanding of painting, one can name, at first glance, each painting: Rembrandt, van Ostade, Cuyp, Veronese, Correggio, del Sarto. . . . Today there is a miserable promiscuity. The line of descent is effaced. Nothing is left but the mark of a general debility and common ugliness."[18] Writing in 1861 Maxime du Camp agreed: "This fine French School, of which we have been so proud, now wanders haphazardly like a battalion of deserters in full flight; the gold standard has been changed into base coin, its hallmarks erased. Everyone imitates everyone else, and in this epidemic of imitation, it is natural that nothing new appears. The salon of 1861 resembles that of 1859, which resembles that of 1857."[19] Of course, Ingres and the Academy could have replied (and did, as we shall see) that it was not a question of uncritical copying of the work of others, but of a judicious selection. Yet this was dangerous advice, as the influential drawing teacher Horace Lecoq de Boisbaudran recognized: "The path that generally seems to be the surest and easiest is the imitation of those previously honored works, those that are unfailingly exhibited with all due honor and pomp, as if offered as the means to success. Can anyone fail to understand the full significance of such incentives when most candidates abandon their own inspirations to follow slavishly the path recommended by the Ecole, and who, consequently, are blessed by success?"[20]

Lecoq's opinion was shared by Eugène Delacroix, who stressed in his *Journal* the need to overcome the weight of tradition:

> Some artistic temperaments are strong enough to absorb and take advantage of everything. In spite of being brought up in ways that would not have come naturally to them, they find their own path through the mazes of other men's precepts and examples. They benefit by what is good, and although they sometimes bear the mark of a particular school, they develop into artists like Rubens, Titian, or Raphael. It is absolutely essential that at some moment in their careers, artists should learn not to

> despise everything that does not come from their own inspiration, but to strip themselves of the almost always blind fanaticism which prompts us all to imitate the great masters and to swear by them alone.[21]

By this Delacroix did not mean that Rubens, or Titian, or Raphael had learned nothing from the art of the past, only that they remained in control of their individual stylistic vocabulary in spite of examples of monstrously celebrated art on all sides.[22]

Delacroix's conception of a healthy rivalry allows the present to learn the achievements of the past, but this was not a perspective shared by many members of the Academy, whom, faced with the impossibility of "find[ing] their own path through the mazes of other men's precepts and examples," while dismissing as a *copie équivoque* the emulation that addresses the model as motif, took refuge in the authority of the canon. This is the academician Pierre Guérin, writing in 1828, commenting on the progress of students under his care at the Académie de France in Rome: "The works of this immortal painter [Raphael] appear to be the most proper to oppose the direction that the arts have taken in France and which threatens to hasten its decadence. The clarity, the noble and gracious simplicity, as much as the naturalism that reigns in the productions of this divine master, must make him preferable to Michelangelo whose genius, if misinterpreted, may easily lead his imitators astray."[23]

Indeed, treating Raphael as a salutary, and Michelangelo as a dangerous, example, Guérin adds a dimension of prohibition—the exclusion of those models (in this case the work of Michelangelo), that threatened to challenge the reasoned order of the canon. It had a long history. As early as 1668 Fréart de Chambray had contrasted the decorum of the former to the *terribilità* of the latter: "Michael-Angelo, superior in Fame, but far inferior to [Raphael] in Merits, shall by his extravagant Compositions, amply furnish us to discover the Ignorance and Temerity of those libertines, who trampling all the Rules and Maxims of Art under their feet, pursue only their own Caprices."[24]

But many artists and critics in the nineteenth century were less interested in establishing the present's rapport with a given canonical artist than in setting up a frame of reference in which the canon functioned as a benchmark of excellence—a benchmark, that is, of the most atemporal and legislative kind. As the *Dictionnaire de l'Académie des Beaux-Arts* noted with considerable understatement, "The choice of model is not a matter for indifference for the progress of the young student."[25] In commenting on the *envois* sent back to Paris by the *pensionnaires* of the Académie de France in Rome, the judges withheld unequivocal praise from an otherwise excellent copy by Joseph-Désiré Court because the artist had chosen as his model a painting by Valentin de Boulogne, who was, in the opinion of the judges, "not of that number who recommend themselves by a noble character or grandeur of style."[26] In the same vein the jury formed to review the *envois* of 1838 criticized Eugène Roger for choosing as a model a work by Titian that "could not offer any of the precious qualities recognized in the work of this great master"—thereby at a stroke absolving Titian from any fault while blaming Roger for his choice of Titian in the first place.[27] In 1817 the weight of the Academy's criticism fell on Léon Pallière's choice of model, Caravaggio's *Supper at Emmaus*. Although the authors of the report, Antoine-Jean Gros and Pierre-Narcisse Guérin, took care to suggest that blame might lie with Caravaggio, their displeasure is aimed squarely at the student copyist who was responsible either way for making a choice outside the canon: "Keeper of those principles that uphold the dignity of art, the Academy must stipulate that students should turn their brushes away from everything—even masterpieces—that tend to degrade the representation of nature."[28] While the canon was made up of masterpieces, the qualities generally held to signify a masterpiece were not sufficient reason for a given work's inclusion in the canon. To win that honor, the work must "uphold the dignity of art," and demonstrate not just its paradigmatic status as a masterpiece but also its canonical status as a model of emulation.[29]

Unsurprisingly, avant-garde critics such as Théodore Duret saw canonicity less as the operation of a gold standard and more as a counterfeit authority impeding progress. As he argues in his salon of 1870 with reference to Henri Regnault's *Salome* (fig. 4.2), the young artist, seen by many as the best hope for the rejuvenation of establishment values, was little more than a opportunistic thief exploiting the canon for his own ends:

> But here I see some reader take me by the arm to say: And M. Regnault? Is he not a newcomer? And do you not think he shows enough brilliance? Why do you pass him by in silence? It is true that, among the last to arrive, M. Regnault has caused a stir; he is a bird dressed in a brilliant plumage, and nothing is more pleasant than to see the gullible stop dumbfounded in front of him. If we have nothing to say, it's that, of all the feathers with which he has adorned himself, it is impossible for us to distinguish those which properly belong to him. It seems to us that M. Regnault pilfers everywhere, and the only talent he possesses that, at the time of speaking, we cannot argue with, is a marvelous capacity for making art out of the most diverse materials.[30]

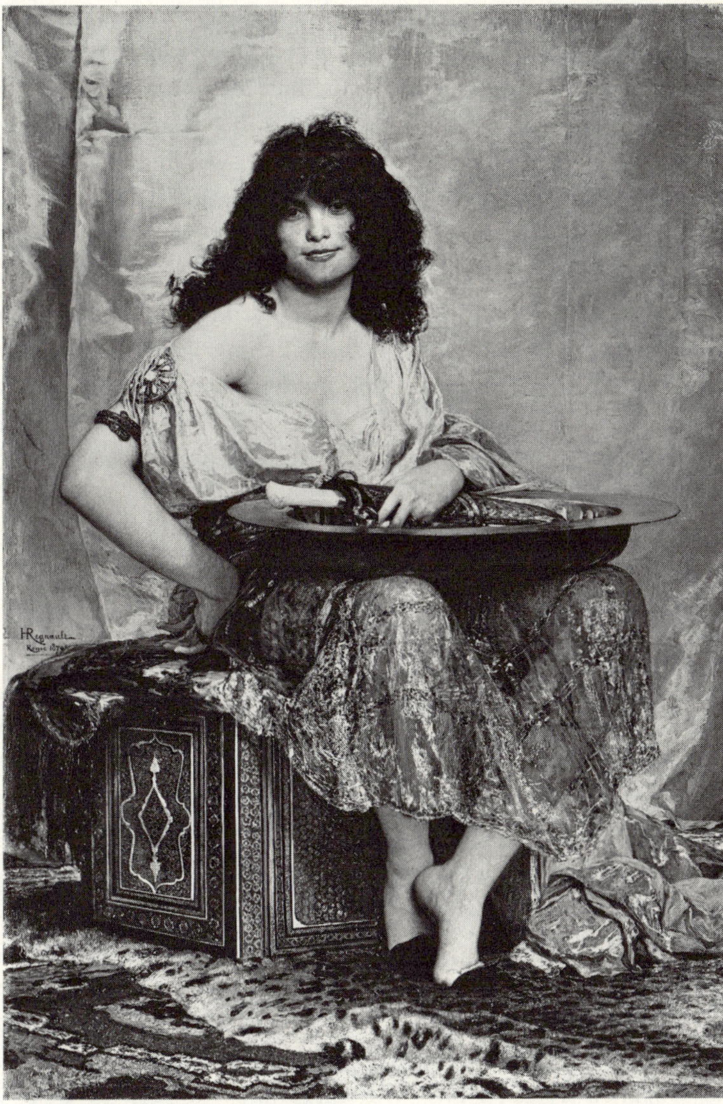

4.2. Henri-Alexandre-Georges Regnault, *Salomé*, 1870, oil on canvas, the Metropolitan Museum of Art, New York.

Paradoxically, given Regnault's referencing of the art of the past, it is the *lack* of origin that best describes his painting. Although he was held by many to be the personification of canonicity, in reality the canon was a modern invention, its professed qualities matching not those of past art, but offering a context to artists such as Regnault whose self-perception was based on presenting himself as the inheritor of a great tradition. Indeed, while such painting may appear to be formally contiguous with that of earlier centuries, in fact it represents a break between past and present. The past was finally, and fatally for the authority of the canon, no longer a living organism.

We have only to recall that Raphael's self-appointed spokesperson Ingres likened the Renaissance master to "a god descended to earth"[31] and remarked that "when one is in front of his works, it is like being a second creator," to see the operation of canonicity in its plenitude: "For a long time, my works have recognized no other discipline other than that of the old masters, that is to say, the great masters who flourished in that century of glorious memory when Raphael set the eternal and incontestable bounds of the sublime in art. . . . I am thus a *conservator* of good doctrine, not an *innovator*, nor am I as my detractors pretend, a servile imitator . . . although I know enough to take advantage of more of the fruits than they know how to see."[32] For Ingres, the art of Raphael is the conduit through which his own art must pass. When he says, "I know enough to take advantage of more of the fruits than they know how to see," he is consciously pitting himself against his contemporaries as an imitator of the artist the nineteenth century regarded as quintessentially canonical, not to rival Raphael but in order to demonstrate his superiority over his contemporaries. Ingres does not identify with Raphael as much as he identifies himself as Raphael's follower, his amanuensis in the modern world of decadent values and lost greatness. Raphael, we might say, is a mirror in which Ingres sees himself reflected. It is an image that the less clairvoyant are unable to see, for it reflects Ingres's revolutionary status as the conservator of past greatness.

When he said in 1820 of a recently completed painting, the *Christ Giving the Keys to St. Peter*, "finished, but never sufficiently,"[33] Ingres was articulating a firm belief that no single pictorial statement could ever stand independently of the tradition of which it was part. This is a point that has been argued by Norman Bryson, who writes that Ingres's most emulative painting, the *Vow of Louis XIII* (fig. 4.3), "implies a suite of *permutations* in which no combination can be final or definitive; it opens on to a vista of alternative dispositions

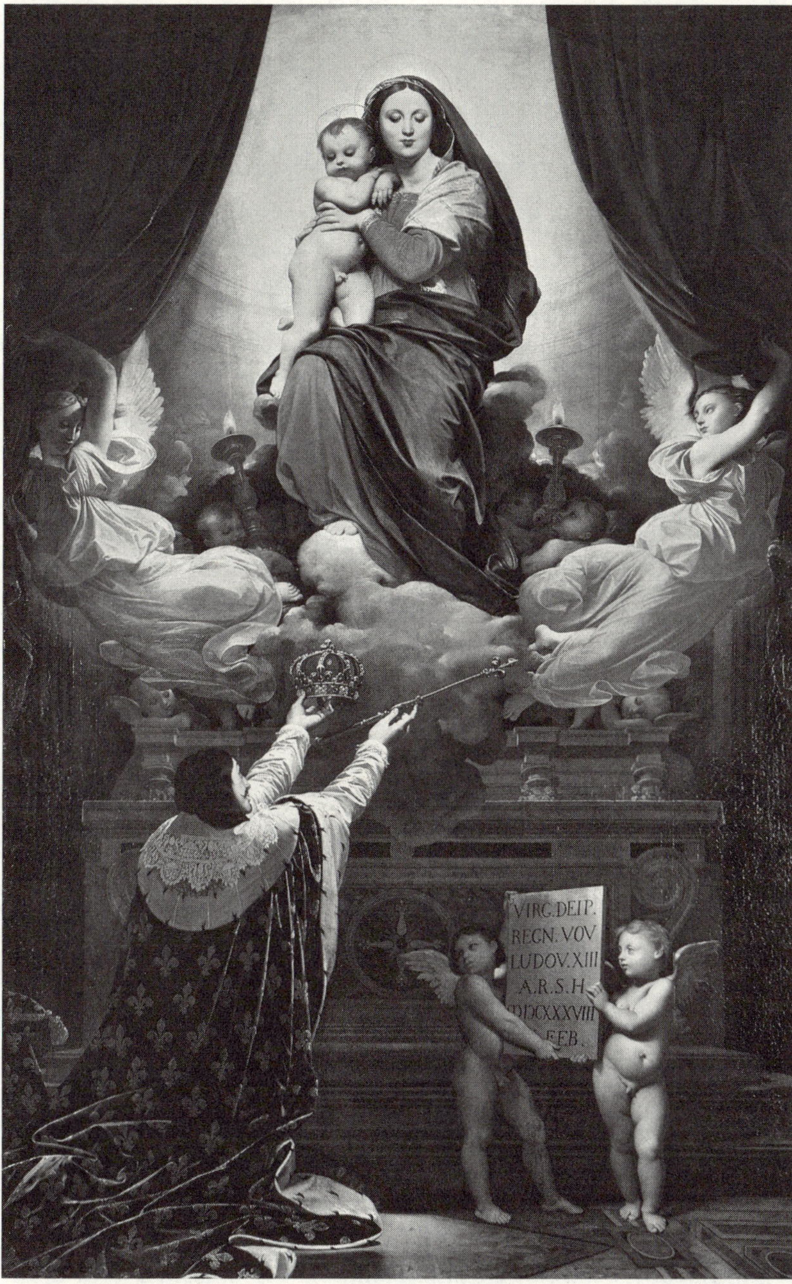

4.3. Jean Auguste-Dominique Ingres, *Vow of Louis XIII*, 1824, oil on canvas, Notre Dame Cathedral, Montauban. Photo: Erich Lessing/Art Resource/New York.

incapable of closure or completion."[34] We should recognize what this means for our understanding of canon maintenance. Ingres saw emulation of the canon as a process of assembling those elements of preexisting perfection that constituted the building blocks of timeless beauty. When Amaury-Duval first visited Ingres's studio with a view to training as a painter, Ingres showed him the *Vow*: "You see this . . . it's beautiful, isn't it? . . . Of course I don't mean the painting; the painting, the newspapers say, is a pastiche, a copy of Raphael." Examination of the painting reveals not only Ingres's profound veneration of Raphael, but also the subtlety of his procedure. When he says, "it's beautiful, isn't it?" and then adds, "of course I don't mean the painting," he operates within the mindset of the classicizing artist for whom the present articulation of the ideal is but a particular, and provisional, reiteration of canonical values that lie both in the past (insofar as his models are necessarily anterior) and in the present—where Ingres's *oeuvre* will attain its timeless realization.

At this point in the discussion of the *Vow*, Amaury-Duval reported, Ingres became animated, and his eyes shone with passion: "Well! this is no pastiche, this is no copy. . . . I've also left my mark. . . . Certainly I admire the masters, I bow before them . . . above all before the greatest [Raphael] . . . but I don't copy them. . . . I have drunk their milk, I have nourished myself on it, I have tried to appropriate their sublime qualities . . . but I have not pastiched them."[35] This is, of course, an instance of the operation of a visual ideology—in this case Ingres's image of himself in relation to the art of the past, which, in the manner of a mirror, he looked into for self-recognition. In this sense his identification with the art of the past is the deployment of a visual paradigm that made a model for emulation out of past art that had, in reality, no obvious or compelling connection with the present. Rather, Ingres constructed a position of subordination for himself vis-à-vis past art that he believed to be imposed solely by the weight of Raphael's reputation. Accepting Ingres's relationship to the past as paradigmatic, we should consider the discourse around canonicity in nineteenth-century France less as a process through which the present inherits the past, and more as the construction of a contemporary identity predicated on identity with the canon.

The progressive marginalization of the canon during the nineteenth century, carrying as it does a sense of the permeability of the hitherto firm categorical distinctions between the genres, is alone sufficient cause to explain the horror with which the Academy learned of the proposals for the reform of art education published in the *Moniteur universel* of November 15, 1863.[36] Two days before, the emperor had signed a decree that deprived the Academy of the privilege of directing the École des Beaux-Arts and the Academy in Rome, of organizing its competitions, or of judging the Grand Prix. Those who formulated the changes—Prosper Mérimée, Eugène Emmanuel Viollet-le-Duc, and the superintendent of fine art, the comte de Nieuwerkerke—introduced a series of measures designed to modernize art instruction.

A principal measure sought to promote the importance of painting at the expense of drawing (formerly only drawing, as the common foundation of the visual arts, had been taught). As a first step, three successful academic artists—Gérôme, Cabanel, and Pils—were appointed to head the new painting studios. Most significant of all, however, is what these measures meant for the role of the canon in art education. In particular, the shift in emphasis away from drawing to painting moved the center of gravity away from the study of the canonical masters toward fostering originality in the young artist.[37] This claim may seem exaggerated, until we realize that drawing was inextricably tied to the study and reproduction of examples of past art: Amaury-Duval recalled how, in 1825, on his first day as a student of Ingres, he was set to copying engravings after Raphael. Writing over fifty years later, Amaury-Duval recalled, "I can see them now, a Christ and an Apostle . . . and, having pointed out to me all their merits, I was advised to copy them with devoted precision."[38]

Unsurprisingly, the initiative was strongly contested by some members of the Academy. Arguing that "drawing is everything" and that the "material processes of painting are very easy and may be learned in a week," Ingres opposed instruction in painting on the grounds that the old masters had not proceeded in this way: "The great masters have left us, in innumerable drawings and compositions after nature, the examples that we should follow, because there is not a single painted study from nature to be found by them; it is from these drawings that they painted their admirable works."[39] Perhaps more to the point, drawing allowed for the reproduction of canonical works as the benchmark and compass of the young student's training, while painting, considered more physical and impressionistic, tempted the student toward interpretation. With great subtlety, the academician Louis Vitet argued that the reforms confused two kinds of originality—"true" and "false." While the first kind is inseparable from native talent and cannot be taught, the second betrayed a love of novelty, exaggeration, capriciousness, and fantasy, a spurious originality based on an emphasis on individual technique—in other words the merely bizarre.[40]

But Vitet and the Academy were swimming against the tide. The proposal was intent on promoting its version of originality, a quality it believed was inhibited by "those more or less absolute doctrines and theories" that kept students prisoners of the canon. "This personal originality, a quality so essential to artists, and one that art instruction tends to develop so little today, is further shackled in a most regrettable manner by the current system of competitions that have become the principal concern of students and teachers at the Ecole des beaux-arts. . . . This sort of progression, which all young artists must endure, seems to be founded on an opinion that is hardly ever contested, namely, that with patience and memory one may attain one's goal."[41] Echoing criticism of the judgments passed on the *envois* from Rome, Nieuwerkerke argued that the institutionalization of mediocrity has led to Prix de Rome winners being selected on the basis of fewest faults, not the most qualities. As Nieuwerkerke put it, "Honest mediocrity has the greatest chance of success."[42]

The Academy reacted to the proposals with disarming frankness. A response to the decree published in *Le Moniteur universel* of January 6, 1864, plaintively noted, "Your Majesty must see that the decree withdraws from the Academy the source of its activity, its intellectual life, and as it were its raison d'être."[43] This was nothing less than the plain truth, and the root of the Academy's distress. In the end a change of regime came to the aid of the Academy, albeit after a painful period of humiliation. Eight years to the day after the original decree, on November 13, 1871, the new Third Republic rescinded most of the reforms. It would be hard to see this action as a reflection on the success or failure of the changes. More plausibly, the Third Republic's new president, Auguste Thiers, and his minister of fine art, Jules Simon, wanted to obliterate as much of the Second Empire's artistic legacy as they could, while the interventionist measures proposed by Nieuwerkerke ran counter to the Third Republic's political philosophy, which saw in the reforms an authoritarian and didactic element little in keeping with the new regime's liberal policies.[44] Yet it is tempting to see neither politics nor aesthetics driving change, rather that the bond between the canon and the Academy, in which the latter was the institutional embodiment of the former, just as the former was the artistic expression (through history painting) of academic association, had finally atrophied into insignificance without anyone in the government or the Academy quite realizing it. From this point of view, the reforms of 1863, which squarely took aim at not just the authority of the Academy but also the authority of the canon, stand as the last attempt by the state to involve itself in the direction of the arts, and the Third Republic's abdication of the role dealt a mortal blow to an institution that, finally, could only thrive with the authority of the canon intact.

The results of this representational order are obvious. Estranged from the dialogue between past and present that had animated artists as different as Poussin and David, nineteenth-century painters found themselves condemned to repeat what they could not transcend. It is this essentially obsolete aesthetic (an aesthetic that appeared whole and immediate in comparison to a fragmented and confused present) that imbricated art practice in a system of values that worked not only to situate contemporary art at the matrix of an imitative web, but also to bestow on the nineteenth century the belief that identification with the canon was the prerequisite for self-identity in the present.[45] Under such conditions institutional art practice could not claim a privileged role in the prosecution of nineteenth-century painting, nor could it be considered the locus of a body of knowledge, whether received wisdom or otherwise. The century's discursive formations, instinctual biases, and seemingly limited perspective force us to conclude that, as a mode of interpretation, the exclusive reliance on canonical values to imbue the art of the nineteenth century with meaning served only to restrict the number of options open to artists.

Ultimately, treating the canon as a transcendental value—untouchable, exemplary, paradigmatic—opened up nineteenth-century art to sudden and catastrophic collapse. For many in the nineteenth century, artists were judged exclusively on their ability to meld disparate visual references into a meaningful statement. Such criticism situates not nature as the object of the artist's enterprise, but only, and always, another work of art. The inevitable result is that much nineteenth-century painting could only ever be defined in terms of past art, of supposed sources and influences. For an academy that was fatally caught between the obligations to an aesthetic that many saw as absolute, and the challenges of a present increasingly indifferent to those values, stasis was the paralyzing response.

Notes

1 For a study of the institutional structure of French seventeenth-century art practice, see Heinich, *Du peintre à l'artiste*; also Thuillier, "Académie et classicisme en France."

2 Testelin, *Mémoires pour servir à l'histoire de l'Académie royale de peinture et de sculpture depuis 1648 jusqu'en 1664*, 1:4.

3 Félibien, preface to *Conférences de l'académie royale de peinture et de sculpture pendant l'année 1667*, [unpaged].
4 Félibien, *Entretiens sur les vies et sur les ouvrages des plus excellens peintres.*
5 The slander is contained in the petition to the crown, "Requête de M. Charmois," reprinted in Vitet, *Académie royale de peinture et de sculpture*, 195–207; see also Testelin, *Mémoires pour servir à l'histoire de l'Académie royale de peinture et de sculpture depuis 1648 jusqu'en 1664*, 1:4–5.
6 Félibien, *Conférences de l'académie royale de peinture et de sculpture pendant l'année 1667*, preface (n.p.).
7 My reading here of canonicity relies heavily on Guillory, "Canon"; see also Sitterson, "Canon"; and the excellent Sarna, Beckwith, and du Toit, "Canon."
8 For the role of instruction in the perpetuation of ideological formations, see Althusser, "Ideology and Ideological State Apparatuses (Notes Toward an Investigation)."
9 Félibien, *Conférences de l'académie royale de peinture et de sculpture pendant l'année 1667*.
10 As one scholar states, "The problem of the canon is the problem of syllabus and curriculum, the institutional forms by which works are preserved as *great* works" (Guillory, "Canon," 240).
11 Testelin, *Mémoires pour servir à l'histoire de l'Académie royale de peinture et de sculpture depuis 1648 jusqu'en 1664*, 1:46–47.
12 Two established studies of art training are Boime, *The Academy and French Painting in the Nineteenth Century*, for the earlier part of the nineteenth century; and Milner, *The Studios of Paris*, for the later decades. See also Benhamou, "Public and Private Art Education in France 1648–1793"; and Goldstein, *Teaching Art*.
13 Van Opstal lectured to the Academy on July 2, 1667; see Félibien, *Conférences de l'académie royale de peinture et de sculpture pendant l'année 1667*, 31–32.
14 Champaigne, "Contre les copistes de manières."
15 The whole question of latecoming has been extensively treated by Bloom, whose *The Anxiety of Influence*, along with Bate's *The Burden of the Past and the English Poet*, set the terms of the discussion in the 1970s; more recently, Bryson has characterized the artists of the early nineteenth century in similar terms in *Tradition and Desire*.
16 Delaborde, *Ingres*, 148.
17 "Copie," *Dictionnaire de l'Académie des Beaux-Arts*, 4 (1884):262–65, esp. 263.
18 Thoré-Bürger, *Salons de T. Thoré 1844, 1845, 1846, 1847, 1848*, 33–34.
19 Du Camp, *Le Salon de 1861*, 5.
20 Lecoq de Boisbaudran cited in Moffett, *The New Painting*, 37–49, 398. For a study that emphasizes Lecoq's aversion to emulation, see Gotlieb, "The Pedagogy of Emancipation."
21 Wellington, *The Journal of Eugène Delacroix*, 321 (entry for September 30, 1855).
22 In his short essay *De Imitatione Statuarum*, written about 1608 but first published by Roger de Piles a century later, Rubens warned that excessive imitation would serve only to crush native creativity; see Muller, "Rubens's Theory and Practice of the Imitation of Art."
23 Lapauze, *Histoire de l'Académie de France à Rome*, 2:179.
24 Fréart de Chambray, *An Idea of the Perfection of Painting*, preface.
25 "Copie," *Dictionnaire de l'Académie des Beaux-Arts*, 4:262–65.

26 *Rapport sur les ouvrages des élèves pensionnaires à l'Académie royale de France à Rome pour l'année 1825*, [unpaged].

27 *Rapport sur les ouvrages envoyés de Rome par les pensionnaires à l'Académie royale de France à Rome pour l'année 1838*.

28 *Registre des procès-verbaux* for Saturday, October 11, 1817.

29 Ibid.

30 Duret, *Critique d'avant-garde*, 51–52.

31 Boyer d'Agen, *Ingres d'après une correspondance inedited*, 297, 333–34.

32 Condon, Cohn, and Mongan, *Ingres, in Pursuit of Perfection*, 14 (translation slightly modified).

33 Ibid., 11.

34 Bryson, *Tradition and Desire*, 149.

35 Amaury-Duval, *Atelier d'Ingres*, 13.

36 Vitet and Viollet le Duc, *Débates et Polémiques*, 147–53; also Laurent, *Arts et pouvoirs en France de 1793 à 1981*, 54–73.

37 Boime, "The Teaching Reforms of 1863 and the Origins of Modernism in France," 13.

38 Amaury-Duval, *Atelier d'Ingres*, 13.

39 Ingres, *Réponse au rapport sur l'Ecole impériale des Beaux-Arts adressé au Maréchal Vaillant*, 8.

40 Vitet, "Les arts du dessin en France," 74–107.

41 "Rapport à Son Excellence le maréchal de France, ministre de la maison de l'Empéreur et des Beaux-Arts," in Vitet and Viollet-le-Duc, *Débats et Polémiques*, 147–53, esp. 150.

42 Nieuwerkerke's argument found an echo in contemporary literature. Edmond Goncourt's and Jules de Goncourt's Garnotelle in their contemporary novel *Manette Salomon* epitomized:

> The case of the artist born without talent but blessed with will-power, thankless persistence, and the courage of mediocrity: patience. Through application and perseverance he had become an almost knowledgeable draughtsman, the best in his studio. His drawing was no better than exact—a dry line, a copied contour, all servile and strained, where nothing breathed that air of freedom characteristic of the great interpreters of form. . . . For this artist color did not exist. His compositions were mediocre, drawing on a second-hand imagination borrowed from a dozen well-known paintings. Garnotelle was, in a word, a man of negative qualities, a student without the vice of originality (my translation, 75).

43 See Académie des Beaux-Arts, "Protestation respectueuse contre les atteintes qui viennent d'être portées à son caractère, à ses droits, à ces attributions."

44 Vaisse, *La Troisième République et les peintres*, 53–8; also Genet-Delacroix, *Art et Etat sous la IIIe République*, 3.

45 For a full account of the Lacanian theme of self-recognition, see Evans, *An Introductory Dictionary of Lacanian Psychoanalysis*, 80–84.

5

Chinese Art, the National Palace Museum, and Cold War Politics

JANE C. JU

The Chinese have been writing about art for over two thousand years. These writings—biographies of artists, technical treatises, essays on art theory, and painting catalogues—were appropriated into the discourse of modern Chinese art history during the last century as part of China's modernization effort. In recent years as scholars in China and in the West have begun to evaluate art historical paradigms, the similarities and dissimilarities between traditional and modern Chinese art history have become one of the points of contention in the debates about the definition of Chinese art and about how it should be studied.[1] It is generally accepted, however, that the Chinese became interested in art in the Western sense in the first decades of the twentieth century, at approximately the same time as they began defining their country in terms of a modern nation-state.[2]

In my previous research, I have found that museums played an important, though largely unacknowledged, role in shaping this modern conception of Chinese art.[3] The republican period, which dates from the fall of the Qing dynasty in 1911 to 1949 and represents the initial stage of modern Chinese nationalism, witnessed countless debates over what the "real" modern China stood for. In those debates the collection of the Beijing Palace Museum, which opened to the public in 1925, was often mentioned, since it was at the center of activities to preserve, study, and define Chinese art. However, it would be a mistake to assume that the modern idea of Chinese art was already well formed during the early republican period. Although China had a long tradition of artistic expression, the term "art," or *yishu*, began to be used only during the republican period, and it was based on the Chinese characters used by the Japanese to translate the term's European meaning.[4] In texts on traditional art and the Palace collection that were written during the republican period, debates about the meaning of the objects almost always go back to the fundamental question of what makes these objects authentically "Chinese" (*Zhongguo*) and thereby sets them apart from Western culture and from the traditional culture appropriated by the Manchu of the recently toppled Qing dynasty.[5]

The modern Chinese nation-state established during the republican period was short-lived. The government formed by the Guomindang (the Nationalist Party) never had complete control over the country. Chinese political development was interrupted first by the warfare against the local warlords, then by the war against the Japanese, and finally by a civil war between the Communists and the Guomindang, which the latter lost, forcing its retreat to Taiwan. John Breuilly has noted that "nationalism is, above and beyond all else, about politics"; it is not an a priori concept.[6] The Guomindang brand of nationalism failed because the party could not achieve its "objectives of obtaining and using state power."[7] In other words, the new Chinese republic was not strong enough to develop and support ideological institutions that were needed to form a definitive national culture. However, most scholars of modern China would agree that the nationalist movement did inspire the Chinese people to think of themselves as a nation.

To be sure there were many points of contention concerning specifics of this shared national identity. In terms of culture, Marxist theorists, such as Qu Qiubai (1899–1935), considered folk art to be the truest representation of the Chinese people. Chen Hengke (1876–1923) and Huang Binhong (1864–1955), in contrast, pointed to works of the literati, the ruling elite of China, as the most important Chinese art of the past and a model for its modern development.[8] Nationalism was used in equal measure by the Communist Party to establish a socialist state on the mainland and by the Guomindang to construct a Chinese state in Taiwan.[9] In this essay I will focus on the Taiwanese context. I will show that the exiled Guomindang government not only continued using the name "Republic of China," but, more importantly, used the ideas developed during the republican period to create a canonical narrative of Chinese culture, which identified the literati tradition as the foundation of Chinese art. Ironically, this definition of the canon was also profoundly influenced by the politics of the cold war and the emerging American cultural hegemony.

America's "China" in Taiwan

In 1949 the Guomindang government was forced to retreat to Taiwan. The problem of recognizing which government had sovereignty over China should have been simple since the Guomindang no longer controlled the mainland. However, the escalation of the cold war and the outbreak of the Korean War created the problem of "two Chinas." Instead of recognizing the legitimacy of the Communist government on the mainland, the United States acknowledged the government of the Republic of China on the island of Taiwan as the official China, giving it substantial economic and military aid.[10] With the mainland Communist government also claiming to represent China, the governments of the United States and the Guomindang faced the serious challenge of identifying Taiwan politically and culturally with the historical China.

With the ultimate goal of acquiring national security for Taiwan during the period of the cold war, the U.S. foreign policy of technical assistance, economic aid, and mutual military defense necessarily overshadowed cultural and educational programs. The extent of American impact on Taiwan's cultural development has been difficult to ascertain because of minimal or sometimes nonexistent documentation. At the same time, educational and cultural exchanges between the United States and Taiwan were construed to be modernizing and positive, and as such were never questioned or critically evaluated. The influence of American cultural policies on the development of modern art in Taiwan is commonly known.[11] Liu Kuo-sung and the Fifth Moon Group are two notable examples. Both created works using traditional Chinese techniques and materials to create modernist forms similar to the paintings of the American abstract expressionist painters.[12]

Not as familiar are the American programs that supported studies of Chinese traditions and modern Chinese history (usually Qing dynasty to the republican period) in Taiwan as well as in the United States.[13] The American presence in Taiwan coincided with the post–World War II process of decolonization. The Americans wanted to distinguish the expansion of their influences on East Asia from that of the former European colonial powers; thus they tended to promote programs within a system of reciprocity, or "mutual aid," a term used by the U.S. Department of State.[14] For example, in 1966, at the suggestion of C. Martin Wilbur of Columbia University, the Conference on Sino-American Cooperation in the Humanities and Social Sciences was held in Taipei.[15] For three days scholars and education administrators from

Taiwan and the United States, many of whom represented the Social Science Research Council, the American Council of Learned Societies, and the National Academy of Sciences, discussed the state of Chinese studies. Many of the recommendations were developed into study programs in the sciences and social sciences. Creation of art history and museum studies programs was also recommended. Programs in Chinese history, language, and the humanities were set up in universities in Taiwan, and Chinese studies programs were also established in major American universities, often with funding from the Ford Foundation. The focus of the research on traditional culture and Chinese history often emphasized the humanistic aspects, and coincidentally worked well with the American government's goal of defining Taiwan as a democratic, humanistic, and modern China in opposition to the Communist, oppressive, mainland China.

In his critical studies of international and area studies during and after the cold war, Bruce Cumings concluded that the forces that shaped the scholarly studies are "economic and political."[16] The funding government agencies, including the U.S. Central Intelligence Agency (CIA), and private foundations supported these programs for the good of Taiwan's development. The Americans, in particular the U.S. government, believed that an understanding of East Asia could be best achieved through modern (Western) methods. This attitude has been called "post-Orientalism" by recent scholars to differentiate American involvement in Asia from Edward Said's analytic designation of primarily pre–World War II European "Orientalism."[17] Cumings, who described this phenomenon in terms of "American hegemony," stated that approaches taken by American scholars in East Asian studies could be explained by "a Foucauldian understanding of power . . . people do things without being told. And often without knowing the influences on their behavior."[18] The focus on literati tradition in the research and teaching on East Asian history and culture in American academia was noted in the 1980s by John K. Fairbank, who wrote in his memoir that American scholars of East Asian studies "can see our survey now as a summary of the Chinese literati-ruling class's view of itself and its achievements."[19] It is within this context that I will examine the U.S. government's funding of the National Palace Museum, including programs that disseminated knowledge about the Palace collection, establishing it as a basis of the Chinese art canon in the West.

Reconstructing Chinese Nationalism in Taiwan

For the Guomindang regime, the other "player" in the cultural engineering of Taiwan, what had to be eliminated was almost as important as what had to be created. In order to identify Taiwan with China, all traces of the Japanese occupation of the island, which lasted from 1895 to 1945, had to be eliminated.[20] The removal of Japanese culture was done through the prohibition of the Japanese language and other local traditions and customs, which created the tension and bifurcation between the local Taiwanese and the mainlanders that remain unresolved today. Although Taiwan was never officially part of China, settlers from the mainland had inhabited the island as early as the seventeenth century. When the Guomindang took over, Taiwan's historical links with China's past were "rediscovered" and the period of Japanese colonization was explained as a "hiatus" in Taiwan's Chinese development.[21] At the same time, the Guomindang appropriated many customs, forms, and cultural meanings from the early republican period to "reconstruct" Chinese traditions and culture on the island.[22] These appropriations created the national tropes that set Taiwan apart from Communist China, wherein new socialist meanings were imposed on the customs and traditions of the common people. While the Communists used the word "people" (*renmin*) in naming their institutions, the Guomindang put "national" (*guoli*) before the names of almost all state-owned organizations and institutions. The most far-reaching appropriation of Chinese culture in Taiwan was the introduction and mandatory use of *guoyu*, a national language based on a Beijing dialect, in schools as well as in all public and official communications.

More important, the Guomindang had actual objects to create links with China's past histories and to reconstruct a collective memory that was advantageous to its political control of the island. In 1949, the retreating Guomindang government brought with it to Taiwan the best pieces from the Palace collection, the contents of the National Central Museum collection, the National Library collection, and historical and archaeological materials collected by the Academica Sinica. James Clifford, in his study of the "predicament of culture," stated that "every appropriation of culture, whether [by] insiders or outsiders, implies a specific temporal position and form of historical narration." The Guomindang's management of the Palace collection is a good example of Clifford's description of museum curators "owning, classifying and valuing" cultural objects in order to create national histories.[23] The catalogues, bibliographies, and books on specific or specialized topics that were published were, to some extent, a continuation of the scholarly studies initiated during the early years of the Chinese republic when histories and objects from ancient China were recontextualized for a modern China. In his attempt to locate the formation of identity in modern China, Prasenjit Duara posits that an unchanging "core of authenticity" was used by the political elites to define the nation during the early republican period. The Guomindang, self-appointed heirs to the early republican nationalists, chose to portray themselves as the legitimate caretakers of the "regime of authenticity," to borrow Duara's term.[24] For the Guomindang elites, the representative figures of this authenticity were the Confucian scholar-officials, or the literati. Hence, the literati's ideals and their works, including literature, histories, and art, were chosen to represent Chinese culture. To police this regime of authenticity, the authoritarian leader Chiang Kai-shek ruled Taiwan based on the ideals of Confucian statecraft. [25]

By the 1960s, while the Americans were embroiled in Vietnam, Taiwan had become an exemplary, industrializing modern state. It had shifted to an export-driven economy and was considered a success story in terms of economic and social development, so much so that the U.S. government decided to terminate economic aid in 1965. But as the country was modernizing and becoming stronger economically, the Guomindang faced a dilemma of how to maintain a modern Confucian society in the midst of a rising influence of American popular culture. At the same time, across the straits, China was experiencing the Cultural Revolution (1966–76), the mass movement that tried to destroy all ancient traditions. Chiang Kai-shek saw these circumstances as reasons for a revival of the nationalist cause, and in 1966 the Chinese Culture Renaissance Movement was officially launched. The goals of the movement, simply put, were to modernize the country, improve international relations, increase foreign exchange, and educate the nation's youth.

Many of the studies on the Chinese Culture Renaissance Movement focus on its political significance. The National Palace Museum and its programs are mentioned in passing, if at all. However, the director of the museum, Chiang Fu-tsung, was a member of the standing committee of the Chinese Culture Renaissance Movement, and the initiative implemented special museum programs, such as exhibitions, workshops, and publications.[26] Ironically, most of the movement's programs also promulgated Confucian ethics. The contradiction in the objectives of the movement often resulted in the sacrificing of elements that were deemed not favorable to the reconstruction of a Confucian state. As a result, modernist artists such as Liu Kuo-sung, and political dissidents, many of whom were trained in the United States, were silenced for their "liberal" opinions.[27] Paradoxically, it was in this spirit of modernizing Taiwan that the public National Palace Museum was built to highlight and celebrate the Chinese past.

Representing Chinese Art Abroad

Although the national identification of Taiwan with China promoted by the governments of the Guomindang and the United States was maintained by military means, since the lifting of martial law in 1987, many Taiwanese still think of their country as a Chinese nation. In fact, most advocates of a Taiwanese independence acknowledge the country's Chinese roots. In other words, the issue of Taiwan's identity seems to be more about its political identity as a Chinese republic and less about its cultural identity. But the question remains: How did a Chinese consciousness become part of the collective memory and identity of the people in Taiwan? The answer to that question is most likely linked to the success of the Guomindang government's cultural and educational institutions. To borrow Benedict Anderson's terms, I will argue that the National Palace Museum played a key role in creating an "imagined Chinese community" in Taiwan by encouraging perception of a shared past through exhibitions and educational programs.[28]

The history of the National Palace Museum, from its opening to the public in 1925 in Beijing to the time when it was transported to Taiwan in 1949, is well documented.[29] However, the period when the collection was stored in caves outside of Taichung (fig. 5.1), in central Taiwan, is generally not known. While in storage, the collection was available for study by scholars of Chinese history and culture as the collection was deemed an important resource in their reconstruction of an authentic, that is, historic, China. The art historians who visited the caves include James Cahill, Chu-tsing Li, Richard Edwards, Laurence Sickman, and many others. In 1956, with funds from the U.S.-based Asia Foundation, a "quasi-nongovernmental organization," an exhibition gallery was built in order to display parts of the collection to the public and, as indicated in the foundation records, allow "for the preservation of Chinese national cultural heritage."[30] At this time when Communism was considered a major threat, there was a sense of urgency to protect the collection, lest traditional Chinese culture be annihilated completely.[31]

The curators, who moved with the collection to Taiwan and were now displaced from their homeland, focused their work on defining the Palace collection as the only authentic representation of Chinese art and culture. They did so by allocating to the objects the same cultural and historical value

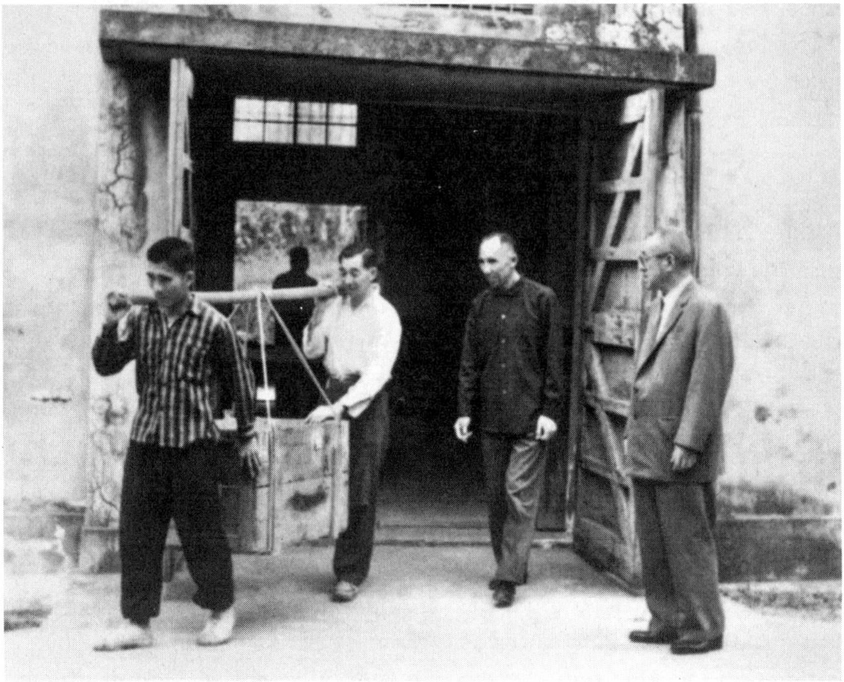

5.1. The entrance to the caves used to store the palace's collection in Peikou, Taichung, Taiwan. Photo: Chao-lin Song, ed., *Gugong kua shiji da shi lu yao* [Major events of the Palace Museum across the centuries] (Taipei: National Palace Museum, 2000).

that the Qianlong emperor had given them when he compiled the collection in the eighteenth century.[32] From the massive and diverse contents of the imperial collection, these curators elected to focus their research and cataloguing work on the objects that were considered important to the literati: paintings and calligraphy, antiquities such as bronzes and jade, and ceramics. For the curators, the Qianlong emperor's admiration of literati culture was an example of a barbarian emperor who was acculturated into the superior Han culture. This "reinterpretation" of the Qianlong emperor's contribution to Chinese culture obscured the anti-Manchu sentiments of the earlier republican nationalists, while validating the Chinese literati and their ideals as the core of Chinese civilization.

American art historians working in the 1950s to 1970s looked at the collection from a perspective of the Western modernist framework.[33] They perceived Chinese art's development in linear terms as an unchanging interest in the literati ideals. Many of these art historians presented Chinese artworks within the framework of cultural history, and not as particular types of curiosities and collectibles prevalent in discussions by the earlier Western Orientalists. Post–World War II American scholars (and other Western art historians) based their work on traditional Chinese art history (Chinese historical texts on paintings and theories and Chinese connoisseurship based on brushwork), which they combined with Western art historical methods, such as stylistic analysis and social history. For the Americans, the literati's emphasis on the individual, self-expression, and allusions to the past demonstrated the presence of a humanist tradition of China's history. In James Cahill's introduction to his *Chinese Painting* (1960), the traditional literati art is described as demonstrating the timeless essence of a Chinese tradition that focuses on expressiveness and humanity.[34] For Cahill and art historians of the post-war period, Chinese literati paintings conveyed the same qualities sought by modernist artists, many of whom believed in the universality of their works. The parallels between the ideals of literati art and modern art were such that the English words used to describe key concepts about literati art, such as "expressive," "individualistic," "spiritual," and so forth, are often the same ones used to describe modern paintings. In other words, the modern discourse of literati art is "translingual," to borrow Lydia Liu's use of the term in her studies of modernity in Chinese literature. Liu's use of the term "translingual" describes the process by which one culture is translated into the language of another when there are equivalences in concepts such as modernity, nationhood, and individuality.[35] Like Liu's analysis of the modern discourse of Chinese literature, therefore, the sources of the Chinese and American art historians' opinions and writings about art cannot be easily isolated from a complex interweaving of ideas, not only from China and the United States, but also from Europe and Japan.

One of the most apparent examples of how complex cultural interactions and special political circumstances made the objects in the Palace collection value-laden with nationalist ideas was the Chinese Art Treasures exhibition of 1961-62, which toured five American cities—Washington, at the National Gallery of Art; New York, at the Metropolitan Museum of Art; Boston, at the Museum of Fine Arts; Chicago, at the Chicago Art Institute; and San Francisco, at the M. H. de Young Memorial Museum (fig. 5.2).[36] True to Stephen Greenblatt's observation that museum exhibitions convey "resonance and wonder" like literary texts, the Chinese Art Treasures exhibition was a "wonder" because it had, in Greenblatt's words "the power to stop the viewer in his or her tracks, to convey an arresting sense of uniqueness, to evoke an exalted

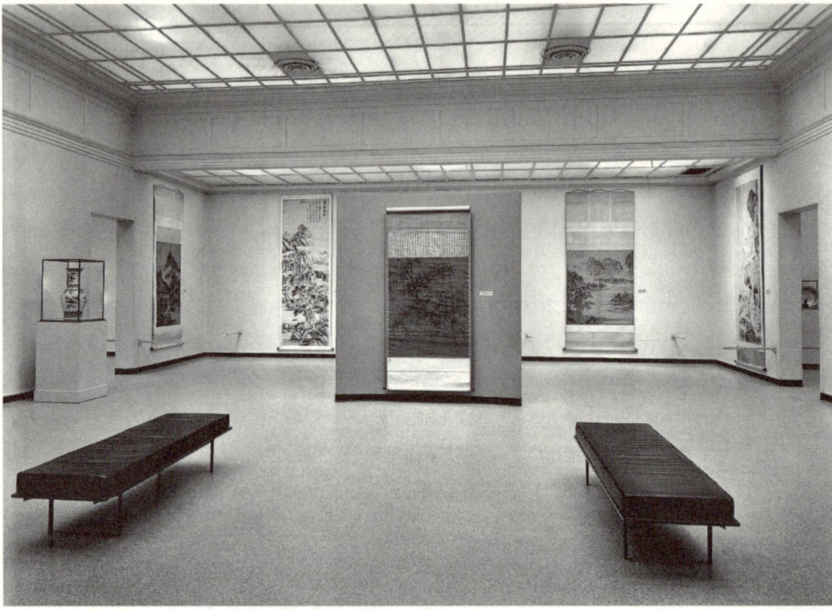

5.2. An installation view of the Chinese Art Treasures exhibition of 1961–62, the Art Institute of Chicago. Photo: The Art Institute of Chicago.

attention."[37] As we shall see, the timing of the exhibition coincided with the period when Americans were becoming increasingly interested in East Asia. The objects in the exhibition, which included scrolls of monumental landscapes, refined and delicate bird-and-flowers images, expressive calligraphy, and imperial ceramic wares of subdued greens and crackled blues, were seen as opening Western (American) eyes to the great artistic traditions of Chinese civilization.

As for Greenblatt's use of "resonance" in analyzing the cultural significance of exhibitions, the Chinese Art Treasures exhibition was from the onset designed with political intentions in mind. Henry R. Luce, a staunch anti-Communist and a friend of Chiang Kai-shek, is recorded to have been the first person to propose the exhibition to Chiang. The issues brought up during the planning of the exhibition were mostly questions of national sovereignty. The final decision to go ahead with the exhibition was made after the Guomindang government received assurances from the U.S. Department of State concerning the safety of the collection from the Communists. The artworks were transported to the United States via an American naval vessel. The preface of the exhibition catalogue explicitly states the political agenda of the show with declarations such as "This exhibition may also serve as a reminder that the free Chinese are fighting to save their cultural heritage as much as to recover lost territories."[38]

The "resonance" of the Chinese Art Treasures exhibition is even more evident in that the exhibition was able, again in Greenblatt's words, "to evoke in the viewer the complex, dynamic cultural forces from which it has emerged and for which it may be taken by a viewer to stand."[39] The thematic focus of the exhibition on the literati tradition transformed earlier Western perceptions of Chinese art.[40] Western preferences in Chinese art before World War II were mostly limited to decorative and functional objects such as furniture, ceramics, and costumes.[41] The Chinese Art Treasures exhibition conveyed the idea that the objects on display had artistic, expressive, and philosophical attributes that made them "art" works. The organizers communicated this message through the exhibition's catalogue as well as the arrangement and presentation of the objects. The introductory essay in the exhibition's catalogue presented a cohesive view of Chinese art, linking carefully selected types of works from different periods to a common aesthetic ideal of the literati culture. The catalogue itself reflected the design methods still in use today: it had an attractive cover, included beautiful reproductions of the works printed on individual pages, and short descriptive discussions of the works. This is very different from the earlier catalogue of the 1935–36 International Exhibition of Chinese Art held in London, in which the Beijing Palace Museum was one of many participants. As stated in its catalogue, the London exhibition attempted to present a "comprehensive" display of Chinese art from museums and collectors throughout the world.[42] Its catalogue itemized listings of the objects as if they were for sale.

Although the gallery displays of the Chinese Art Treasures exhibition varied from museum to museum, they were all consistent in presenting the objects as "art" (see fig. 5.2). The objects were placed individually with ample space between works so that each item would stand out as a showpiece of an artist, a genre, or a period. Lights were also used to dramatize the objects. These display methods were similar to the "white cube" display mode described by Brian O'Doherty as a technique used by modern art museums to emphasize the uniqueness and modernity of their collections.[43] This was a major departure from the usual manner in which Chinese art had been shown in the early part of the twentieth century in shows such as the 1936 London exhibition (fig. 5.3), the Chinese exhibits in the Louisiana Purchase Exposition of 1904 in St. Louis, and the displays in the Beijing Palace Museum.[44] Chinese artworks were no longer stacked together and treated as cultural artifacts in the manner of a display common to history or ethnography museums. Instead, they were

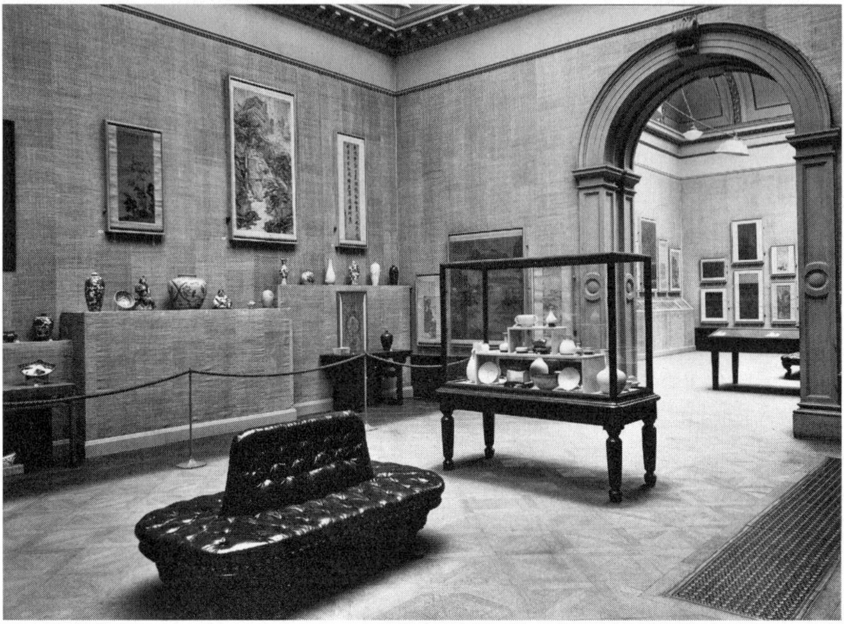

5.3. An installation view of the International Exhibition of Chinese Art of 1935–36, the Royal Academy of Arts, London. Photo: The Royal Academy of Arts, London.

treated as works of art, isolated and endowed with significance as expressions of high aestheticism and skill.

The National Palace Museum as a Reconstructed Cultural Site

In 1965, the Palace collection was moved to its present site in Taipei and was originally to be called the National Palace Museum (a name it still uses). However, to promote the objectives of the Chinese Culture Renaissance Movement, Chiang Kai-shek mandated that the museum be called the Zhongshan Museum in honor of the one-hundredth birthday of Sun Zhongshan (also called Sun Yat-sen), the "father" of the Republic of China. It is recorded that the American government, again, provided partial funding for the construction of the building.[45]

Although the construction of the National Palace Museum may call to mind the politics behind the formation of museums in Great Britain in the nineteenth century as analyzed by Tony Bennett, one must keep in mind the superficial character of such similarity.[46] The establishment of the National Palace Museum was not a product of democracy or a new civic society. The

National Palace Museum was built in a scenic area of Wai Shuangxi, near the planned communities of Yangmingshan and Shilin, rather than in downtown Taipei, where it would have been more accessible to the local residents. It was located in the area where the elites lived—Chiang Kai-shek had a residence in Shilin; in addition, embassies were also located in the area, and many foreign residents, mostly Americans, lived in Yangmingshan or the nearby Tianmu. At the time, most people surmised that the hilly area outside of Taipei was chosen as the site for the museum primarily to protect the objects from air raids and theft. Not as familiar was the other reason for the museum's location. Huang Pao-yu, the museum's architect, pointed out that the museum was easily accessible by foreign tourists, who could come and go from the museum to the international Sungshan Airport and the new modern hotels.[47]

The museum reported that an estimated 350,000 foreign tourists visited Taiwan in 1968. Americans comprised almost half of the total, and more than half of the Americans were servicemen visiting on rest and recuperation leaves from Southeast Asia.[48] By the 1970s, Taiwan had a built-in regular group of American tourists. For these American servicemen, as well as other visitors, a tour of Taiwan usually included a stop at the National Palace Museum, which meant an introduction to Chinese history and culture.[49] One of the responsibilities of the National Palace Museum's education department was to make the collection understandable to foreign guests by providing English tours, bilingual display labels, and exhibition catalogues.

The international recognition of the National Palace Museum as an important cultural site provided comforting assurance to Taiwan's citizens that they had a standing in the world even when many countries questioned the legitimacy of Taiwan's existence as a state. The museum's newsletters regularly listed names of visiting foreign dignitaries.[50] Also, the distance and secluded nature of the museum's whereabouts created an alienating sense of awe for the "national treasure" among the islanders.[51] Although during the 1960s and 1970s relatively few Taiwanese visited the museum, with the exception of students who were periodically bused there as part of their extracurricular activities, the National Palace Museum was nevertheless perceived by the people of Taiwan as a significant symbol of their past.

The overall design of the museum building was derivative of the imperial palace in Beijing. This use of Chinese motifs was not limited to public structures; many private and commercial institutions also utilized the traditional forms on their logos or in their advertisements. These prevalent uses of images from the past, especially in Taipei, a fast-growing modern city, can be explained as an outgrowth of the Guomindang government's interest in rebuilding and reviving traditional China. In light of recent studies in the development of national culture and identity, however, the building of the museum must also be seen as a "commodification" of Chinese culture for foreign, especially American, consumption. Although Taiwan was not included in Christina Klein's book *Cold War Orientalism*, her study on how American filmmakers, writers, and producers of popular or "middlebrow" culture "sold" Asian culture to Americans parallels the American involvement with the National Palace Museum.[52]

Wang Chen-ho, a renowned Taiwanese writer, satirized this commodification of culture in his novel *Rose, Rose, I Love You* of 1984.[53] The story describes a day in the life of a Chinese teacher of English who is hired to teach prostitutes basic English in preparation for the visits of American GIs who will be coming from Vietnam for their R and R. What is most ridiculous in the novel is the teacher's intention of making the prostitutes not only learn basic vocabulary but also represent Chinese culture. One of his ideas is to have the girls wear the *cheongsams*, a modernized form of a traditional Chinese dress. I may seem to have digressed from my discussion, but I bring up this very funny and sad story because the professional museum guides at the National Palace Museum are still required to wear austere looking *cheongsams* and to speak fluent English in addition to having a background in Chinese art and history (fig. 5.4).

It is generally misconstrued that national culture is "pure," "timeless," and untouchable by outsiders, but the American involvement with the National Palace Museum, like the American support of East Asian studies discussed earlier, was not as innocent as it may seem. This complex cultural interaction is evident in the American-inspired mode of exhibition displays and educational programs of the National Palace Museum. Domestically, the museum planned educational programs for school children as supplements to their art and history lessons. There were also special in-service programs for schoolteachers. The museum provided reproductions of canonical works for illustrations in history and literature textbooks. Therefore, even if a student missed one of the school field trips to the museum, he or she would still be exposed to the objects deemed important for a proper understanding of China's past—a certain bronze vessel, a handwritten essay by a famous ancient scholar-official, or a landscape painting found in the museum.

As for the museum's international programs, throughout the 1960s and 1970s the Asia Foundation continued to be an important source of funding for the publication of catalogues that were disseminated to major university and museum libraries worldwide. The Asia Foundation, along with the Ford

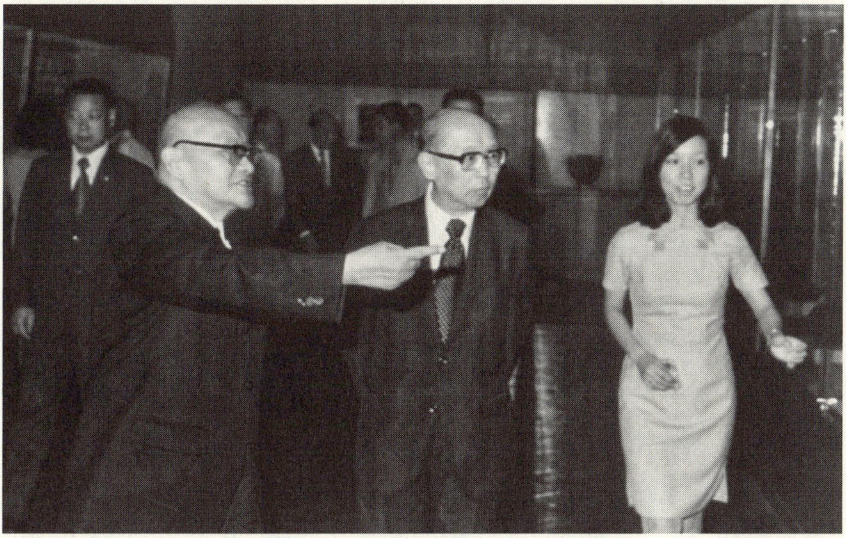

5.4. A docent at the National Palace Museum leading a tour, ca. 1970. Photo: Chao-lin Song, ed., *Gugong kua shiji da shi lu yao* [Major events of the Palace Museum across the centuries] (Taipei: National Palace Museum, 2000).

Foundation, also funded exchanges of scholars and students for short- and long-term research studies at the museum. The museum sent staff members to the United States for further training. The Asia Foundation also helped establish the joint master's program in art history between the National Taiwan University and the National Palace Museum, now a highly regarded graduate program in Chinese art history, which has produced many distinguished scholars in the field. Monographs and papers on artists and painting schools and styles, detailing the authentication of works, were published. The museum organized several influential exhibitions establishing the literati canons, such as the 1975 exhibitions Four Great Yuan Masters and the Ninety Years of Wu School.

Another of the museum's programs was the 1970 International Symposium on Chinese Painting. The fourteen papers presented at the symposium, which were written by the foremost Western and Asian scholars, were groundbreaking for their time and still remain important even as the methodologies on which they were based are being reevaluated. Again, while the scholars did not have political agendas, they reflected a Western modernist bias in their discussions about Chinese art. For instance, Laurence Sickman, a co-chair of the symposium, remarked that the art historical studies and research in the West and the National Palace Museum have been able "to make . . . a better understanding of the profound spirit and humanistic significance of Chinese painting."[54]

Conclusion

For most Chinese who have grown up in Taiwan from the 1960s to the present, the works in the National Palace Museum are the tangible expressions of their past and heritage. For local and international scholars and students of Chinese art and culture, the museum is still an important center for the study of Chinese art. A visit to the museum continues to be mandatory, a sort of pilgrimage necessary for validation of their scholarship. The political context has gone through many changes, however. In 1979, the United States recognized and resumed diplomatic relations with the People's Republic of China, which has slowly recovered from the Cultural Revolution and opened itself to the world. But in spite of the changes in the climate and relations, the "two Chinas" issue remains unresolved, owing to a large extent to the continuing relationship between Taiwan and the United States under the latter's Taiwan Relations Act. Although Taiwan and China maintain a "nondiplomatic" relationship, there have been ongoing "unofficial" educational and cultural exchanges. Business ventures are allowed and have led to economic interdependence. One could say that the two countries look upon one another more as estranged siblings working together in a dynastic family business, rather than as hostile political enemies.

Today, without the political power of the governments of the Guomindang and the United States to hold together the idea of Chinese nationalism in Taiwan, the exclusivity of literati art as Chinese art is faltering. Instead, Chinese art is being redefined in "native" Taiwanese terms. These changes have caused the staff of the National Palace Museum to reconsider the goals and purposes of the institution. They must redefine the meaning of the word "national" for the museum. They also now face a new generation as an audience, both in Taiwan and abroad, that does not think of the island as China. This sharp reversal in thinking, or what Bruce Cumings calls "parallax visions,"[55] of East Asia has led to the shifting of American focus and funding of Chinese studies from Taiwan to China. Meanwhile, on the other side of the straits, Chinese nationalism is in full force in a newly transformed Communist China. The nationalist rhetoric used by the enterprising capitalist Chinese "communists" has led to a revival of interest in images of the past, including those represented by the Palace collections in both Beijing and Taipei. Numerous younger art historians who came of age after the Cultural Revolution, many of whom were trained in American universities and have remained in the United States as university professors and museum curators, continue to focus their research on the literati aspect of Chinese art.

Paradoxically, as Taiwan and China are redefining themselves as distinctive Chinese states, the Guomindang chapter of their national narratives has been forgotten or obscured. In this essay, I hope to have redressed this omission by demonstrating how the nationalism of the Guomindang and the politics of the cold war affected the creation of the National Palace Museum in Taipei and hence the canon of Chinese art. Whether the Confucian literati narrative of Chinese art history will endure in either the People's Republic of China or the Republic of China depends on how nationalism, a modernist concept, will work in a postmodern world. After all, the present Chinese nation-states of Taiwan and China are comparable to dysfunctional families; "home" for many Chinese is no longer a fixed destination but rather multiple locations in Taipei, Hong Kong, Shanghai, Beijing, Los Angeles, or New York. Multiculturalism in everyday living is now the norm rather than the exception. Today, in both China and Taiwan, there has been an increase, both domestically and internationally, in the display, buying, and selling of traditional Chinese art and culture through museum exhibitions, antique sales, and heritage sites. This would seem to indicate that capitalism has erased the symbolic and spiritual significance of national culture by introducing destructive elements of market values, profit, and competition to the cultural superstructure that many consider essential and timeless. But as Duara has observed, the commodification of culture can lead to an intensification of nationalism as the value of one of its icons—art—increases.[56] What this all means with regard to the definition of Chinese art in the future remains to be seen. For now, it will suffice to conclude that Chinese nationalism, in its various political dimensions, has defined, and continues to maintain, a semblance of canonicity for the art forms of the Confucian literati.

Notes

1 For two examples, see Fong, "Why Chinese Painting Is History"; and Hay, "Toward a Disjunctive Diachronics of Chinese Art History."

2 Two recent works that probe these issues are Croizier, *Art and Revolution in Modern China*; and Wong, *Parting the Mists*.

3 Ju, "The Palace Museum as Representation of Culture."

4 Liu, *Translingual Practice*, 302–5.

5 *Zhongguo* literally means "Middle Kingdom." The English words used to translate the compound word vary from "China" to "Chinese" to "national." The ancient origins

and meanings of the word are highly controversial and still unsettled as indicated by a series of lively online discussions on the "evolution of the concept 'Zhongguo'" in September 2003, on H-Asia of H-Net Humanities and Social Sciences Online, *http://h-net.msu.edu/~asia/*.

6 Breuilly, *Nationalism and the State*, 1.

7 Ibid., 1, 252.

8 Chen reorganized various past concepts into a cohesive set of ideas in his essay "The Value of Literati Painting." Huang equated the monumentality of Song landscapes as expressions of national character, which he believed should be revived. For illustrations of Huang's paintings, see Kuo, *Innovation within Tradition*. Although there are many available materials on traditional painters from this period, not much scholarly work has been done on them because most understand modernity in Chinese art to signify Western-influenced painting. Recent studies such as Wong's *Parting the Mists* are reevaluating these traditional painters' contributions to China's modernity and their definition of a "Chinese" or a "national" art.

9 Most scholars of modern China regard 1949 as the end of the "nationalist" or "republican" China, and they consider Chinese nationalism to have ended at that time. They treat the concepts of nationalism used by the Communist Party and the Guomindang in Taiwan to be different from that of the republican period. However, in line with Hughes, *Taiwan and Chinese Nationalism*, I believe that both parties continued to use a form of republican Chinese nationalism to achieve their political goals.

10 For more information on U.S. aid to Taiwan, see Jacoby, *U.S. Aid to Taiwan*.

11 In terms of the arts, studies have illustrated how the U.S. Information Agency (USIA) and the Museum of Modern Art in New York disseminated American modernist art and ideals to the world after World War II through exhibitions and exchange programs. For one example, see Guilbaut, *How New York Stole the Idea of Modern Art*.

12 Chu-tsing Li and Thomas Lawton, two scholars of Chinese art who were doing research work at the National Palace Museum during the 1960s, wrote introductions for the 1966 American Federation of Arts catalogue of the traveling exhibition of Liu's landscapes. See Li and Lawton, *The New Chinese Landscape*.

13 For a discussion of American studies in Chinese history, see Cohen, *Discovering History in China*; and Duara, *Rescuing the Nation from History*.

14 See Jacoby, *U.S. Aid to Taiwan*.

15 The minutes and reports of the conference can be found in the C. Martin Wilbur Collection, Box 11, Rare Book and Manuscript Library, Columbia University Library.

16 Cumings, *Parallax Visions*, 174.

17 Klein, *Cold War Orientalism*, 15.

18 Cumings, *Parallax Visions*, 174.

19 Fairbank, *Chinabound*, 375.

20 Although Taiwan was not officially part of China in the early republican period, as part of Japan's surrender to the Allied powers in 1945, the island was "returned" to China, which was then under the Guomindang. The Nationalist government sent military and civil administrators from China to rule Taiwan until 1949. When the Guomindang was defeated by the Communists, it retreated to the island with its entire political and military personnel.

21 See the introduction in the exhibition catalogue of traditional painting sponsored by the Taiwanese government, *Painting and Calligraphy of Taiwan during the Ming and Ch'ing Dynasties*, 9.

22 For a critical analysis of this reconstruction, see Johnson, "Making Time."

23 Clifford, *The Predicament of Culture*, 232. See also his "Collecting Ourselves."

24 Duara, "The Regime of Authenticity."

25 For a discussion of how Chiang Kai-shek and other leaders of modern Asian states reinterpreted the Confucian classics to achieve their political goals, see the last chapter, "Claiming the Canon," in Nylan, *The Five Confucian Classics*, 307–81.

26 During his tenure as the director of the museum, Chiang wrote many essays relating to the National Palace Museum and the Chinese Culture Renaissance Movement. These have been compiled by Chiang as *Zhonghua wenhua fuxing yundong yu gugong bo wu yuan* [The Chinese Culture Renaissance Movement and the Palace Museum].

27 Liu was accused of being a Communist because of his anti-traditional modernist paintings. See the written debates between Liu and Hsu Fu-kuan, one of the most esteemed Confucian scholars, about the meaning of modernism, now collected in the Kuo, *Dang dai Taiwan hui hua wen xuan 1945–1990* [Writings on contemporary Taiwan painting 1945–1990], 226–35.

28 Anderson, *Imagined Communities*.

29 For an outline of the National Palace Museum's history, see Song, *Gugong kua shiji da shi lu yao* [Major events of the Palace Museum across the centuries].

30 Special issue, *Program Bulletin* (Asia Foundation) 40 (August 1966), 19. In 1980 the U.S. government acknowledged that the CIA had funded the Asia Foundation's activities. See *The Asia Foundation*, 1–2.

31 See Jayne, "How Safe Are the Chinese Treasures in Formosa?"; and Lippe, "Art Journey to Formosa." Both authors were staff members of American museums, and Jayne, who was especially concerned about the safety and preservation of the collection stored in the caves, recommended that it be moved to the United States temporarily for safekeeping.

32 The museum's most recent exhibition, recorded in Feng, *Emperor Ch'ien-lung's Grand Cultural Enterprise*, presents a critical evaluation of Qianlong's taste and at the same time affirms the emperor's influence on our understanding of Chinese art. Please note that "Ch'ien-lung" and "Qianlong" refer to the same person. In this essay I have used the pinyin system (Qianlong) for the romanization of Chinese names except for author's names and titles of works originally employing the Wade-Giles system (Ch'ien-lung).

33 Hay, "Toward a Disjunctive Diachronics of Chinese Art History" is one of many recent studies that discusses this East/West dichotomy in Chinese art historical methods. But like many of these studies, modernity is seen from a Western perspective. The existence of a Chinese modernity is obscured, and if it is discussed, it is considered a "borrowed" modernity.

34 Cahill, *Chinese Painting*.

35 Liu, *Translingual Practice*, 1–42.

36 Information on the exhibition is discussed in the memoirs of several curators who were involved. For an example, see Li, *Guo bao fu mei zhanlan riji* [Diary about the Na-

tional Treasures Exhibition in America]. Other details can be found in the Files of the Planning Committee for the Exhibition to the United States, National Palace Museum, 1960, Taipei.

37 Greenblatt, "Resonance and Wonder," 42.

38 *Chinese Art Treasures*, 8.

39 Greenblatt, "Resonance and Wonder," 42.

40 In addition to the positive reviews of the Chinese Art Treasures exhibition in art journals and magazines by scholars of Chinese art, daily newspapers also reported its importance as the best of Chinese art. For example, see the *New York Times*, September 16, 1961; September 17, 1961; October 15, 1961; and the *New York Times Magazine*, April 9, 1961.

41 Clunas has made these observations about the changing Western perceptions of Chinese art in different studies; most pertinent in this context is "China in Britain."

42 See the preface to the *Catalogue of the International Exhibition of Chinese Art*.

43 O'Doherty, *Inside the White Cube*.

44 Photographs of the 1904 St. Louis Exposition are reproduced in Cheng-hua Wang, "Chen xian 'zhongguo'" [Representing "China"].

45 The U.S. Agency of International Development is specified as the source of partial funding in Hartmann, "The National Palace Museum," 305. I have not been able to find USAID records on the funding.

46 Bennett, *The Birth of the Museum*.

47 P. Huang, "Zhongshan bo wu yuan zi jian zhu" [The construction of the Zhongshan Museum].

48 *National Palace Museum Newsletter* 1, no. 4 (February 1969).

49 For more on the discussion of American tourists in Asia during the period of the cold war, see Klein, *Cold War Orientalism*, 100–42.

50 For an example, see *National Palace Museum Newsletter* 2, no. 7 (May 1970), which lists the following distinguished guests: a thirty-six-member mission from the Smithsonian Institution in Washington; astronauts of Apollo 12 and their wives; a trustee of the Cleveland Museum of Art; Japanese art collectors; and ministers from Barbados and El Salvador.

51 Tu Cheng-sheng, the first museum director appointed by the first non-Guomindang president of Taiwan, wrote in his inaugural message to the public, "In the new century, the museum will step down from its imperial throne into the life of the local community." See Tu, "A Message from the Director."

52 Klein, *Cold War Orientalism*.

53 Wang, *Rose, Rose I Love You*, 71.

54 *Proceedings of the International Symposium on Chinese Painting*, 729.

55 See Cumings, *Parallax Visions*, 1–8.

56 Duara, "The Regime of Authenticity," 381.

6

Masculine Reason or Feminine Spirit: Gender Battles in the Werkbund's Canonization of National Style

DESPINA STRATIGAKOS

In September 1907, an exhibition opened in the gallery of the Berlin Secession that prompted one reviewer to comment that the usual clarity, order, and good form of these rooms, normally dedicated to displaying modern art, had succumbed to the chaos of "bric-a-brac."[1] The cause of this disruption was an arts fair hosted by the Women's Employment Association, an organization that promoted economic opportunities for women. Antique dealers were invited to participate in the fundraising event, and old Gobelins, Madonna statues, Meissen knickknacks, chalices, giant amethysts, and even mammoth bones commingled with handicrafts by the association's members (fig. 6.1).[2]

Reviews in the popular press emphasized the jarring contrast between this jumble of artistic wares and the sobriety associated with the Berlin Secession's own exhibition methods. The vast quantity and variety of objects displayed at the women's show—heaped together with little regard for categories—were described as confusing and overwhelming, but also as intimate and cozy. If the Secession, according to reviewers, now resembled more "a great colorful bazaar" than a "little temple of art," the transformation was not unpleasant.[3] For in the thick stew of bric-a-brac, one could immerse oneself in the visual and tactile pleasures of excess, heterogeneity, and disorder.

While enthusiastic crowds shopped at the exhibition of the Women's Employment Association, a group of artists, architects, critics, and business owners met in Munich to found the German Werkbund.[4] They came bearing different ideologies but a common goal: to save German culture from bric-a-brac. From the perspectives of those gathered in Munich, the Berliners' chaotic indulgences were symptoms of a national malady. The confusion of styles, the popularity of kitsch, and the allure of the fantastic were signs of the disintegration of German *Geist*, the nation's cultural glue, in the face of modern economic and social pressures. Members of the Werkbund mourned the common spirit that they believed had integrated cultural forms in the precapitalist era. Yet if bric-a-brac signified modern soullessness, it could also be a site for intervention. Rejecting the elitist approach to art reform represented by the Berlin Secession (all the more striking when its pristine gallery was briefly usurped by lace makers and curio-hunters), the artists of the Werkbund directed their aesthetic discipline to everyday spaces and habits, focusing on the home and the consumer commodities that filled it. They hoped that in this down-to-earth environment a modern *Wohnkultur*, or culture of dwelling, would arise to unite deeply rooted German spiritual values with the forces of industrialization. National style would return as "the sign of an integrated culture, the aesthetic evidence of a life free from alienation."[5]

The bric-a-brac pleasures of the Women's Employment Association exhibition were considered by many in design reform circles to be typically feminine vices. In their call for a return to order, Werkbund spokesmen—and spokeswomen—were not gender-neutral. When Karl Scheffler, an art critic and an influential Werkbund theorist, declared that "the battle of the Werkbund is . . . a campaign to achieve a new masculine reason," he meant it literally.[6] Although others countered that design reform needed a feminine viewpoint, the belief that the "battle" of aesthetic renewal was a gendered one emerges repeatedly in Werkbund writings.

In this essay, I explore how the agendas of male and female reformers collided in the Werkbund's often acrimonious struggle to define and bolster a national style during its early years. I ask how competing notions of modernity, informed by shifting gender roles in German society, produced deeply divergent attitudes in the organization toward women as objects and subjects of reform as well as toward the design values driving its aesthetic interventions. What was at stake in emphasizing the differences between men and women at this moment of canonizing a (promised) national style ostensibly intended to unite?

Women and Everyday Objects

The presence of women in the Werkbund has been all but unrecognized by historians. Nonetheless, women artists, writers, and entrepreneurs were among those who enthusiastically took up the Werkbund banner. From a small but distinguished cohort among the principal founders, the number of women grew significantly in the organization's early years. The most prominent of the early female members were designers, including Anna Muthesius

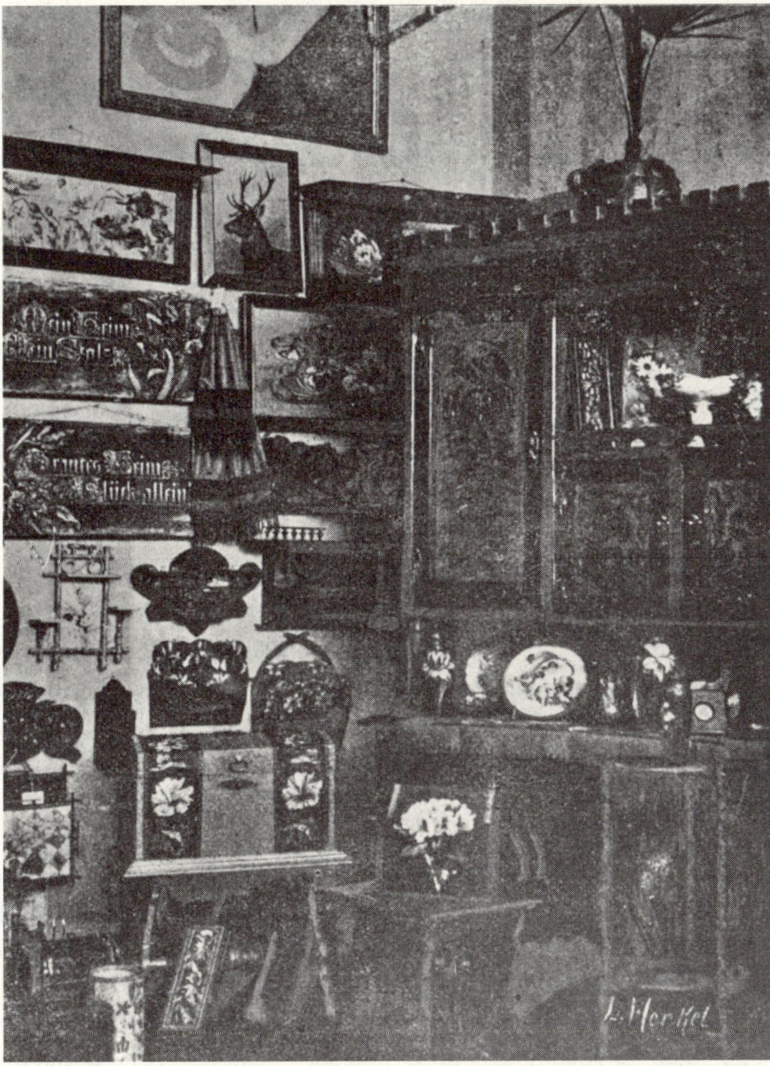

6.1. "Bric-a-brac in the Secession": The Women's Employment Association exhibition, Berlin, 1907. Photo: *Frauen-Leben und -Erwerb* 3, no. 20 (1907): 159.

(1870–1961), a leader of dress reform and the wife of Werkbund co-founder Hermann Muthesius; Else Oppler-Legband (1875–1965), the director of the Werkbund's school for display art, the Höhere Fachschule für Dekorationskunst in Berlin; and Fia Wille (1868–1920), the co-owner of one of the most successful design firms in Berlin.

Acclaimed and confident artists, these women brought their own theories of design reform to the Werkbund, ideas that were shaped in part by contemporary discourses in the applied arts but also by other radical currents at the turn of the century, including dress reform and the women's movement. They envisioned a vital role for women in German aesthetic culture as mediators between old and new, bringing traditional feminine values to bear on a modern *Wohnkultur*. At the same time, they shared with their male Werkbund colleagues certain assumptions about feminine vices—indeed, loudly proclaimed their dangers—but argued that they alone could eradicate them. Women in the Werkbund presented themselves as the "natural" teachers of other women on the basis of a shared feminine sensibility and an understanding of the domestic realm. They thus insisted on their centrality to the organization's educational efforts, particularly in bringing the reform message to German housewives, shop girls, and other women artists.

To vanquish bad taste, Werkbund strategists knew they must first win over the consumer. As long as German consumers delighted in *Schund*, or junk, manufacturers had no incentive to offer anything better. Germans had to be made to understand the cultural significance of consumption and the national consequences of their personal choices.[7] Here the reformers could not ignore women, who formed a broad segment of the buying public—as much as 90 percent, according to some estimates.[8]

Exploiting the commonly held view that female taste was conservative, the Austrian theorist and Werkbund initiator Joseph August Lux denounced the regressive rule of female consumers. In an article written at the time when the idea for the Werkbund was germinating (and almost certainly read by its future leaders),[9] he bluntly declared: "The intellectual backwardness of women is one of the greatest spiritual obstacles with which progress must struggle. Men are ruined not so much by wicked females as by stupid ones." Unfortunately, these fools had a great deal of economic power "because women are the clientele for the important, large sector of industry that creates for the furnishing and design of daily life, for the visual culture of the everyday." Their influence, he warned, encouraged the production of shoddy goods.

But women were not entirely at fault. Lux admonished educated men for relinquishing control of this domain. By claiming "not to understand anything about these matters, [men] leave care of the house and home—on which the essence of the city, life, and thus pretty much everything depends—to women, who usually understand even less." The result was an economic and spiritual disaster: "Through [women], who determine public taste, sentimentality waltzes in the door" in the fashionable "ultra-curlicued" clothing of mass-produced commodities.[10] Almost as if speaking to cuckolds, Lux rebuked men for doing nothing to stop their kitsch-embracing wives.

Equally harsh criticism of women was voiced by Else Warlich, a writer living in Kassel.[11] Her polemical essay, "The German Werkbund and the Woman," appeared in the inaugural volume of *Das Werk*, the Werkbund's first publication. Commenting on the "hot" cultural wars fought by the Werkbund, Warlich identified the female consumer as the "arch enemy." Responsible for making the home beautiful, modern women failed because they preferred cheap imitation to authenticity. Lacking the "proper judgment and appreciation for quality work," women alone were to blame for the household junk choking the modern dwelling.[12]

Warlich pleaded with the Werkbund leaders to address women, thereby implying that they conceived their audience as primarily male. In making her case, she likened the female consumer to a "deep, gnawing wound" and "a great barbarian," and the Werkbund to her surgeon and civilizer.[13] Tapping into broader fears of cultural degeneration and evoking the language of race and disease common in debates about German colonialism, such metaphors were intentionally alarmist. Warlich's essay was, in essence, a manifesto intended to refocus the group's energies onto women. Although censorious, she did not advise, as did Lux, that husbands play a greater role in domestic consumption. Rather, she argued for reforming the female shopper and believed it would be other, better educated women who would administer the cure. Warlich's attack reaffirmed the centrality of the female shopper, a key difference from Lux.

The argument that women's immersion in the world of everyday objects placed them at the center of commodity reform was also employed by Fia Wille. Addressing window displays, an art that figured prominently in the Werkbund's concern with the appearance of consumer goods, she argued that women, as the intended audience, must instigate change. Published in a popular women's journal shortly before the Werkbund was founded, her article explained to its female readership what to expect and demand from shop displays.[14] Wille, together with other female members, continued to use the women's press as a mouthpiece for reform in the early years of the Werkbund. Their writings disseminated the organization's message to an important general readership not as easily reached by its own more specialized publications.

When we focus on the female shopper in the Werkbund discourse, our understanding of what was at stake in the reeducation of the consumer shifts. It was a question not only of *what* the consumer would buy—whether quality goods or *Schund*—but also of *who* would make purchasing decisions. Elisabeth Altmann-Gottheiner (1874–1930), an economist and a prominent figure in the bourgeois women's movement, asserted that middle-class female consumers were driving the dramatic growth in luxury commodities.[15] For Wille and her female colleagues in the Werkbund, this affirmation of women's economic power was professionally desirable: a strong woman consumer represented a persuasive claim to influence within the organization. But this very recognition could lead to a reactionary stance, as represented by Lux. Precisely because women were seen as all-too-powerful consumers, men (and specifically, educated, middle-class men) must be rallied to the shops. The Werkbund's leaders' insistence on addressing their fellow men (as suggested by Warlich) thus makes sense despite claims by Lux and others that it was women who dominated the consumer market for everyday commodities. In the context of male anxiety about women's economic influence, a new reading of the Werkbund's consumer reeducation program is necessary: it was not only about making better shoppers, but also, and importantly, about convincing men that shopping was a gentleman's affair.

To her plea for a change of priorities within the organization, Warlich added a warning: men may well be the founders and leaders of the Werkbund, but women would determine its success. The "public" spoken of in Werkbund propaganda, she pointed out, was overwhelmingly composed of women. In addition to consumers, women were the majority of sales personnel "in the entire garment industry, in department stores, in gold and silverware shops—there where all the thousand little embellishments for our life and home are sold." The salesperson's position, with its power to shape consumer choices, was viewed by the Werkbund as one of tremendous responsibility, and Warlich decried the harm being done by tasteless saleswomen pushing "ugly, false, and cheap rubbish" on their customers. Warlich demanded that the Werkbund concentrate on training female sales personnel, who, multiplied by the thousands, would become the foot soldiers of its reform campaign. For Warlich, the ideal saleswoman would be from the educated middle classes, and on the basis of her education and culture would "bear the truly well-made and beautiful to the widest strata of our people."[16]

Writing in *Deutsche Kunst und Dekoration* a few years later, Karl Widmer, a Karlsruhe-based professor and Werkbund member, recommended educated female sales personnel for arts and crafts shops. He did so reluctantly, believing that modern social conditions compelled women to seek careers instead of their "natural occupation," motherhood. Widmer opposed allowing women access to "male" professions but could foresee an expansion into areas for which women were particularly suited, such as crafts retail. Women constituted the main market for handicrafts, he argued, and they, much more than men, felt the lure of fashion and the need for advice. As sales personnel, women were particularly good at giving this kind of advice and were "naturally" interested in the objects for kitchen and dwelling that comprised the bulk of production in the arts and crafts industry. Widmer may have sought to diminish the distasteful monetary aspect of this exchange by subordinating the saleswoman's role in fulfilling material needs to a higher cultural duty, the education of taste. At this level of responsibility, technical knowledge alone did not suffice; one had to be cultured. Echoing Warlich, whose article he may have read, Widmer declared that educated, middle-class women were desperately needed, but he feared that the shame associated with working outside the home would keep them from the retail profession.[17]

Although Widmer based his argument for the saleswoman partly on gender-based needs and skills, both Widmer and Warlich emphasized her middle-class status. The Werkbund's class-driven goals, which strove to impose middle-class tastes across German society, were easily allied with the efforts of the bourgeois women's movement to broaden employment possibilities for middle-class women.[18] If, as discussed below, women as artistic producers were resisted within the Werkbund, they may have been perceived as useful allies at the level of retail. Educated, middle-class men would not accept such socially inferior employment.[19] But if educated, middle-class women could be persuaded to go in their place, they could serve as the retail missionaries the Werkbund needed for the successful propagation of middle-class taste.

As an appeal for the recognition of women as partners in design reform, Warlich's essay began, at first glance, rather oddly. She discussed the inherent conceptual limitations that prevented women from achieving greatness in "masculine" artistic fields, such as architecture.[20] Her views recalled Karl Scheffler's theories on women and creativity published a year earlier in his influential book *Die Frau und die Kunst*.[21] Labeling female artists perverse, he alleged that women who strove toward masculine genius endangered German culture and themselves, becoming prostitutes and lesbians.[22] Calculated to stem the advancing tide of productive (rather than reproductive) women before it was too late, the treatise found a receptive audience in design reform circles (and beyond), judging from the discernable imprint of its theories on later publications by Werkbund members Otto Bartning, Robert Breuer, Paul Klopfer, Paul Westheim, and others. Scheffler's ideas were further disseminated in the journals of prominent publishers in the Werkbund.[23]

The reason why *Die Frau und die Kunst* found adherents among men in the Werkbund is not difficult to imagine. Many had begun their careers in arts academies and architecture schools and were newcomers to the design of everyday commodities. Their attempt to create a new field of professional activity for themselves was opposed by the craftsmen who dominated the traditional arts and crafts.[24] Standing on contested ground, male reformers reacted antagonistically to the competition represented by yet another group of newcomers. Women, also seeking new professional markets, turned to design in increasing numbers after the turn of the century. Evoking their customary role as arbiters of taste in the home, they now sought to exercise this monopoly on a professional level. The appeal of Scheffler's vilification of women artists must be considered in light of the struggle by different groups—voiced in the Werkbund's debates—to control this field of culture at the moment when it was becoming commercialized and professionalized.

In this context, Warlich's appropriation of Scheffler, far from signaling a concession, served to reinforce a proprietary bid. Agreeing with Scheffler that women's artistic talents were not equal to those of men, she countered that those differences were precisely the source of women's special talents in domestic design. Where the male artist "strives in vastness," the woman excelled in "the small and fine, the fragile and ornamental." In her ability to think on an intimate scale, she surpassed the man, and the art of the home, Warlich maintained, should belong first and foremost to her.[25] A potential liability was thus transformed into a strategy for intervention in the heart of Werkbund territory, the realm of everyday objects.

Despite their being a minority, Warlich imagined an essential role for women as artistic producers in this domain. Who could better understand and educate the public in the art of the home than the woman artist who possessed first-hand knowledge of daily domestic life? She would counsel women seeking to beautify their homes far more effectively than men estranged from such desires.[26] With the female designer's intercession, Warlich's argument came full circle. Her account of the Werkbund's relationship to women proceeded from the sins of fallen shoppers to their redemption by the all-knowing female creator of daily life. Simply put, the bad women destroying German culture would be saved by the good women belonging to the aesthetically enlightened. Warlich thus situated women at the center of the Werkbund's design crusade, which was to be fought, literally, on the home front.

Another potential liability for the woman artist—the stereotype of the eternal feminine—was tactically deployed in a 1906 article on Else Oppler-Legband. The author, Irma Schneider-Schönfeld, gave a feminist inflection to the theory common among German design reformers that modern form had its roots in the (imagined) golden era of their forefathers. Oppler-Legband was portrayed as a female Janus, balancing "ancient feminine capacities" with "the educated and self-empowered intelligence of the modern woman." Rather than being the vehicle for kitsch—Lux's accusation against women—Oppler-Legband mobilized a lost, authentic German spirit in her modern designs. To the quest for style, Schneider-Schönfeld avowed, women brought a particular feminine balance that united a spiritual connection to the past with a contemporary sensibility.[27]

(En)Gendering Good Form

Efforts to position women at the center of the Werkbund's reform project thus sought to reinforce and capitalize on their identification with the objects and spaces of everyday life. Whether learned or innate, women designers' gender-specific knowledge was posited as grounds for professional privilege. This claim did not go unnoticed or uncontested. Men seeking professional sovereignty over the same realm could not present equivalent credentials. But in their differences they, too, saw an opportunity. On the basis of defending good form, the signifier of national style, male design reformers made their own gendered counterclaim to the everyday.

With hundreds of affiliates, the Werkbund never represented a unified or—as underscored by the much-discussed debates about types between Hermann Muthesius and Henry van de Velde—consistent viewpoint on design reform. Nonetheless, two interrelated concepts dominated the Werkbund's definition of good form: *Qualität* (quality) implied solid, honest materials and unalienated workmanship; and *Sachlichkeit* connoted a sober, rational approach to design that rejected nostalgia for past styles and excessive ornament. Both concepts assumed rigorously trained artists uniting the latest machine technology with traditional German cultural values.

The relationship of women to quality was the subject of an essay by the Swiss economist Wilhelm Wirz (b. 1890–d. unknown), which was published and reprinted in journals owned by Werkbund members Eugen Diederichs and Alexander Koch.[28] Wirz wished to assess the impact of female psychology on the production of quality goods. Quoting the art critic Oscar Bie, Wirz stated that there were two types of people: "those who have a need for ornament, an external ideal of riches, and those who possess the organ for function, for the inner construction of things and for bringing out the anatomy."[29] For Wirz (and Bie), these categories were distinctly gendered: men possessed the "organ for function" (that is, *Sachlichkeit*) that women lacked. Citing Scheffler and Warlich, Wirz argued that women's ornamental taste, having no critical or constructive depth, was drawn to appearance rather than to substance.[30]

Unlike Lux and Scheffler, Wirz concluded that female psychology was not a source of bad design. But it was not a positive force either: "The predominance of the decorative over the constructive does not predispose women to further the quality movement."[31] The aesthetic creation of the home at the "tectonic" level must be left to male designers. Women had a role to play in functional, modern design at the level of refinement, which consisted of softening its "hardness" with the female flair for intimacy. Wirz ended his essay with a quote from Oscar Wilde: "She has nothing essential to say, but says the unessential with great charm."[32]

In 1912, critics were given an unprecedented opportunity to evaluate women designers' contributions to the quality movement. The German Lyceum Club, an elite professional association for women, hosted a monumental exhibition in Berlin entitled Women in the Home and at Work. Oppler-Legband and Wille were among the principal organizers, and the work of women designers dominated the exhibits. Three complete dwelling interiors created for the upper, middle, and lower classes attracted particular attention. These exhibits represented an important public statement about a new, professional design relationship between women and the home. Extensive coverage by the national and local press as well as an astonishing half a million visitors temporarily focused the limelight on women designers.[33]

Reviewing the work of his female colleagues, the critic Paul Westheim condemned the triumph of the decorative over the tectonic, evidence of the continuing "problem" of women's artistic activity.[34] He also sensed the lingering presence of the *Dilettantin* (the woman dilettante), who was identified by her tendency toward kitsch, the signifier of aesthetic lack.[35] Almost as if describing their makers, he called the displayed ceramics "wretched little ornaments, little pictures, craftily coiffured, old-maid kitsch." The embroidered pictures of one artist prompted Westheim to note "how easily something like this can sink down to the level of old-maid arts." Even favorable impressions stirred up bad memories of earlier, amateurish efforts (that is, progress was marked by a reminder of how bad things used to be).[36]

This is not to say that Westheim's criticism was wholly unwarranted; with thousands of objects on display, a range of quality was inevitable. Notable, however, is how readily the charge of dilettantism in particular was levied against the woman designer. To prove herself as a professional, the woman designer had to banish the ghost of Christmas fairs past. In the contemporary discourse on the woman designer, education was, for many critics, the key to her rehabilitation. Outspoken Werkbund members Karl Gross and Margarete von Brauchitsch lobbied for equal training to produce "quality craftsmen" of both sexes.[37] But others in the organization doubted that education would lead women from dilettantism to quality. Scheffler believed that dilettantism was a woman's natural (and only) artistic state.[38] Klopfer, director of the Royal Building College in Weimar and an influential critic, took a similar view, blaming frivolous and incompetent female students for trivializing applied arts schools.[39] Women designers struggled to distance themselves from this damaging cliché. Organizers of the 1912 exhibition, for example, sought to impress upon the German public that women's dilettantism was a thing of the past.[40] The selection of displayed objects was carefully controlled, and education in all branches of women's work was made central to the exhibition. As we will see below, the claim to quality and *Sachlichkeit* at the Haus der Frau was based on the total repudiation of the *Dilettantin* and the un-Werkbund-like attributes she represented.

The turf war between men and women over the aesthetic creation of everyday life was thus entrenched in the rhetoric of sexual difference. From Wirz's probing of the psychology of taste to Schneider-Schönfeld's search for a connection to the past, reformers argued over the significance of a person's gender for achieving the goals of the design reform movement. Supporters of women designers emphasized their familiarity with day-to-day domestic practices and eternal feminine values that tapped an older, purer German spirit. They also emphasized the difference between "reformed" women, who belonged to a design elite, and their dilettantish Other. Those advocating a supreme role for male designers adopted a similar strategy promoting difference: by defining quality and *Sachlichkeit* partly against so-called feminine flaws, they portrayed good form as the more "natural" product of men. On the basis of the Werkbund's "new masculine reason," men could appropriate everyday design for themselves.

The House That Women Built

In 1914, the Werkbund summoned an international audience to an exhibition in Cologne that demonstrated in visual form, and on a monumental scale, the organization's efforts to resuscitate German style. Female associates were invited to participate with their own building, the Haus der Frau, which was intended as a showcase of their achievements in the applied arts. The pavilion was well located, sharing a plaza with Henry van de Velde's theater, Peter Behrens's Festhalle, and Walter Gropius's factory administration building. Amid these leading modernists, the Haus der Frau boldly asserted women's role in the design reform movement. Employing the visual signs of sobriety and restraint, it announced the arrival of the *sachlich* woman designer. In its "feminine" conception and organization, the pavilion also proclaimed her difference.

The organizing committee of the Haus der Frau, headed by Anna Muthesius and Else Oppler-Legband, reserved the pavilion as an exclusive realm for women's artistic labor.[41] In promotional literature, they stressed the project's disciplining standards.[42] An early notice stated that it was conceived not "as a sanctuary for female handiwork of a dilettantish sort, which otherwise could not find a place in the German Werkbund exhibition, but rather as a fully valid certificate of female artistry."[43] Work submitted by women artists and designers was subject to close scrutiny: objects shown at the Haus der Frau were juried three times.[44] Oppler-Legband indicated what was at stake: "This is the first time that women's achievement in the applied arts is being tested in such a united format [and] under such high demands." In addition to being a test of women's abilities, the Haus der Frau would set a standard, according to Oppler-Legband, serving "as a criterion for selection among the great numbers of those who feel called" to the design profession.[45]

The stark physical appearance of the building signaled this new discipline. Chosen in a competition open to German and Austrian women architects, the winning design was submitted by Margarete Knüppelholz-Roeser (b. 1886–d. unknown), an architect living in Berlin. The pavilion was a low, tripartite structure with an impressive horizontal span. From the front, a striking feature was the total absence of windows on the wings (fig. 6.2). Entrances to the building were framed by two monumental portals in blue ceramic tile by the Munich artists Johanna Biehler (1880–1954) and Minnie Goossens (b. 1878–d. unknown). At the rear of the building, a garden terrace faced the Rhine (fig. 6.3). Except for the tiled portals at the front and band molding at the rear entrance, the building was unornamented. It was also insistently rectilinear

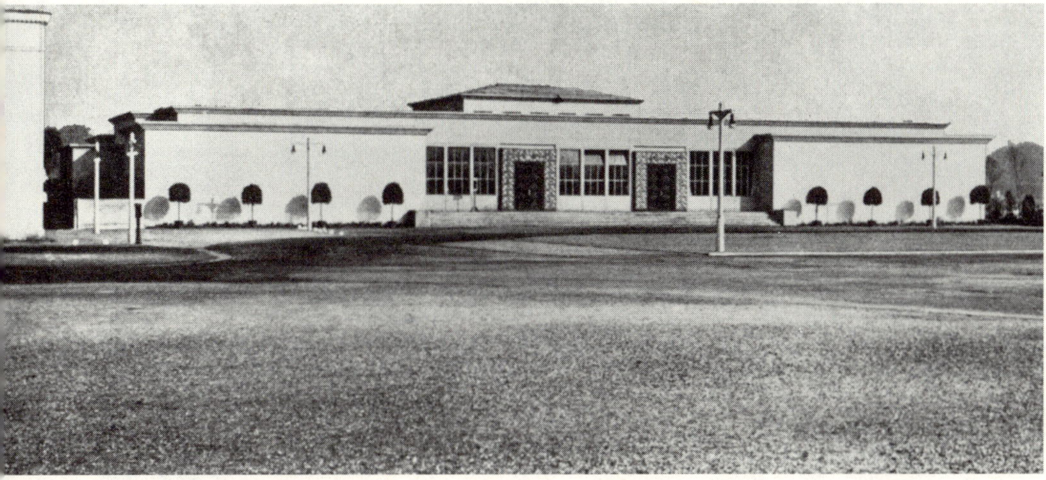

6.2. Margarete Knüppelholz-Roeser, Haus der Frau, front façade, Werkbund exhibition, Cologne, 1914, destroyed. Photo: Wilhelm Schäfer, "Die Baukunst der Deutschen Werkbund-Ausstellung in Köln," *Die Rheinlande* 14 nos. 8–9 (1914): 295.

in its forms, with no rounded elements. The only exceptions were the small domed trees that the architect, who designed the gardens, included at the front of the building.

Writing about the building in the Werkbund's *Jahrbuch*, Oppler-Legband extolled the design's fundamental restraint, particularly in its approach to ornament: "simple, without pretensions, and clear in all parts," it eschewed "covering up honest ability and good taste through sumptuousness and invalid means, and thereby simulating more than is really there—the fundamental evil of every false decorative style." In its shorn state, the "succinctness, strict *Sachlichkeit*, and material solidity" of the architecture evinced the program of the Haus der Frau as a whole.[46] Although she explained the refusal to embellish in the familiar moralistic Werkbund rhetoric of good form, in the context of a women's pavilion, this plainness bore other levels of meaning. The extent of the nakedness of the building, shocking to many visitors, suggests that the organizers were determined to avoid the criticism of excessive ornament so readily flung at women designers. The bare, expressly "tectonic" surfaces can be seen as a visual retort to Scheffler, Westheim, and their like-minded Werkbund colleagues. But the association of the feminine with the decorative was so ingrained in architectural discourse that, as we will see below, some critics had difficulty conceiving this as a women's pavilion.

Oppler-Legband's no-frills design philosophy exemplified the approach to

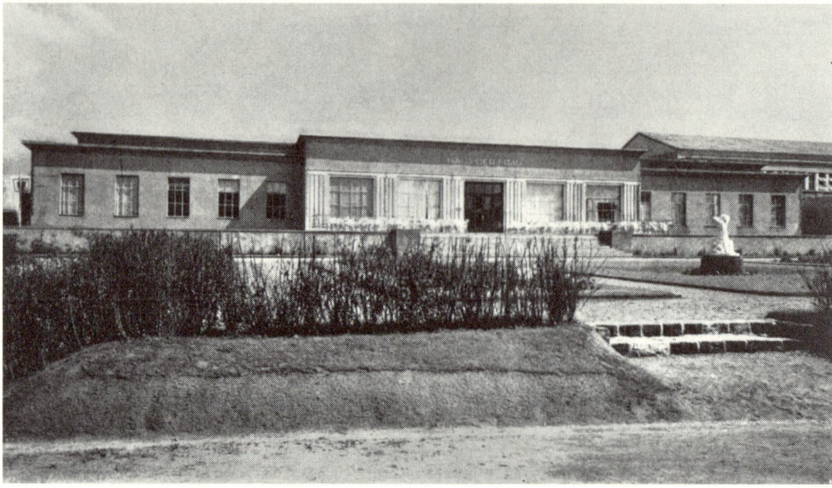

6.3. Margarete Knüppelholz-Roeser, Haus der Frau, rear façade (facing river), Werkbund exhibition, Cologne, 1914, destroyed. Photo: Fritz Stahl, "Die Architektur der Werkbund-Ausstellung," *Wasmuths Monatshefte für Baukunst* 1 (1914): 176.

modern architecture advocated by Henry van de Velde and Hermann Muthesius, who used clothing reform as "a literal model for design practice." Rejecting fashion, they believed that architects should prioritize utility, "stripping off the excess layers of ornament to liberate and mobilize the underlying structure."[47] As leaders of the dress reform movement, Anna Muthesius and Else Oppler-Legband clothed women in loose garments that minimized surface ornament, followed the natural contours of the uncorseted body, and promoted freedom of movement. Strong parallels exist to the design of the Haus der Frau, which similarly emphasized a naked façade, clearly articulated structure, and physical movement in the internal layout. In conceiving a building for modern women, the designers of the Haus der Frau chose an architectural form that, like the new clothing, represented and facilitated the dynamism of emancipated female bodies. By eliding plain architecture and the unencumbered woman, the pavilion introduced a socially progressive vision of the female body into the quest for national style at the Werkbund exhibition.

Another facet of the modern woman's liberation evoked by the Haus der Frau's design was her freedom from fashion. Compared to most of the exhibition's buildings, the Haus der Frau's simple, unornamented surfaces refused any hint of architectural modishness. Werkbund theorists considered fashion to be one of the most powerful capitalist forces destabilizing German

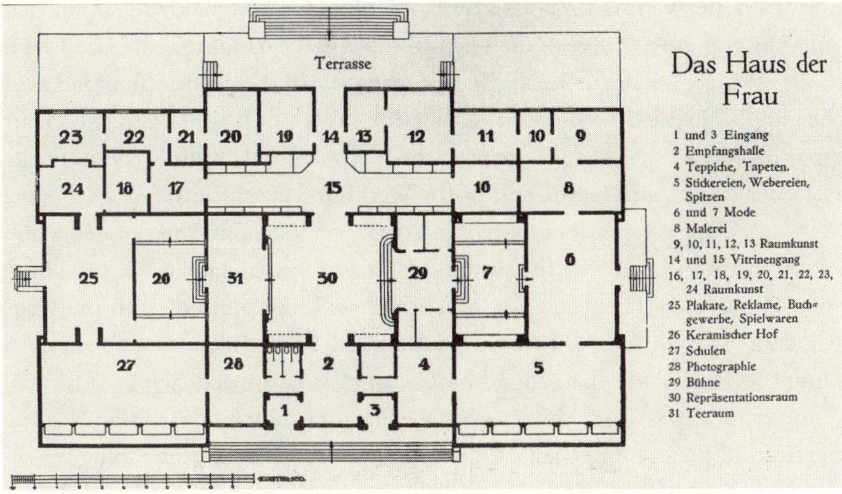

6.4. Plan, Haus der Frau, Werkbund exhibition, Cologne, 1914, destroyed. Photo: *Offizieller Katalog der Deutschen Werkbund-Ausstellung Cöln, 1914*, 2nd ed. (Berlin, 1914), 262.

society. It could be combated only through the creation of a lasting national style. Fashion was, furthermore, a vice explicitly associated with women and the female clothing industry, and their enslavement to foreign (specifically, Parisian) tastes.[48] In her writings on dress reform, Anna Muthesius argued that dress reform was an "anti-fashion" that fostered women's search for personal style.[49] As chairperson of the Haus der Frau, she applied the idea of anti-fashion to women's architecture, thereby situating the building in the Werkbund's utopian realm of true style.

Upon entering the Haus der Frau, visitors encountered a series of variously sized rectilinear spaces, at the center of which stood a large square room designed by Oppler-Legband (fig. 6.4, no. 30). Flanked by a stage on the right side (no. 29) and a tearoom on the left (no. 31), this space was intended for social functions. These consisted primarily of artistic performances by women and afternoon teas, which were organized by a special committee of women from Cologne. The exhibit rooms, which Oppler-Legband called the "purely practical section," were arranged around this active, social core.[50] Items displayed included tapestries, embroidery, designs for women's and children's clothing, books, posters, toys, jewelry, paintings, photographs, and even models by women architects.[51] The largest section, at the back of the building, was devoted to interior decoration, with individual rooms assigned to different designers. Among the few surviving images of the Haus der Frau's interior is one of a dining room by Annemarie Moldenhauer, a designer from Offenbach am Main (fig. 6.5). It reveals the uncluttered visual harmonies associated with modernist display aesthetics, in sharp contrast with the chaotic abundance of the 1907 Women's Employment Association show (see fig. 6.1). Fritz Stahl, art critic for the *Berliner Tageblatt*, praised the "practical and tasteful" rooms of the Haus der Frau as among the best of the Werkbund exhibition.[52]

A broad cross-section of women's artistic products thus surrounded a hub of activity at the center of the pavilion. This organizational scheme presented women's creative talents as part of a larger synthesis embodied in the Haus der Frau. Specifically, visitors to the Haus der Frau encountered a modern feminine *Wohnkultur* that united *sachlich* objects and spaces with traditional domestic practice. The exhibition catalogue, for example, noted that "for the duration of the exhibition, a social committee of women from Cologne will practice the art of hospitality and through artistic events of many different sorts variously complement the strict *Sachlichkeit* of the Haus der Frau."[53] *Sachlichkeit* and hospitality were portrayed as arts balanced in a women's pavilion. More vaguely, Oppler-Legband insisted that "each department should act not as an austere exhibition object, but rather as a space formed with love and care, so that . . . the true womanly gift to decorate and make livable is expressed. True womanliness—that is the general motto for the whole enterprise. The Haus der Frau is intended not as presumptuous competition to men's work, but rather as a balancing regulator and valuable complement to it."[54] This "womanly gift" to animate spaces and objects, then, also served to deflect potential criticism that women designers were competing with men: feminine practice or spirit, posited as integral to female-designed objects, made the latter somehow fundamentally different.

The Haus der Frau, therefore, was conceived as a domesticated (that is, livable) example of modern design. In its internal decoration, comfort, and hospitality, the women's pavilion was a kind of home; but it was also a place of work created by professionals. The *Sachlichkeit* of its displays and spaces belonged to the sphere of the woman professional, while the life within arose from the female bearer of domestic culture. Each was posited as integral to the other in the creation of the modern home. The conception of the pavilion can be seen as involving a dual self-representation of modern women as feminine and domestic, on the one hand, and as professional (or *sachlich*) artists, on the other. Although the Haus der Frau's organizers viewed these qualities as complementary, not all visitors agreed.

Critics of the Haus der Frau ignored the importance ascribed to practice in mediating form, even though it exemplified the Werkbund's conception

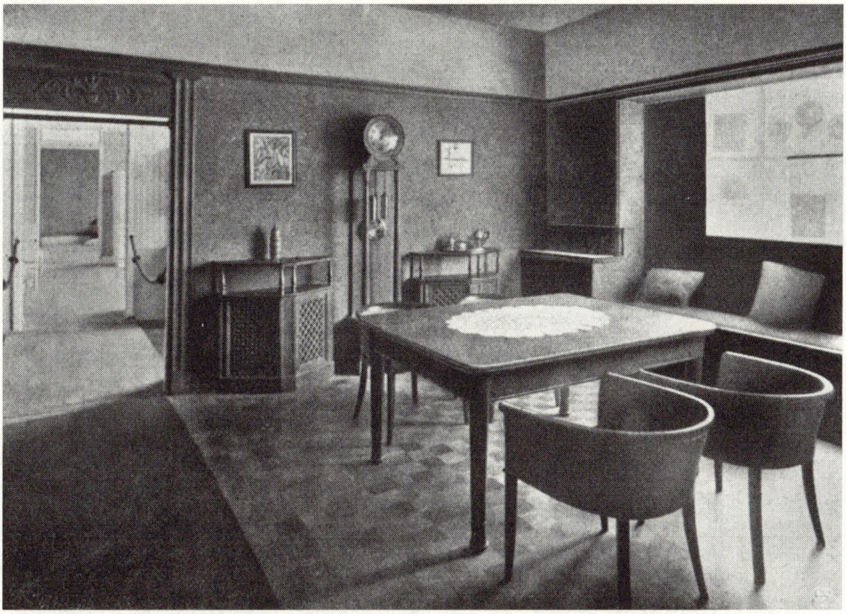

6.5. Annemarie Moldenhauer, dining room in the Haus der Frau, Werkbund exhibition, Cologne, 1914, destroyed. Photo: Wilhelm Schäfer, "Die Baukunst der Deutschen Werkbund-Ausstellung in Köln," *Die Rheinlande* 14 nos. 8–9 (1914): 297.

of *Wohnkultur* as a lived aesthetic. Rather, adopting a purely visual approach, reviewers of the women's pavilion focused exclusively on appearances, and many expressed unease with what they perceived as its unmoderated *Sachlichkeit*. The building's minimal ornamentation and windowless wings, in particular, seemed to confuse visitors who found it bare, austere, and expressionless.[55] This sense of an absence or barrenness in the Haus der Frau related directly to its femininity. Joseph Löttgen, writing on the Haus der Frau for *Deutsche Bauhütte*, complained that he could not detect a hint of "feminine grace" in this overwhelmingly masculine pavilion.[56]

The apparent masculinity of the Haus der Frau, implied by the absence of feminine signifiers such as ornament, represented for some critics, ironically, a kind of architectural falsehood. One reviewer mocked the pavilion as "a lot of mannerism . . . and playing the muscleman. . . . The power that seems to reside in [the Haus der Frau] is borrowed, is a reflected radiation [of the energies emitted by the other exhibition buildings]. On its own, the [women's] building does not contribute anything because it does not have any character, or rather pretends a false character. This *Sachliche* and only *Sachliche* is contrary to the spirit of woman."[57] To these critics, the Haus der Frau's masquerade in men's clothing resulted in sterility, offering only a false semblance of life in a sea of productive male virility.

Like its detractors, champions of the Haus der Frau tended to focus on what it was not. Noting that some female visitors found the building without charm, one writer countered that the artistic charm of the building lay precisely in the absence of all charming things.[58] Several other reviewers praised the women artists and designers for having emancipated themselves from dilettantism.[59] In these favorable assessments, the Haus der Frau's success was attributed to a double negative: it had eradicated aesthetic lack. As Wirz might say, women had developed the masculine "organ for function." Thus, their shame—their aesthetic castration—no longer need be feared: measuring up to "the best and biggest" of the German art world, the Haus der Frau could "by all means let itself be seen beside the others."[60] On the question of a positive contribution, however, even the most outspoken supporters were vague on what the marriage of femininity and *Sachlichkeit* produced.

If admirers had trouble defining the hybrid values promoted by the Haus der Frau, critics were quick to identify a dangerous blurring of the natural order of the sexes.[61] Reviewing the Haus der Frau and its exhibits, Wilhelm Schäfer, editor of the journal *Rheinlande* and a member of the Werkbund, defended normative boundaries in the division of creative labor between men and women.[62] He detected originality only within traditional branches of female artistry (such as textile work). Similarly, commenting on the Haus der Frau, Peter Jessen, the influential library director of the Royal Applied Arts Museum in Berlin and a founding member of the Werkbund, suggested that "[the woman designer] serves herself and the fatherland best when she seeks the field for her ambition there where she is superior to man according to her nature and therefore can create fully from her own spirit."[63] For him, the appropriate "field for her ambition" was not architecture but needlework.

Fears of professional competition from women strengthened this resistance to the perceived transgendering of artistic labor. Oppler-Legband's assertion that the Haus der Frau complemented the male design sphere did little to stem accusations of competitive intentions. Such professional ambition on the part of women was regarded as one of the unsettling products of modernity and its destabilization of gender norms. The reviewer who rebuked the Haus der Frau for playing the muscleman associated its gender confusion with "the modern woman who in her mounting sense of self wishes to enter into serious competition with man."[64]

The Werkbund's mission to restore cultural harmony through the aesthetic transformation of daily life could not help but become entangled with the changes in gender roles that were uprooting the very patterns of that existence. Women's "mounting sense of self"—expressed in their claims to cultural authority and professional practice—represented a new kind of agency that impinged upon the organization's call to order. From the beginning, the structure of the Werkbund's discipline was put into question: its roles and methods of policing were contested between men and women, both of whom proffered the supposed differences of their gender as the basis for their authority. The object of aesthetic discipline was also disputed. Warlich, Widmer, Wille, and others argued that women's cultural and physical proximity to everyday objects should be harnessed as a vehicle for change. Other commentators, from Lux to Klopfer to Wirz, believed the solution lay in educating and empowering men to reclaim the aesthetic creation of daily life from women, whether in the shops, classrooms, or design studios. Attending to these debates brings the reality of gendered everyday lives into the Werkbund's theoretical discourses on culture and style.

Women's "mounting sense of self" also challenged the adequacy of the design values at the core of the Werkbund's national agenda. Accepting the desirability of quality and *Sachlichkeit*, women designers and reformers nonetheless insisted on a broader notion of good design, one that reconciled "masculine" reason with their commitment to a modern "feminine" spirit. At the Haus der Frau, the organizers' attempts to define feminine *sachlich* form, their search for gender complementarity, and their demand for the segregation of men's and women's artistic labor (echoed by their critics) put on display the struggle over the meaning of gender for modern design. By claiming to have incorporated the modern within the feminine, however, the Haus der Frau provoked a backlash: thus, a building recognized as an exemplar of Werkbund design principles ("*Sachliche* and only *Sachliche*") was simultaneously attacked as an utter failure of femininity. The perceived incompatibility of the feminine and the modern at the Haus der Frau exposes the deeply gendered meanings of the aesthetic values that were meant to redeem culture.

With the outbreak of World War I, the exhibition in Cologne came to an abrupt end. It was soon to be resurrected, however, in the legend of modernism, which was already being written by the 1920s. Design histories give the impression that the Haus der Frau, arguably among the most modern of the exhibition buildings, never existed. Other sources and voices introduced here as part of our analysis of the Werkbund's engagement with the gendered complexities of modern identity similarly have been overlooked. In light of these absences, we might usefully direct the questions asked in this essay about the relevance of gender to the Werkbund's project to the inclusions and exclusions of its history. To what extent have we adopted the viewpoint of the Haus der Frau's critics, divorcing architectural form from lived practice, the "feminine" from the modern, and the notion of reason (intellectual-rational or technological) from other approaches to design? By reinscribing such values, we crown victors in the Werkbund's gendered battles, forgetting that in 1914 the picture was far messier and infinitely more interesting.

Notes

1 A longer version of this chapter appeared as "Women and the Werkbund: Gender Politics and German Design Reform, 1907–14," *Journal of the Society of Architectural Historians* 62, no. 4 (2003): 490–511.

2 Mäcen, "Bric-à-brac in der Sezession," 1497; review in *Das Deutsche Blatt*, reprinted in *Frauen-Leben und -Erwerb* 3, no. 19 (1907): 150. Founded in 1899, the organization assisted middle-class women forced to work outside the home and created new markets for their products. Selected reviews of the exhibition were reprinted in its journal *Frauen-Leben und -Erwerb*.

3 Mäcen, "Bric-à-brac in der Sezession," 1497; review in *Berliner Lokalanzeiger*, reprinted in *Frauen-Leben und -Erwerb* 3, no. 20 (1907): 159; review in *Norddeutsche Allgemeine Zeitung*, reprinted in *Frauen-Leben und -Erwerb* 3, no. 18 (1907): 146; review in *Das Deutsche Blatt*, reprinted in *Frauen-Leben und -Erwerb* 3, no. 19 (1907): 149; review in *Danziger Zeitung*, reprinted in *Frauen-Leben und -Erwerb* 3, no. 18 (1907): 145.

4 On the history of the founding of the Werkbund, see Campbell, *The German Werkbund*; and Junghanns, *Der Deutsche Werkbund*.

5 F. Schwartz, *The Werkbund*, 18.

6 Scheffler, "Gute und schlechte Arbeiten im Schnellbahngewerbe," 42; quoted and translated in F. Schwartz, *The Werkbund*, 229 n. 135.

7 See Breuer, "Der Einkauf als Kulturelle Funktion."

8 I. Wolff, "Die Frau als Konsumentin," 893.

9 L[ux], "Erziehung zur Sentimentalität." Lux published his article in *Die Hohe Warte*, which he also edited. Among the chief contributors to this design reform journal were later leaders of the Werkbund, including Hermann Muthesius and Paul Schultze-Naumburg. In 1909 it became *Das Werk*, the first publication of the Werkbund, as noted below.

10 L[ux], "Erziehung zur Sentimentalität."

11 Else (Elisabeth) Warlich (née Zahn, 1873–1942) does not appear on Werkbund membership lists. Her husband, Hermann Warlich (1865–1920s), was a Werkbund member and a writer on design reform.

12 Warlich, "Der Deutsche Werkbund und die Frau," 104.

13 Ibid.

14 Wille, "Das Schaufenster als Erzieher," 251–53.

15 Altmann-Gottheiner, "Die Frau als Konsumentin."

16 Warlich, "Der Deutsche Werkbund und die Frau," 104, 109. Warlich may have known

of the 1907 national census, which revealed that three-quarters of retail sales personnel were women. The majority came from working-class families and had only an elementary-school education. Adams, *Women Clerks in Wilhelmine Germany*, 14, 18. On the role of sales personnel for the Werkbund, see F. Schwartz, *The Werkbund*, 102.

17 Widmer, "Die Gebildete Frau im Kunstgewerbehandel," 63, 65, 69.

18 On the role of class in the Werkbund's mission, see Jarzombek, "The Discourses of a Bourgeois Utopia, 1904–1908, and the Founding of the Werkbund"; and F. Schwartz, *The Werkbund*, 39–43. For an introduction to the campaigns for women's education and employment led by the bourgeois women's movement, see Frevert, *Women in German History*, 107–30.

19 Within the clerking profession, men preferred the more prestigious office and managerial positions to retail sales. See Adams, *Women Clerks in Wilhelmine Germany*, 12–14.

20 Warlich, "Der Deutsche Werkbund und die Frau," 103.

21 Scheffler, *Die Frau und die Kunst*. For a discussion of Scheffler's views on female creativity, see Stratigakos, "Architects in Skirts."

22 Scheffler, *Die Frau und die Kunst*, 91–103, 109.

23 Bartning, "Sollen Damen bauen?"; Breuer, "Die Frau als Möbelbauerin"; Klopfer, "Die Frau und das Kunstgewerbe"; Westheim, "Die Frauenausstellung." See also note 28.

24 Campbell, *The German Werkbund*, 51–52.

25 Warlich, "Der Deutsche Werkbund und die Frau," 103.

26 Ibid., 109.

27 Schneider-Schönfeld, "Eine moderne Kunstgewerblerin."

28 Wirz, "Frau und Qualität," *Wolhfahrt und Wirtschaft* 1, no. 4 (1914):196–200; reprinted in "Dekorative oder Konstruktive Gestaltung," *Deutsche Kunst und Dekoration* 18, no. 12 (1915): 426–27; and "Die Frau und die Qualitäts-Bewegung," *Innen-Dekoration* 25 (1914): 391–98.

29 Bie, *Das Kunstgewerbe*, 18; quoted in Wirz, "Frau und Qualität," 197.

30 Wirz, "Frau und Qualität," 197–98.

31 Ibid., 200.

32 Oscar Wilde quoted (in German) in Wirz, "Frau und Qualität," 200.

33 Stratigakos, "Skirts and Scaffolding," 231–55.

34 Westheim, "Die Frauenausstellung," 270, 275.

35 My use of this term is inspired by Calinescu's description of kitsch as "aesthetic inadequacy." See Calinescu, *Five Faces of Modernity*, 236. In light of views expressed at the time, exemplified by those of Wirz, that women's design abilities suffered not from a weak "organ for function" but rather from its absence, I believe "aesthetic lack" is, in this gendered context, the better term.

36 Westheim, "Die Frauenausstellung," 271–73, 275.

37 Wolff, "Die Frau als Kunstgewerblerin," 53.

38 Scheffler, *Die Frau und die Kunst*, 42.

39 Klopfer, "Die Frau und das Kunstgewerbe," 216–18.

40 Heyl, "Die Ausstellung 'Die Frau in Haus und Beruf,'" 129.

41 On the founding struggles of the Haus der Frau and its reception, see Stratigakos, "Skirts and Scaffolding," 323–53.

42 Oppler-Legband, "Das Haus der Frau auf der Werkbundausstellung"; and *Offizieller Katalog der Deutschen Werkbund-Ausstellung Cöln 1914*, 1st ed., 199–200.
43 *Für die Frau Meisterin*, no. 14 (1913): 3.
44 Correspondence from Lilly Reich to Agnes Grave, December 30, 1913, DWK/203/76, and March 28, 1914, DWK/203/91, Karl Ernst Osthaus-Archiv, Karl Ernst Osthaus-Museum, Hagen.
45 Oppler-Legband, "Das Haus der Frau auf der Werkbundausstellung."
46 Ibid.
47 Wigley, *White Walls, Designer Dresses*, 142.
48 F. Schwartz, *The Werkbund*, 26–41.
49 Muthesius, "Die Ausstellung künstlerischer Frauen-Kleider im Waren-Haus Wertheim-Berlin," 441–42.
50 Oppler-Legband, "Das Haus der Frau auf der Werkbundausstellung."
51 Lists of participating artists and objects displayed in the Haus der Frau are included in the rare second edition of the official exhibition catalogue. See *Offizieller Katalog der Deutschen Werkbund-Ausstellung Cöln 1914*, 2nd ed., 262–91.
52 Stahl, "Der Werkbund, seine Idee und seine Ausstellung."
53 *Offizieller Katalog der Deutschen Werkbund-Ausstellung Cöln 1914*, 1st ed., 200.
54 Oppler-Legband, "Das Haus der Frau auf der Werkbundausstellung."
55 Weber, "Der Werkbund in Köln"; "Die Deutsche Werkbund-Ausstellung."
56 Löttgen, "Von der deutschen Werkbundausstellung in Köln."
57 Fb., "Deutsche Werkbund-Ausstellung."
58 Jatho, "Werkbundgedanken III," 513.
59 Rehorst, "Lage und Plan der Werkbundausstellung," 12; Koch, "Die Deutsche Werkbund-Ausstellung Cöln 1914," 97; Haas, "Die deutsche Werkbundausstellung Köln 1914," 694.
60 Gallwitz, "Das Haus der Frau auf der Werkbundausstellung in Köln," 593; Haas, "Die deutsche Werkbundausstellung Köln 1914," 694.
61 Löttgen, "Von der deutschen Werkbundausstellung in Köln."
62 Schäfer, "Die Baukunst der Deutschen Werkbund-Ausstellung in Köln," 293.
63 Jessen, "Die Deutsche Werkbund-Ausstellung Köln 1914," 30.
64 Fb., "Deutsche Werkbund-Ausstellung."

7

Courbet, the Decorative, and the Canon: Rewriting and Rereading Meier-Graefe's *Modern Art*

JENNY ANGER

In memory of Kermit Swiler Champa

The art historian Julius Meier-Graefe wrote in 1905 that "perfect completion [*Vollkommenheit*] appears as necessity, as the most striking contrast to chance."[1] His subject was the artistic masterpiece and the apprehension thereof, but he may well have been discussing the canon. The apparent completeness of the canon produces the effect of inevitability, that is, that the artists and works included seem essential to the unfolding of the narrative. Meier-Graefe's own *Entwickelungsgeschichte der modernen Kunst* (Developmental history of modern art, 1904, which was translated and published as *Modern Art*, 1908) has been understood in just such terms. Hans Belting, for example, wrote in 1987 that Meier-Graefe had identified the "correct moderns [*richtige Moderne*]."[2] Belting implies that history eventually recognizes the right artists and works, and that Meier-Graefe's greatness was to identify them so early.

One might criticize the canon (for its hermetic ontology), and one might fault Belting (for mistaking the canon's production for its revelation), but in this essay I want to explore how the effect of *Vollkommenheit* is achieved. Meier-Graefe's own epic history provides an excellent case study, because—despite its apparent wholeness—it did not appear all at once. Rather, it was written and rewritten over many editions and one crucial translation into English. For example, soon after publishing the *Entwickelungsgeschichte* in 1904, Meier-Graefe wrote a little book, *Corot und Courbet: Ein Beitrag zur Entwicklungsgeschichte der modernen Kunst* (Corot and Courbet: A contribution to the developmental history of modern art, 1905). The artists Jean-Baptiste Camille Corot and Gustave Courbet had barely appeared in the first edition of the *Entwickelungsgeschichte*. As Meier-Graefe wrote in the preface to *Corot und*

Courbet, he hoped to correct this oversight—his "unforgivable offense"—with this slim volume, the contents of which were largely incorporated into the English version of *Modern Art* and significantly affected, as we will see, the emphases of Meier-Graefe's narrative.[3] Not everything from the book on Corot and Courbet made it into the English volumes of 1908, however. In fact, the sentence mentioned above was left out, identifying it, ironically, not as an integral part of the text, but as a double, unacknowledged supplement: to the text on Corot and Courbet and to the original history of the period.

Meier-Graefe's sentence on *Vollkommenheit* thus becomes emblematic of the supplementary logic that, I contend, structures the canon. Jacques Derrida's *The Truth in Painting* is in part a meditation on the role of the supplement in Kantian aesthetics, whereby something thought to be extraneous to the object turns out to be essential to it.[4] What might the supplement mean for looking at specific works of art and interpreting them and their history? To begin to answer that question, I want to explore the mechanism that leads most readers to accept Meier-Graefe's *Modern Art* as a narrative wholly consistent with and constitutive of the canon of modern art. I will explore what Meier-Graefe added to and subtracted from various editions, revealing that the addition of Courbet in the English version may have obscured a significant subtraction, that of the decorative, which had been an integral part of Meier-Graefe's aesthetic up to that point. Indeed, Courbet not only compensates for this loss, but his inclusion negates the value of the decorative, laying the groundwork for the familiar canon of modernism.

Published references to Meier-Graefe's book reveal how quickly it became a foundational text across Europe.[5] Charles du Bos, reviewing the first edition in the *Gazette des Beaux-Arts* in 1906, wrote: "We are indebted to his monumental work, the first in which an effective synthesis of this vast ensemble—Modern Art—is attempted."[6] Count Harry Kessler noted in *Kunst und Künstler* in 1905 that James Abbott McNeill Whistler had sometimes been accused of affectation, and that "[a] shadow of this view falls as far as the book by Meier-Graefe."[7] Kessler apparently did not need to give the book's title or date or even Meier-Graefe's full name; it was understood that readers would know exactly which book he meant. By 1946, when the German immigrant John Rewald published his classic *History of Impressionism* in America, he had no choice but to concede that Meier-Graefe had written "the first broadly conceived general history that assigns a dominating place to the individual impressionists."[8]

Rewald, as we shall see, maintained the Meier-Graefian canon. He had owned the first edition of the *Entwickelungsgeschichte*, but his account's emphases more closely reflect those of Meier-Graefe's English version or the subsequent German edition.[9] His annotated bibliography does not note the differences, however, other than to say that the second edition was "enlarged."[10] Kenworth Moffett, the author of the sole monograph on Meier-Graefe to date (1973), acknowledged that *Modern Art* had been reworked, but he maintained that "the essential structure of the book as a whole . . . remained the same, a testimony to how little his basic ideas had altered through the years."[11] The scholarly appendages to later German editions (including paperbacks in 1966 and 1987) do announce that there was an earlier version, but they, too, downplay the changes. As Benno Reifenberg wrote in 1966, the main difference is Meier-Graefe's use of language.[12]

These editorial reassurances that nothing essential had changed have no doubt reinforced any reader's desire to see *Vollkommenheit* where it did not exist in any material form. Ironically, Meier-Graefe, who purportedly had not expected the changes to be so great, tried to alert readers to them. Reinhard Piper, who began to publish the second edition in 1914, relates in his memoirs that "what Meier-Graefe feared, happened: looking through the text produced a completely different book." Piper admits: "Afterward we said to each other that it was too bad to have given the new book the old title."[13] In fact, in Meier-Graefe's foreword to the second edition, he distanced himself profoundly from the earlier version, claiming that he had "confused the development of art with [his] own development." He even wrote: "Gott verzeih mir das Buch [God forgive me for that book]."[14]

Although Piper's and Meier-Graefe's own testimonies locate great changes between the first and second German editions (1904 and 1914+), I suggest that the changes were well underway with the English translation of 1908.[15] What became manifest in 1914 was already pushing at the seams in 1908. Catherine Krahmer, one of the few scholars to recognize differences among Meier-Graefe's editions, has identified two motivations in his texts: "his desire for a far-reaching movement that would combine all the arts and give all of daily life a harmonious face and his inclination toward pure painting and sculpture that he calls 'abstract' art."[16] I argue here, however, that in the 1904 edition these two interests are intertwined and interdependent: pure form depends for its articulation on multiple arts embedded in the fabric of life.[17] In 1908, as we will see, the strands unraveled.

Meier-Graefe was actively engaged with the widespread decorative arts movements (*art nouveau* and *Jugendstil*) circa 1900: he both owned a Parisian boutique, *La Maison Moderne*, and co-edited a journal titled *Dekorative Kunst*.[18]

Meier-Graefe's commitment to the decorative is fully evident in the *Entwickelungsgeschichte*, even though it is mostly about painting. The first edition appeared in May 1904 and bore the subtitle, *Vergleichende Betrachtung der bildenden Künste, als Beitrag zu einer neuen Aesthetik* (A comparative consideration of the fine arts, as a contribution to a new aesthetic).[19] An admirer of French Impressionism and a conflicted defender of *art nouveau* and *Jugendstil*, Meier-Graefe proposed, I contend, that the future of art might lie in their fruitful union, leading to the production of the decorative *as* painting.

Meier-Graefe's "history" represents an appeal to young artists. In his final chapter on art,[20] "The Generation of 1890," Meier-Graefe identifies the future "of a rational decorative art" with Germany. The "great period" of French art may have "come to an end,"[21] he writes, but: "Our grandsons will say two things of our age: that it had a proud art, which was above it, a conscience of which it knew nothing; and that it acquired an industry, a new grandiose means of subsistence, in which it did not dare rejoice. It will be the part of our grandsons to amalgamate the two. Our own efforts threaten but to injure the one or the other."[22] Admittedly, Meier-Graefe's frustration both with his own generation of artists in Germany and with the current state of the decorative arts is palpable. Nevertheless, he presents a model and a challenge for the young German artist to follow.

Meier-Graefe traces the beginning of pictorial art to Ravenna's Early Christian mosaics. These he explicitly hails as "decorative."[23] Meier-Graefe writes, however, that "the rapidity with which the decorative ideals of the mosaicists disappeared is remarkable. In his mosaics, as in his gigantic Madonna-pictures, Cimabue still shows the decorative grandeur of an art directed to the ornamentation of vast interiors. In Giotto's hands, painting is already pictorial." Meier-Graefe places Giotto at this inauspicious juncture because "the Chapel of the Arena was the first picture-gallery. . . . The picture has already become something we must look at alone, divorced from its surroundings and governed by its own laws."[24] He mourns this change: "It seems incomprehensible that we should have given up the one thing—this splendid unity—to nurture the other—the art that Giotto inaugurated."[25]

Meier-Graefe writes with the awareness, though, that Western art *did* in fact pursue autonomy in painting, however detrimental the pursuit may have been. His text reveals a search for the lost ideal in the new medium: a successful fusion of decorative color and ornamental line in a constricted, flat picture plane, powerful enough to evoke the grandeur of the vast spaces of the past.[26] His heroes are four of the Impressionists, Edouard Manet, Paul Cézanne, Auguste Renoir, and Edgar Degas. Meier-Graefe christens them the "pillars of modern painting," thereby firmly establishing them within the canonical house. It may surprise readers today, however, that in the first edition the contribution of these artists is understood in terms of the decorative. Meier-Graefe writes that "Manet's doctrine was the recognition of painting as flat decoration; the ruthless suppression of all those elements used by the old masters to seduce the eye by plastic illusion; and the deliberate insistence on all the pictorial elements in their stead."[27] Summarizing the feats of the four "pillars," Meier-Graefe writes: "Manet set forth the general programme: the new art was to be decoration pure and simple; Cézanne exhibited the texture of the stuff; Renoir painted exquisite fragments for it, the feminine element that must be in all real painting; Degas drew for it."[28] In fact, Meier-Graefe defines "texture" in reference to Cézanne as textile, thus incorporating a decorative art into a description of painting: "Occasionally he did not even trouble himself to cover over certain small blank spots on his pictures. . . . But this superficial defect is really nothing more nor less than the frayed out corner of a splendid old tapestry."[29] The tapestry metaphor also appears in conjunction with Vincent van Gogh. Describing two paintings in Théodore Duret's collection, Meier-Graefe declared that "they are tapestries, worked in yellow and blue and notably red, painted quite flat—which was unusual in his case—encircled in a completely ornamental fashion with uniform red outlines that enclose the exquisite purple tones in gleaming fire."[30]

Although the *Entwickelungsgeschichte* appears to be a tribute to the decorative in painting, specific references already suggest its contingency. Renoir's "exquisite" contributions are "fragments," not wholes. They are also characterized as "feminine," a subject to which I will return. In addition, the characteristic that leads Meier-Graefe to consider a painting by Cézanne a tapestry is its "blank spots," its lack that must be compensated for by memory of a time-worn carpet. This contingent supplementarity also appears in the illustrations. While the *Entwickelungsgeschichte* includes reproductions of many paintings, it also contains many reproductions of abstract ornamental designs by artists such as Otto Eckmann (fig. 7.1) and Henry van de Velde (fig. 7.2), as well as designs for decorative arts objects, such as a table by Peter Behrens, fabric by William Morris, a carpet by Aristide Maillol (fig. 7.3), and an actual interior, decorated by Morris and Edward Burne-Jones. These illustrations, however, do not coordinate directly with the text, even as they contribute to the book's cumulative articulation of a decorative, pictorial aesthetic.

Although carpets provide an honorable metaphor for the Cézannes and van Goghs, and illustrations of carpets and tapestries adorn the pages of the book, Meier-Graefe, surveying earlier nineteenth-century art, writes: "In all

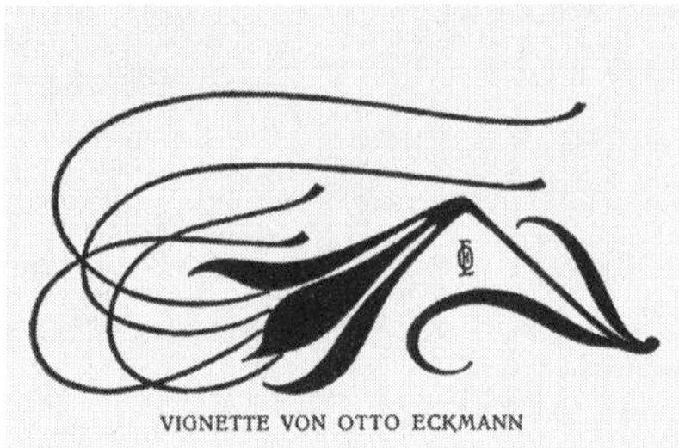

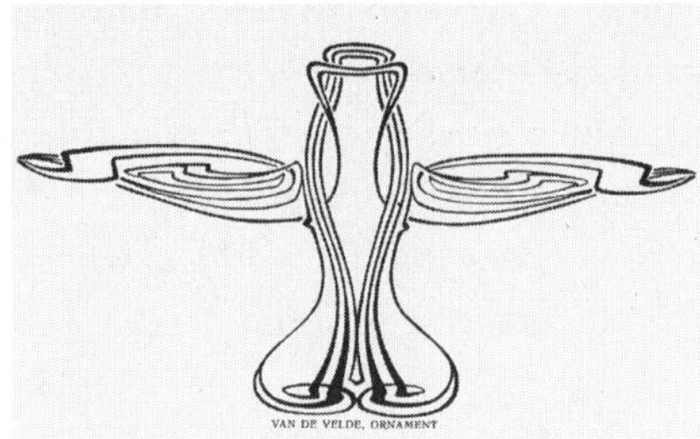

7.1. Otto Eckmann, vignette, n.d. Image: Julius Meier-Graefe, *Entwickelungsgeschichte der modernen Kunst* (Stuttgart: Hoffmann, 1904), 2:148. Image © Board of Trustees, National Gallery of Art, Washington. 7.2. Henry van de Velde, ornament, n.d. Image: Julius Meier-Graefe, *Entwickelungsgeschichte der modernen Kunst* (Stuttgart: Hoffmann, 1904), 2:674. Image © Board of Trustees, National Gallery of Art, Washington.

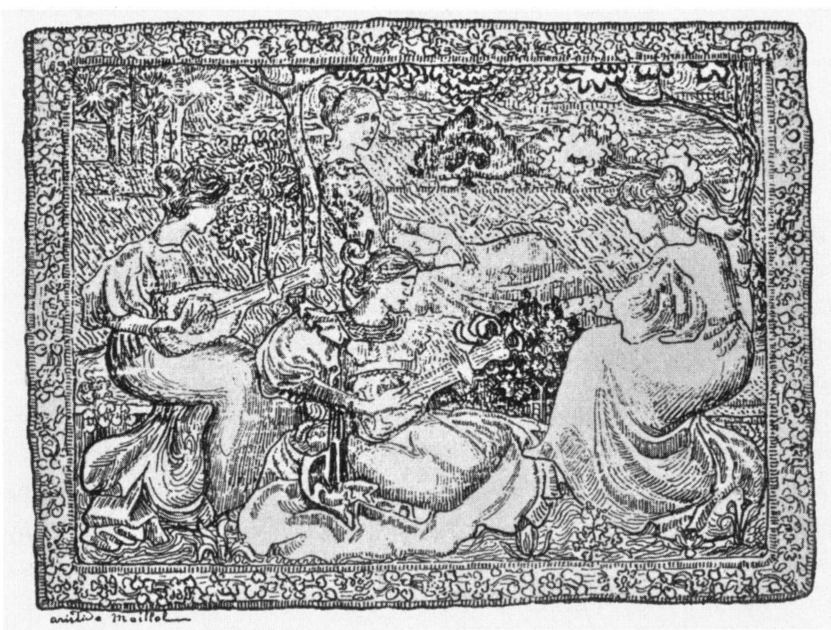

7.3. Aristide Maillol, design for carpet, n.d. Image: Julius Meier-Graefe, *Entwickelungsgeschichte der modernen Kunst* (Stuttgart: Hoffmann, 1904), 1:401. Design © 2004 Artists Rights Society (ARS), New York / ADAGP, Paris. Image © Board of Trustees, National Gallery of Art, Washington.

appreciation of Delacroix's colour . . . we must be careful not to value him only for his palette. We can make carpets with colour, but not pictures."[31] A long passage tucked into Meier-Graefe's survey of Georges Seurat and other "Neo-Impressionists" provides his most sustained rumination on the perceived problem:

> If we are to believe that the external fusion of the elements in a picture is unnecessary to the picture in everything outside the pure colour harmony, and that this alone is enough to fulfill the purpose of a work of art, we find ourselves in the domain of more or less abstract ornament. Indeed, a masterly juxtaposition of splashes of colour *will* produce ornamental effects. If this be the object in view, it is difficult to see why every means should not be employed to make these effects as rich as possible, and it is obvious that artists like [Edouard] Vuillard or [Pierre] Bonnard, who bring all the possibilities of mosaic effects into their domain, are richer than the Neo-Impressionist, who admits but a limited number of these possibilities. But if it is merely a matter of ornament, the discussion comes to an end, after it has gradually dawned upon souls fully alive to ornament that ornament for its own sake is a lovely but peculiarly superfluous pastime. . . . [32]

In this passage Meier-Graefe appears to condemn what he praises elsewhere. In most of the text, "decorative" signifies color, and "ornament," line; here, "ornament" is bad pictorial effects in implicit opposition to "decoration" as good pictorial effects. But one would be hard-pressed to identify the character of the actual difference. Here Meier-Graefe marks, however, the vulnerability of the decorative in the house of modern art. Its position was about to crumble.

The cover of the 1908 English translation seems to identify the decorative in painting *as* modern art. An image-free 1904 cover was replaced by one with a reproduction of Maurice Denis's painting *The Nymphs in the Hyacinths* (1900, fig. 7.4), which van de Velde incorporated into his designs for Count Kessler's home in Weimar in 1903.[33] The contents of the English *Modern Art*, however, suppress the decorative. Although the reproductions of applied arts and the previously quoted text are included, the latter is tempered by substantial changes. A chapter on Whistler is added, and chapters on Corot and Courbet are lifted from the book on Corot and Courbet of 1905. In 1904, there were four "pillars of modern painting": Manet, Cézanne, Renoir, and Degas.

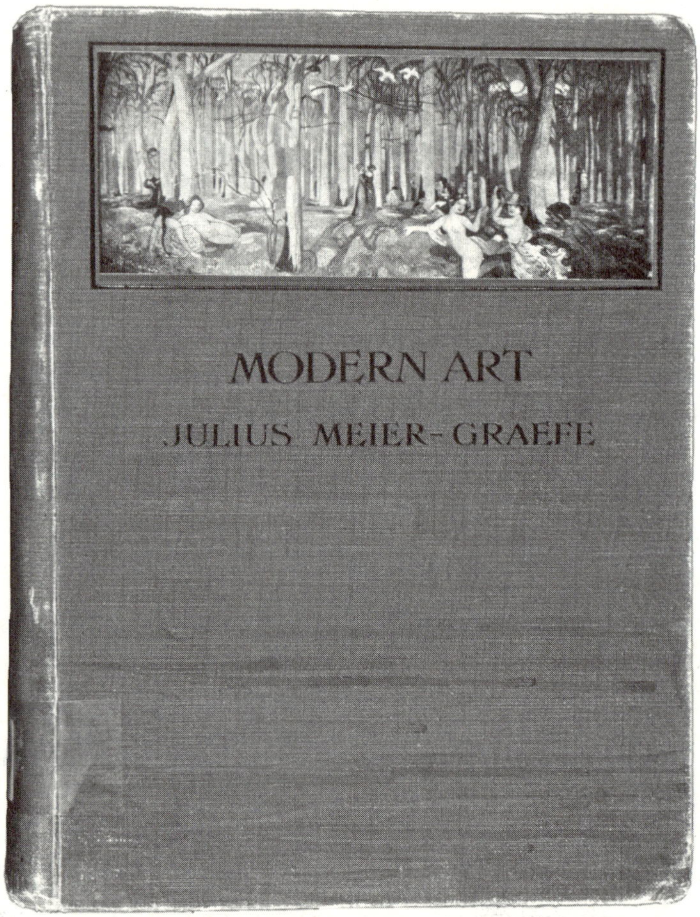

7.4. The cover of Julius Meier-Graefe's *Modern Art* (New York: Putnam, 1908), with a painting by Maurice Denis (*The Nymphs in the Hyacinths*, 1900). Painting © 2004 Artists Rights Society (ARS), New York / ADAGP, Paris. Book in Burling Library Collection, Grinnell College, Grinnell, Iowa. Photo © Karen Hueftle.

In 1908, Courbet becomes their very foundation.[34] Courbet is a supplement; however, his addition changes everything.

In the text, Meier-Graefe negotiates the addition of Courbet by claiming that Jean-François Millet "gave no stimulus and could give none, to the most important school of the nineteenth century. The conquering spirit of our modern painting derives from Courbet."[35] The assertion that Courbet is necessary to the development of modern art is followed up with even grander claims. Acknowledging previous criticism of Courbet and even some fault in his "lack of a certain harmony," Meier-Graefe goes on to compare the artist with Michelangelo and Jesus Christ! He writes: "Harsh judgment of him [Courbet] belongs to the same category as the censure audaciously meted out to Michelangelo for centuries. . . . Men who give their all must sometimes give fragments. The defect is a result of their richness, of natures absorbed in production, of a hatred of all compromise. What is wanting in them is supplied by their followers, who gather round such geniuses as the disciples round Christ, and do their part towards turning gold into current coin."[36]

By placing Courbet within a lineage of the greatest men of all time (although inadvertently suggesting another lack that must be filled), Meier-Graefe stresses the overt masculinity of this lineage. He introduces a virile gender profile of the artist:

> Not the art alone, but the whole being of this artist was conquest. There is nothing timid, childlike or good-natured about Courbet. He was the individualist with strong elbows. . . . In Paris this unpolished fanatic was like a bear in a nest of bees. . . . We shall find all sorts of things in him, save only the typical French qualities. Nothing classical, nothing lyrical, nothing decorative after the manner of the great eighteenth-century landscape painters; no trace of the playful charm of the Watteau school, nor of Delacroix'[s] dramatic quality.[37]

The boorishness of Courbet is familiar in art history. The muscular aggression we see emphasized here is, however, so pronounced that it reads as a defensive declaration. Why masculinity had to be stressed is not especially clear until Meier-Graefe catalogues the qualities that Courbet and his art are *not*: not classical, not lyrical, and, *not decorative*. Courbet may very well have been a rough man, but was Meier-Graefe focusing on his masculine attributes so as to subdue the feminine association of the decorative? Although Meier-Graefe *expressly* associated the decorative with the "feminine" only infrequently in *Modern Art* or in the first edition of the *Entwickelungsgeschichte* (recall Renoir's "feminine fragments"), the decorative traditionally had feminine connotations.[38] Courbet's hypermasculinity, in effect, drew out the latent femininity of the decorative, and devalued both femininity and the decorative.

There are other consequences as well. Meier-Graefe asserts that apart from one painting, in which he claims Courbet tried to paint didactically, "all the rest, from the first portrait of himself to the grandiose Stag-pictures and *The Wave*, are pure art."[39] If Courbet is anti-decorative, "pure" art thus becomes anti-decorative. In addition:

> Two things compete in Courbet to heighten expression: the plastic and the pictorial tendency. The one indicates a very great artist of the older style, who aims at plastic form, who therefore seeks to suppress all suggestion of his implement, and to paint as smoothly as possible. The other a great artist of the new style, relying more upon instinctive creation, and getting form out of the brush-stroke; a flat painter, the heir of Rubens, Rembrandt and Velazquez, a creator of material.[40]

The "plastic" is the new emphasis here, at least in its positive valuation. Meier-Graefe, we recall, had written approvingly of Manet's "ruthless suppression of all those elements used by the old masters to seduce the eye by plastic illusion." Manet had been praised specifically for *not* being plastic, and for recognizing "painting as flat decoration."[41] The plastic continues to be posited as the antithesis of the formal and flat, but whereas that pole had previously been called pictorial and/or decorative, it is now exclusively pictorial. In this representation, Courbet battles with the plastic and the pictorial. If the pictorial bears any residue of the decorative, the implication is that Courbet could overcome that aspect with his plasticity. The plastic also nicely anticipates and describes Courbet's representational project, because, as Meier-Graefe writes, surfaces "did not suffice him. His rhetoric demanded a personification—not that of genre, he was too deeply imbued with the old masters and too honest for that; but at least the significant presence of man and beast in the landscape."[42]

The positive revaluation of "plastic" and the exclusive use of "pictorial" instead of "pictorial" *or* "decorative" would seem to give Meier-Graefe a way to discuss formal effects *sans* the decorative, and in most cases this assumption proves to be correct. Therefore, we would also expect him to marshal the "plastic" and the "pictorial" to analyze Courbet's *Painter's Studio* (1855)—but he does not. Instead, he makes a surprising declaration: "What we see is a magnificent piece of *decoration*."[43]

Why does the decorative slip back in? Meier-Graefe's description does focus on formal qualities, especially color (although not plasticity): "The center of the composition is the painter in a dark gray jacket, his fine profile relieved against the beautiful work on the easel—a brown wooded landscape with a blue sky, closely related to the exquisitely outlined naked model, whose carnations [flesh-colored tones], naturalistically treated in reddish gray tones, shed a mild radiance throughout the picture" (*MA*, 1:234–35). Moving outward from the central group, Meier-Graefe does not review the various other figures, but, rather, he extends his description beyond the literal frame of this already huge painting:

> In the Defossés collection this picture enjoys a rare privilege accorded to our pictorial art. The enthusiasm of the collector has moved him to a princely deed. He has devoted a whole room to the work, a vast interior lighted from above, finely proportioned and gorgeously fitted. Heavy gilded architecture alternates with panels of Gobelin tapestry, which accustom the eye to a gray-blue basis. At the upper end of the room, extending across the whole width, the picture is enframed in massive gilded pilasters. The effect is highly impressive. It affords a proof, unique of its kind, that this much despised realism, the value of whose existence has been at times limited to unessential verities, may compete with the greatest art that has decorated churches and palaces. . . . (*MA*, 1:235)

Here one can see that Meier-Graefe's taste had not metamorphosed completely between editions. In 1908 he still seeks to resurrect the ancient decorated interior within modern painting, and he locates a "unique" success in a painting lovingly ensconced in an interior. He even calls it a "decoration." However, I submit that most readers have missed these points, and with good reason: the rest of the Courbet chapter foregrounds the "plastic" and militates against the decorative both in its elision of the decorative arts and in its valorization of the masculine at the expense of all things feminine.

Another added chapter underscores these shifts and suggests how the emphasis on Courbet influences the appreciation of other artists. Whistler appeared in 1904 in a relatively short (and generally unfavorable) comparison with Manet. In 1908, Meier-Graefe accorded Whistler an entire chapter, but he ridiculed him, going so far as to claim that some of his works "are only so far painting that they were executed with a paint-brush" (*MA*, 2:208). Whistler's art was "not indispensable to modern art-development" (*MA*, 2:200). It was "unmodern . . . or, in plain words, insufficient," and his art suffered from an incapacity "for preserving the relation of the parts in the attempted plasticity." The failed plasticity—Courbet's great strength—results, as we might expect, in feminized decorativeness. The *White Girl* "remains merely glass eyes, false hair, clothes, carpet and curtains" (*MA*, 2:202). Regarding the *Symphony in White*, the "dubious element is . . . to create human beings by means of the higher decorative arts" (*MA*, 2:203). Furthermore, there are direct and emasculating comparisons with Courbet, including: "The Courbet-like character studies inaugurated by these heads [by Whistler] had no further results. The tendency of the elegant portrait painter admitted of no ruthless sincerity. To achieve originality and dexterity on this road demanded more earnest efforts than the indication of enthusiastic girlish emotion" (*MA*, 2:205).

The invective is striking. Krahmer notes that Meier-Graefe had first voiced disapproval of Whistler, and already in comparison with Manet, in 1899.[44] This twenty-seven page rant in the 1908 book seems excessive, however, especially since he granted the conqueror of modern painting, Courbet, only five pages more. Meier-Graefe appears hell-bent on replacing the decorative (which a feminized Whistler is now consigned to represent) with the muscular plasticity of Courbet.

Could Courbet have been portrayed otherwise? Kessler's defense of Whistler in 1905 suggests that he could have been. In the Whistler essay, Courbet is as much a canonical hero—"all of modern art stands on his shoulders"—as he will be in Meier-Graefe's 1908 edition of *Modern Art*.[45] However, Kessler unabashedly admires this Courbet for his decorative qualities: "When one sees Courbet's pictures hanging in the Louvre next to Rousseaus, Millets, and Delacroixs, they have the effect of Gobelins: no sharply framing coulisses in the foreground, no holes, no interruptive darks or lights, but, instead, every picture a calm surface that builds a complete, unbroken area for itself on the wall."[46] Or the following: "Courbet suggests heavy silk, splendid damask. . . ."[47] Kessler shows that Courbet's materiality, even his plasticity, did not necessarily have to be figured as brutish anti-decoration. It could, rather, be praised for its substantial decorative effect, for its rich, rough texture or its grand presence in an interior.[48]

Why, then, did Meier-Graefe seek to vanquish the decorative, to write it out of *Modern Art*? There is no one fully satisfactory answer to this question, although various partial ones offer themselves. Elsewhere I have suggested that in the early years of the twentieth century, misogyny combined with the commercial failures of the decorative arts to produce a distrust of feminized domestic wares and taste.[49] Meier-Graefe suffered from this general failure personally: he had to sell his boutique, *La Maison Moderne*, at a loss in April 1904, a month before the first edition of the *Entwickelungsgeschichte* appeared.[50] Kessler's diary records that the enterprise was failing, not only financially, but also morally and psychologically, long before that. After visiting Meier-Graefe's shop in December 1901, Kessler recorded: "In Meier-Graefe's store it's almost all junk [*Schund*] now. So in his eagerness to fight junk he has become a dealer. But dealing forced its rules on him. In order to keep the store running, he was forced at first to sell some junk and now to sell almost all junk. The means have become master over the purpose. Psychological drama."[51] In this account, the highly principled campaign to make fine goods available to all through an enlightened production of and commerce in the decorative arts lost out to the need to "get by." It is tempting to see this personal failure as a factor in Meier-Graefe's growing pessimism about the decorative arts.

That did not mean that the decorative *tout court* had to be abandoned or suppressed, however, as Kessler's praise of Courbet has shown. Still, it largely was. The roles that Courbet and, to a lesser extent, Whistler, might play in this revaluation are not self-evident. I believe they were simply brought to Meier-Graefe's attention, and they facilitated his war against the decorative. Their addition was not inevitable. Courbet had been highly esteemed by Emile Zola and the German art historian Franz von Reber, but he barely appeared in the exhaustive Parisian centennial exhibition of 1900.[52] Meier-Graefe had had at least six years in the preparation of the *Entwickelungsgeschichte* to consider the importance of Courbet, but he did not come to the conclusion that he was pivotal. Indeed, the contemporary reviewer in the *Gazette des Beaux-Arts* did not note the omission, signaling that Meier-Graefe was not alone in his (early) lack of estimation of Courbet.[53] Kessler, writing his essay on Whistler in 1905, did declare that "Courbet's role in art history is still strangely underestimated."[54] Kessler's essay, itself inspired by two major Whistler exhibitions (at the International Society in London and the Académie des Beaux-Arts in Paris), was too late to cause Meier-Graefe to write on Courbet, but its pairing of Courbet and Whistler may have stayed with Meier-Graefe and encouraged him to position Whistler in opposition to his hero Courbet in 1908.[55]

But why Courbet, and why so late with such a vengeance? Alfred Lichtwark, the director of the Hamburg Kunsthalle, explained the shift in a letter in 1908: "When his book about the developmental history of French [*sic*] art had appeared, [Paul] Cassirer said to him: But you have forgotten Courbet. He hit himself on the head and went off and wrote a book about him. Later [Emil] Heilbut said to him: Why did you ignore Corot?"[56] It is indeed possible that Meier-Graefe simply forgot and then remembered—or was reminded of—these major artists, but this account suggests a confidence in a complete canon a priori to the writing of the history, a canon that was waiting to be articulated. Krahmer seems closer to the truth when she declares that Meier-Graefe's "entire art-writing corpus is a sort of work-in-progress, a lifelong improved and expanded *Entwickelungsgeschichte*."[57]

Some research into contemporary artistic events in Paris offers other possible occasions through which Meier-Graefe's memory may have been pricked. While I have not addressed the specific content of Meier-Graefe's chapter on Corot, the potential impetus for his becoming attuned to Corot is noteworthy. The standard Corot *catalogue raisonné* first appeared in 1905.[58] It was based on notes by Alfred Robaut and written by Étienne Moreau-Nélaton. As David Ogawa argues, Moreau-Nélaton shaped his narrative on Corot so as to position him most positively within an evolving historical narrative of Impressionism, and he did this not only because of his admiration for Corot, but also because he was himself about to give his large and extraordinary collection of paintings—from Barbizon painters through the Impressionists—to the Louvre.[59] Meier-Graefe's own book on Corot (and Courbet) also appeared in 1905, but one can only imagine that Meier-Graefe, closely attuned to the Parisian art world, was aware of the fact that the major *catalogue raisonné* was about to come out. He may even have seen an advance copy, because, as Ogawa argues, Moreau-Nélaton produced a Corot who was very different from the one recorded in Robaut's unpublished notes, and Meier-Graefe's biographical emphases exactly match those of Moreau-Nélaton.[60]

I do not mean to imply that Meier-Graefe plagiarized Moreau-Nélaton. The claim is more mundane, but more far reaching: I believe that Corot did not of necessity fit into Meier-Graefe's canon, but, rather, that he fell into it belatedly because Meier-Graefe's awareness of him was heightened later. Moreau-Nélaton's project was a likely impetus, and the correspondence of narratives supports that assessment. However, if Ogawa is right that Moreau-Nélaton rewrote Corot in a bid to secure the artist and his lineage, then it is interesting, to say the least, that Courbet's paintings were not in that large and extraordinary collection.[61] Here was another major modernist narrative that did not feature Courbet.

Courbet—skipped over in the Parisian centennial exhibition, absent from the Moreau-Nélaton narrative, not missed by Meier-Graefe's reviewer—simply was not *essential* to the canon. He became essential, however, for a canon stripped of the decorative. What brought Meier-Graefe to that solution? The biography in the Courbet *catalogue raisonné* (compiled much later, in 1977) includes only one entry for the three years (1902–4) before the book on Corot and Courbet was published. Is it fortuitous that it is a book by Théodore Duret on *Whistler* (1904)? Meier-Graefe definitely knew Duret (recall that he praised the tapestry-like qualities of the van Goghs in Duret's collection), and he also knew the book was coming out (in the 1904 *Entwickelungsgeschichte*, he expresses his anticipation of the forthcoming book).[62] The book's references to Courbet are somewhat disappointing in their blandness, however. Duret simply notes that Courbet had admired Whistler's painting *At the Piano* (1859), and that "Courbet had been the first of the older artists to appreciate and praise him, and Whistler had been very grateful to him. Between them was the distance which separates the man arrived at great fame from the young man who is beginning."[63] These references alone are likely not enough to have made Meier-Graefe reconsider Courbet, but Duret's other connections with Courbet may have cumulatively influenced him. For example, Duret's collection included at least twenty Courbets, and Meier-Graefe had reproduced one of them (*The Beach, Trouville* [1866]) in the first edition of the *Entwickelungsgeschichte*. (In *Modern Art*, the same painting appears in the chapter on Whistler, because Courbet painted it during one of the two summers that he and Whistler painted together at Trouville.) Equally important to Duret's collection, perhaps, is that there was a sale of thirty Courbets in March 1905 in Paris. Meier-Graefe, who facilitated scores of art sales over several decades and knew dealers and collectors intimately, was almost certainly aware of this one. And of special note is that the preface to the sales catalogue was written by Duret.[64]

It is in the end impossible to pinpoint what or who provoked Meier-Graefe to write about Courbet (as well as Corot and Whistler) and to change the *Entwickelungsgeschichte* so drastically, but it should be clear that chance was involved as much as was necessity. What we know for sure is that history and its ideals as Meier-Graefe reconceptualized them became canonical. I have argued that great ambivalence about those changing ideals can be located in the English edition, but it is the second German edition that represents that canon unequivocally. With little exception, the decorative had been *the* goal for painters in the first *Entwickelungsgeschichte*, and the English translation's essays on Courbet and Whistler undermined that goal significantly. The second edition, however, absorbed the thrust of those new essays through and through. That is, by 1914 Meier-Graefe had extricated the decorative completely from his masculinized ideal of abstract painters and painting. Specifically, *all* of the passages I have quoted in the early part of this essay—that is, *all* of the quotations from the *Entwickelungsgeschichte* that were not in the chapters on Courbet or Whistler—*disappeared*. So did all of the explicitly decorative or ornamental images from the first German edition and the 1908 English version. The metaphor for a Cézanne is no longer a splendid tapestry; it has been transformed, rather, into "pure music."[65] Music has its own history as a metaphor for abstract form, and it appears regularly throughout all of the editions, but here it represents the complete occlusion of the decorative.[66]

John Rewald's *The History of Impressionism* provides a classic and pithy example of how the artists of the second-edition Meier-Graefian canon became synonymous with the ideals he endorsed on their behalf. In the middle of roughly twenty-five pages devoted to Courbet's powerful influence on all of the Impressionists, Rewald laments that Whistler eventually turned against Courbet. He writes: "By turning his back on nature, by ignoring Courbet's message, Whistler henceforth condemned himself never to penetrate beneath the surface of appearances, to be satisfied with decorative arrangements."[67] The sentence is packed with cliché and sexualized innuendo. Whistler's contentment with the decorative, in this account, leaves him impotent, unable to penetrate to the interior ever again. By negative implication, Courbet's virility is celebrated.

The rhetoric that took shape in 1908 (*Modern Art*) and crystallized in 1914 (the second edition of *Entwicklungsgeschichte*) continues to this day. Some of it is likely based in truth, but my point is not to question its validity, but, rather, to consider its genesis and its effects. The latter are far reaching and insidious, even as some feminists have tried to combat them. Linda Nochlin, for example, has criticized the "unequivocally male" painter in Courbet's *Painter's Studio*, a painting in which, she claims, "gender is overtly and blatantly positioned as opposition—and domination."[68] Although she argues convincingly that the central figures present an Oedipal triangle that reinscribes a masculine canon, I wonder whether her anger is overdetermined, causing her to miss a potentially more productive target: not Courbet, but rather, the canon as produced by Meier-Graefe and his followers. If the canon had not been structured around a hypermasculinized Courbet, might Nochlin have been able to see his painting differently, to see, perhaps, a decorative Courbet à la Kessler?[69] It is impossible to know, because we readers today all learned the modernist narrative that devalues the feminine and the decorative and heroizes the aggressively masculine in the name of Courbet. It is difficult to take on that narrative, because, as Meier-Graefe wrote, "perfect completion appears as necessity, as the most striking contrast to chance."[70] We have seen, however, how great a role chance plays in providing the fragments necessary to produce the effect of the whole canon. This gives us all the more reason to question the "necessity" of the canon. Otherwise, we leave what we see in art to chance.

Notes

1 Meier-Graefe, *Corot und Courbet*, 221. Translations are mine unless otherwise noted.

2 Belting, afterword to *Entwicklungsgeschichte der modernen Kunst* (1987); also in Paul, *Hugo von Tschudi und die moderne französische Kunst im deutschen Kaiserreich*, 163 n. 135. The title of this edition reflects the modern spelling of *Entwicklung*. In the essay, I use the spelling current at the time of the first edition, *Entwickelung*.

3 Meier-Graefe, *Corot und Courbet*, 1.

4 Derrida, *The Truth in Painting*, esp. 51–82. See my reading of this text in Anger, *Paul Klee and the Decorative in Modern Art*, 7–13. Thanks to Marcia Brennan for alerting me to its relevance for (its supplementarity to?) this essay as well.

5 Meier-Graefe's exhibition planning also contributed to the canon. See Krahmer, "Tschudi and Meier-Graefe." Krahmer also maintains that major public and private collections bear the stamp of Meier-Graefe ("Tschudi and Meier-Graefe," 372, 376 nn. 23, 24).

6 Du Bos, "Bibliographie." Despite such praise, Meier-Graefe's history has not retained such prestige in France. According to Catherine Krahmer, Meier-Graefe, "who had lived in France for many years, remained as good as unknown there." Krahmer wrote this in the context of failed negotiations in 1907 to produce a French translation of *Modern Art*, thereby suggesting that French language insularity may be to blame. Krahmer, *Julius Meier-Graefe*, 358.

7 Kessler, "Whistler," 445.

8 Rewald, *The History of Impressionism*, 448.

9 The first edition of the *Entwickelungsgeschichte* at the National Gallery of Art library in Washington, D.C., comes from the John Rewald Collection. The second German edition, which modernized the title's spelling to *Entwicklungsgeschichte*, came out in stages: vol. 1 appeared in 1914, vol. 2 in 1915, and vol. 3 in 1924.

10 Rewald, *The History of Impressionism*, 448.

11 K. Moffett, *Meier-Graefe as Art Critic*, 177 n. 418.

12 Reifenberg, "Introduction" to Meier-Graefe, *Entwicklungsgeschichte*, reprint of 3rd ed., edited by Reifenberg and Meier-Graefe-Broch, 25. Echoing the prejudices of later volumes, Reifenberg does note that "one understands that the new edition appropriately cleaned up [*gehörig aufräumte*] the pre-Raphaelites, the confusions around the decorative arts [*den Wirrnissen der Stilfragen*] at the turn-of-the century, and the ornamentation, out of which one van de Velde grew" (23).

13 Piper, *Mein Leben als Verleger*, 259.

14 Meier-Graefe, "Foreword to the Second Edition," *Entwicklungsgeschichte* (1914), repro. in reprint of 3rd ed. (1966), 42–43.

15 Meier-Graefe worked with Florence Simmonds on the translation, which he told van de Velde would be "admirable." Meier-Graefe to van de Velde, April 14, 1905, in Krahmer, "Meier-Graefes Weg zur Kunst," 224.

16 Krahmer, "Meier-Graefes Weg zur Kunst," 169.

17 Paul comes closer to this account, writing that "Meier-Graefe's promotion of a painterly art found its roots in his enthusiasm for the decorative arts movement." Paul, *Hugo von Tschudi und die moderne französische Kunst im deutschen Kaiserreich*, 172.

18 See Krahmer, "Meier-Graefes Weg zur Kunst," esp. 173–93; Troy, *Modernism and the Decorative Arts in France*; and Anger, "Forgotten Ties," and "Modernism at Home."

19 The introductory chapters were serialized as early as 1899–1900 in *Die Insel*. See Krahmer, "Meier-Graefes Weg zur Kunst," 219. Paul notes that large portions of Meier-Graefe's earlier books, *Manet und sein Kreis* (1902) and *Der moderne Impressionismus* (1902) were also incorporated. Paul, *Hugo von Tschudi und die moderne französische Kunst im deutschen Kaiserreich*, 168. Thus, the first edition was already a mosaic composed in part with recycled pieces.

20 The German first edition has additional chapters on aesthetics, focusing on Goethe and Diderot, Nietzsche and Wagner. These chapters, which do not appear either in the English edition or in subsequent German editions, raise issues beyond the scope of the present essay.

21 Meier-Graefe, *Entwickelungsgeschichte der modernen Kunst*, 2:703–4 (hereafter simply *Entwickelungsgeschichte*); and Meier-Graefe, *Modern Art*, 2:311. Unless otherwise noted, here and below I quote the English translation (*Modern Art*) and note its source in the 1904 edition of *Entwickelungsgeschichte*.

22 Meier-Graefe, *Entwickelungsgeschichte*, 2:726; and Meier-Graefe, *Modern Art*, 2:324.

23 Meier-Graefe, *Entwickelungsgeschichte*, 1:23–38; and Meier-Graefe, *Modern Art*, 1:11–20, passim.

24 Meier-Graefe, *Entwickelungsgeschichte*, 1:39–40; and Meier-Graefe, *Modern Art*, 1:21.

25 Meier-Graefe, *Entwickelungsgeschichte*, 1:41; and Meier-Graefe, *Modern Art*, 1:22.

26 Jay A. Clarke notes that Meier-Graefe had already aligned the decorative with color (and the French) and ornament with line (and the Germans) in his book on Félix Vallotton in 1898. See Meier-Graefe, *Félix Vallotton*; and Clarke, "Munch, Liebermann, and the Question of Etched 'Reproductions,'" 54.

27 Meier-Graefe, *Entwickelungsgeschichte*, 1:160–61; and Meier-Graefe, *Modern Art*, 1:264.

28 Meier-Graefe, *Entwickelungsgeschichte*, 1:179; and Meier-Graefe, *Modern Art*, 1:277.

29 Meier-Graefe, *Entwickelungsgeschichte*, 1:165; and Meier-Graefe, *Modern Art*, 1:266.

30 Meier-Graefe, *Entwickelungsgeschichte*, 1:170; and Meier-Graefe, *Modern Art*, 1:270.

31 Meier-Graefe, *Entwickelungsgeschichte*, 1:93; and Meier-Graefe, *Modern Art*, 1:154.

32 Meier-Graefe, *Entwickelungsgeschichte*, 1:240–41; and Meier-Graefe, *Modern Art*, 1:320.

33 I offer an extended analysis of this painting and its setting in relation to the *Entwickelungsgeschichte* in Anger, "Modernism at Home."

34 The metaphor is not yet explicit in 1908, but I hope to show that it may as well have been. In Meier-Graefe's handwritten notes within the pages of the first edition, notes presumably not written until the second (German) edition was undertaken, he writes, following allusion to the "four pillars": "The house stands on a solid, widely projecting foundation: Courbet." See Meier-Graefe, *Entwickelungsgeschichte*, 1:139, in Meier-Graefe, Prosa 90.100.1, Deutsches Literaturarchiv, Marbach am Neckar. This volume shows many other additions, crossed-out sections, and pages cut out to facilitate merging the original text and other material (for example, the chapters on Corot and Courbet) for the new German edition. The notes do not match the second edition precisely, however, suggesting that Meier-Graefe began rewriting wholesale somewhere else. Complicating matters, there are also at least two hands: Meier-Graefe's old German script (nearly illegible) and an unknown Latin script.

35 Meier-Graefe, *Modern Art*, 1:219. Courbet's role was more humble in 1904. There, in a paragraph in the Millet chapter that was not carried over into the 1908 edition, Meier-Graefe writes: "The realism that followed in France had nothing to do with Millet. Millet was a great synthesist, Courbet an accomplished painter, the creator of a marvelous material. . . . Courbet's significance lies in the area that Manet exhausted, and that taught our eyes to see materially." Meier-Graefe, *Entwickelungsgeschichte*, 1:110.

36 Meier-Graefe, *Modern Art*, 1:238.

37 Meier-Graefe, *Modern Art*, 1:219.

38 This association dates at least to Cicero's comparison of unadorned prose and unadorned women—although it is ironic that even in that metaphor, the women are specifically *not* ornamented.

39 Meier-Graefe, *Modern Art*, 1:221. The painting purportedly painted "to illustrate a theory" is *Aumône d'un Mendiant*.

40 Meier-Graefe, *Modern Art*, 1:225.

41 Meier-Graefe, *Entwickelungsgeschichte*, 1:160–61; and Meier-Graefe, *Modern Art*, 1:264. Although these lines remain in the 1908 edition, Manet's reputation suffers in other passages due to the new emphasis on Courbet. Manet is not credited with as much of an influence himself. In 1904, Meier-Graefe wrote that "Manet left behind a development; he had cleft the earth with mighty strokes of the spade, and bequeathed us not only brilliant works, but a fruitful manner in which to conceive of new things" (*Entwickelungsgeschichte*, 160). In 1908, one finds the following: "Courbet had cleft the earth with mighty strokes of the spade, and bequeathed us not only brilliant works, but the possibility of a new conception of Nature. Manet realized this possibility beyond all expectation, and in spite of all he owed to Courbet and to others, appears as the more harmonious, the more fruitful artist" (*Modern Art*, 264). In an altogether new paragraph in 1908, Meier-Graefe suggests that Manet's advantage is mere appearance, however, and one that masks a certain decorativeness: "He [Manet] appears as the higher manifestation of Courbet, purified but stripped of certain advantages in the process. He subdued the animality of Courbet, but he never produced works so moving as the *Enterrement* and *La Vague*. The *Olympia* and *Déjeuner sur l'herbe*, in which, moreover, there are obvious traces of the predecessor, contain a decorative art, which, as much, minimises the degree of dramatic directness, which Courbet achieved in his happiest moments" (*Modern Art*, 263).

42 Meier-Graefe, *Modern Art*, 1:232.

43 Ibid., 1:234, emphasis added. Subsequent consecutive citations to Meier-Graefe's *Modern Art (MA)* are cited parenthetically in the text.

44 Meier-Graefe, "Die Stellung Manets," *Kunst für Alle* 15 (November 1899), in Krahmer, *Julius Meier-Graefe*, 357–58.

45 Kessler, "Whistler," 453.

46 Ibid.

47 Ibid.

48 As Susan Strauber has pointed out to me, these qualities imply the decorative on a grand scale, not an intimate or intricate rococo. She reminds us of the decorative's wide range of possibilities, *all* of which Meier-Graefe sought to quash.

49 See Anger, "Forgotten Ties."

50 Troy, *Modernism and the Decorative Arts in France*, 31–46.

51 Kessler, "December 29, 1901" in Kessler, *Das Tagebuch*, 3:452.

52 See Paul, *Hugo von Tschudi und die moderne französische Kunst im deutschen Kaiserreich*, 38–44, 125; and *Exposition universelle de 1900*.

53 In his review for *Die Zukunft*, Scheffler also failed to note any lack of appreciation for Courbet; see Scheffler, "Meier-Graefe," 324–30.

54 Kessler, "Whistler," 451. Krahmer notes that this was an "indirect criticism of the *Entwickelungsgeschichte*." Krahmer, *Julius Meier-Graefe*, 358.

55 After reading the Whistler essay, Meier-Graefe wrote to Kessler that he looked forward to hearing the latter's response to his book on Corot and Courbet, which he noted would be out in six weeks. Meier-Graefe to Kessler, August 8, 1905, in Krahmer, *Julius Meier-Graefe*, 49–50.

56 Alfred Lichtwark, letter, September 17, 1908, in Pauli, *Briefe an die Kommission für die Verwaltung der Kunsthalle in Auswahl*, 2:251. I am grateful to Catherine Krahmer for sharing the contents of this letter with me.

57 Krahmer, *Julius Meier-Graefe*, 338.

58 Robaut and Moreau-Nélaton, *L'oeuvre de Corot*.

59 Moreau-Nélaton's collection included gems such as Manet's *Déjeuner sur l'herbe*. He gave the collection to the Louvre in 1906. David Ogawa, "Alfred Robaut, Étienne Moreau-Nélaton, and Writing Corot," 329. I am grateful to David Ogawa for sharing this research with me.

60 Ogawa argues that "Moreau-Nélaton's work involved a wholesale transformation of his source material [Robaut's personal notes from years of acquaintance with the artist]." For example, according to Ogawa, "Robaut's account is carefully balanced across the mother-father axis . . . [whereas] Moreau-Nélaton represents the parents as utterly polarized in terms of character." In this construction, Corot's father emerges as "the embodiment of petit bourgeois pettiness when Corot announces his wishes to become a painter." Ibid., 328, 330. It is the latter story that Meier-Graefe retells.

61 Ogawa, correspondence with the author, July 6, 2004. Moreau-Nélaton did possess some drawings by Courbet. See *De Corot aux impressionists*, 214–15.

62 Meier-Graefe, *Entwickelungsgeschichte*, 1:158; and Duret, *Histoire de J. McN. Whistler et de son oeuvre*.

63 Duret, *Whistler*, 21, 98. I am loathe to use a later translation without comparing the original, but in this case I have not been able to locate the original and must therefore take my chances with its accuracy!

64 "Vente succession Félix Gérard père—30 oeuvres de Courbet—Paris, H.D., S. 1, les 28 et 29 mars 1905. Préface de Th. Duret. Mes Chevallier et Mauger, C.-P., MM Georges Petit et Jules Féral, exp." Fernier, *La vie et l'oeuvre de Gustave Courbet*, 2:353. Duret published several essays on Courbet and finally published his own book on the artist in 1918; see Duret, *Courbet*. Beyond Duret, another possible prompt was Meier-Graefe's visit to the Defossés collection, which he described in *Modern Art* as having immediately followed an exhibition of "Primitives in Dusseldorf." Meier-Graefe, *Modern Art*, 1:235. This was likely a major exhibition in 1904. See Clemen, *Meisterwerke westdeutscher Malerei und andere hervorragende Gemälde alter Meister aus Privatbesitz auf der Kunsthistorischen Ausstellung zu Düsseldorf 1904*.

65 Meier-Graefe, *Entwicklungsgeschichte*, 2nd ed., 3:584. The third volume of the second edition, in which this quote appears, was not published until 1924. The sections on Cézanne draw heavily from Meier-Graefe's book on the artist from 1918, however, in which the decorative has already been purged. Cf. Meier-Graefe, *Cézanne und sein Kreis*.

66 For the position of music in the discourse of the era, see especially Champa, *The Rise of Landscape Painting in France, Corot to Monet*. I discuss musical metaphor in Meier-Graefe's writings in Anger, "Modernism at Home."

67 Rewald, *The History of Impressionism*, 148.

68 Nochlin, "Courbet's Real Allegory," esp. 31.

69 Michael Fried has argued that Courbet's paintings reverse the gendered oppositions historically attributed to the gaze in Western painting, rendering them structurally feminine. Nochlin vehemently denies this possibility, and this may be one such case whereby the hypermasculinization of the canonized Courbet has prevented the reader and viewer from being able to acknowledge representational effects that she might otherwise have hailed. See Fried, "Courbet's 'Femininity,'" and his revised version in Fried, *Courbet's Realism*, 189–222.

70 Meier-Graefe, *Corot und Courbet*, 221.

8

The Multiple Masculinities of Canonical Modernism: James Johnson Sweeney and Alfred H. Barr Jr. in the 1930s

MARCIA BRENNAN

Among the familiar iconic images in canonical modernist art history, the flowchart that Alfred H. Barr Jr. constructed as the cover design for the exhibition catalogue *Cubism and Abstract Art* (Museum of Modern Art, 1936) remains one of the most prominent (fig. 8.1).[1] In this diagram, Barr famously outlined a series of interconnected relationships between the various movements of modern art. Working along a chronological axis that spanned the period 1890 to 1935, Barr traced an elaborate network of successive artistic developments that extended from Post-Impressionism through Fauvism, Cubism, and other contemporary European avant-garde practices ultimately to culminate in the two distinct, parallel trajectories that he labeled "geometrical abstract art" and "non-geometrical abstract art." Given its long-standing historical significance and high degree of visibility within American art historical discourses, it is not surprising that Barr's flowchart has become a focal point for much partisan debate, as scholars have examined the ideological investments underpinning Barr's modernist project and its legacy for a present-day audience. Indeed, Barr's vision of modernism has been interpreted as representing everything from a scholarly model of "historical truth and internal coherence" that also served as a powerful "proselytizer" of "the Gospel of modern art" (Robert Rosenblum), to a codified statement of gender oppression reflecting the historical exclusion of female artists (Griselda Pollock), to a myth-making declaration in support of the modernists' elitist "quest for purity" at the expense of the "colonized subjects [who] play the Other to the idealist dialectics of abstraction" (W. J. T. Mitchell).[2] Such discourses have shed much light on the networks of privilege and exclusion that have underpinned the modernist project historically. Yet the familiar polemic between traditionalist modernist accolades and their corresponding revisionist critiques largely overlooks another more subtle yet extremely powerful aspect of Barr's project: namely, the dialogical theorization of gendered subjectivity embedded within the aesthetic structures of canonical modernism.

While *Cubism and Abstract Art* occupies a unique if controversial position in the history of modernism, it has an important precedent in a much less familiar text, *Plastic Redirections in 20th Century Painting*, which was published in 1934 by Barr's close associate, the critic and curator James Johnson Sweeney. Although Barr has repeatedly been singled out within critiques of canonical modernism, his analysis in fact belonged to a complex discourse that also included Sweeney's contemporary theorizations of aesthetics and gendered subjectivity. In their texts, both Barr and Sweeney adopted a genealogical approach for tracing the evolutionary development of the plastic sequence in modern art, and for mapping its corollary characteristics onto conceptions of modernist selfhood. Much like the chronological axis of Barr's flowchart, Sweeney's narrative extended from developments in later nineteenth-century Impressionism to the abstract psychological works of "Superrealism" (what we now call Surrealism). Of the two, Barr's model of modernist aesthetics and subjectivity may have worn its dialectics more visibly on its sleeve (of the book jacket). Yet both Sweeney's and Barr's texts were based on parallel conceptions of modernist subjectivity that encompassed the aesthetic, material, ethical, and spiritual domains. In their texts, the abstract qualities of modernist artworks were repeatedly characterized as symbolic analogues of an idealized conception of modernist selfhood, with its ambivalent capacity to express rationality and emotion, intellect and intuition, logical calculation and mystical ecstasy. When viewed today, Sweeney's and Barr's studies seem almost to anticipate the internal tension between opposing forces that, as Anna Brzyski incisively points out in her introduction to this volume, now characterize the contested status of the canon itself and the epistemologically fragile boundaries that distinguish modern from postmodern production.[3] Yet at the time of their production, Sweeney's and Barr's canonical texts provided a contemporary audience with structurally reassuring guides for the intellectual comprehension of challenging modernist artworks, and with imaginative models for the active reconceptualization of modernist selfhood.

The resonance between Sweeney's and Barr's texts is not surprising. While the two men were in their thirties and forties, they were close colleagues at the Museum of Modern Art. Barr was the founding director of the museum, and Sweeney (who made New York his primary residence in 1934) organized a number of high-profile exhibitions and served as a member of the museum's Advisory Committee.[4] In the acknowledgments to *Cubism and Abstract Art*, Barr thanked Sweeney for his assistance in assembling the exhibition

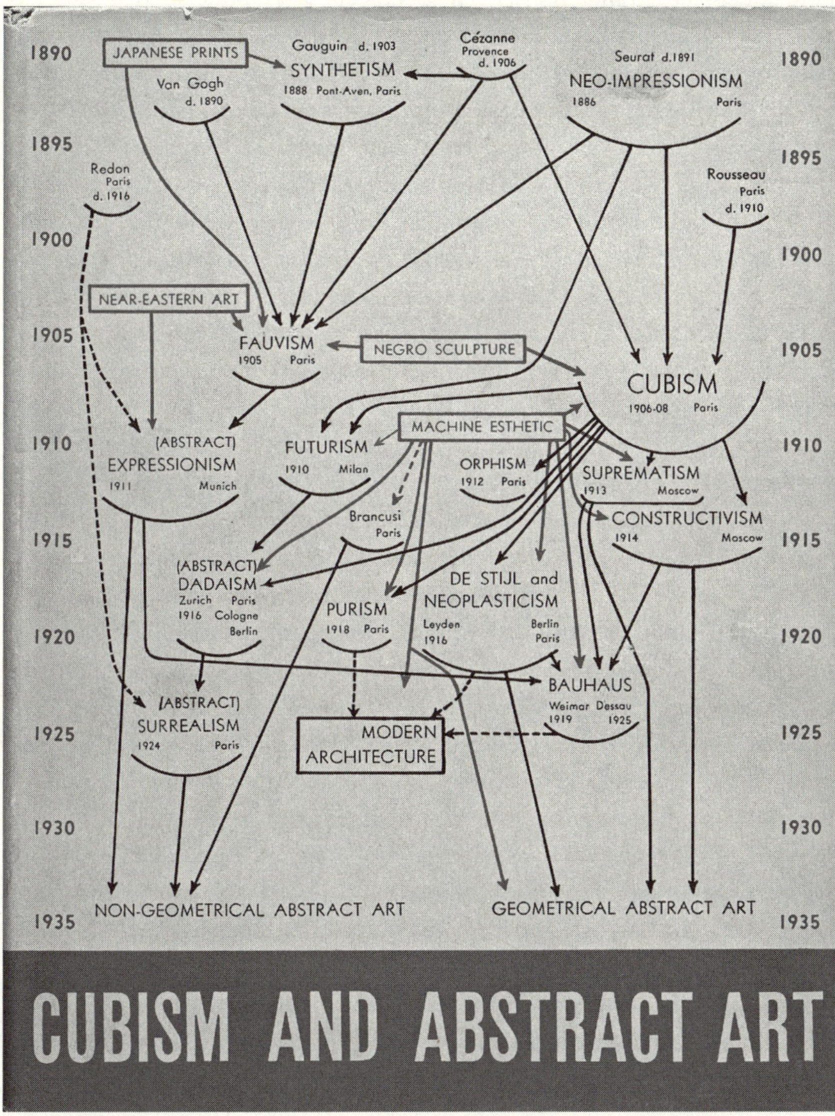

8.1. Alfred H. Barr Jr., cover of the exhibition catalogue *Cubism and Abstract Art*, 1936, the Museum of Modern Art, New York. Digital Image © the Museum of Modern Art, Licensed by SCALA/Art Resource, N.Y. The Museum of Modern Art, New York, N.Y., U.S.A.

and preparing the accompanying catalogue.[5] Although technically Barr was Sweeney's superior at the museum during the 1930s, their relationship was far more collegial than hierarchical. The personal correspondence that Sweeney and Barr exchanged throughout the decade clearly indicates that the two men shared avid mutual interests in non-Western art and twentieth-century modernism.[6] During the 1930s Sweeney was a highly influential figure in the New York art world, serving as a respected guest curator for prominent shows at the Museum of Modern Art. Having come from a prosperous family, he was also actively building his private art collection and owned Mondrian's *Composition with Large Red Plane, Blue, Gray, Black and Yellow* (1921, fig. 8.2), which he loaned anonymously for the *Cubism and Abstract Art* show.[7] Sweeney was also an important figure in the New York literary world, serving as an associate editor of *Transition* (1936–38), an avant-garde art and literary quarterly, and as an influential art critic for *The New Republic* (1935).

In the summer of 1934 Sweeney organized an important exhibition of contemporary artworks at the Renaissance Society of the University of Chicago. Entitled *A Selection of Works by Twentieth-Century Artists*, this exhibition seemed to foreshadow Barr's much larger and better-known show. An image of Calder's organic yet mechanomorphic mobile sculpture *Object with Red Disks* (1931)—another work that would later become part of Sweeney's personal art collection—appeared prominently on the cover of the catalogue (fig. 8.3).[8] In addition to two Calder mobiles, the show also featured works by Arp, Brancusi, Braque, Gris, Hélion, Léger, Miró, Mondrian, and Picasso. Sweeney arranged the selection and installation of the exhibition, and his critical writings are quoted at length in the accompanying catalogue. That same year, Sweeney's *Plastic Redirections in 20th-Century Painting* was published jointly by the Renaissance Society and the University of Chicago Press.

Sweeney and Barr also moved in overlapping intellectual circles. During the mid-1930s, both participated in a highly selective, informal study group organized by the art historian Meyer Schapiro. On March 8, 1935 Schapiro invited Barr to take part in the group, proposing an outline of its goals and a potential list of its membership:

> Would you be interested in the formation of a group for the discussion of modern, and especially contemporary, art? It would consist of several scholars and writers, meeting informally once a month in New York. I have in mind the following persons—yourself, Sweeney, Panofsky, Goldwater, Jerome Klein, myself, Tselos, Lozowick, Abbot, and others whom you might suggest. Mumford would probably be interested, and

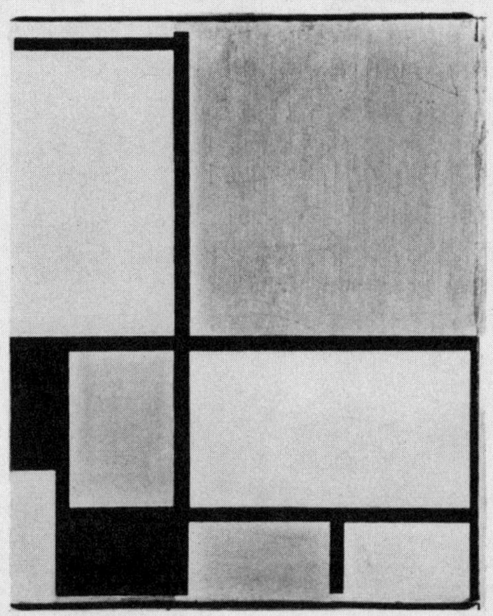

PLATE XV. PIET MONDRIAN, "COMPOSITION," 1921

8.2. Piet Mondrian, *Composition with Large Red Plane, Blue, Gray, Black and Yellow*, 1921, oil on canvas. Image: James Johnson Sweeney, *Plastic Redirections in 20th-Century Painting* (Chicago: University of Chicago Press, 1934). Image © 2004 Mondrian/Holtzman Trust, c/o *hcr@hrcinternational.com*.

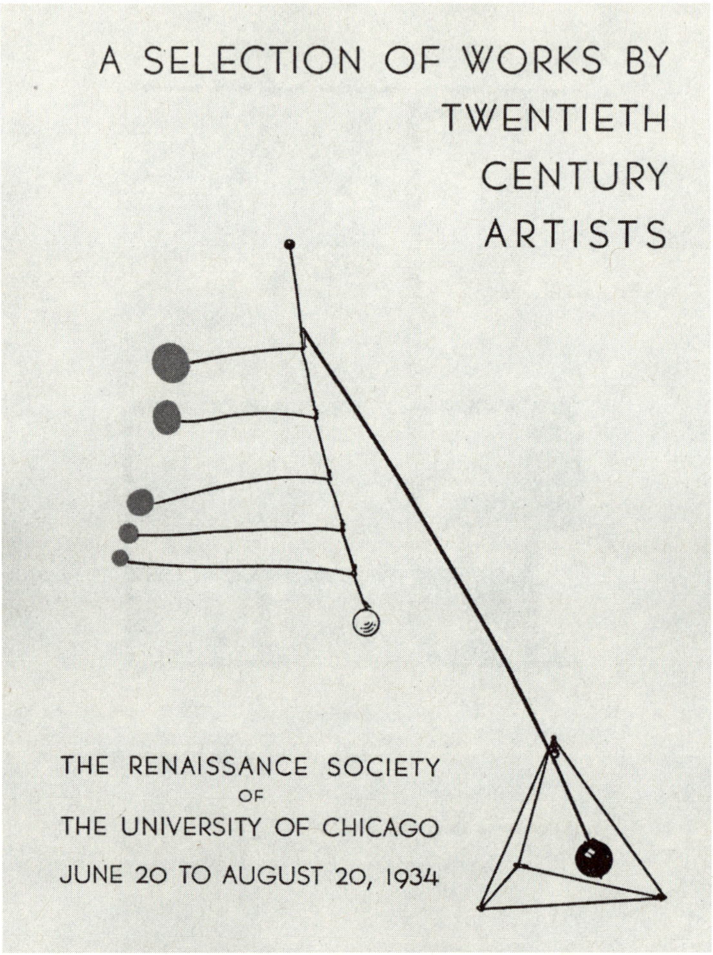

8.3. Alexander Calder, *Object with Red Disks*, 1932, appearing on the cover of E. W. Schütze, *A Selection of Works by Twentieth-Century Artists* (Chicago: Renaissance Society of the University of Chicago, 1934). © 2004 Estate of Alexander Calder/Artists Rights Society (ARS), New York.

> there are perhaps several people in Philadelphia and New Haven who might be desirable members of such a group. The number should be sufficiently small to permit informal discussion, and large enough to produce variety of opinion and alert criticism. Papers would be read and submitted for discussion, or an informal talk on a general question of common interest would open a discussion. Tell me if you are sufficiently interested to wish to participate in such a group.[9]

Three days later Barr not only responded positively to Schapiro's invitation, but he offered to make the facilities of the Museum of Modern Art available as a host location for the gatherings. As Barr told Schapiro: "I think that if the meeting were held in the evening I could offer the Museum Library as a place. It has a very large oval table about which we could sit and its location might be conveniently between uptown and downtown. Books in the Library would, of course, be immediately available."[10]

In addition to this intellectual forum, during the mid-1930s Sweeney also had a pedagogical framework available for the expression of his modernist ideas through the graduate courses he taught at New York University's Institute of Fine Arts.[11] Sweeney's course, "Tendencies in Modern Art," offered twice from 1934 to 1936,

> considers from a plastic point of view and in their relationships to the society and culture of the period those directives in painting which mark the first three decades of the twentieth century. The lectures begin with a brief consideration of the nineteenth-century background and a cursory résumé of the developments in painting that led up to Impressionism. The plastic approach of Impressionism and those movements immediately succeeding it will be analyzed. The discussion will consider the work of Cézanne and Van Gogh, the theories of Serusier, and of the "Symbolists" and the "Art Nouveau" and "Jugendstil" groups as well as the art of primitive peoples, in its influence on and importance for twentieth-century painters up to Fauvism. Such phases of twentieth-century development as cubism, futurism, dada, neoplasticism, expressionism, constructivism, Superrealism, the "new romanticism," and the "new objectivism" will be studied in relation to the general social and cultural character of the period.[12]

The following year he participated in a team-taught course that examined "Aspects of Modern Art" from the 1890s to the present; Sweeney's portion of the class was devoted to developments in recent painting.[13] Significantly, the audience for Sweeney's class extended directly to Barr himself. In a letter to Sweeney dated September 11, 1934, Barr told Sweeney that "Marga [his wife] looks forward to attending your course at New York University. I hope I can join her."[14]

In his graduate courses at New York University, Sweeney followed much the same historical and interpretive trajectory that he outlined in *Plastic Redirections in 20th-Century Painting*. In the book, Sweeney not only established an evolutionary formal model for tracking the plastic sequence in modernism; he simultaneously associated contemporary artistic developments with a corresponding conception of modernist subjectivity that placed a dual emphasis on intuitive psychic energies and plastic formal organization, on atavistic archaism and innovative modernist renewal. In so doing, Sweeney situated the development of modernist painting within a paradoxical framework that was based on the integration of a series of collapsed dualisms, as modern artworks were described as complementary embodiments of matter and spirit, subjectivity and objectivity, instinctive emotion and structural balance, masculine virility and formal abstraction. And just as these terms were applied to works of visual art, the artworks themselves became characterized as "subjective representation[s] by plastic means,"[15] and thus, as symbolic expressions of the creative subjectivities who produced them.

At the very outset of *Plastic Redirections*, Sweeney invoked the language of zeitgeist by asserting that the twentieth century has been characterized by "a revision of spiritual values," a tendency that "is especially evident in the plastic arts" (3). Sweeney anchored this theme in dramatic images of historical disjunction and organic renewal. While the nineteenth century saw the ascendancy of science, reason, and Cartesian philosophy, the twentieth century required a "complete severance from all the dominant trends of the preceding century—a break and a new beginning. It was realized that a new epoch could grow only out of a new archaism. The surface soil had become exhausted. It had to be turned deeply and completely to produce anything young in vigor or sap"(3). At the conclusion of this essay, Sweeney extended this theme by advocating an instinctive, almost primordial mode of expression in the visual arts:

> The final years of the nineteenth century marked the close of the rationalistic era. In it, art had been conceived as a rational ideal—a painful striving toward intellectual perfection. The period ended with an acute consciousness of its own sterility. To the future, it offered no illusions, no hopes, no creeds. The twentieth century has been characterized by a

gradual return to origins, to a new archaism—a prelogical mode of expression—to art as something necessary and organic: a vital element in the world about us, not merely a reflection of it. (35)

Thus in *Plastic Redirections* Sweeney self-consciously addressed the current perception of modern art's relationship to its times. Situating modernist aesthetic production within an overarching narrative that contrasted the outdated propensities toward rationalist sterility with the unfolding, vital promise of archaistic renewal, Sweeney established the specific positions of the various avant-garde movements. He wrote that in response to a sense of disenchantment with Impressionism's "disinfected scientific documentation," the Post-Impressionists cultivated instead "a return to structural interests in painting." This could be seen in the pronounced pictorial emphasis that Cézanne placed on the geometrical forms that he perceived as underlying natural objects (4, 7). According to Sweeney, "It was this that made Cézanne so popular when the Cubists were feeling their way back to structure by analytical methods" (9). Yet this emphasis on structure, geometry, and analytical reasoning represented only a portion of the modernists' pictorial innovations; another crucial component lay in the artists' exploration of the instinctive and emotional qualities of non-Western art. Sweeney wrote that, in addition to Cézanne, the Cubists' structural analyses of pictorial forms were also shaped by Seurat's "intuition of formal relationships" (10). Yet while Seurat's followers became mired in "pseudo-scientific color experimentation," Gauguin "point[ed] the way out" by "submit[ing] readily to the influences of the Orient" (11). Sweeney wrote that Gauguin's practice initiated "a new plastic direction" that Matisse subsequently pursued through his "frank profession of the major tenets of oriental plasticism" and his emphasis on "the purely decorative function of painting" (12, 14). As a result, modern European art became infused with vitality through its contact with the imagery of non-Western cultures. In both African sculpture and in the paintings of Matisse and Picasso, Sweeney perceived similar subjective and emotional responses embedded within tightly crafted architectonic compositions, just as the artists' intuitive impulses ostensibly guided the formal processes of pictorial organization.

In particular, Sweeney found such "intensity of visualization" "in primitive Negro art." He reproduced in *Plastic Redirections* an African copper, brass, and wood ancestor figure that Barr subsequently exhibited in the *Cubism and Abstract Art* show (fig. 8.4). In such "primitive" sculpture and in abstract modernist paintings, the viewer encountered "the same scrupulous craftsmanship, the same sensibility to plastic fundamentals, and the same intu-

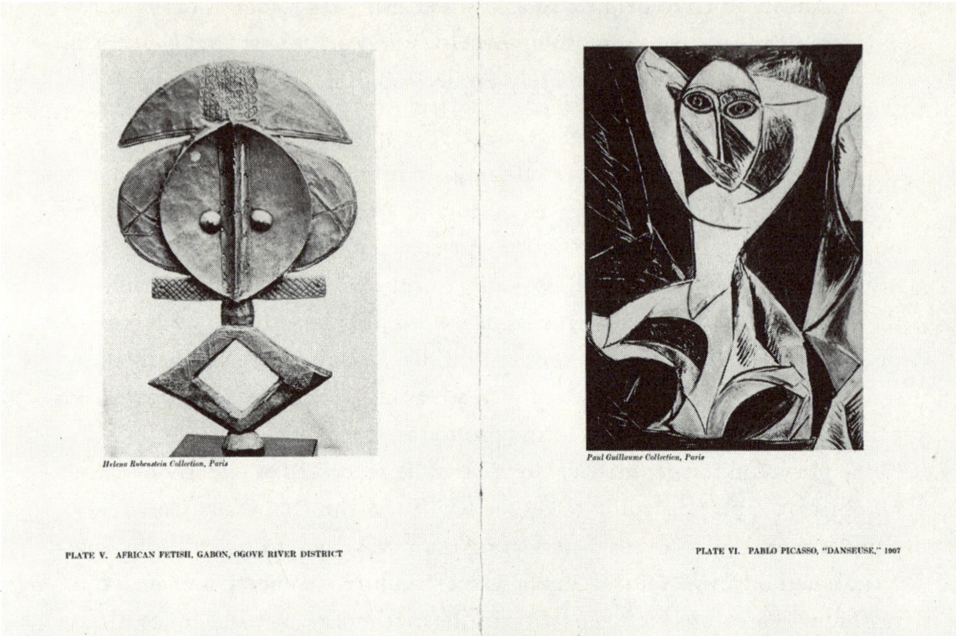

8.4. Reliquary figure, Kota, Gabon, or People's Republic of the Congo, wood, copper, and brass; and Pablo Picasso, *Danseuse* [The dancer], 1907, oil on canvas. Images: James Johnson Sweeney, *Plastic Redirections in 20th-Century Painting* (Chicago: University of Chicago Press, 1934). © 2004 Estate of Pablo Picasso/Artists Rights Society (ARS), New York.

itive interest in the architectonic interplay of abstract forms" (17). Sweeney further noted that the influence of African sculpture extended from the German Expressionist paintings of the Brücke group to Picasso's proto-Cubist experimental figures, such as *Danseuse* (The dancer) of 1907 (see fig. 8.4). Significantly, Picasso's *Danseuse* was reproduced in both *Plastic Redirections* and in *Cubism and Abstract Art*, where it was similarly juxtaposed with an image of an African copper and wood reliquary figure.[16] Sweeney's comparative allusion to Picasso in *Plastic Redirections* was meant to demonstrate the extent to which "the Negro image-maker intuitively resolved his volumes into their constituent elements, with every inessential shorn away. Nevertheless, the whole was held in an architectonic unity by the artist's single-minded intensity of emotion."[17] Thus in African sculpture and in archaistic examples of European modernism, Sweeney identified a similar synthesis of aesthetic and subjective qualities that encompassed intuition, emotion, and rational structural clarity.

Once the European modernists had internalized the powerful example of African art, the next step in their developmental trajectory entailed the rejection of naturalistic reproduction. According to Sweeney, this step was realized in Picasso's and Braque's analytical Cubist experiments of 1909, which displayed "a sort of mosaic of such perspective 'boxes' or areas, more or less fused—their organization based solely on formal or chromatic relationships" (23). Such progressive formal simplification of elemental pictorial units subsequently led to "a new sense of clean surfaces and a plastic organization stripped of all extra-plastic, sensuous, or associational charms." For Sweeney, the final turn in the modernist narrative entailed a shift in emphasis away from the external world and toward the internal one: "Only one further step now remained: to carry the integrity of the plastic conception, out of the objective, into the subjective." In the art of the Surrealists, particularly Chirico, Ernst, Arp, and Klee, Sweeney identified "the magic realism of the dream-world" (30). He found comparable, albeit pictorially distinct, examples of such complete artistic freedom in the stark planar simplicity of the de Stijl group's imagery, such as Mondrian's *Composition with Large Red Plane, Blue, Gray, Black and Yellow* of 1921 (see fig. 8.2)—a work from Sweeney's personal art collection that was illustrated in both *Plastic Redirections* and *Cubism and Abstract Art*. Sweeney likewise praised Miró's fantastic, lyrical paintings, images in which "no intellectual control whatsoever seems to come between the artist's free intuitional response to his materials and the plastic result" (35).[18] One such example can be found in Miró's *Composition* of 1933, a dialogical, biomorphic abstraction that was exhibited both in Sweeney's 1934 show at the Renaissance Society and, two and a half years later, in Barr's ground-breaking exhibition *Fantastic Art, Dada, Surrealism* (Museum of Modern Art, 1936–37). Following the latter show, Sweeney acquired this painting from the Pierre Matisse Gallery for his own personal art collection.[19]

The idealized conception of modernist identity that Sweeney described in *Plastic Redirections* was an implicitly gendered one, as all of the artists discussed in the study were male. And if there were any question about the gendering of this artistic construction, the masculinist associations of these themes became explicit both in the Renaissance Society's exhibition catalogue and in a related article that Sweeney published in *The New Republic* (April 10, 1935). When critiquing the pervasive tendency toward naturalism in the visual arts, Sweeney observed: "Nature, as Nietzsche warned us she would, has taken her revenge on us for disregarding the myth, for allowing it to decline to a 'fairy-tale,' for not bringing it back to virility. In short, for 'the abstract character of our mythless existence.' Esthetically we have become a dry, colorless people . . . our art has decayed either into a hackneyed academicism, or an illustrational attitudinizing, both finally dependent on technical virtuosities." In order to transcend this state of cultural "decadence" and achieve the restoration of "virility," it is necessary to "learn to see with young eyes to respect the intensity of intuitions."[20] In a slightly later piece published in *The New Republic*, Sweeney remarked that

> men like Matisse, Braque, Vlaminck and Derain in the opening years of the century were looking to all sides for a suggestion toward some idiom in which to assert their protest against academicism and impressionism other than in the emasculate decorative tradition of Serusier, Denis and Signac. The expressionistic as well as the more strictly formal sides of primitive art appealed to them as in keeping with [the] formal and expressionistic sides of their so-classed 'Fauve' work of the same period.[21]

Thus by rejecting the "emasculated" decorative qualities of their European counterparts and productively embracing the vital example of "primitive art," the Fauves found an "antidote for the weakness of our esthetic expression" that fostered the production of "exquisite sensibility and creative genius."[22]

As these quotations exemplify, the term "decorative" functioned as an ambivalent signifier in Sweeney's writings. Just as Sweeney praised Matisse's emphasis on "the purely decorative function of painting," he subsequently critiqued what he perceived to be the Nabis's "emasculate decorative" tendency toward superfluous ornamentation devoid of underlying structural depth. Yet whether the decorative was assigned a positive or a negative valuation, in all instances the term was deployed to reinforce a particular formalist conception of masculine creativity. Indeed, the discursive production of gendered modernism in both Sweeney's and Barr's texts was achieved precisely through such placement and displacement of key descriptive terminology.[23]

Following his exhibition at the Renaissance Society in 1934, Sweeney's next major show, *African Negro Art*, was held at the Museum of Modern Art during the spring of 1935. Sweeney served as the director of the exhibition and as the author of the accompanying catalogue and of a related promotional article in *The New Republic* (April 10, 1935).[24] In both the essay and the catalogue, Sweeney emphasized the "essential plastic qualities" of African sculpture and their generative influence on such modernist painters as Picasso, the members of the German Brücke group, and the Fauves.[25] When discussing the significance that African art held for a contemporary American audience, Sweeney remarked: "It is the vitality of the forms of Negro art, that should speak to us, the simplification without impoverishment, the unerring emphasis on the essential, the consistent, three-dimensional organization of structural planes in architectonic sequences, the uncompromising truth to material with a seemingly intuitive adaptation of it, and the tension achieved between the idea or emotion to be expressed through representation and the abstract principles of sculpture."[26] While emphasizing the formal, plastic appeal of African sculpture's abstract structures, Sweeney also commented on their special shamanic qualities and magical functions. In addition to objects produced for the practices of ancestor worship (such as in fig. 8.4), the Museum of Modern Art show also included fetish objects that assisted in promoting an "animistic" connection between the human and divine realms, as "trees, streams, rocks, even animals, take the character of minor supernatural forces and have their cults celebrated by rituals in which sculptured masks and fetishes play an important part."[27] Sweeney further pointed out that many of the ritual objects displayed in the show were associated with the processes of healing, fertility, conjuration, and other magical and protective functions. Placing a dual emphasis on the formal and spiritual properties of these objects, Sweeney wrote that "what is finest in African art was intimately bound up with religion," just as for the Cubists, the Fauves, and the German Brücke group the value of these works lay in their powerful expressionistic and formal qualities.[28] As we have seen, in *Plastic Redirections* Sweeney advanced just such a formalist interpretive model to emphasize the expressive, vital, and spiritual qualities that he perceived in modern European artworks.

In *Cubism and Abstract Art*, Barr similarly proposed a progressive teleological model for the development of modern art. Viewed historically, Barr's catalogue proved to be so appealing in part because it offered a clear, chronologically organized, schematic overview of the various movements of modern art, a complex subject that still lacked just such conceptual clarity for many contemporary viewers. Like *Plastic Redirections*, *Cubism and Abstract Art* also offered its readers something more—namely, a parallel theorization of modernist aesthetics and subjectivity. This complementary interpretive structure becomes evident in the important transitional section of Barr's text that appeared at the conclusion of his introductory discussion of modernism and just prior to his in-depth analysis of its specific artistic movements. At this crucial interpretive juncture, Barr presented his vision of the "two main traditions of Abstract Art." Barr's analysis deserves to be quoted in its entirety:

> At the risk of grave oversimplification the impulse towards abstract art during the past fifty years may be divided historically into two main currents, both of which emerged from Impressionism. The first and more important current finds its sources in the art and theories of Cézanne and Seurat, passes through the widening stream of Cubism and

> finds its delta in the various geometrical and Constructivist movements which developed in Russia and Holland during the War and have since spread throughout the World. This current may be described as intellectual, structural, architectonic, geometrical, rectilinear and classical in its austerity and dependence upon logic and calculation. The second—and, until recently, secondary—current has its principal source in the art and theories of Gauguin and his circle, flows through the *Fauvisme* of Matisse to the Abstract Expressionism of the pre-War paintings of Kandinsky. After running under ground for a few years it reappears vigorously among the masters of abstract art associated with Surrealism. This tradition, by contrast with the first, is intuitional and emotional rather than intellectual; organic or biomorphic rather than geometrical in its forms; curvilinear rather than rectilinear, decorative rather than structural, and romantic rather than classical in its exaltation of the mystical, the spontaneous and the irrational. Apollo, Pythagoras and Descartes watch over the Cézanne-Cubist-geometrical tradition; Dionysus (an Asiatic god), Plotinus and Rousseau over the Gauguin-Expressionist-non-geometrical line.[29]

After establishing the thematic and stylistic parameters of these "two main currents," Barr conceded that "often, of course, these two currents intermingle and they may both appear in one man."[30] Yet after acknowledging this intertwining, Barr returned to his previous dialectical formulation, as he placed the central formations of modernism—its rigid geometry and its primordial organicism—in a state of mutual stylistic opposition in which "the shape of the square confronts the silhouette of the amoeba."[31]

As these passages reveal, one of the most suggestive ways in which Barr established a dialogical aesthetic and subjective framework for modern art was by drawing on a Nietzschean-inflected critical discourse that contrasted Apollonian and Dionysian art forms. In *The Birth of Tragedy* (1871), Friedrich Nietzsche identified the classical gods Apollo and Dionysus as two dominant typological embodiments of the "mystical doctrines of art."[32] Nietzsche wrote that Apollo is associated with conceptions of tranquility, morality, control, order, rationality, restraint, wisdom, light, philosophical interpretation, and cognitive power. In contrast, Dionysus is linked to enchantment, awe, intoxication, emotion, extravagance, excess, rapture, organicism, pantheism, passion, imagination, freedom, and the glorious transports of mystical ecstasy. While both gods were personified as male deities, Dionysus is directly associated with phallic power through the symbols carried in his ceremonial festival processions. In *Cubism and Abstract Art*, Barr identified Dionysian mystical and ecstatic energies as being evident in the curvilinear, decorative, organic, biomorphic forms of "non-geometrical abstract art." In contrast, he characterized architectonic, classical, Apollonian elements as the bases for "geometrical abstract art."[33]

Although they were positioned as contrasting elements, these dualistic qualities became productively synthesized within the overall structures of Barr's theoretical model. This occurred in two ways. As Barr himself acknowledged, in certain instances these two stylistic "currents intermingle" and may "appear in one man." Barr identified just such a porousness of categorical boundaries in the works of Picasso, Mondrian, the Bauhaus artists, Kandinsky, Picabia, Duchamp, Arp, and Calder.[34] Yet another highly suggestive way in which the distinctive strands of Barr's theoretical model became productively conjoined was in the overall structures of his flowchart. Prima facie, Barr's chart appears to be a rather rigid linear document fixed in its classifications. Yet the flowchart is built on the contradictory premise of a dualism that is, ultimately, unstable. It posits an ideal, organic sense of unity even as it overtly displays the patterns of its own internal disjunctions. When viewed as a whole, a series of categorical differentiations *and* generative interconnections becomes evident between the rational and spiritual domains of modernist aesthetics, between austere logical calculation and intuitive imagination, and between sublimated intellectual theorization and passionate organic vitality. The result is a highly ambivalent sense of duality *and* of the reconciliation of duality within both Nietzsche's and Barr's typological formulations of masculine creativity, and in the organizing taxonomic structures of canonical modernist art history itself.[35]

An idealized conception of gendered subjectivity is also clearly at stake in Sweeney's and Barr's visions of modernism. Not only did their critical models apply almost exclusively to male artists, but in their writings modern art itself was constructed as a kind of symbolic masculine presence whose generative qualities were hyperbolically differentiated yet dualistically synthesized in the production of a vital, "virile" new art.[36] For both writers, this interpretive process specifically entailed a deep intertwining of ambivalent aesthetic categories that attached a heightened cultural value to the masculine subject position.[37] Throughout Sweeney's and Barr's writings, these thematic structures encompassed notions of the rational and the mystical, the modern and the primitive, reason and passion, abstraction and organicism, the analytical and the spontaneous, intellect and emotion, formal purity and physical sensuousness. Through the sustained discursive efforts of their writings, Sweeney and Barr actively dislodged associations that had previously been ascribed to the feminine subject position in order to recuperate these qualities within a revised, and powerfully paradoxical, conception of modern masculine subjectivity. As such, the new typological model of the male artist was one that successfully managed to merge and to separate these ambivalent gendered qualities. However, such a dialogical formulation of masculine creativity left little space for modern female artists.[38] Indeed, the great success of Sweeney's and Barr's aesthetic models seemed to be based in part on the displacement of the feminine so that a range of traditionally masculine *and* feminine qualities could be absorbed within an expanded conception of masculine subjectivity.[39]

Given their shared intellectual pursuits and the prominent historical roles that Sweeney and Barr played as active creators of the modernist canon, it is not surprising that *Plastic Redirections* and *Cubism and Abstract Art* generated notably similar responses from their critical reviewers. In a discussion of *Plastic Redirections* in the *New York Times* (August 26, 1934), Sweeney was praised for "present[ing] his argument in a scholarly fashion, carefully annotated and documented. A valuable feature of the book (whose first edition, we learn, was virtually sold out before the work went to press) is a set of biographical notes, which should prove extremely convenient for reference."[40] Writing in the *Chicago Daily Tribune* (August 25, 1934), the curator Daniel Catton Rich similarly noted that *Plastic Redirections* "is packed with original thought, clear in its expression, and level in its judgments."[41] Barry Byrne of *Commonweal* (November 23, 1934) enthusiastically endorsed "the culture and detachment with which the work is assayed. With the publication of these lectures comes the promise of a continued appearance of thoroughgoing art criticism allied to a distinctive literary style."[42] Yet as positive as these reviews are, the most important intellectual endorsement that Sweeney received came from the eminent art historian Erwin Panofsky, another proposed member of Schapiro's reading group. Writing in *The Bulletin of the Museum of Modern Art* (November 1934), Panofsky praised *Plastic Redirections* as "one of the few attempts at approaching the problems of contemporary art from the standpoint of scholarly art history." He proceeded to note: "Mr. Sweeney, combining detachment with subjectivity, has now proved that it is, after all, possible to apply the methods of art-history to contemporary art."[43] As the critical reception of *Plastic Redirections* clearly indicates, during the 1930s Sweeney was able to promote a powerfully ambivalent discourse that seamlessly conjoined the dignified professionalism and erudition of his interpretive approach with the cultural cachet of modernist aesthetics and the liberating promise of intuitive, archaistic impulses. Even if critics did not fully restate Sweeney's position in their reviews, they implicitly supported his message through the positive reception of the text.[44]

Similar rhetoric recurred two years later in the critical reception of Barr's *Cubism and Abstract Art.* In an extended appreciation of the text in the *New York Times* (June 7, 1936), Edward Alden Jewell observed that Barr's catalogue "represents a work of permanent value within its field, especially as a volume for source references. Mr. Barr, in his always painstaking manner, has gone into this subject with thoroughness, providing a general survey of the still controversial movement itself and engaging in documented consideration of artist protagonists who may be esteemed of major and minor importance to the modern movement's growth."[45] Barr's study was similarly praised in *Commonweal* for its careful enumeration of the various classificatory categories of modern art, which lead the reviewer to characterize Barr himself as performing the quasi-divine act of evolving "beauty and the splendor of order" out of "ugliness" and "chaos."[46] Notably, the one rigorous challenge that Barr received to *Cubism and Abstract Art* came from within his own contemporary intellectual circle. Writing in *Marxist Quarterly* (January-March 1937), Meyer Schapiro drew on Barr's canonical leitmotifs in order to call his theorization of modernism into question. Schapiro pointedly emphasized the necessity of historicizing abstract art rather than presenting modernism as an aestheticized expression of pure form.[47] Schapiro insightfully remarked that coextensive with Barr's conception of formalist aesthetics is a preoccupation with primitive society and collective spiritual life. Noting pronounced shifts in the historical valuation of this material, Schapiro observed: "What was once considered monstrous, now became pure form and pure expression, the aesthetic evidence that in art feeling and thought are prior to the represented world. The art of the whole world was now available on a single unhistorical and universal plane as a panorama of the formalizing energies of man."[48] As a result, "in the distorted, fantastic figures [of primitive art] some groups of modern artists found an intimate kinship with their own work. . . . The highest praise of their own work is to describe it in the language of magic and fetishism."[49] Anticipating postcolonial critical discourses, Schapiro argued that such assertions overlooked the historical relationship between the development of modern art and the workings of "colonial imperialism," particularly its economic and cultural exploitation of "subjugated peoples."[50] Ultimately, Schapiro criticized Barr's conclusion that "by a remarkable process the arts of subjugated backward peoples, discovered by Europeans in conquering the world, became aesthetic norms to those who renounced it. The imperialist expansion was accompanied at home by a profound cultural pessimism in which the arts of the savage victims were elevated above the traditions of Europe. The colonies became places to flee to as well as to exploit."[51] Thus, just as Sweeney's and Barr's dialogical constructions of modern masculine subjectivity combined qualities traditionally associated with masculine and feminine subject positions, Schapiro similarly reconstructed the ways in which a parallel occurred through the modernists' appropriation of the subjective qualities associated with subjugated, colonized peoples.

As we have seen, Sweeney and Barr perceived a multifaceted conception of modernist subjectivity as being visibly evident in the formal structures of modernist artworks. As such, the artistic *objects* displayed in their exhibitions became symbolically invested with *subjective* human attributes. In the process, Sweeney and Barr established a further philosophical resonance between canonical modernism and shamanic magic, as they formulated an alternative conception of modernist subjectivity that collapsed modern and premodern perspectives. One of the central characteristics of shamanic objects is the notion that supernatural beings can inhabit their physical structures—or the idea that "the spirits may also take temporary abode in certain inanimate objects," thereby establishing a fluid sense of reciprocity between the material and spiritual domains.[52] The philosopher Charles Taylor has located such beliefs within a premodern worldview, since "the boundary between the psychic and the physical [worlds] had not yet been sharply drawn"; instead, they remained suggestively open, a perspective that "made possible a serious belief in magic."[53] Sweeney identified one such example of premodern magical structures in the practices of ancestor worship associated with the African reliquary guardian figure that he reproduced in *Plastic Redirections* and in *African Negro Art*, a work that Barr also exhibited in *Cubism and Abstract Art* (see fig. 8.4). When discussing this and other similar objects, Sweeney observed that "ancestor-worship is elaborated primarily among peoples who through seeing men wielding great power in this world come to feel that the souls of the great should still be powerful after death. This is the cult that in many regions of Africa has been productive of the finest sculpture, not only through symbolizing the dead as in the stylized burial fetishes of the Ogove River district in Congo (Nos. 378–387), but also through actual portraits."[54] Just as Sweeney was aware of the magical functions that such objects performed as mediators connecting the world of the living with the spirits of the dead, Barr too drew on the suggestive notion that the presence of powerful guardian figures—from Apollo, Pythagoras, and Descartes to Dionysus, Plotinus, and Rousseau—became intrinsically associated with works of modern art.

Significantly, Sweeney's and Barr's interpretive strategies are consistent with the various meanings associated with the term "canon." According to the *Oxford English Dictionary*, the multiple definitions of the word encompass the designation of consecrated persons and authentic and sacred texts, as well as the rational, systematic classification of knowledge.[55] As a result, canonical processes of ritual sanctification *and* of intellectual codification connote a privileged sense of cultural authority. In so doing, the definitional boundaries between sacred subjects, intellectual codes and practices, and broader accounts of social and cultural values become so fragile—both for Barr and Sweeney, but also within the creation of the modernist canon itself—that they collapse entirely, leaving these interpretive categories not merely coextensive, but mutually entwined in their significations.

The paradoxes embedded in Sweeney's and Barr's modernist narratives can be located within larger dialogical patterns that thread through modern intellectual history, from Nietzsche to Freud to Weber.[56] As these writers have famously observed, just as the demands of modernity placed a privileged emphasis on rationality, progress, reason, discipline, and control, a counter-discourse advocated instead an alternative conception of ideal subjective authenticity that was associated with notions of personal liberation, uninhibited self-expression, and individual autonomy. Thus in different yet complementary ways, Sweeney's and Barr's texts addressed precisely the long-standing relationship between the conflicting anxieties and desires of modernist subjectivity. Both writers drew on and actively constructed a common corpus of artistic imagery—the canon of modern art—as they rehearsed the familiar tropes of modernism's oppositional dualisms and offered potential solutions to the conflicting impulses of modernist selfhood. In so doing, the discourses they advanced in *Plastic Redirections* and in *Cubism and Abstract Art* posited a conceptual model in which works of art could serve as visual analogues of modernist subjectivity itself, as impelled by its own highly ambivalent, reciprocal capacity and desire for dualism and for integration. Thus, whether tracking the plastic sequence of modern art in *Plastic Redirections* or diagrammatically charting its trajectories in *Cubism and Abstract Art*, Sweeney and Barr mapped a territory that at once designated patterns of artistic form and states of subjective consciousness.

As prominent cultural mediators *and* active creators of the modernist canon, Sweeney and Barr moved fluidly between the domains of avant-garde modernism and archetypal primitivism, between the specialized world of scholarly discourse and a broader engagement with an educated general public. Just as they cultivated the dignified bearing of their professional identities—personas that served them well within the context of New York's elite culture—both men worked dynamically between the intellectual rationalism of their analytical methodologies and the transformative capacities and magical qualities of modernist aesthetics. In so doing, they created texts in which the intellectual and mystical domains remained territorially distinct even as they productively converged to form a multidimensional modality and composite mode of consciousness. The resulting vision of modern art was also an idealized vision of the modern self, a subject who was multiple and yet unbroken.

Notes

Many individuals offered valuable assistance in assembling the primary archival materials that are foundational to this essay. I would like to thank Edwina Ashie-Nikoi, the archival assistant at the New York University Archives; Jon Evans of the Hirsch Library, Museum of Fine Arts, Houston; Randolph Tibbits of the Fondren Library, Rice University; and Kathleen Tunney, the assistant to the Library and Museum Archives at the Museum of Modern Art. Heather Schweikhardt expertly produced several of the photographs that accompany this essay. I am also grateful to Jenny Anger, Hajime Nakatani, and Caroline Quenemoen for their close readings and insightful comments on this essay, and to Anna Brzyski for her generous invitation to participate in *Partisan Canons*.

1 Regarding Barr's flowchart, see Kantor, *Alfred H. Barr, Jr. and the Intellectual Origins of the Museum of Modern Art*. For additional discussions of *Cubism and Abstract Art*, see Marquis, *Alfred H. Barr Jr.*, 150–56; and Sandler's introduction to Sandler and Newman, *Defining Modern Art*, especially 22–27.

2 Regarding these discourses, see Robert Rosenblum, Foreword, 3–4; Pollock, *Vision and Difference*, 50–51; and Mitchell, "*Ut Pictura Theoria*," 366, 367.

3 Regarding the categorical relations between modernism and postmodernism, see also Berger, *Postmodernism*; and the introduction to Brennan, *Modernism's Masculine Subjects*.

4 Sweeney would later briefly become the director of the museum's Department of Painting and Sculpture from January 1945 until November 1946. Sweeney's appointment was announced in *The Bulletin of the Museum of Modern Art* 12 (January 1945): 20; his resignation from this position, which was precipitated by a new administrative structure that placed limitations on his authority, was noted in *The Bulletin of the Museum of Modern Art* 14 (fall 1946).

5 Barr, *Cubism and Abstract Art*, 7–8.

6 Sweeney's and Barr's correspondence of the 1930s can be found in the Alfred H. Barr Jr. Papers of the Museum of Modern Art.

7 See Joosten, *Piet Mondrian*, 2:163, 292–93. This painting was one of four works by Mondrian that Sweeney would eventually own.

8 In the Renaissance Society exhibition catalogue, this work is listed as *Object with Red Disks* and dated 1931. Sweeney acquired the sculpture directly from Calder some time

after the Renaissance Society's exhibition. For provenance information on this work, see *Property from the Estate of the Late James Johnson Sweeney*, item #1, n.p.

9 Meyer Schapiro to Alfred H. Barr Jr., March 8, 1935, in the Alfred H. Barr Jr. Papers [AAA: 2165; 981], The Museum of Modern Art Archives, New York.

10 Alfred H. Barr Jr. to Meyer Schapiro, March 11, 1935, in the Alfred H. Barr Jr. Papers [AAA: 2165; 980], The Museum of Modern Art Archives, New York.

11 In the biographical entry for *Who's Who in American Art*, Sweeney is listed as holding a visiting lecturer position at New York University's Institute of Fine Arts until 1940. See Gilbert, *Who's Who in American Art*, 415.

12 This course description appears in the *New York University Graduate School of Arts and Science Bulletin* (1934–35), New York University Archives, 88.

13 This course description appears in the *New York University Graduate School of Arts and Science Bulletin* (1936–37), New York University Archives, 99.

14 Alfred H. Barr Jr. to James Johnson Sweeney, September 11, 1934, in the Alfred H. Barr Jr. Papers [AAA: 2165; 582], The Museum of Modern Art Archives, New York. Notably, in the spring of 1927 Barr had taught an art history class at Wellesley College that examined the development of modern art from nineteenth century painting through the influence that "primitive and barbaric art" exerted on contemporary visual production. See Kantor, *Alfred H. Barr, Jr.*, 103–4.

15 Sweeney, *Plastic Redirections in 20th-Century Painting*, 75.

16 Just as Sweeney juxtaposed images of the African reliquary figure with Picasso's *Danseuse* on facing pages of *Plastic Redirections*, William Rubin also juxtaposed illustrations of these same works on facing pages of his essay on Picasso in W. Rubin, *"Primitivism" in 20th-Century Art*, 1:268–69. For a critical discussion of this exhibition see note 23 below. Regarding the recurrence of this imagery in *Cubism and Abstract Art*, see Barr, *Cubism and Abstract Art*, 32–33, figs. 13 and 14.

17 Sweeney, *Plastic Redirections*, 23.

18 Ibid., 35. Sweeney developed his multifaceted conception of modernism further in the final two sections of *Plastic Redirections*, "From This Side of 'Cubism'" and "Superrealism." A preliminary version of these ideas can also be found in his October 1933 essay "Painting," which was published in *Museum of Living Art*, n.p.

19 Information regarding the exhibition history and provenance of the Miró painting can be found in *Property from the Estate of the Late James Johnson Sweeney*, item #4, n.p. This painting is now in the collection of the Musée National d'Art Moderne, Centre Georges Pompidou, as Pierre Matisse donated the work to the French state in 1991. See Dupin, *Joan Miró*, 2:72.

20 Sweeney's statement, which was originally published in *Cahiers D'Art* (1932), was quoted at length in the foreword to Schütze, *A Selection of Works by Twentieth Century Artists*, n.p.

21 Sweeney, "African Negro Art," 244.

22 Ibid., 244. For critical discussions of the gendered implications of the modernists' engagement with primitivism, see Steiner, *Venus in Exile*; and Chave, "New Encounters with *Les Demoiselles d'Avignon*," 597–611.

23 For a gendered theorization of the decorative in the art of Paul Klee, see Anger, *Paul Klee and the Decorative in Modern Art*.

24 For a review of this catalogue, see Mather, "The New Books," 25. For notices of this exhibition and related period commentary, see *The Bulletin of the Museum of Modern Art* 5 and 6–7 (February 1935 and March-April 1935).

25 In his critical response to the highly controversial exhibition *"Primitivism" in the 20th Century* (Museum of Modern Art, 1984), Hal Foster commented on the various ways in which the discourses of primitivism have been deployed to support the patriarchal project of modern Western culture. See Foster, "The 'Primitive' Unconscious of Modern Art," 58–70. Regarding primitivism's long-standing association with Western colonial practices, see also Nelson and Shiff, *Critical Terms for Art History*, 1st ed., 170–84. For a historical overview of the cultural debates surrounding primitivism, see the introduction to Flam and Deutch, *Primitivism and Twentieth-Century Art*, 1–22.

26 Sweeney, *African Negro Art*, 21.

27 Ibid., 19.

28 Sweeney, "African Negro Art," 244.

29 Barr, *Cubism and Abstract Art*, 19.

30 Ibid.

31 Ibid. Regarding the ambivalent nature of Barr's aesthetic interests, see Kantor, *Alfred H. Barr, Jr. and the Intellectual Origins of the Museum of Modern Art*, 120.

32 Nietzsche, *The Birth of Tragedy*, 19. Notably, despite their mutually distinct characteristics, both Apollo and Dionysus are deities associated with healing, prophecy, and fertility.

33 Barr, *Cubism and Abstract Art*, 19.

34 Regarding this stylistic intermingling, see Barr, *Cubism and Abstract Art*, 98, 142, 156, 172, 186, 190, 197.

35 During the following decade the critic Clement Greenberg would also draw on these Nietzschean signifiers in his discussion of modern art. It was precisely this contrasting yet complementary notion of Apollonian balance, classicism, and logic, coupled with a Dionysian sense of "great passion," that Greenberg referenced in his important critical essay "The Present Prospects of American Painting and Sculpture" (*Horizon*, October 1947). This essay is reproduced in Greenberg, *The Collected Essays and Criticism*, 2:160–70.

36 Notably, in Barr's *Cubism and Abstract Art* women artists are included in the sections on theater, typography, and posters. Although their works are not treated in the same level of detail as those of their male counterparts, Barr offers brief discussions of the female Russian modernists Lyubov Popova, Natalia Gonchorova, and Varvara Stepanova.

37 Regarding issues of interpretive valuation, see Connor, *Theory and Cultural Value*.

38 Regarding the displacement of the feminine in twentieth-century aesthetics, see Steiner, *Venus in Exile*, 32–71.

39 Jenny Anger's excellent comments were instrumental in helping me to develop the gendered implications of Sweeney's and Barr's interpretive positions.

40 "Modern 'Redirections,'" *New York Times* (August 26, 1934), 6x. Sweeney's text was awarded a second review in the *New York Times*; see Jewell, "New Books on the Arts," 21.

41 Daniel Catton Rich's review appeared in the *Chicago Daily Tribune* (August 25, 1934), 6.

42 Barry Byrne's review was published in *Commonweal* 21 (November 23, 1934), 125.

43 Panofsky, "Book Comment," 3.

44 Significantly, the one genuinely negative response to these themes came from Thomas Craven, a vociferously anti-modernist critic and partisan of the Regionalist painters Thomas Hart Benton and Grant Wood. Writing in *The Nation* (September 26, 1934), Craven dismissed Sweeney's book as an elitist "show of erudition," noting that "his tract is a museum dish for pallid aesthetes with no stomach for an art enriched by the impurities of the real world, a morsel of consolation for those whose convictions and investments are at stake." See Craven, "Art," 360. Regarding the tensions that played out during the 1930s between the critical proponents of modernism and the Regionalist artists and critics, see Brennan, *Painting Gender, Constructing Theory*, 202–31.

45 Jewell, "The Anatomy of Cubism and Abstract Art," 8.

46 This review appears in *Commonweal* 24 (July 3, 1936), 272.

47 Meyer Schapiro, "Nature of Abstract Art," originally published in *Marxist Quarterly* (January-March 1937), 77–98, and reprinted in Schapiro, *Modern Art, 19th and 20th Centuries*, 187. Regarding Schapiro's response to Barr, see Kantor, *Alfred H. Barr, Jr. and the Intellectual Origins of the Museum of Modern Art*, 328–31. Kantor also mentioned that Schapiro "served on the board of trustees of the Museum for a period" (451 n. 59).

48 Schapiro, *Modern Art, 19th and 20th Centuries*, 186.

49 Ibid., 200.

50 For a discussion of the Surrealist artists' protest of French colonial practices through their polemical exhibition *The Truth about the Colonies* (1931), see Mileaf, "Body to Politics," 239–54.

51 Schapiro, *Modern Art, 19th and 20th Centuries*, 201. It should be noted that, while Schapiro's revisionist critique has received significant scholarly attention, his commentary represented a reactive polemical response to the initial interpretive challenge Barr posed when he conspicuously contested Schapiro's interpretation of Cubism in the introductory section of the catalogue. See Barr, *Cubism and Abstract Art*, 15. Not surprisingly, after the publication of Schapiro's essay in *Marxist Quarterly*, the volume of personal correspondence that Barr and Schapiro exchanged during the 1930s dropped off sharply.

52 On this subject, see Schulz-Weidner, "Shamanism," 13:1.

53 C. Taylor, *Sources of the Self*, 191.

54 Sweeney, *African Negro Art*, 19. For a more extended discussion of these works, see Geoffroy-Schneiter, *Tribal Arts*.

55 See the entry for the term "canon" in Simpson and Weiner, *The Oxford English Dictionary*, 2:838.

56 In addition to Nietzsche's *The Birth of Tragedy*, an engagement with the ambivalent themes of modernity can be found in Sigmund Freud's *Three Essays on the Theory of Sexuality* (1905) and his *Civilization and Its Discontents* (1930); and in Max Weber's discussion of ideal social typologies in Runciman, *Max Weber*.

9

"Gardner" Variety Formalism: Helen Gardner and *Art through the Ages*

BARBARA JAFFEE

Love them or loathe them, art history survey texts are a staple of the discipline. Yet insofar as they define simultaneously the subject area and the method—the "what" *and* the "how"—of art history, survey texts also are places where debates over the formation of art historical canons are most visible. *Gardner's Art through the Ages*, for years the traditional alternative to the dynamic but highly subjective and personalized text *History of Art* (written by Horst W. Janson and first published in 1962), hardly seems the stuff of controversy. The book probably enters the collective memory of American art history students with its fifth edition, revised in 1970 by Horst de la Croix and Richard G. Tansey. But its real story—and thus its interest for an anthology organized around the idea of partisanship and canon formation—begins much earlier.

Helen Gardner, the author of *Art through the Ages*'s first three editions (1926, 1936, 1948), was familiar with both the high and the low ends of academic art history. Trained at the University of Chicago but working as an instructor of artists at the School of the Art Institute of Chicago for almost thirty years, Gardner was part of a generation of scholars and progressive educators who sought to marry their commitment to industry and the applied arts with an emphasis on visual form as a unique and significant vehicle for understanding. She was, in a word, a formalist—but not, as we will see, in the sense associated today with the reductive theory of modernism promoted in the 1940s and 1950s by the American art critic Clement Greenberg.

In the first two editions of her book, Gardner successfully produced an outline of world history and a canon of art that are familiar to today's readers. However, Gardner's third edition, which appeared posthumously in 1948, presents a different case entirely. In this unprecedented (and today virtually unknown) volume, Gardner announced her intention to survey the world horizontally rather than vertically, thereby avoiding what she described as "our Europocentric [*sic*] attitude towards art." True to her word, Gardner provided her readers with an ecstatic vision in which "Medieval" Chinese artifacts commingled with the "Renaissance" art of Northwest Coast Indians, the whole culminating optimistically in a chapter devoted to the international "Arts of the Machine."

From our vantage point, Gardner's 1948 edition looks remarkably prescient. Beginning in the 1970s, the pressure applied to mainstream art history from once marginalized constituencies resulted in the expansion of old survey texts and the creation of a number of new, more inclusive ones. Yet the schema proposed by Helen Gardner in 1948 was vehemently rejected by the Yale team that began revising her text in the 1950s, and by those who returned in subsequent editions to a more conventional canon emphasizing Europe and the "high" arts of painting, sculpture, and architecture. Apart from the vestigial presence implied in her book's proprietary retitling as *Gardner's Art through the Ages*, after 1959 the historical Helen Gardner plays no role in art history's own history. Why did Helen Gardner shift the narrative and canonical focus of her 1948 edition? What models and/or methods did she use to arrive at her expanded canon? Why was Gardner's new canon rejected by subsequent revisers of the text? And what does this earlier case have to tell us about our own efforts to refashion the canon for mass consumption?

To answer these questions and to better understand what was at stake for Gardner in 1948, I offer a close reading of Gardner's three editions along with considerations of the author's background and training at the University of Chicago in the 1910s, of the role of art history at the School of the Art Institute of Chicago—where Gardner's survey supplied the unifying narrative for an increasingly fragmented and specialized educational discourse—and of larger patterns of politics and art in the immediate postwar era. The process of rereading Gardner should bring into focus not only the surprising range of interests and preoccupations addressed by modernist formalism, but also the politically charged relationship between canon and method.

Method and Meaning 1926–36

Published in 1926 by Harcourt, Brace and Company, New York, Helen Gardner's *Art through the Ages* was if not the first single-volume history of art in the United States then the first to achieve widespread popularity. The book went through three editions and thirty-nine printings between 1926 and 1948 for a total of 446,479 copies, of which 97,196 were sold in bookstores and the rest, 349,283 were sold as textbooks.[1] Following the author's death in 1946, the book's title became the more familiar *Gardner's Art through the Ages* for the fourth edition, revised by Sumner McKay Crosby and the Yale Department of the History of Art and published in 1959. De la Croix and Tansey collaborated on the next five editions of the book (1970–90), with contributions to the ninth edition made by Diane Kirkpatrick. The tenth edition of *Gardner's Art through the Ages*, revised by Tansey and Fred S. Kleiner, appeared in 1995. Despite considerable competition in the university market—beginning most notably with the 1962 publication of Janson's *History of Art*—*Art through the Ages* continues to find readership worldwide.

In one way, *Gardner's Art through the Ages* has not changed at all since 1926. Its reputation today rests firmly on the quantity and quality of its photographic illustrations, images that have made *Gardner's*, for decades, the most inclusive art history textbook available. Unfortunately, the book is to some degree a collection of images awaiting a thesis (an advantage, it must be said, as far as many survey lecturers are concerned). When praised in today's marketplace, in which most survey texts wear their methodologies on their sleeves, it is for its objectivity—a euphemism, perhaps, for the book's "fair and balanced" if a bit dull reporting of the history of art. If there is a method to *Gardner's*, it is a somewhat old-fashioned documentary ideal associated with older models of cultural history.

Yet Helen Gardner's original *Art through the Ages* had a thesis, one so robust, in fact, that it gave the book its distinctive shape (thirty chapters, all save one with identical outlines), a muscular symmetry that was the product of Gardner's desire to define art—all art—as something we would call today the applied arts, or crafts: the skilled manipulation of materials for socially useful and/or decorative purposes. Art is never for its own sake, according to Gardner, but is always (at least ought to be) fully integrated into society. In her words, "The statue may be a decoration of a building, an integral part of the structure and determined by it. The painting frequently decorates a great wall surface or the page of a manuscript and much of its composition and color is determined by its use and its technique. The stained-glass plays its part in the whole interior ensemble and is not merely an example of the minor arts. . . ."[2]

The artist as craftsman is a model that works especially well in her early chapters. From prehistory through the Gothic period and in her discussion of the Americas, India, China, and Japan, the arts of design including jewelry, manuscripts and books, textiles, furniture, ceramics, metalwork, and bone carving featured prominently as examples of creative ability and expression equal in every way to painting, sculpture, and architecture. Gardner's discussion of the Italian Renaissance took pride of place in the central four chapters of the book, one each devoted to architecture, painting in Florence, painting in central and northern Italy, and sculpture together with minor arts. Gardner lauded the Italians for their versatility and noted approvingly that art was at the center of public life: "specialization was the exception, not the rule. Art meant not simply to erect a building or to carve a statue or to paint an altarpiece or to decorate the walls of a chapel, but also to set a jewel, to carve and paint a chest, to decorate a banner with the heraldic device of a noble family or brotherhood, to fashion costumes and properties for a pageant or church festival, to make designs for embroideries and tapestries, or to illumine a book. . . ."[3]

Gardner's treatment of the national schools of modern Europe and the United States (more or less from the beginning of the fifteenth century to the end of the nineteenth) followed the pattern as well. Each country is discussed in its own chapter. Spain and Flanders are praised for their strong guild traditions, Holland for the creation of a middle-class art, Germany for its continuity with the Middle Ages, and England for its protest (of which William Morris is described as representative) against the ugliness wrought by the Industrial Revolution. The art of the United States from its colonization to 1900 largely is dismissed as derivative. Gardner's most developed discussion in this period is of France, which she praised for the high standards of workmanship resulting from the state control of its applied arts. The chapter on France is organized around the principle of revolution—first the concentration of power in the monarchy and then the overthrow of the old order. These shifts are registered closely in French architecture, sculpture, and, especially, its painting, according to Gardner; the relevant artists are the "Classicists" David and Ingres, the "Romanticist" Delacroix, the naturalists of the Barbizon school, and the realists Courbet and Daumier. In conclusion, she observed that the political situation of revolution and counterrevolution eventually turned the French art world on itself. The revolt against academicism begun by Manet and taken up by the Impressionists produced its own counterrevolution with Cézanne, described by Gardner as "the culmination of the nineteenth century in France and also the starting-point of the various schools that have arisen in Europe since about the year 1900."[4]

The present, however, defied integration. Describing it as a "transitional age," Gardner explained that

> art has become segregated from the affairs of life as something to be treated with indifference, or disregarded, or as a luxury, something to be indulged in, upon occasions, or as a means of ostentation. It is the age of the museum and the exhibition—both unnatural. That impulse of the people as a whole which impelled the craftsman to use time and patience to make the church vessel or the everyday utensil expressive and beautiful, which recognized good taste and sound craftsmanship, and which rose in certain individuals to a degree that enabled them to create masterpieces—that impulse finds no expression today, because machinery has taken away the opportunity for self-expression, and because taste has been dulled by our being compelled to accept the uniform and standardized products of a commercial world that frankly looks to profit first.[5]

As a result, her final chapter, "Contemporary Art in Europe and America, 1900–1925, A.D.," contained only a very brief discussion of the contemporary situation, with political, intellectual, industrial, and technological developments named, though not examined. She noted her exclusion of the minor arts, the result of what she described as the detrimental effects of industrialization, and the related (and equally unfortunate) emphasis on individualism and unintelligibility in painting and sculpture.

Gardner was considerably more optimistic about the prospects for art in 1936. Two exceptions to Gardner's 1926 critique were contemporary Russian art, by which she meant the ensemble work of the Ballet Russe, and the collective activity associated with the creation of the modern skyscraper. She praised architects in general for their "logical constructive thinking," yet mentioned no individual by name. Her 1936 edition continued to explore these extremes in a completely rewritten section entitled "Modern Art: The Nineteenth and Twentieth Centuries," comprising chapters on France, the United States, and "The Art of Today." In the new text, Gardner found the true modernism of American architecture in such unabashedly anonymous, industrial forms as grain elevators, and she reserved her highest praise for painters who revived archaic or traditional forms—contemporary indigenous artists of the American Southwest and those engaged in the Mexican mural movement (she also mentioned the public face of contemporary painting represented by Thomas Hart Benton's murals for the New School of Social Research and John Norton's murals for the *Chicago Daily News* Building [fig. 9.1]).

What links these otherwise opposed impulses—industrialized functionalism in architecture with "primitivizing" or ethnic styles in painting—is

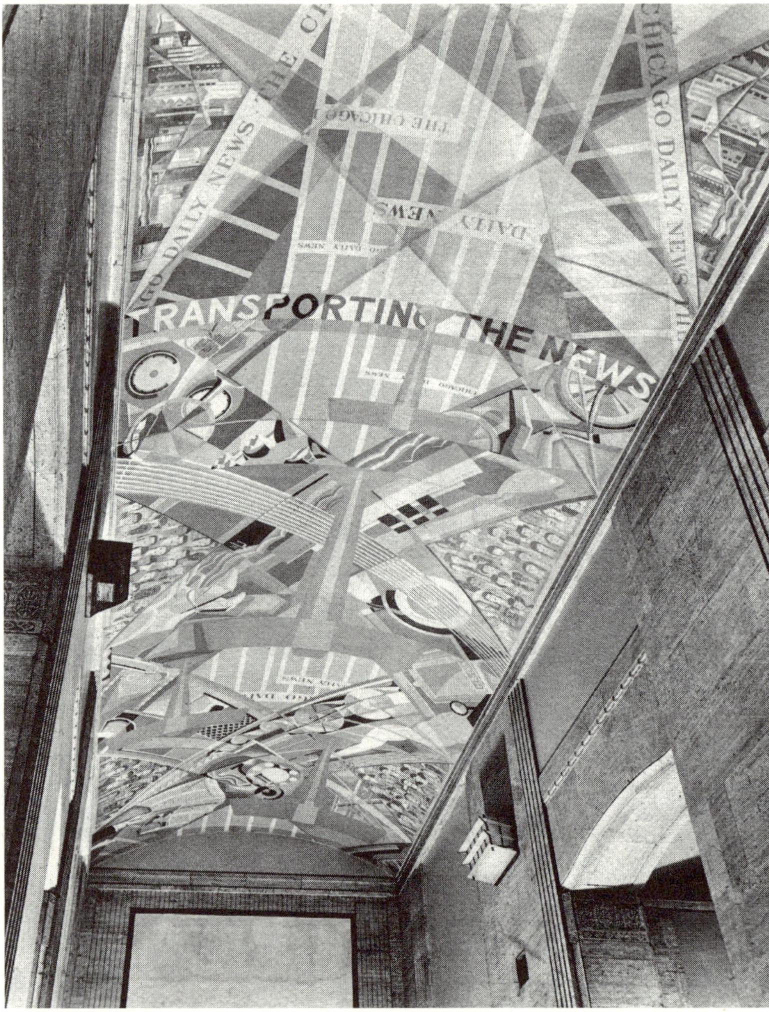

9.1. John Warner Norton, *The Chicago Daily News*, 1929, mural for concourse of the *Chicago Daily News* Building, 400 W. Madison St., Holabird and Root, architects, 1929–37. Photo: © 2004 Art Institute of Chicago, Ryerson and Burnham Libraries, Historic Architecture and Landscape Image Collection, Ryerson and Burnham Archives.

Gardner's celebration of these activities as instances of contemporary artists operating successfully within mainstream social and economic systems. By contrast, she lamented, most contemporary painting remained "privatized," that is, circulating only through the essentially anti-social mode of exhibition. The chapter closed with an enthusiastic discussion of developments in the industrial arts (textiles, glass, typography, and so forth), which, according to Gardner, indicated that art was in the process of being "reintegrated into the cultural fabric." In other words, by 1936 Gardner's *Art through the Ages* was well on its way to creating a canon of modern art that disrespected painting in favor of the "beauty of a gauge and a seaplane."[6]

Modernized Art Education in Chicago

How did this happen? Helen Gardner based *Art through the Ages* on the survey course she had created for students at the School of the Art Institute of Chicago beginning in 1920. Gardner was the school's first art historian, hired at a time when, according to no less an authority than Erwin Panofsky, art history existed in the United States only in hopeless entanglement with practical art instruction, art appreciation, and what Panofsky dismissed derisively as "that amorphous monster 'general education.'"[7] Nowhere are these complications closer to the surface than in the history of art and design education in Chicago.[8]

The Art Institute of Chicago, despite having acquired a reputation as a conservative academy in the style of the Beaux-Arts, was in the early twentieth century a pioneer in integrated industrial and fine arts education. Founded in 1878 as the Chicago Academy of Fine Arts, out of the ashes of an older, artist-run organization, the Art Institute of Chicago (AIC) and its school (the name was changed in 1882) was the project of a group of businessmen convinced that arts education was vital to the commercial success of their city. Their new School of the Art Institute of Chicago (SAIC) was eclectic in its pedagogy. It offered academic life-drawing classes alongside vigorous technical training: Saturday and evening classes in ornamental design, woodcarving, frescoing, mosaics, and stained glass were attended throughout the 1880s mainly by men engaged in decorative arts and design and working in Chicago's vast commercial lithography industry. Applied arts courses would be fully integrated with the academic day program by 1897, the year that programs in what were described as the "modern arts" of illustration and advertising were introduced as well.[9]

Although it was hardly a unanimous decision, the progressive educator

George William Eggers was elected acting director of the Art Institute of Chicago and its school in August 1916.[10] Eggers moved quickly to make the SAIC a center for "scientific" art pedagogy, as part of a national, patriotic drive, formed in the wake of World War I, to reform the tastes of working-class families. His vision emerged in full force in SAIC's catalogue for 1918–19, which shows that the new program was based on a division into three parts: an introductory program called the Lower School, which offered basic courses in drawing and design to all untrained students; a Middle School in which design, normal and commercial art, illustration, and crafts were pursued side-by-side with elementary painting and sculpture; and an Upper School, in which advanced students pursued painting and sculpture in an atelier system with recognized masters. "This reorganization," Eggers wrote, "recognizes not only the responsibility which the art school owes to American industry, but takes full cognizance of the responsibility of the school to the individual whose vocation must render him a livelihood."[11] In hiring Gardner, Eggers was following the advice of the renowned Arts and Crafts designer Ernest Batchelder, who in 1910 had called for designers to study history, geography, archaeology, and ethnology, stressing the streamlined efficiency of earlier epochs in choosing the "line of least resistance in the development of art forms."[12] Art history, then, entered SAIC as part of Eggers's efforts to rationalize its curriculum. By 1926, the year Gardner's book appeared, art history was described in the school's catalogue in unabashedly compensatory terms, as "an intensive study of certain phases of art so presented as to be of particular value to students as their training becomes more specialized."[13] To borrow the vernacular from the machine age, *Art through the Ages* represented the singular and authoritative position from which the automated assembly line of modernized art education acquired its meaning.

Helen Gardner was more than prepared to meet the challenge. Gardner's formative educational experiences were a close encounter with both the elite *and* the popular practices of art history. Born March 17, 1878 in Manchester, New Hampshire, Gardner graduated from the University of Chicago with a degree in Latin and Greek in 1901 and became a teacher and later an assistant principal at the Brooks Classical School. In 1915, Gardner was accepted as a graduate fellow in the art history department of the University of Chicago. Although the university had offered neither practical courses in art nor courses in art history when it first opened in 1892, the reform-minded charge of its first president, William Rainey Harper, was to focus on the relationship between industrialism and democracy in the urban setting. This attracted a number of faculty interested in the sociological dimension of art and aesthetics.[14]

Early offerings in art history at Chicago (beginning in 1902) drew on faculty whose primary appointments were with other departments, notably archaeology and the Semitic languages and literature. They also included courses on "modern" art, that is, of the Renaissance and after, and American art taught by George B. Zug, an artist who was a graduate of the university. By the time Gardner arrived, however, Zug was gone, and the modern portion of Chicago's historical sequence was being taught by the young art historian Richard Offner.[15] Offner, a specialist in Florentine painting, was steeped in the tradition of psychological aesthetics and formalism that had marked the birth of art history as a modern academic discipline in Germany during the 1880s and 1890s.[16]

Another recent addition to the faculty of Chicago's art history department was Walter Sargent, an artist, progressive educator, and former director of drawing and manual training for the city of Boston.[17] That there is a significant connection between Gardner and Sargent is clear from her acknowledgment of him in the first edition of *Art through the Ages*. Even as she continued her research with Offner, having been the recipient of a fellowship for further study in 1917–18 (with the intention of completing her Ph.D.), Gardner was elected in 1920 to the executive committee of the Renaissance Society, an organization founded at the University of Chicago around the time of the Armory Show. In its lectures and exhibitions, the young society (today recognized as a leading forum for the exhibition of innovative contemporary art) expressed its commitment to modernist ideals through an active exploration of Japanese art. It was then, if not before, that Gardner encountered Walter Sargent, who was the society's president from 1918 to 1920. Gardner never finished her Ph.D.—by the time Offner left Chicago for Harvard, Gardner was already teaching at SAIC—but she audited Sargent's Color in Decorative Art, an education class offered through the University of Chicago's art history department, in 1922.

Like his colleagues at the Art Institute, Sargent saw the First World War as an opportunity. In an essay written for the federal government's biennial study of art education in 1918, Sargent observed that "art education related to industries has been prominent in America for many years. It is receiving fresh impetus at present from the prospect that, after the war, the United States will have to depend upon its own resources more than in the past, not only for designers but also for styles of design. A kind of originality must be developed that can produce things which are not only new but fine in quality."[18] His ideas were put to real test in 1924, when he was named a professor and the chairman of the University of Chicago's newly reformed and renamed Department of Art. As chairman of a department in which history, theory, and practice commingled, Sargent presided, in the three years before his death in 1927, over a program that reflected the most progressive factions of modernism in Chicago—a remarkably diverse collection of designers, artists, and art historians.[19]

Implicit in the name Sargent gave his new department was his belief that the values and order of art were independent of and separate from any particular instance. On April 17, 1927 the following notice appeared in the *Chicago Tribune*:

> Plans to establish the University of Chicago as a center of artistic influence . . . will be presented on Thursday by Walter Sargent, chairman of the art department, to members of two women's organizations which have been leaders in furthering an appreciation of the fine arts. . . . Mr. Sargent . . . has four main objectives in his program: to offer all students an opportunity to develop an intelligent enjoyment of the world's artistic inheritance; to reach a much wider sphere by training teachers in the history, theory, and practice of the arts who will be able to present art in such a way that it will enter into the daily life of students; to offer some experience with the materials of art; and to forward appreciation of industrial art and to cooperate with the rapidly growing interest in giving to possessions and surroundings greater charm and distinction. . . .[20]

Although plans for Sargent's institute foundered with his death, a commitment to "present art in such a way that it will enter into . . . daily life" is what Gardner learned from Sargent; it is the lesson of *Art through the Ages* as well.

Toward 1948

There is another way in which history is represented in survey texts and, as I suggested at the beginning, it is in this direction that the real radicalism of the 1948 edition of *Art through the Ages* lies. Periodization was not particularly of interest to Gardner in 1926. Her close, chronological survey of what she described as "successive" civilizations (that is, those in which so many elements from a preceding age are contained that it is impossible to understand in isolation) resulted in a series of linked, cultural units, each analyzed briefly first in terms of natural environment (climate, geography, natural resources), social, economic, and political conditions, and religious beliefs. After careful consideration of the period's characteristic art forms, Gardner summarized each chapter by drawing connections between the art and the history in broad strokes. She composed each of her first twenty-nine chapters identically, in this fashion: historical background followed by expositions of architecture, sculpture, painting, and what she called the minor arts, followed by a final summary.

Lurking just below the surface of Gardner's carefully orchestrated symmetry, however, was the chaos of phenomena—and what escaped Gardner's organization is, of course, telling. Continuities in time and space serve her fairly well from prehistory through the Roman era, after which there is an implicit, if unacknowledged break. Though there are no headings larger than chapter, Gardner's focus shifts to an array of belief systems, including early Christianity and Islam, and styles—Romanesque, Gothic, Renaissance—before returning to variously periodized considerations (post-Renaissance–1900) of the modern nation states of Spain, Flanders, Holland, Germany, France, England, and the United States. Finally, Gardner's chronology falters fatally when confronted with the task of integrating the precolonial Americas, India, China, and Japan, each of which is treated in its own chapter appended awkwardly to the end of her narrative.

Gardner "corrected" these problems in 1936. Still comprised of thirty chapters, the revised book imposed order through nine major divisions: "Prehistoric Art in Europe," "Art of the Ancient Near East," "Classical Art," "Medieval Art" (Russia now joined Gardner's survey of religious expression from the early Christian through the Gothic to Islam), "Renaissance Art" (including Italy 1300–1600 and a new chapter on the Baroque), "Renaissance and Post-Renaissance Art in Northern and Western Europe and in the United States" (a title curiously precise and vague at once), "Primitive Art," "Oriental Art," and the previously mentioned "Modern Art: The Nineteenth and Twentieth Centuries." Also new was a brief introduction, in which Gardner considered the presumably fixed and universal fundamentals of design in relation to innovations in materials and techniques over time and space. In other words, her new, stricter adherence to the ideal of chronology contributed to the impression, reinforced by her textual additions and the inclusion of a number of unusual analytic "diagrams" (fig. 9.2), that art itself developed independently of culture.[21]

This was a decisive shift from her earlier book. But when Gardner's new enthusiasm for the transcendent powers of form met the political realities of the Second World War, the results were extraordinary. "Because today and only today, the concept of one total world inescapably thrusts itself forward," Gardner wrote in 1948, "I have been motivated in preparing this third edi-

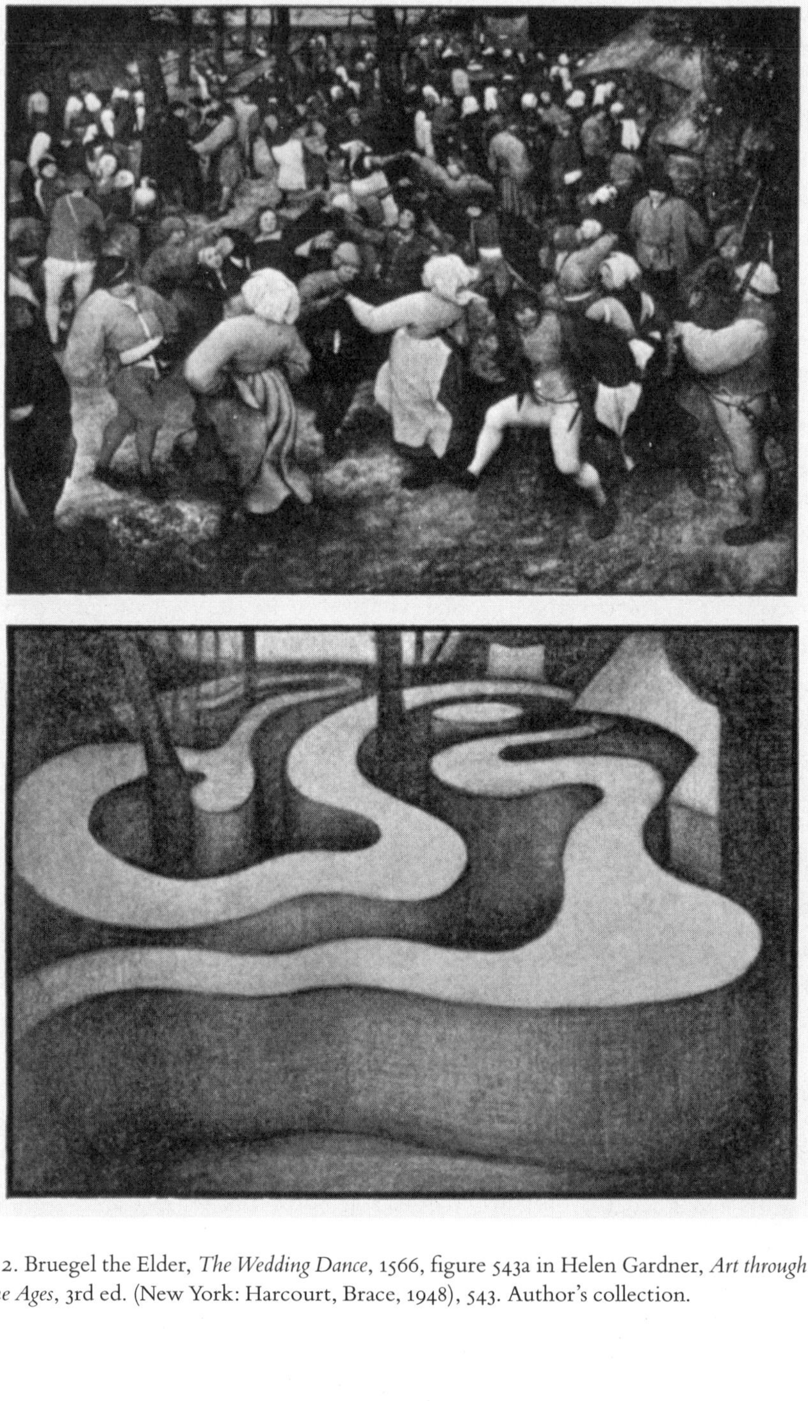

9.2. Bruegel the Elder, *The Wedding Dance*, 1566, figure 543a in Helen Gardner, *Art through the Ages*, 3rd ed. (New York: Harcourt, Brace, 1948), 543. Author's collection.

tion of *Art through the Ages*, both in the incorporation of new material and in the reorganization of the old, by a desire to present a world panorama of art."[22] Her method was, for its time, ingenious. Gardner took the four, great chronological periods that had dominated the writing of human (that is, Western) history, "Ancient," "Medieval," "Renaissance," and "Modern," and used them against their narrative grain to present hefty cross-sections of the simultaneous rather than the relentless forward march of the sequential. Some of the effects are striking: Asian art takes its place among the "Ancient" and "Medieval" traditions of the Near East, the Mediterranean, and Europe, as does the art of Africa, Oceania, and the Americas; "Renaissance Art" includes remarkable chapters on "Latin American Art," "French American Art," "English American Art," and American Indians of the Northwest Coast, the Great Plains, and the Southwest. Others leave something to be desired: African and Oceanic art appear only in the Medieval period, under the unfortunate rubric of "Primitive Art."

Yet there *is* a grand narrative to the third edition of 1948, which Gardner makes clear in her brief preface:

> *Part One* presents a panorama of the arts in ancient times and shows how great cultures arose and evolved on all the continents, largely in isolation yet with some vital contacts that affected the forms of expression. *Part Two* continues the panorama through the Middle Ages when the contacts between Asia, Northern Africa, and Europe became more pronounced and a lively intercourse brought about mutual exchanges of ideas, motifs, and forms. *Part Three* shows the Renaissance as the period when the world began to shrink at an ever accelerating rate. This was the age of discovery, exploration, and colonization. It witnessed the transplanting of European arts to large sections of the world, most important of which was the hitherto unknown western hemisphere, where the conflict or assimilation of European arts with the indigenous American arts transformed them into American-European styles. *Part Four* reveals the world, through unbelievable advances in transportation and communication, as one world in which the nations are becoming acquainted with each other, are learning from each other, and are to a considerable extent producing works of art which, despite national divergencies, come within an international framework.[23]

The "one world" of which Gardner spoke was the resonant title of Wendell Wilkie's memoir of his travels in 1942 to the Middle East, the Soviet Union, and China. A corporate lawyer and a progressive Republican, Wilkie had challenged Franklin Roosevelt unsuccessfully for the presidency in 1940. It was a case of a liberal internationalist running as the candidate of a conservative, isolationist party. His vision of international cooperation became a shibboleth of liberal internationalism in the immediate postwar era, as the nuclear devastation of Nagasaki and Hiroshima deepened the urgency with which liberals called for global unity. Two weeks after the atomic bombing, the editor Freda Krichwey was insisting in *The Nation*, an independent journal of politics and culture, that a world government to control nuclear weapons was the only means of saving civilization from annihilation.[24] Chicago became a center for the world government movement with the formation of the Committee to Frame a World Constitution at the University of Chicago in November 1945.[25]

Gardner rehearsed in spectacular fashion Wendell Wilkie's utopian vision of coming world fusion in her final chapter (the 1948 edition has a total of forty-six), which was entitled "The Arts of the Machine." Here she evoked the thrill of "a streamlined railroad car" or airplane, and the delights of "the mechanized kitchen" and the "simple, gaily colored gadget from the five-and-ten." Even some painters were applauded for "designing machine-made articles as well as ballet-settings" and "reaching out into the fields of weaving, ceramics, and glass," though the exclusive practices of the majority Gardner continued to dismiss as "devoid of function."[26] Gardner concluded in unequivocal terms that the present age would bear witness to the emergence of a new, unified style based in science and technology.

Art History and Politics in the Postwar Era

Passionate though it may be, Gardner's is not the model on which postwar American art history built its narratives. And it has even less to do with the transcendentalist terms by which abstract expressionist painting emerged eventually (though not inevitably) as the paradigmatic postwar avant-garde.[27] Any explanation must acknowledge the political reality that the severing of "high" and "low" (the so-called Great Divide of twentieth-century culture) was the product of arguments in the 1940s that painting and sculpture were privileged forms that were ideally suited to furthering the progress of the human spirit—and thus the focus of the American project of "saving" Western civilization from itself.

It had been the dream projected in 1928 by R. L. Duffus, whose study was financed by the Carnegie Corporation, that a truly American art, which he described as an art equal parts poetry and pragmatism, would issue from the SAIC: "To make the commercial arts finer and the fine arts, if not more commercial more practical[, i]n this direction, if anywhere, must lie our approach toward an American Renaissance—the birth of a new national art. For it means that the artist will come out of the most powerful forces of his own time. Such, one feels, is the vision taking form at Chicago. The Art Institute is, at all events, in a good position to train just such artists. . . ."[28] In fact, the AIC's George Eggers had invited a group of local manufacturers, designers, and educators to meet at the museum in the spring of 1919, and, as a result, had formed a permanent organization, the Alliance of Art and Industry. Reorganized as the American Arts and Industries Society in August 1921, this group was a precursor to the Association of Arts and Industries—best known for bringing László Moholy-Nagy and the New Bauhaus to Chicago in 1937.[29]

In the highly charged atmosphere of the immediate postwar era, the big news in Chicago's art world was the passing of what were described as "New York-type" galleries (small spaces showing only two-dimensional works) in favor of a new type—commercial studios integrating art, architecture, and design.[30] These "Chicago-style" galleries, as the critics dubbed them, took their cues from the synthesis of art and commerce long encouraged in the city. It seemed likely to many that an international avant-garde, centered in Chicago, was about to emerge. However, many of the figures prominent in the collaborative design studio-galleries of the 1940s soon were caught up in an ambitious new arena: the massive urban renewal efforts that had begun as federal funding intended to resurrect the public housing programs of the 1930s, but that had become available for inner-city development after 1949. As a result, the confident commitment to the idealism of the immediate postwar period would find expression through Chicago's civic and commercial aspirations—in the optimism of international-style architecture and urban planning, and in a powerful language of advertising and design. The less obviously practical arts of painting and sculpture were cut adrift from their links to a synthesis of art, architecture, and design, and the once-promising "Chicago-style" gallery of the 1940s degenerated into an eclectic boutique—seen increasingly by artists and critics as regressive.[31]

The end of the dream of a synthetic American art was encouraged as well by the imperatives of the cold war, beginning with the rejection of the "degraded" products of mass culture in Clement Greenberg's essay "Avant-Garde and Kitsch" (1939) and continuing with such arguments as those in Alfred H. Barr Jr.'s essay "Is Modern Art Communistic?" (1952), a defense of avant-garde painting and its "democratic" values. Anti-Communism had a dramatic impact in Chicago. The AIC's 1948 Annual Exhibition of American Art, organized by Katharine Kuh, the curator of modern painting and sculpture, had focused on the nonobjective style favored by Chicago's nascent avant-garde. But conservative and moderate critics alike condemned the exhibition, prompting the AIC director, Daniel C. Rich, to attempt to clarify the show's message. In a strongly worded argument published in the *Atlantic Monthly*, Rich defended what he described as the "Freedom of the Brush" only to find himself accused in Congress of communist leanings by Representative George A. Dondero of Michigan. In a speech delivered to the House of Representatives on August 16, 1949, Dondero quoted extensively from Rich's *Atlantic Monthly* article as evidence that the AIC director was an encourager of "international art thugs" set on destroying American art and principles.[32] As a result, curators in Chicago moved quickly to demonstrate their solidarity with East Coast advocates of Abstract Expressionism. The education of painters and sculptors became increasingly subjective, in Chicago as elsewhere.

For a moment in the early 1940s, it seemed as if things might be otherwise. Transformations in the journal *Parnassus* (the precursor of today's *Art Journal*, first published by the College Art Association [CAA] in 1929), may be taken as representative of the general mood. In its twelfth year, the journal reinvented itself: "Devoted to Modern Art, Art Criticism, Art Education, and Art News" a new masthead proudly proclaimed across its October 1940 issue. Inside, the incoming CAA president, Ulrich Middeldorf, a refugee intellectual who had arrived at the University of Chicago from Italy in 1935, described the rejuvenated publication as providing the common meeting ground for scholars and artists by addressing living questions of art criticism and art education.

At the new *Parnassus*, the progressive, or general education model ruled. For some eight issues between October 1940 and May 1941, *Parnassus* continued to promote the integration of intellectual ideals with more specialized, technical concerns in teaching art. In article after article celebrating the potential of the new university art department—in which the liberal arts of philosophy and history would be taught by competent scholars with the primary purpose of inspiring potential young artists—the journal's editors made clear that nothing less than America's resistance to Fascism was at stake. In the words of Lester Longman, "It can be argued today that liberal culture has vanished on the continent of Europe, and that we are faced with the alternative of maintaining and cultivating it here, or instead taking satisfaction in the demise of a culture we never fully understood, condoning our provincialism with belligerent delight, praising indiscriminately all things American as we cast ourselves adrift from the European culture of the past, and joining with Hitlerian vigor in the 'new order' of the twentieth century. . . ."[33]

In May 1941, this synthetic and partisan approach came to an abrupt end. As the new CAA president, Sumner Crosby, announced in that month's issue, the publication of *Parnassus* was to be suspended permanently. Crosby cited the conclusion of the association's directors that the group's primary responsibility was to the teaching of art history, theory, and criticism—and that these pursuits found their most profound resonance with the humanistic disciplines rather than with the teaching of art practice. Crosby did acknowledge the association's continued interest in the interrelationship of instruction in art history and in art practice and, to that end, the monthly illustrated *Parnassus* was replaced with a "more modest, quarterly trade journal."[34] With this ended a chapter in the history of art instruction in this country, of which Helen Gardner had been a typical participant, and began a new chapter on the repression of the underlying social, political, and economic bases of American formalism.

Conclusions

Not surprisingly, little of Gardner's utopian scheme survived the 1959 revision of her text accomplished by Yale University's art history department under the direction of Sumner Crosby—the same Crosby who had suspended publication of *Parnassus*. The imperialistic "universalism" of this much better known edition knowingly recapitulated the divisions of the new world order and represented a return to "normalcy" in its rejection of globalism, reinstatement of traditional hierarchies, and reinforcement of temporal and spatial boundaries. As Crosby wrote in his preface:

> Although Miss Gardner's organization of the Third Edition provided many opportunities for interesting comparisons and made it possible to study in adjacent chapters what was occurring in different parts of the world during more or less the same historic periods, this organization often obscured the intrinsic qualities and especially the development of the different styles. As our table of contents indicates, we have presented the arts of different periods and countries in a more normal order.[35]

"Normal" meant the imposition of four major divisions, "Ancient" (Prehistoric, Egyptian, Middle Eastern, Aegean, Greek, Etruscan, and Roman), "European" (Early Christian and Byzantine, Medieval, Renaissance, Baroque and Rococo, Colonial American, and Russian), "Non-European" (Islamic, Southeast Asian, Chinese, Japanese, Pre-Columbian Mayan, Mexican, Andean, North American Indian, and primitive), and "Modern" (painting, photography, sculpture, and architecture in Europe and America). In this way, the presumably distinctive stylistic coherence of European art was preserved, but at considerable expense: not only would the anonymously produced objects so important to Gardner's discussion no longer appear side-by-side with works bespeaking individual genius, as traditional, canonical works were reinscribed into the realm of pure art, but the modern, industrial design that had been the goal of Gardner's insistent teleology simply disappeared.[36]

Of course, by 1959 the possibility of East-West cooperation had long since vanished: Winston Churchill delivered his famous Iron Curtain speech in 1946; the American Marshall Plan began two years later to pump $12 billion into that part of Europe that included a West Germany made up of American, French, and British occupation zones. These and other events mark these years as the first major turning point of the cold war conducted between the United States and the Soviet Union after World War II.

It would take the end of the cold war to produce as inclusive a canon as Helen Gardner's again. Although the major revision of *Gardner's "Art through the Ages"* by Horst de la Croix and Richard Tansey in 1970 resulted in a volume celebrated for its "objectivity" and breadth, the authors made no pretext of disrupting, as Gardner did in 1948, the traditional art historical story of stylistic development or of extending their evenhandedness to the nineteenth and twentieth centuries (the discussion of which is dominated by individual artists presented within the narrative as visionaries and innovators). New survey texts introduced in the 1970s reflected methodological changes in the discipline, particularly those associated with Marxist or social history, yet their interference with the traditional canon was minimal. It was not until Marilyn Stokstad's 1995 *Art History* that the canon would be seriously, though respectfully, challenged. Yet despite the similarity of Stokstad's and Gardner's canons, the contrast of their methods—between Gardner's atomic-age liberal internationalism and Stokstad's multiculturalism—could not be greater.

Despite its intentionally slow progress, Helen Gardner's *Art through the Ages* was at heart a story of continuities. Thus her book gives lie to the idea that the modernist/formalist tradition was (necessarily and ruthlessly) exclusive in its rush to use the past to explain the present. Were the American discipline of art history able to embrace its origins in progressive education, or at least to recognize the common ground between progressivism and the European tradition of critical art history, then it might be possible to make informed decisions about the kinds of textbooks we need today.[37] At the very least, it is time to write a history of formalism that can account for its complexities.

Notes

1 These figures are according to Gardner's devoted student, the photographer Harold Allen, who penned her entry in *Notable American Women*. See Allen, "Helen Gardner."

2 Gardner, *Art through the Ages*, 1st ed., iii–iv.

3 Ibid., 235.

4 Ibid., 373.

5 Ibid., 467.

6 Gardner, *Art through the Ages*, 2nd ed., 742. Gardner is quoting Read's *Art and Industry*, 108.

7 Panofsky, *Meaning in the Visual Arts*, 321–46.

8 See Jaffee, "Before the New Bauhaus."

9 The Art Institute of Chicago, *School Catalogue*, 1901.

10 The AIC Board of Trustees was divided at the time between a small but influential progressive faction, including its powerful president Charles Hutchinson, and a more traditional majority (cf. note 7, above).

11 *Catalogue of the Art School of the Art Institute of Chicago, 1918–1919*, 10–11.

12 Batchelder, *Design in Theory and Practice*, 233.

13 *Catalogue of the Art School of the Art Institute of Chicago, 1926–1927*, 13.

14 Thomson, "Thorstein Veblen at the University of Chicago and the Socialization of Aesthetics," 3–15.

15 Richard Offner taught at the University of Chicago from 1915 to 1920. After two years at Harvard, he spent the majority of his long and distinguished academic career on the faculty of the Institute of Fine Arts at New York University. Offner died at the age of seventy-six in 1965.

16 This tradition, according to Michael Podro, had as its objective the exploration of works of art in light of principles that were understood to govern the artistic enterprise as a whole. See Podro, *The Critical Historians of Art*.

17 Sargent had joined the University of Chicago's School of Education in 1909 as professor of manual training and art in relation to education. The origins of a link between Gardner and Sargent are suggested in Sargent's change of title in 1912 to professor of fine and industrial art in relation to education—after his practical courses began that year to be cross-listed between Chicago's School of Education and its art history department. Sargent's reconfigured appointment is indicative of the growing importance of the education school at Chicago, at the time one of the largest in the country and a center for the new empirical "science" of education.

18 Sargent, *Instruction in Art in the United States*, 29–30.

19 *Register of the University of Chicago, 1924–1925*.

20 From art department files, University of Chicago archives.

21 Gardner began to assign her students the task of diagramming canonical artworks in order to ensure their internalization of the principles of design. The purpose of these

exercises, she wrote in 1940, was to ensure that the art student, "interested vitally in the immediate present, [would] find in the observable formal elements a common denominator for present and past. . . . The primitive method of dissecting a form of nature and reassembling the parts and several aspects of one part according to aesthetic requirements differs but little from the method of Picasso and Bracque [*sic*]. In fact, it was basic in the work of the ancient Egyptian painter." Many of these student exercises illustrate Gardner's "The Analytic Method." I discuss these and similar practices in detail in Jaffee, *Diagrammatics*.

22 Gardner, *Art through the Ages*, 3rd ed., ix.

23 Ibid.

24 Krichwey, "One World or None."

25 The committee was formed despite the initial isolationism of Robert Hutchins, then the president of the university. After first providing a haven at the university for the Manhattan Project (which resulted in the first self-sustaining nuclear reaction in December 1942), Hutchins found in the utopianism of the Italian poet Giuseppe Antonio Borgese, who had joined the university's faculty in 1936 and was a passionate advocate of the idea of world government, a match for his own idealism. The two were instrumental in the formation of the committee. See J. Allen, *The Romance of Commerce and Culture*.

26 Gardner, *Art through the Ages*, 3rd ed., 782.

27 As in Sandler's *The Triumph of American Painting*.

28 Duffus, *The American Renaissance*, 139.

29 The SAIC had proved itself long before to be no Bauhaus. George Eggers, the architect of the SAIC's integrated arts program, was out by October 1921.

30 Trier, "New Chicago Outlook," 48. Principal among the new studios, according to Trier, was Baldwin Kingrey. Backed by the architect Harry Weese, the gallery opened in the summer of 1947 with a show of decorative arts and furniture design in combination with fine art.

31 This view was articulated by A. James Speyer, an architect (and later, the AIC curator of twentieth-century painting and sculpture) who began reporting on art in Chicago for *ARTnews* in September 1955. Reviewing works by the Italian painter Guido La Regina at the Myrtle Todes Gallery, Speyer noted, "It is difficult to have looked at this work in a gallery which emphasizes furniture and fashionable accessories and fits painting between home furnishings. The paintings were superior to the competitive paraphernalia, and yet they were disturbingly too comfortable there . . ." Speyer, "Art News from Chicago," 11.

32 Rich, "The Freedom of the Brush," and Dondero, "Modern Art Shackled to Communism."

33 Longman, "On the Uses of Art History," n.p.

34 This was the *College Art Journal*, later the *Art Journal*.

35 Crosby and the Department of the History of Art at Yale University, *Helen Gardner's "Art through the Ages,"* xi.

36 A new chapter on the "artistic history" of photography took the place of Gardner's discussion of the industrial arts.

37 Although she makes no mention of Gardner specifically, Stankiewicz has made an ex-

ceptional case for the importance of women and women's education in general to the development of art history as an academic discipline in the United States in her essay "Virtue and Good Manners: Toward a History of Art History Instruction." For more on the historical role played by women as art students and educators, and by women's institutions in shaping the practice of art in colleges and universities, see Singerman, *Art Subjects*, 41–66.

10

The Rembrandt Research Project: Issues and Controversies Raised by a Canonical *Oeuvre*

LINDA STONE-FERRIER

In 1968, the Dutch government—specifically the Netherlands Organization for the Advancement of Pure Research—funded what has since been called the Rembrandt Research Project to determine precisely those paintings that can be firmly attributed to Rembrandt's hand. The mission of the project resulted from two concerns. First, the long-perceived canonical significance of this seventeenth-century Dutch artist and his work warranted such an in-depth and expansive determination of his autograph paintings. Rembrandt's name enjoys a celebrity and iconic status among the public today that marketing and advertising executives have appropriated to position and promote products from artists' paints to toothpaste.[1]

Second, in Rembrandt's own time, but also since, an enthusiastic production of copies and forgeries has flooded the art market. Rembrandt's style was emulated in various ways and times more than that of any other seventeenth-century Dutch artist. The Rembrandt Research Project dedicated itself to sorting out his autograph works from copies that, by definition, lacked the canonical superiority of paintings executed by Rembrandt. After creating a repertoire of known characteristics of Rembrandt's painting materials and methods, the project aimed to examine disputed paintings and eliminate those that had significant qualities that were inconsistent with Rembrandt's working methods.

That was the assumption behind the project; however, side-by-side examination of Rembrandt's paintings with those by copyists and imitators has proven to be a complex and difficult enterprise. The Rembrandt Research Project has employed all of the traditional means at the disposal of art historians to determine correct attributions. It has also employed newly developed and sophisticated scientific techniques. Over the course of five years, members of the project team visited art collections all over the world in order to examine every painting that had been seriously attributed to Rembrandt.[2] In the late 1990s, after having spent $5 million on the still incomplete project, the Dutch government withdrew its financial support,[3] which was replaced, in part, by the University of Amsterdam and various public and private sources.

The project has radically reduced the number of paintings soundly attributed to Rembrandt. Yet, ironically, as Rembrandt's autograph *oeuvre* has shrunk, his canonical status has enjoyed a higher profile than ever by virtue of "mere exposure"[4] to the project's judgments, the resulting controversies, and those paintings under scrutiny. The project's efforts follow a long succession of late nineteenth- and twentieth-century scholarly catalogues that also attempted to define the size of Rembrandt's autograph *oeuvre*. Like the Rembrandt Research Project, the sheer number of such publications over a long time span has contributed significantly to Rembrandt's canonical status through "mere exposure." In their 1897 to 1905 publication, Cornelis Hofstede de Groot and Wilhelm Bode identified 595 autograph paintings, which Adolf Rosenberg decreased in 1906 to 558. In 1909, Willem Valentiner increased the number to 606 in his edition of Rosenberg's publication, and then in 1921, Valentiner increased the number to 711 in his own assessment. Subsequent publications reduced the number of autograph paintings: that of Abraham Bredius (1935) to 630; of Kurt Bauch (1966) to 562; and of Horst Gerson (1968) to 420.[5] Ultimately, the number of paintings authenticated by the research project is expected to drop to less than 300.[6]

Although the project has attempted to categorically determine Rembrandt's *oeuvre*, ironically, its efforts have led to an increased perception of uncertainty that has given rise to a range of questions and controversy. If the authenticity of Rembrandt's full *oeuvre* cannot, in fact, be determined with finality, does that affect his canonical status? How many universally agreed upon, attributed paintings are required in order to warrant canonical status? Do de-attributions erode or destroy that status? Are there, in fact, specific paintings on which Rembrandt's canonical status depends? Is canonical status defined by both quality and quantity? Do collaborative paintings by Rembrandt and his pupils contribute to, or detract from, Rembrandt's canonical status? To whom should such collaborative works be attributed? Whose *oeuvre* do they help define? Do copies of Rembrandt's paintings by his pupils, and paintings done in Rembrandt's style by his pupils that the teacher instructed his students to produce, contribute to, or detract from, Rembrandt's canonicity? The emergence of these questions has raised doubts as to whether it was possible or appropriate for the Rembrandt Research Project to have embarked on its mission.

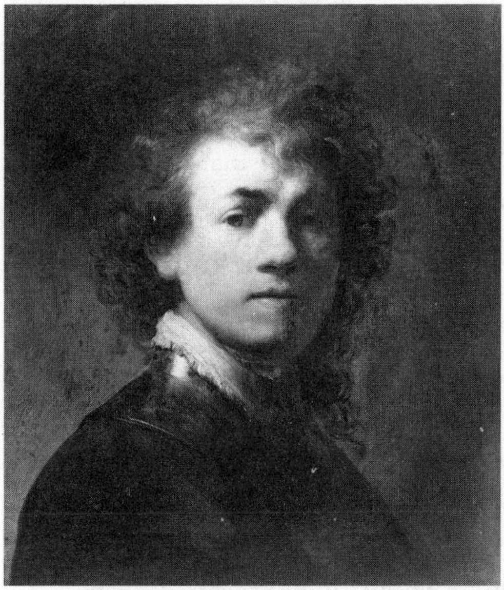

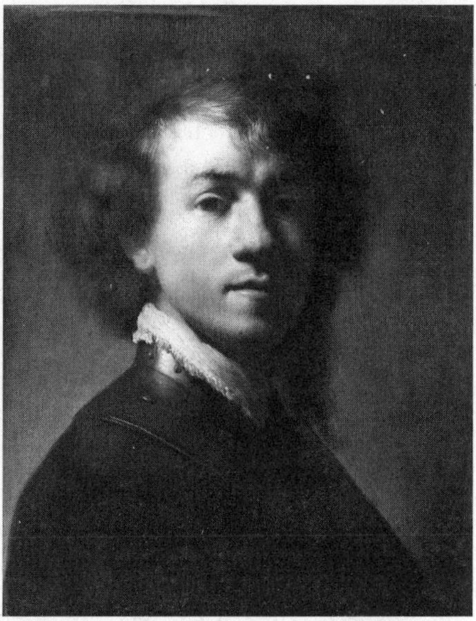

10.1. Rembrandt(?), *Self-Portrait with Gorget*, ca. 1629, oil on panel, Germanisches Nationalmuseum, Nuremburg. 10.2. Anonymous artist after Rembrandt(?), *Portrait of Rembrandt with Gorget*, oil on panel, Royal Cabinet of Paintings Mauritshuis, The Hague.

Two portraits of Rembrandt appropriately serve as a starting point for our discussion (fig. 10.1 and fig. 10.2). All scholars agree that both paintings are portraits of Rembrandt painted in the late 1620s. And all scholars agree that one of these paintings is a self-portrait. But which one? It depends on whom you ask. Some experts argue vehemently that the painting in Nuremburg is a self-portrait and that the painting in The Hague is a portrait of Rembrandt by someone else. Other scholars argue the reverse just as passionately.[7] The remarkably heated argument over these two attributions will serve well as an introduction to the intensity of such differences of opinion. The controversy played itself in various forums, but none was more heated than that via e-mail on a listserv for historians of Netherlandish art. Scholars contributed arguments with sometimes personal attacks on each other. Some participants labeled others' opinions as despicable, dogmatic, pompous, irrational, arbitrary, ignorant, insulting, or comically mean-spirited.[8] Not surprisingly, no one changed anyone else's opinion.

How did the rarified world of Rembrandt connoisseurship get to such an unrarified plane of discourse? I hope to provide here the context for understanding such intense controversy. In the first part, this essay will explain the history and the mission of the Rembrandt Research Project and the legacy of attributions and de-attributions that the project inherited. It will also examine the issues and controversies that lurk among the members of the project (as opposed to those controversies between the members of the project and non-members). The second part will explain some of the analyses and tests with which the Rembrandt Research Project has proceeded in its attribution efforts, as well as the opportunities and limitations of those methods. The third and last part will deal with the issues that have been raised by scholars who are not members of the project.

The Project

The conclusions of the Rembrandt Research Project have been published so far in four of an originally projected total of five volumes referred to collectively as *A Corpus of Rembrandt Paintings*.[9] Each published volume covers a number of chronological years of Rembrandt's working lifetime. Published in the 1980s, the first three volumes address paintings from the late 1620s, during Rembrandt's earliest years as an artist in Leiden, through the early 1640s, when he was an accomplished painter in Amsterdam.[10] Each of the published volumes of the *Corpus* includes various scholarly essays, enormous amounts of information on Rembrandt's painting methods, and three different categories to which paintings have been assigned. Section A is for paintings firmly attributed to Rembrandt based on a closed-doors consensus about which Josua Bruyn, the first director of the research project, provocatively stated: "The way decisions on a final opinion of authenticity have been made . . . would be worthy of a socio-psychological study."[11] Section B of the *Corpus* includes paintings that have not been positively accepted or rejected as by Rembrandt. Section C includes paintings definitely not by Rembrandt.[12] A Section D was originally planned for fakes, but subsequent examination suggested that there were actually not many of them.[13]

Man in a Golden Helmet (ca. 1650–1655; Gemäldegalerie, Staatliche Museen Presussischer Kulturbesitz, Berlin) is a well-known and much admired painting that is no longer attributed to Rembrandt.[14] Such paintings have been otherwise attributed in numerous imprecise ways, as an imitator of Rembrandt; in the circle of Rembrandt; as a follower of Rembrandt; as someone working in the style of Rembrandt; as a copy after Rembrandt; as a copy after a former pupil of Rembrandt; as a studio copy after Rembrandt; as a Rembrandt forgery; as a partial copy after a contemporary of Rembrandt; as someone working in the style of Rembrandt executed in the seventeenth century;

or possibly as someone working in the style of Rembrandt executed in the eighteenth or nineteenth century.[15]

In spite of the extensive and high-tech ways in which Rembrandt's paintings have been examined, there has sometimes been a lack of consensus among the members of the Rembrandt Research Project.[16] At times the members have vacillated with regard to the value placed on one method of examination and its findings over others. For example, in the case of a given painting, one scholar may decide that the information revealed by scientific examination outweighs the same project member's assessment of the surface brushwork. To make matters even more complicated, the same scholar who placed priority of importance on the physical evidence of a painting over its surface appearance may then reverse the significance given to these matters in the attribution of another painting.[17] In sum, there have been no uniform standards to which everyone consistently subscribed.

A lack of uniform standards makes clear that attribution of a painting cannot always be based on a definable litmus test. Yet, the longevity of the nineteenth-century concept of the artist as genius who produced only "innovative"[18] paintings inhibits the identification of autograph works that do not meet the litmus test on which the designations of genius and canonical have been based. Further, whatever uniform standards the members may sometimes have agreed upon represent the judgments of only a small number of (by definition) partisan individuals—all of whom are Dutch men.[19] Who was entrusted, and on what basis, with the selection of the members of the project? Dozens of other Rembrandt specialists—Dutch and non-Dutch, male and female—have no voice in determining the uniform (or not uniform) standards on which the project's members base their deliberations or publications. How can we know whose opinions among *all* Rembrandt specialists are most discerning?

Some differences of opinion among members of the project with regard to attributions have resulted from changes in membership. In 1984, Bruyn tentatively suggested that *The Polish Rider* (ca. 1655; Frick Museum, New York City) was painted by Willem Drost rather than Rembrandt. After Bruyn's retirement, the attribution of the painting was restored to Rembrandt by the project. However, Ernst van de Wetering suggested that the painting was unfinished in certain sections and that another hand executed the "shank of the boot and the folded-back tail of the coat and possibly his hose."[20] Yet the project's members have not articulated what aspects or what percentage painted by Rembrandt of a collaborative painting between Rembrandt and a student qualify it for inclusion in the artist's canonical *oeuvre*. Does inclusion depend upon Rembrandt's responsibility for the painting's conception and *disegno*? And/or does inclusion depend upon the size of the surface area of paint on the panel/canvas that can be attributed to Rembrandt?

Controversy among the members also occurred when the project's basic direction changed from a chronological organization to a thematic one. In 1993, the original five-man membership of the project disbanded because of the disagreement that they had with their colleague, van de Wetering, who wished to discard the attribution categories of A, B, and C.[21] Van der Wetering prevailed and was appointed the new head of the project. He argued that the former chronological approach of the project's investigations "was based too much" on the assumption that "Rembrandt had a constant style that gradually evolved."[22] As a result, the fourth and forthcoming fifth volumes (University of Amsterdam, publisher) are arranged "thematically rather than chronologically."[23] However, a selective, thematic organization, rather than a chronological one, similarly imposes upon Rembrandt's *oeuvre* organizing principles of value that the project privileges.

Volume 4 addresses "the function, meaning and authenticity of Rembrandt's self-portraits including etchings and drawings" as well as a reconsideration of works already published in earlier, chronological volumes of the *Corpus*.[24] In announcing that this volume includes reconsidered opinions, the research project acknowledges that definitive attributions are not always possible, and that the project's conclusions may be considered as unstable in perpetuity. Future reconsiderations may be forever fueled by changing notions of what is canonical about Rembrandt's *oeuvre*. Volume 5 will examine small-figured history paintings attributed to Rembrandt. All findings not published in the volumes of the *Corpus* will go into a Digital Rembrandt Archive that will cost another $5.5 million.[25]

The Methods

What means have been employed by the Rembrandt Research Project to attribute or de-attribute paintings, that is, to define the Rembrandt canon? The project scrutinizes paintings attributed to Rembrandt for their ability to fit into the canonical parameters that they have established, rather than to stretch them. The project's modus operandi emphasizes the typical, the characteristic, the formulaic in Rembrandt's artistic production, allowing little if any room for the anomaly, and even less room for a painting deemed to be unworthy of attribution solely on the basis of quality. Did Rembrandt never waver in his production practices or in his ability to produce an "innovative" painting? When the size of the artist's *oeuvre* has been reduced, and only rarely increased, the research project offers no discussion of how a newly attributed or de-attributed painting alters our understanding of the Rembrandt canon. However, a reduction in the quantity of authenticated paintings does not affect Rembrandt's canonical status, which once bestowed on an artist is rarely if ever revoked.[26]

Before the establishment of the project, a winnowing of the number of paintings attributed to Rembrandt resulted from the scrutiny of connoisseurs in various traditional ways. These experts rejected a painting when they felt that the visual appearance of the surface of the painting was inconsistent with that of the undisputed paintings by Rembrandt, such as *Aristotle with a Bust of Homer* (1653; Metropolitan Museum of Art, New York; fig. 10.3). Other factors that contributed to firm attributions included unbroken documentation of ownership; the extent to which a painting's iconography conformed to Rembrandt's established pictorial interests; and the connoisseur's response to the work's quality.

Today, scrutiny of a painting by the project also includes the scientific examination of the paint materials through various means. By first examining those paintings by Rembrandt the attribution of which is certain, the project's members have determined the chemical composition of the paints that Rembrandt consistently used, the characteristic ways in which he prepared a panel or canvas, and how he typically executed a painting. The numerous revelations can be fascinating. Rembrandt, for example, often painted on panels made of mahogany—a wood not native to the Netherlands.[27] Such mahogany panels came from dismantled packing boxes that had been used to ship sugar to Amsterdam by the Dutch West India Company.[28]

After creating a repertoire of known characteristics of Rembrandt's painting materials and methods, the project then examines disputed paintings and eliminates those that reveal qualities that are inconsistent with Rembrandt's working methods. Confusion, however, has arisen by virtue of the fact that Rembrandt consistently taught his pupils his own methods for mixing paint, preparing panels and canvases, and building up paint layers. Therefore, in many cases one cannot distinguish with certainty the work of the master from the work of his pupils.

The scientific examinations, however, have been useful when distinguishing Rembrandt's paintings from copies made outside of his workshop or created at a later time. For example, if the scientific examinations reveal deviations from the ways in which Rembrandt prepared a canvas or panel and

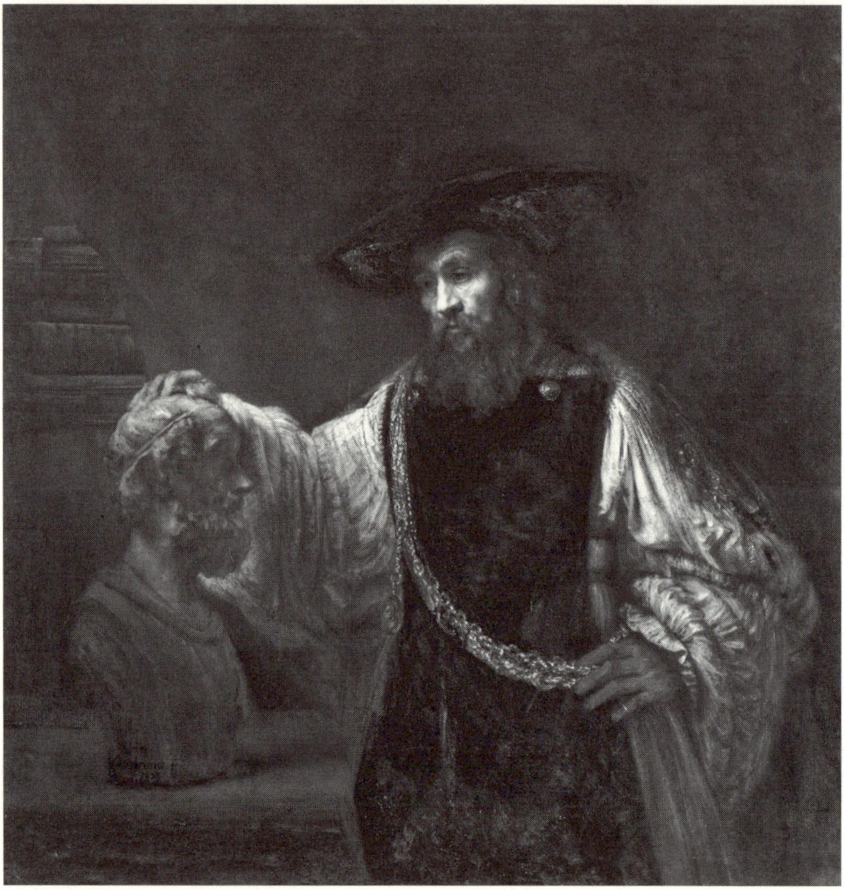

10.3. Rembrandt, *Aristotle with a Bust of Homer*, 1653, oil on canvas, Metropolitan Museum of Art, New York.

how he subsequently built up the painting layers, then that could serve as the grounds for deciding that the work was not painted by Rembrandt or his pupils. Similarly, if the disputed work exhibits paint, the chemical makeup of which did not exist in Rembrandt's time, the picture could not have been painted by Rembrandt or by a pupil. If the disputed painting was on panel, with dimensions that were not standard for Rembrandt's time, then the painting most likely was not by Rembrandt or by a contemporary.[29] If the wood on which a work was painted dates from later than the seventeenth century, then the disputed work had to have been painted by a later copyist.

Forms of scientific scrutiny by the Rembrandt Research Project include what is called "x-radiography," "autoradiography," and "infrared reflectography," sophisticated forms of x-rays that can reveal aspects of a painting beneath the surface.[30] Such scientific examination of the painting's physical structure can reveal a painting's ground,[31] underdrawing,[32] or the monochrome blocking out of the composition[33]—terms that refer to the preliminary design of the image that the artist made on the panel or canvas. Such scientific methods of examination can also reveal a painting's underpainting, a term that refers to the layers of paint beneath the surface.[34] Through such examination, one can also see changes made in the painting, which are obscured by the surface image.

Paintings attributed to Rembrandt also undergo other scientific scrutiny, including pigment analysis of minuscule cross-sections that reveals the chemical component of paint layers and the sequence in which the layers have been built up.[35] The findings from a disputed painting can be compared to the proper sequence and the quantity and composition of paint materials that are known to have been used by Rembrandt.

Dendrochronology, a method of dating wood objects,[36] determines whether a particular painting on wood could date from Rembrandt's lifetime. The tree rings visible in the panel may reveal that the painting dates from a more recent period and is, therefore, a later copy or a fake. A tree ring pattern can also provide positive identification for the very piece of lumber from which a panel was taken.[37] For example, tree rings in the panels of four paintings dating from the 1630s revealed that the wood all came from the same tree.[38] The research project assumed that Rembrandt purchased the panels that came from the same tree at the same time even if he did not paint on those four panels in the same year.[39] Such dendrochronological evidence establishes another variable in support of the paintings' attribution to Rembrandt or to his pupils.

When a work has been painted on canvas instead of on panel, members of the research project compute the thread density, that is, the number of warp and weft threads per square centimeter. They then compare the thread count of the painting with hundreds of x-rays that reveal the thread count of paintings attributed to the artist.[40] The time-consuming process of counting threads and gauging their thickness can be used to help identify the bolt of cloth from which the canvas was taken.[41] The examination of many authenticated canvases in this way has revealed that small groups of Rembrandt's paintings on canvas were cut from the same bolt of cloth. Thread density in a questionable painting that matches that of an autograph work contributes one more variable in favor of the former's attribution to Rembrandt or a pupil.[42]

Still another way in which attributions have been made has been through the standard comparative method of connoisseurship based on the examination of consistently depicted, commonly occurring details in pictures, such as facial features or lace collars. This method assumes that the ways in which artists repeatedly painted such commonly occurring details form a kind of signature of their respective styles. One can compare the details in an authenticated Rembrandt painting with those in a disputed painting to come to some conclusion about the latter's attribution. This type of stylistic scrutiny has been referred to as the Morellian method.[43]

In addition to determining the signature way in which Rembrandt depicted facial features, the members of the project have determined the signature ways in which he painted lace—a common detail of his portrait paintings.[44] Typically, Rembrandt's signature style includes, not surprisingly, the meticulous manner in which three-dimensionality, structure, and the diaphanous and supple quality of the lace are convincingly suggested.[45] The project's members describe in great technical detail the specific ways in which Rembrandt attained these illusions. In contrast, a painted lace collar that lacks Rembrandt's signature style is rendered—as van de Wetering describes—in a "nervous and chaotic way" that "does not at any point offer a persuasive clarity of structure."[46] Remarkably, based upon the analysis of lace in portraits, the project's members have suggested that there may be very few portraits painted by Rembrandt alone.[47]

Although the Morellian method reveals a signature way in which an artist consistently paints eyes, mouths, lace, and so on, the examination of actual signatures on paintings, that is, the artist's signed name, has played a relatively minor role in the authentication of paintings by Rembrandt.[48] Problems in the attribution of a painting on the basis of Rembrandt's signature are many. For example, over time, Rembrandt varied the way he signed his paintings, using either his first name or his monogram in cursive or in printed letters.[49] One might think that one could identify a prototype for Rembrandt's signature in a notarized document that he signed with pen and ink on paper. However, it is difficult to compare a signature written with pen and ink on paper to a signature written with paint and brush on panel or canvas.[50]

Further complicating the authentication of attribution via signatures, Rembrandt may have placed his signature on the paintings of his pupils, which, it has been suggested, was allowed by guild regulations.[51] What role, then, in the attribution of a painting can an autograph signature by Rembrandt play? Does such a signature by the master artist on a workshop copy bestow on the copy autograph status as a painting? Does such a claim by Rembrandt to authorship of a workshop copy supercede the standards for attribution of the research project? In its refusal to accept a workshop copy with Rembrandt's autograph signature as a work by the master, the project is using standards for attribution that are at odds with seventeenth-century practice, and, therefore, are ahistorical. Exacerbating the attribution dilemma further, Rembrandt's pupils also may have signed his name, in his writing style, on their own Rembrandt-like paintings.[52] Further, around 1800 in particular, collectors and connoisseurs added Rembrandt's signature to paintings they newly attributed to him.[53] Not surprisingly, Bruyn concluded that "chaos" reigns with regard to "non-authentic signatures."[54]

The Controversies

Although no one has formally challenged *or* justified Rembrandt's canonical status—a curious fact in light of the expense of the Rembrandt Research Project—the project has engendered various kinds of issues and disagreements among non-members. Owners of de-attributed paintings have been known to challenge the project's judgments, or to ignore its conclusions. One can imagine the collective dismay, for example, of the proprietors of the Wallace Collection in London when the members of the project reduced the number of authentic works by Rembrandt in the collection from twelve paintings to one (*Portrait of Titus*, ca. 1660).[55]

Other disagreements among non-members of the research project abound. Some have complained that the project has too rigid a conception of the consistency of Rembrandt's style and technique over the course of his working life.[56] The decision to change the focus of the last two volumes of the *Corpus*, that is, to abandon the organizing principle of chronology and to turn to a thematic examination of Rembrandt's work, also met with much criticism from at least one non-member of the project. Walter Liedtke, the curator of Dutch and Flemish paintings at the Metropolitan Museum of Art, complained that the chronological classifications of the multivolume publication should not be changed mid-course. "It's as if the *Encyclopaedia Britannica* ran A through L," he stated, "and then said they would change their approach and cover M through Z through great themes—love, death, whatever—regardless of whether the subject [of a theme] begins with P or Z."[57] Such criticism suggests that disagreements over the organizing principles and standards for attribution of the research project have taken precedence in some observers' minds over questioning the project's most basic goals. Such criticism does not challenge the fact that some of the research project's assumptions about Rembrandt as an artistic genius, about his "innovation," and about his signature works are at odds with seventeenth-century practice.

Non-members of the project have sometimes argued vehemently with *each other* on the attribution to Rembrandt of many paintings.[58] In a major exhibition from 1995 entitled *Rembrandt/Not Rembrandt*, the catalogue ultimately had to be published in two volumes because Liedtke and Hubert von Sonnenburg, the museum's conservator, had conflicting opinions regarding the attributions of paintings in the collection of the Metropolitan Museum of Art.[59]

To what can we attribute such a broad spectrum of circumstances under which paintings meant to look like those by Rembrandt were produced in the seventeenth century? To a very large extent, the attribution dilemma results from the organization of Rembrandt's workshop, and from his manipulation of the marketplace.[60] Rembrandt specifically trained his pupils in his workshop to paint in his style and to paint copies of his paintings, which resulted in the many works that intentionally mimicked his own.[61] As Bruyn has concluded, "These paintings were meant to resemble Rembrandt's art to a deceptive degree."[62] As early as the mid-1630s, the training of pupils in Rembrandt's studio included drawing or painting copies of the master's own artwork, especially his self-portraits,[63] which Rembrandt sold for his own profit.[64]

Rembrandt's pupils were eager to learn their teacher's style because his paintings sold very well.[65] The pupils hoped to capitalize on Rembrandt's success by learning his painting method. Arnold Houbraken, a seventeenth-century Dutch biographer of artists, documented this workshop practice when he first described Rembrandt's fame and then wrote that "artists were forced (if they wanted to have their work accepted) to accustom themselves to [Rembrandt's] manner of painting. . . . This was why Govert Flinck and others joined Rembrandt's school."[66] The biographer also revealed that viewers and collectors were often unable to determine with certainty the authentic from the inauthentic Rembrandt painting.[67]

Paintings by pupils in Rembrandt's style were marketed as authentic works by the master and were probably signed by him, a practice allowed by some guild regulations.[68] In the 1656 inventory of his possessions, Rembrandt listed at least two paintings as his own works that were actually painted by his pupils: Ferdinand Bol's *Resurrection* and Barent Fabritius's *Woman Holding a Child*.[69] Such workshop production defies the premise of the research project that a single canonical artist produced singular paintings. However, the research project rejects Rembrandt's claim that his pupils' paintings in his style constitute his own work.

Why would Rembrandt have encouraged his pupils to produce paintings in his own style as well as to produce copies of his own paintings? What advantage was there for him? According to Joachim Sandrart, a German painter, writer, and contemporary of Rembrandt's, the latter profited financially from this arrangement.[70] He received large sums from the sale of his pupils' paintings in return for the privilege of training and working in his shop. Such an arrangement was common at this time in master artists' workshops.[71] As more and more paintings in Rembrandt's style, especially copies of his self-portraits, came available on the growing art market, Rembrandt benefited by the increased recognition of his style, his name, and, therefore, his fame. This, in turn, increased the demand for his paintings by the public, which often did not distinguish between paintings by Rembrandt and paintings in his style by his pupils. Thus, Rembrandt greatly contributed to his own "public prominence, peer regard, and critical claim" through "self-promotion"[72] and "mere exposure."[73] Rembrandt purposely caused the market to swell with paintings by his students that deceptively copied his style, as well as paintings by his students that deceptively copied actual paintings by him. Critical acclaim resulted from the proliferation of a style by Rembrandt and his pupils that originated with him, rather than from a singular production of that style.

Based on this information with regard to Rembrandt's control over the style and sale of his pupils' paintings, Svetlana Alpers, a critic of the Rembrandt Research Project, argued that Rembrandt manipulated the market for his paintings through the organization of his workshop. He was, in her view, "an entrepreneur of sorts," "an entrepreneur of the self," whose school was a studio for "the commodity—the *Rembrandt*."[74] In a rebuke of the project, Alpers concluded that Rembrandt was "an artist whose enterprise is not reducible to his autographic *oeuvre*."[75] Therefore, should the paintings in Rembrandt's style that are attributed by the research project to his known pupils actually be considered part of Rembrandt's *oeuvre*? If Rembrandt intended for the public to accept pupils' copies of his paintings, as well as their paintings executed in his painting style as works by him, then why don't we? Rembrandt's conception of his authorship of paintings is at odds with the assumptions regarding attribution that the Rembrandt Research Project adopted at the beginning.[76]

One wonders whether the seventeenth-century public cared if the paintings that they purchased were autograph Rembrandts or works by his pupils. The evidence is inconclusive and somewhat contradictory, and, therefore, it suggests a fluid value system. In the first half of the century, and in particular in the 1630s, documentation shows that some, but not all, collectors carefully distinguished between an autograph Rembrandt painting and a painting in Rembrandt's style.[77] Records from an auction reveal that an authentic Rembrandt painting was referred to as a *principael*.[78] An unauthentic work was referred to in one document of 1608 as "apprentice work," a term probably generated from the fear of being overcharged for a copy,[79] and elsewhere as "after Rembrandt (*naer Rembrandt*)."[80]

Some evidence suggests that after 1650 collectors noted much less often the distinction between authentic and copied paintings owing probably to the extent to which workshop production of copies had become commonplace.[81] Documentation from the mid-century attests to the fact that master artists regularly presented copies from their workshops as their own autograph paintings. As a result, at least one painters' guild stiffened the language that required autograph paintings from master artists. The 1644 regulation of the Utrecht painters' guild stipulated that "every painter belonging to this college [was required to provide] a piece of work done by him." This regulation was changed in 1664 to state more emphatically "a piece of work done by him himself, worked up wholly by his own hand."[82]

In some contrast to this assumption that after the mid-century master painters typically presented workshop copies as their own work, other documentation and research by John Michael Montias suggests that many, if not most, collectors placed higher value on the authenticated attribution of a painting to an important artist than on the subject matter of the image.[83] Montias based his conclusions on extensive research in the Delft archives of inventories of seventeenth-century collections.

Each of Rembrandt's pupils learned and perpetuated in his workshop only the specific painting style that his teacher employed during the limited number of years that the student studied with him.[84] Such limitations on pupils' production of Rembrandt's style to the time they spent in his workshop reinforce Rembrandt's claim that workshop production in his style constituted autograph paintings by him. Rembrandt's painting style changed dramatically from decade to decade. A pupil who studied with him in the 1630s learned a very different Rembrandt painting style from that adopted by a different pupil in the 1640s or the 1650s. One can determine the approximate decade in which a known pupil studied in Rembrandt's workshop by identifying the time period of the master painter's style that the pupil emulated. After leaving Rembrandt's workshop, all but one of his pupils adopted their own distinct painting styles different from that of their teacher.

Only Aert de Gelder (1645–1727), a pupil of Rembrandt's probably in the early 1660s, continued to work in the Rembrandtesque style he had learned in his teacher's workshop after he left to work on his own.[85] A similar palette of warm colors and very loose brushwork can be seen in both Rembrandt's *Self-Portrait* (1658; Frick Museum, New York), and in Aert de Gelder's *Portrait of Rembrandt* (Staatsgalerie, Stuttgart). And here we have come full circle in this discussion, returning to a self-portrait by Rembrandt—although now late in his life—and a portrait of the aged Rembrandt by a pupil. However, with this late pair—unlike the first two portraits of Rembrandt as a young man with which we began—we know for certain which painting is by Rembrandt and which is not.

In conclusion, the dilemma we are left with regarding Rembrandt attributions is whether or not to accept his attitude toward autograph paintings, which was different from that of the research project. In its attempt to distinguish carefully between Rembrandt's autograph paintings and pupils' copies and paintings in his style, the research project has adopted post-eighteenth-century assumptions about the artist as a genius who produces singular works. However, such canon building is counter to Rembrandt's own claims for the extent of his *oeuvre* and, therefore, such canon building is ahistorical. If Rembrandt regarded a painting by a pupil that was painted in his style to pass as a painting by him, then why don't we? Further, we do not allow for the possibility that some autograph paintings by Rembrandt may not conform to the project's definition of the canonical quality of his *oeuvre*, which has been superimposed upon his body of work from a long historical distance. We do not allow for the possibility that a painting by a student could surpass the work of his famous teacher. We do not allow for the value of a painting to be preeminently inherent in its success as a work of art, divorced from its attribution to a canonical artist. We do not acknowledge that fluctuating tastes over time affect judgments as much as do the results of scientific examination of paintings attributed to Rembrandt. Therefore, whose contributions to canon building are most historically or qualitatively immutable: those of the Rembrandt Research Project or those of Rembrandt?

These issues challenge the existing assumptions about canonical art and artists. Instead of defining the worth of a work of art on the basis of the canonical status of the artist who made it, we should recognize the false limits and restrictions of an ahistorical history of art that first defines a canon, values paintings that belong to that canon, and de-values the same paintings if and when they are de-attributed and thus fall from canonical favor. The irresolvable lack of consensus among members of the Rembrandt Research Project, between members and non-members of the project, and among non-members themselves testifies to certain problems and fallacies inherent in attempts to categorically determine a seventeenth-century *oeuvre* using sometimes ahistorical twentieth- and twenty-first-century assumptions concerning the basis on which the canon is defined.

Notes

1 Two examples are Rembrandt Acrylic Colours, © 1999 Royal Talens, Apeldoorn, Netherlands; and Rembrandt Whitening Toothpaste, © 2004 Oral-B Rembrandt. Walter Liedtke also discusses "'Rembrandt' as a qualitative distinction or even slang for masterpiece" in Liedtke et al., *Rembrandt/Not Rembrandt in the Metropolitan Museum of Art*, 2:5, 36 n. 13.

2 Hochfield, "What Is a Real Rembrandt?" 93. After the fact, Ernst van de Wetering stated that such travel was premature. If he had a chance to do such investigations differently, he "would first analyze 10 or 20 paintings very meticulously, with no limit to time or energy, and try to learn from that, and only then start to travel to study the paintings in situ." Ibid.

3 Hochfield, "What Is a Real Rembrandt?" 90–91.

4 See Cutting's essay in this volume.

5 Hochfield, "What Is a Real Rembrandt?" 85; and Liedtke et al., *Rembrandt/Not Rembrandt in the Metropolitan Museum of Art*, 2:4.

6 Liedtke et al., *Rembrandt/Not Rembrandt in the Metropolitan Museum of Art*, 2:4.

7 For comments by Ernst van de Wetering on the production of self-portraits and portraits of Rembrandt in his workshop, see Hochfield, "What Is a Real Rembrandt?" 93.

8 See G. Schwartz, The Schwartzlist.

9 Bruyn et al., *A Corpus of Rembrandt Paintings*.

10 Hochfield, "What Is a Real Rembrandt?" 86.

11 Ibid., 87.

12 To date, the Rembrandt Research Project has examined 280 paintings and has assigned them to the following categories: 146 to A; 12 to B; 122 to C.

13 Hochfield, "What Is a Real Rembrandt?" 85, 87. For the definition of a "fake," see Liedtke et al., *Rembrandt/Not Rembrandt in the Metropolitan Museum of Art*, 2:5. The members of the Rembrandt Research Project identified very few "fakes" that dated later than the seventeenth century. Ibid., 2:3–5. See also von Sonnenburg, *Rembrandt/Not Rembrandt in the Metropolitan Museum of Art*, 1:7.

14 Von Sonnenburg, *Rembrandt/Not Rembrandt in the Metropolitan Museum of Art*, 1:4.

15 Such examples of re-attributions, in this case by non-members of the Rembrandt Research Project, appear in von Sonnenburg, *Rembrandt/Not Rembrandt in the Metropolitan Museum of Art*, 1:x, plus catalogue entries; and Liedtke et al., *Rembrandt/Not Rembrandt in the Metropolitan Museum of Art*, 2:x, 3, 33–35; plus catalogue entries.

16 Hochfield, "What Is a Real Rembrandt?" 87, 88, 91. Although Ernst van de Wetering stated that "unanimity among the members was rarely breached," he contributed "minority opinions" to the *Corpus* that "reflected my conviction that connoisseurship by committee does not bring a greater truth. . . . If you analyze these catalogue entries,

they are remarkably clever, but you could also make another argument. It all depends on the basis on which your argumentation is built, and that basis is shaky." Hochfield, "What Is a Real Rembrandt?" 88, 91.

17 "Once the hand of Rembrandt has been recognized or rejected, the Rembrandt Research Project is sometimes obliged to dismiss as irrelevant technical evidence of the kind which it otherwise considers corroboratory. . . . These examples . . . show that a 'good' painting retains its power of conviction, even in the absence of the qualities which are supposed to make it good, while no surfeit of technical evidence will make a 'bad' one look any better." G. Schwartz, "Connoisseurship," 203.

18 See Jensen's essay in this volume. "To identify an artist and his work as exemplary of the canonical," Kjellman-Chapin lists the requisite features as "innovation, precocity, originality, and unique authorial identity." See Kjellman-Chapin's essay in this volume.

19 See Brzyski's introduction to this volume.

20 Van de Wetering, *Rembrandt, the Painter at Work*, 207, 209–11; Hochfield, "What Is a Real Rembrandt?" 90; Carol Vogel, "Rembrandt at Frick Passes," *The New York Times*, October 24, 1997, section E, part 2, 34; and Gary Schwartz, "The Polish Rider," Consortium of Art and Architectural Historians listserv, November 1, 1997. Like Bruyn, von Sonnenburg suggested that the *Polish Rider* was painted by Willem Drost. Von Sonnenburg, *Rembrandt/Not Rembrandt in the Metropolitan Museum of Art*, 1:6, 35.

21 Hochfield, "What Is a Real Rembrandt?" 90–92.

22 Ibid., 92.

23 Ibid., 91–92.

24 Ibid., 92–93.

25 Although only scholars will have access to certain information, most of the database will be available to any interested parties. The digital archive will result from the cooperative participation of various institutions: the University of Amsterdam's Art History Institute, the Netherlands Institute for Art History, the Rembrandt Information Center of the Rembrandt House Museum, the Digital Production Center of the University Library of Amsterdam, the Amsterdam University Press, and the Rembrandt Research Project. Ibid., 93.

26 See Jensen's essay in this volume.

27 Van de Wetering, *Rembrandt, the Painter at Work*, 16 and nn. 15–17.

28 Ibid.

29 Ibid., 11–17.

30 See von Sonnenburg, *Rembrandt/Not Rembrandt in the Metropolitan Museum of Art*, 1:12–14; van de Wetering, "The Invisible Rembrandt," 97, 98, 102; and van de Wetering, *Rembrandt, the Painter at Work*, 150.

31 Van de Wetering, *Rembrandt, the Painter at Work*, 17, 21–23, 129–30, 211, 214. See also van de Wetering, "The Invisible Rembrandt," 96.

32 Van de Wetering, *Rembrandt, the Painter at Work*, 23–24, 27.

33 Ibid., 140.

34 Van de Wetering refers to the stages of underpainting as first "tonal dead color," or monochrome, and second as "the working up of color onto the monochrome." However, "dead color" could also include "lightly-applied colour," as mentioned with re-

gard to the paintings of Anthony van Dyck in the publication by Thomas Marshall ca. 1640–50. Van de Wetering, *Rembrandt, the Painter at Work*, 23, 25, 27, 30–36. See also van de Wetering, "The Invisible Rembrandt," 96–97.

35 Van de Wetering, *Rembrandt, the Painter at Work*, 32–44. "Pigment analysis was of limited value in settling questions of authenticity, for by far the majority of dubious paintings must have been executed in Rembrandt's workshop. It did, though, tell us a great deal about the procedures followed in the studio." Van de Wetering, "The Invisible Rembrandt," 96. For a reproduction of pigment analysis of Rembrandt's *Flora* (National Gallery, London) magnified 175 times, see van de Wetering, "The Invisible Rembrandt," 97, fig. 119.

36 Dendrochronology "measures climatically induced variations in the width of annual growth rings on the cross-cut sides of oak panels." Van de Wetering, "The Invisible Rembrandt," 90. Rembrandt used standard sizes of panels for his paintings. Van de Wetering, *Rembrandt, the Painter at Work*, 15.

37 Van de Wetering, "The Invisible Rembrandt," 90.

38 Van de Wetering, *Rembrandt, the Painter at Work*, 16; and van de Wetering, "The Invisible Rembrandt," 91, figs. 108–11.

39 "Because of the remarkable resemblance in both size and composition of certain panels that were evidently manufactured in one and the same 'series,' it is probable that Rembrandt bought several panels at a time . . . and the discovery by Prof. Dr. J. Bauch that in a number of cases two or more panels used by Rembrandt came from the same tree trunk is evidence for the correctness of this assumption." Van de Wetering, "Painting Materials and Working Methods," 1:17.

40 Van de Wetering, "The Invisible Rembrandt," 94; and van de Wetering, *Rembrandt, the Painter at Work*, 91–110, and, as an example, see figs. 123–25 for reproductions of the canvas threads of *Still-life with Peacocks* (1639; Rijksmuseum, Amsterdam).

41 Van Wetering, *Rembrandt, the Painter at Work*, 96ff., 100. The canvas used for paintings was not originally intended for this purpose, but rather "as a covering for mattresses and quilts, sailcloth, produced for shipyards, and linen cloth intended for clothing, bedding, and the like." Ibid., 95 and nn. 32, 33.

42 Ibid., 109–10. For an interpretation of the cusping on canvases, see ibid., 111ff.; and van de Wetering, "The Invisible Rembrandt," 94.

43 For discussions of the Morellian method, see the preface to Bruyn et al., *Corpus*, 1:xiv; von Sonnenburg, *Rembrandt/Not Rembrandt in the Metropolitan Museum of Art*, 1:11; van de Wetering, *Rembrandt, the Painter at Work*, 171, 173; and van de Wetering, "Rembrandt's Manner," 24–26. For a discussion of two other methods that had similar goals, see the preface to Bruyn et al., *Corpus*, 1:xiv. For a specific comparison, see van de Wetering, *Rembrandt the Painter at Work*, 172 and figs. 214–21.

44 Van de Wetering, "Problems of Apprenticeship and Studio Collaboration," 2:60, 63–77.

45 Ibid., 2:64–65, 69–71.

46 Ibid., 2:73.

47 Bruyn, "Studio Practice and Studio Production," 3:30; and Bruyn, "Rembrandt's Workshop," 77.

48 Bruyn, "A Selection of Signatures, 1632–1634," 2:106.

49 See, for example, Bruyn, "A Descriptive Survey of the Signatures," 1:53–59; and Bruyn, "A Selection of Signatures, 1632–1634," 2:99.

50 Bruyn, "A Descriptive Survey of the Signatures," 1:53.

51 Ibid., 1:59; Bruyn, "A Selection of Signatures, 1632–1634," 2:105; Bruyn, "A Selection of Signatures, 1635–1642," 3:51; and Hochfield, "What Is a Real Rembrandt?" 84.

52 Hochfield, "What Is a Real Rembrandt?" 84; and Bruyn, "A Selection of Signatures, 1635–1642," 3:55. Copies of Rembrandt's paintings were readily available by the mid- to late 1630s. Hochfield, "What Is a Real Rembrandt?" 84.

53 Bruyn, "A Selection of Signatures, 1632–1634," 2:104.

54 Bruyn, "A Selection of Signatures, 1635–1642," 3:56.

55 Hochfield, "What Is a Real Rembrandt?" 86; and Liedtke et al., *Rembrandt/Not Rembrandt in the Metropolitan Museum of Art*, 2:4.

56 Hochfield, "What Is a Real Rembrandt?" 87.

57 Ibid., 92.

58 Ibid., 89.

59 For example, see von Sonnenburg, *Rembrandt/Not Rembrandt in the Metropolitan Museum of Art*, 1:6, 61, 100–104; and Liedtke et al., *Rembrandt/Not Rembrandt in the Metropolitan Museum of Art*, 2:74–76.

60 See Alpers, *Rembrandt's Enterprise*, whose arguments are based on this premise; Bruyn, "Rembrandt's Workshop," 68; and van de Wetering, *Rembrandt, the Painter at Work*, 6, 8 and n. 15. Scholars today do not agree on the organization or size of Rembrandt's workshop. Hochfield, "What Is a Real Rembrandt?" 84, 89. Nor do scholars agree as to whether or not some of the pupils functioned more as assistants. See Bruyn, "Rembrandt's Workshop," 69.

61 Van de Wetering, "The Invisible Rembrandt," 90.

62 Bruyn, "Rembrandt's Workshop," 70.

63 Hochfield, "What Is a Real Rembrandt?" 93.

64 Bruyn, "Rembrandt's Workshop," 75.

65 Ibid., 69–70.

66 For the full quotation, see ibid., 70.

67 Ibid., 70.

68 Ibid., 70, 79; von Sonnenburg, *Rembrandt/Not Rembrandt in the Metropolitan Museum of Art*, 1:6. For a counterargument to the assumption that pupils' paintings were sometimes signed by the master or signed by the pupil with the master's name, see Liedtke et al., *Rembrandt/Not Rembrandt in the Metropolitan Museum of Art*, 2:24.

69 Bruyn, "Rembrandt's Workshop," 70, 79.

70 Ibid., 69–70.

71 Ibid., 71.

72 See Brzyski, "Making Art in the Age of Art History, or How to Become a Canonical Artist" in this volume, in which the author discusses this phenomenon with regard to modern Polish artists in Cracow.

73 See Cutting's essay in this volume.

74 Alpers, *Rembrandt's Enterprise*, 101, 102, 118. See also Liedtke et al., *Rembrandt/Not Rembrandt in the Metropolitan Museum*, 2:6, which takes issue with Alpers's argument by stating that "the Rembrandt style was an integral part of Dutch culture and not a tale of

genius and its dim reflections, much less a matter of Rembrandt marketing his own image and student pictures in his style."

75 Alpers, *Rembrandt's Enterprise*, 122.

76 In order to counter this argument, Ernst van de Wetering states:

> Might it not, as some art historians have indeed written—be an urge nurtured by the nineteenth century's cult of the genius that drives one to sift the *oeuvre* of a master—in our case, Rembrandt—trying to separate out at all costs the products that came about from a form of cooperation such as Rembrandt and his contemporaries evidently found perfectly normal? The need, with an artist of this stature, to follow his personal development through study of autograph work seems a legitimate reason for trying to achieve clarity on this point. In itself, it is disturbing to realize that the amount of artistic pleasure the viewer derives from one and the same painting seems liable to considerable variation, depending on one's ideas about the authenticity of the work in question; not to mention the changes in the painting's monetary value. Absurd though this phenomenon may appear at first sight, knowing whether a painting is a derivative product or not is, in itself, of considerable significance when assessing it. The important question here remains, of course, whether our obsession with problems of authenticity ought not to be regarded as anachronistic. (Van de Wetering, "Problems of Apprenticeship and Studio Collaboration," 2:60)

77 Bruyn, "Rembrandt's Workshop," 70. Most painted copies by Rembrandt's pupils date from the later 1630s. Ibid., 77. Von Sonnenburg claims that no documentary evidence exists that reveals how the seventeenth-century collector regarded a painting by a Rembrandt pupil that could be mistaken for an authentic work by the master. Von Sonnenburg, *Rembrandt/Not Rembrandt in the Metropolitan Museum of Art*, 1:36.

78 Van de Wetering, *Rembrandt the Painter at Work*, x; and Bruyn, "Rembrandt's Workshop," 70.

79 Van de Wetering, "Problems of Apprenticeship and Studio Collaboration," 2:60.

80 Bruyn, "Rembrandt's Workshop," 70.

81 Ibid., 70–71, 79.

82 From 1644: *yder schilder, onder dit Collegie resorteerende . . . een stuk werks, bij hem gemaakt.* From 1664: *een stuk werks, by hem zelfs gedaan, principaal geheelyk opgemaakt.* These requirements are cited and discussed in van de Wetering, "Problems of Apprenticeship and Studio Collaboration," 2:60–61.

83 Ibid.

84 Haverkamp-Begemann, "Rembrandt as Teacher," 27–29. In contrast, Albert Blankert suggests that Rembrandt's painting style had an effect on some of his pupils' paintings long after they left his studio. Cited in Liedtke et al., *Rembrandt/Not Rembrandt in the Metropolitan Museum of Art*, 2:24.

85 Liedtke et al., *Rembrandt/Not Rembrandt in the Metropolitan Museum of Art*, 2:31–32; and Bruyn, "Rembrandt's Workshop," 84 fig. 104, 85–86. The Stuttgart *Portrait of Rembrandt* has also been attributed to "Circle of Rembrandt" and by some to Rembrandt himself. Von Sonnenburg, *Rembrandt/Not Rembrandt in the Metropolitan Museum of Art*, 1:7–8.

Making Art in the Age of Art History, or How to Become a Canonical Artist

ANNA BRZYSKI

What does it take for an artist to enter the canon? How precisely is the consensus formed as to who the great artists are? The traditional responses to those questions have always pointed to the work as the self-evident foundation of aesthetic judgments. Great artists are great because they create great works. The masterpieces provide the evidence necessary to confirm an artist as a "genius," or, to use somewhat less dated terms, to recognize his (and it has been mainly "his") "historic significance." Robert Jensen's essay in this volume provides an important update of this position. Jensen argues that canonical status is a result of a consensus that forms regarding the significance of a particular work or body of works among practitioners inhabiting a particular field of cultural production and consumption. Although canonical status is established relationally, it is not just a matter of perception. It is based on the recognition of concrete and identifiable achievement understood as a significant innovation, which creates conditions for production of future works. Within the logic of this argument canonicity must be earned. The status of the work vis-à-vis the art historical narrative is never determined by purely contextual considerations, much less by ideological imperatives, but rather by historic evidence of the work's impact on contemporary and subsequent practice—an impact that is assumed to reflect the work's character and as such to be empirically available for observation and analysis, but not subject to external revision or manipulation. Value and by extension canonicity are, in other words, created within the historic record through the impact on subsequent art practice, not on the pages of art history books.

In both views of canonical status, the traditional and the empirically based, the relationship of the art historian to his subject is well defined and unambiguous: art historians study art. The artist and the work of art (together with their historic context and affinities) are identified as the focal points of disciplinary inquiry; conversely, those things that do not fit the rubric of "art," though often referenced in discussions, are positioned on the periphery of the main project. Since a canonical work of art (once it securely achieves a place in the canon) is assumed to be qualitatively superior to and hence more "historically significant" than noncanonical works, it becomes virtually unavoidable as an object of study.[1] Its place in the art historical narrative, which guarantees its visibility and ensures its reproduction both as an image and as a referent within the shared disciplinary knowledge base, compels the production of discourse. It motivates seemingly endless observation, description, analysis, critique, interpretation, and reinterpretation by successive generations of art historians, whose methodologies and conclusions may have varied and may have changed over time, but whose focus has remained surprisingly constant ever since the nineteenth century.

Throughout this period, the consumers and the producers of art history texts (those published as well as those delivered in oral and visual forms, as lectures, courses of study, exhibitions, museum installations, and so forth) have assumed a lack of direct connection or reciprocity between the observed evidence (visual and documentary) and the observing scholar, whose noninvolvement (and presumed disinterest) has served as a guarantee of objectivity and impartiality of the investigation and its outcomes.[2] The artist, considered as the creator of the work, has been viewed in a similar manner. His persona—a representation predicated as much on the cultural assumptions and expectations concerning the species "artist" as on any factual information—has been treated as a raw material for disciplined conversion into historical and critical knowledge. But, is such a presumption of distance and disengagement, enshrined by the rhetoric modes of art historical presentation, warranted? When constituted as a historic subject, the artist comes to occupy a position vis-à-vis the art historian that is not dissimilar from that occupied by the Oriental vis-à-vis the Orientalist scholar.[3] The fundamental and, in the end, all important difference between the Orientalist and art historical discourses has been that in the symbolic economy of art history, the artist, especially the canonical great master, has functioned as a positive representation of the Self—the superaltern reflecting our idealized self-image. In Orientalism and colonial discourse in general, the Oriental has functioned as the ultimate Other—the subaltern *against* whom the Self is defined. In both cases, however, the relationship of the scholars to their subjects has been configured as a power relationship of ownership and control of the production of knowledge. It is a relationship predicated on the denial of agency to those being observed—no matter whether they occupy the sub- or the superaltern position. The observers do not admit the possibility that their subjects can be aware and cognizant of the full spectrum of positive and negative consequences of being observed, much less react in a meaningful way by modifying their actions in response to the observers' expectations or claiming for themselves the observer position.

In art history, the passivity of the art historical subjects is further guaranteed by the presumed existence of an unbridgeable temporal gap between the present of art historical discourse and the past of the art's history. Despite growing self-consciousness of the effects and consequences of the present location of the production of disciplinary knowledge, that fundamental assumption of distance has not been questioned. The ongoing debates have tended to focus on the issues of art historical practice—how is the validity of statements to be judged, what is the relationship of the historic record to history, is it in fact possible to retrieve historic information and achieve objectivity, and so on—not on art history's presumed autonomy vis-à-vis the more or less (depending on the perspective) autonomous field of art.

It is ironic, given art history's traditional investment in maintaining the distinction between works of art and artifacts, that it has shared this observer-observed distinction with anthropology, its often unacknowledged sister discipline, which entered the university at approximately the same time as art history, namely in the last decades of the nineteenth century. Although the conceptual framework that has supported the faith in distance and non-interference has been vigorously questioned within cultural anthropology since the 1980s, leading to a much more nuanced understanding of the complex interactions occurring within the dynamic of fieldwork, the same self-consciousness has not registered within art history.[4] This is remarkable when one considers that in art history the observer and the observed not only belong to the same culture but coexist within and co-produce the system that evaluates and confers value on art. It is not uncommon to see the origins of art history traced all the way back to Vasari, though more often and more assuredly they are identified with Winckelmann and the eighteenth century. Even if we assume the more recent founding date, the undeniable historic reality is that the discourse of art history has coexisted with the production of art for over two hundred years. The term "coexisted," which implies the autonomy of and the separation between the two discursive domains—that of art history and that of art practice—may in fact be inappropriate and misleading, when one considers that since the eighteenth century, if not before, Western artists have not only received instruction in art history but have been explicitly encouraged by their professional and cultural environments to think of their practice in historic terms.

Although one could insist, perhaps with some validity, that work produced prior to the eighteenth century was not affected in a significant way by historicist considerations, no such claim can be made for the subsequent period in which art history came to function as the dominant value conferring discourse. The academic professionalization of art history in the twentieth century makes it easy to forget that from the Renaissance through the early twentieth century the production of art historical discourse had been the proper domain of artists, a domain that they shared with a host of other practitioners. The professional art historian, a creature of the university and a product of specialized disciplinary and disciplined training, is a relative latecomer to that group. The notable exception is the German context, in which art history became a university discipline in the first half of the nineteenth century, though there too the production of texts that were understood as "art history" was by no means an academic monopoly. In the second half of the nineteenth century, a period when art history entered public consciousness as the dominant way of thinking about art, the verbal art historical discourse was produced by a wide range of figures with varying expertise, affiliations, and interests: historians, classicists, philologists, philosophers, "men of letters," critics, amateur connoisseurs, assorted "art lovers," journalists, dealers, collectors, and, of course, artists. The distance and boundaries between art history and art criticism were neither established nor policed, and art history, or perhaps more accurately the emerging paradigm that defined art as a historic phenomenon, established a frame of references and terms within which art's value, meaning, and legitimacy were being actively negotiated for the present.[5]

If we assume that contemporary artists were aware of the impact of art historical narratives on the perception of value of past and present art practice and, moreover, were involved, both directly and indirectly, in the production of art historical discourse, then we have to rethink our assumptions concerning the relationship between art history and art practice in the nineteenth century and ever since. The postcolonial theory has amply shown that "the subaltern can know and speak itself" and through speaking can intervene in and affect the colonial discourse.[6] We may now have a more formalized division of labor between art and art history, but the codependence of the two fields is no less in evidence. In fact, one could argue, that at no other time has the perception of art's value been more dependent on its art historical framing.[7] If we assume that art history has been assigning value under the guise of historic significance to works and artists ever since the nineteenth century (a value that has been not just symbolic but economic as well), then how likely is it that artists who have received training in art history, have been fully aware of the benefits conferred by the canonical designation, and have had opportunities to participate in the production of the art historical discourse would not attempt (consciously or unconsciously) to affect their own standing within the system?[8] Within this context, Jensen's claim that artists, not curators or academic art historians, make canons, or at least the canons that matter, may indeed prove to be very true, though perhaps not exactly in the way that the author intended.

Art History as Metadiscourse

The term metadiscourse has been defined in linguistics as a discourse about discourse. On the level of the individual text, metadiscourse describes those features that do not necessarily contribute specific information but rather help to organize a text as a communicative structure. They include logical connections, rhetorical frames, attitude, personal and relational markers, references to sources, transitions, and so forth that not only guide the reader's comprehension but identify a text's meanings in relation to a broader discursive and cultural context.[9] This framing function of metadiscourse has led to the extension of the term to cover not just specific rhetorical features but entire rhetorical systems within which meanings are produced. In a study on parliamentary debates, for instance, C. Ilie defines metadiscourse as "a set of rhetorically structured communicative and interactional strategies used by speakers to signal, highlight, mitigate, or cancel parts of their ongoing discourse and their varying relevance to different addressees and/or audience members."[10]

In his studies of communication theory, Robert T. Craig has expanded the reach of the concept to cover the entire spectrum of theory because of its functions as "a discourse on discourse" in relation to communicative practice.[11] I would like to propose that the art historical discourse occupies a similar metadiscursive position vis-à-vis the art practice, especially if that practice is conceived not as an empirical given but as a complex discursive system operating across both the verbal and the visual fields. In other words, art history is a discourse on art discourse. The art discourse within this context comprises both verbal and visual components—it encompasses art theory, art criticism, and art practice. Since the advent of art academies and the rise of aesthetics as a distinct field within philosophy, art has been highly theorized and self-conscious as a practice. The reflexive discourse on art, namely discourse about art practice, has been produced by the practitioners as well as those not directly involved in the production of art. Since the eighteenth century, that reflexive art discourse has centered on three interdependent issues: art's definition, value, and history. If one assumes that art practice and reflexive art discourse are not independent of one another but merely occupy different positions along the theory-practice continuum—a continuum that precludes a possibility of either pure practice or pure theory—then one must consider that art history, as a discourse about art discourse, has a metadiscursive character.

Although the existing linguistic research has dealt extensively with functional aspects of metadiscursive practices, it offers little guidance in the analysis of the relationship between metadiscourse and value. The observations I offer here in reference to art history are based primarily on my own research and are presented with a full awareness of their preliminary character. More work needs to be done and in no way does this essay exhaust the complexity of the issue. Keith Moxey has observed that "art historians tend to assume that the history of art is an epistemological enterprise rather than a rhetorical one"[12] even though "*all* historical writing is by definition an art of persuasion."[13] For Moxey, the practice of rhetorical persuasion describes the interpretive work of art history as a disciplinary discourse. But limiting the rhetoric function of art history to its analytic project fails to take into account its impact on art practice. The success of rhetorical persuasion that secures particular meanings for specific phenomena also guarantees a discursive and hence historic location for those phenomena. Such a location is never neutral. It confers significance on objects and artists that enhances their symbolic and economic standing within the commercial exchange markets as well as markets involved in the negotiation of professional reputations and status.

Since the emergence in the nineteenth century of art history as a metadiscourse, an event that coincided with what Foucault diagnosed as a shift from a classical episteme to a modern one dominated by historicism,[14] the economic value of artworks and the status of artists have been closely correlated with the perception of their actual or potential historic significance. The shift in perception is perhaps most obvious in the assessment of the value and significance of the old masters—and the expansion of this group during the nineteenth century to include such hitherto "underrated" figures as Vermeer and Velázquez—which came to be increasingly determined by the location of the works by old masters within a narrative framework of art's history, rather than in reference to a set of ahistoric and universally valid criteria. The value of works produced by contemporary artists was similarly determined. As a consequence, the question of how to become a canonical artist, or, in other words, how to gain recognition as a historically significant figure (an artist without whom the history of a particular period or "national school" could not be told), became more than just an existential quandary facing ambitious artists as they contemplated their own practice in relation to the artistic tradition; it became the overarching rationale for all production conducted within the discursive space of "Art." To make work outside the historic paradigm was to leave in effect that discursive space and to enter the space of pure commerce. A work that was made primarily for the market, or, more importantly, that was judged to have been made primarily with the market in mind, fell outside the scope of art history and professional legitimacy. Its value was only related to its immediate function as decoration or commemoration, rather than its potential significance as Art—a category defined through Kantian aesthetics of disinterest and nonutility.

Given what was at stake, it is important to consider the criteria that determined the perception of historic significance of works and artists in the nineteenth century and before. Although etymological origins of the concepts of "genius" and "masterpiece" can be traced to classical antiquity, the roots of their modern definitions are much more recent. They can be linked to the mid-eighteenth century efforts to identify art as an autonomous tradition and practice. Within this context, the influence of German idealist philosophy, in particular of Kant and Hegel, on the pan-European art discourse can not be sufficiently emphasized. As I have argued elsewhere, even as the terms of that discourse began to shift in the mid-nineteenth century, the conceptual framework provided by those two philosophers was largely left intact, profoundly affecting, for instance, Baudelaire's views on art.[15] Throughout this period, Kant and Hegel were cited as undisputed authorities throughout the Western sphere of cultural influence. Whether credited or not, by the end of the nineteenth century, their views, or rather the views they had promoted. had become to such an extent part of the discursive fabric that any discussion of art, in particular when the issue of value was at stake, drew on concepts that could be ultimately traced to their work.

This is not necessarily to claim that either Kant or Hegel was uniquely original. Their observations and conclusions were based on existing paradigms and knowledge. But, they did provide a convenient synthesis of those views and presented them in a manner that was *designed to* enter a rapidly growing and consolidating discourse. Although both Kant's *Critique of Judgment* and Hegel's *Aesthetic Lectures* were addressed to a specific audience of peers, they were read widely by artists, critics, and others with professional or personal interest in the arts. Both works were widely disseminated, translated, and republished throughout the nineteenth century in Europe and beyond, producing a veritable flood of commentaries, responses, and direct and indirect applications. One could argue, in fact, that the main assumptions of Kant's and Hegel's definitions of art, genius, and masterpiece were not questioned until well into the twentieth century, and that even now they continue to affect our perception of art and art's history.

In the *Critique of Judgment*, Kant provides a succinct definition of artistic greatness. "*Genius* is the talent (or natural gift) which gives the rule to art. Since Talent, as the innate productive faculty of the artist, belongs itself to nature . . . Genius is the innate mental disposition (*ingenium*) *through which* nature gives the rule to art."[16] The link drawn by Kant between genius and nature is of key importance here since it takes production of art out of the contingent realm of culture and locates it firmly in the non-contingent realm of nature. In this context, not only is the masterpiece identified as a concrete and "natural" manifestation of the "rules" of art, but the rules themselves are implicitly given the status of natural laws. In other words, what Kant implies is that we, the viewers, owing to our limitations, may not realize the nature of those laws; however, our inability to articulate or comprehend them does not deny their empirical existence. Because the laws of art are natural laws, they cannot be legislated, only "discovered." To clarify this point, Kant states: "1. that genius is *talent* for producing that for which no definite rule can be given; it is not a mere aptitude for what can be learned by a rule. Hence, *originality* must be its first property. 2. But since it also can produce original nonsense, its products must be models, i.e. *exemplary*, and they consequently ought not to spring from imitation, but must serve as a standard or rule of judgment for others."[17]

In identifying the properties of genius, Kant in effect sets up the criteria for evaluating significance in art and creates a conceptual framework on which the narrative of art's history can be "objectively" constructed. These Kantian "truths"—that genius can not be learned; that an artist can not will him- or herself to be great, but must be born as such; that great artists are above all original; and that true originality (unlike original nonsense) must be exemplary, namely that it must serve as a model for emulation by others, and, because of that, it can be used as a yardstick for judging quality (one evaluates an imitation by comparing it with the original)—became the basic tenants of nineteenth-century art history and, ultimately, provided a compelling rationale for the legitimacy of modern art.

Although it is more common to trace the origins of the historic consciousness to Hegel rather than to Kant, it is important to note that Kant's notion of exemplary originality was used by nineteenth-century authors, including Hegel, to argue that art had both continuity and temporal dimension—namely, that it functioned as a tradition. Since the exemplary work was defined as a work worthy of emulation, the designation of genius depended not only on the intrinsic character of the artist's *oeuvre* but on the artist's influence on others and ultimately his impact on the artistic tradition. The implicit logic behind this argument was used to explain the rise of schools and styles, two basic taxonomic categories of nineteenth-century art history, and to argue that innovation was not merely valid but was in fact superior to emulation.

The implied temporal succession of great masters, each born rather than made, each giving rise to a school of followers, each giving a new impetus to art, underpinned a historic narrative of change, if not necessarily of progress. In Hegel's conception of art's history, which is usually identified with the teleological paradigm, the historic development in art is not synonymous with progress toward a particular goal but with evolution, which is understood as the accommodation of art practice to ever changing conditions. According to Hegel, the historic evolution of art followed a deterministic process of the Spirit's quest for self-consciousness. Although art evolved through time because of its association with the evolving consciousness of the Spirit, it did not necessarily progress in a qualitative way. Rather, it changed in form and content in keeping with the zeitgeist of the age that produced it.[18]

For Hegel, the seventeenth and the eighteenth centuries, in particular the development of the type of naturalism epitomized by Dutch genre painting, represented the dissolution of the tenuous union of form and spiritual content that still existed in Romantic art, defined by Hegel as postclassical, Christian art. From that point on, art ceased to evolve or to reflect the zeitgeist. Released from the demands of the evolving Spirit, art became autonomous. "From this point onward it is from himself that the artist receives his content," wrote Hegel. Art became a domain of "the Spirit of man assigning to himself its own boundaries, contemplating, experiencing and giving utterances to the infinitude of his emotions and situations."[19] Because art practice was freed from its subordination to spiritual concerns and because artists increasingly came to question the inevitability of particular forms, art in the present (the nineteenth century) "became a free instrument which [was] qualified to exercise itself relatively to every content, no matter what kind it may be, agreeably to the principles or criteria of the artist's own peculiar craftsmanship."[20]

With Kant's exemplary originality and Hegel's historic cultural framework, the canonical art history of the Western artistic tradition assumed its familiar shape. By the mid-nineteenth century, it was well established that art was a historic phenomenon—a continuous and autonomous tradition defined by canonical figures and schools and connected to the changing historic circumstances through the concepts of zeitgeist and style. These basic assumptions were shared by both the opponents and the proponents of modern art. Baudelaire, for instance, described the history of art in "The Painter of Modern Life" in terms of smooth transitions and continuity between various styles. Comparing artistic development to biological evolution, he implied both an element of inevitability and necessary historic dependence between the various stages.[21] A few years earlier, writing about Delacroix in his review of the 1846 salon, he noted that without the artist "the great chain of history [would break], [it would fall] to the ground."[22] The notion of a chain of history, which recalls the metaphor of "the chain of being" familiar from natural history and the discourse that surrounded contemporaneous debates on evolution, suggests that even at this early date Baudelaire distinguished between historic continuity and progress. He did address this issue explicitly in his review of the 1855 Universal Exposition when he noted that the concept of progress was borrowed from the technological sphere and had been misapplied to culture. Echoing both Kant and Hegel, he wrote that unlike in technology, where each successive invention derives from knowledge accumulated in previous discoveries, "in the realm of poetry and art, the great discoverers rarely have precursors. Every flowering is spontaneous, individual. . . . The artist owes nothing to anyone but himself. To future ages he holds out no promises but his own works. He is a guarantor for no one but himself. He dies without offspring."[23]

Baudelaire's comparison of the great work to a "spontaneous flowering" and his insistence that an artist "holds out no promises but his own works" to future generations call to mind Kant's definition of genius; his explicit references to tradition and to "the chain of history" locates all of his assertions within the Hegelian historic framework. For Baudelaire, art's past, present, and future are linked not through the dependence or influence of one artist on another but through mechanics of chronology. The old master, the contemporary artist who still awaits that designation, and the future master not yet born all exist in the diachronic space of art historic time. The position of each within that space and consequently within the implied hierarchy depends on the original contribution of each, or to combine Kant's and Jensen's terms, on the exemplary innovation of each, the evaluation of which is made relationally with reference to past and present production. The artist's visibility within that space is posited as the ultimate proof of significance and the basis of canonical designation.

Baudelaire has acquired a reputation as one of the key theorists of modernism, but his basic assumptions concerning art history and significance were by no means novel, radical, or exceptional. His interpretation of what constituted an exemplary innovation was no doubt highly partisan, but his understanding of the basic conceptual framework of evaluation was not. By the mid-nineteenth century, the idea that the value of artworks and the status of artists were both determined and evinced by their potential or apparent historic significance was widely accepted. Specific value judgments and pronouncements made in the context of art criticism, pedagogy, or practice were made less and less in reference to absolute standards, which was the dominant practice in the eighteenth century and before, and more and more to historic process, within which the ideology of innovation reinforced by market and institutional forces left little room for Kant's original scheme of the rare, lone genius surrounded by a multitude of followers. To make it in the market, the artist had to demonstrate that his work had a potential for historic significance. In this context, the question of how to become a canonical artist became a matter of concern not just for the artistic elites but for all professional artists interested in receiving symbolic and economic rewards for their work, or to put it simply, making a living as professional artists.

The Group Logic

If one assumes that artists' significance and claims to greatness do not depend solely on qualities present in their works but are also determined by the short- and long-term impact of their works on the artistic tradition—that they are, in other words, related to their position within the art historical narrative—then one must consider how the perception of significance was formed at the time of the work's production and sustained later on. Ever since the nineteenth century, art historical discourse has tended to determine that position relationally, by situating the work within a specific narrative framework and by comparing it with other works past and present. The comparative method, promoted by German art history in the final years of the nineteenth century as the primary tool of *Kunstwissenschaft* (the science of art), was an attempt to shift the discussion of significance from the sphere of subjective judgment to a seemingly more solid ground of empirically determined qualitative distinction. Although this approach did succeed in locating the work more firmly in its historic context, its operative assumption, that *Kunstwissenschaft* was as close as one could get to science within the humanities and consequently that it operated with a similar lack of bias, meant that evaluation—and here by evaluation I mean explicit judgments made regarding the importance and superiority of particular works and artists *as well as* their identification as key moments and individuals in the history of art—was never perceived or portrayed as anything but an impartial assessment of quality and historic relevance. Similarly, there was never any acknowledgment that the value system based on the idea of art's autonomy and special status—first developed by the eighteenth-century aesthetic theory, then embraced by the nineteenth-century art academies, and finally revitalized by the end of the nineteenth century by the modernist ideologues and practitioners as a type of fundamentalist reformation preaching a return to purity of idea and practice—had, in fact, a profound impact on the production of art history. It is in this context that a claim that Manet is a more significant artist than Bouguereau—a claim valid only when the modernist grand narrative is accepted as "the story" of art and when qualities found in the work of Manet are valorized, while those found in the work of Bouguereau are denigrated—has been accepted as a fact born out by the historic record, rather than having been seen as a value judgment made in reference to a specific value system, namely modernism.

If the modernist criteria of value and significance are partisan and culturally contingent, if they advance the interests of specific artists, while doing much disservice to others, why has their partisan character not been addressed or challenged until the advent of postmodernism? If, as I have argued, the issue of innovation is not just a matter of art history but of professional survival and success, then, as uncomfortable as it may make us, we should consider the possibility that artists, acting alone or in groups, have been defining and promoting particular evaluative criteria favoring their own practices as well as creating the conditions in which the perception of the innovative character of their works could be formed by their peers as well as various powerbrokers of the art world, including those engaged in the production of art history texts. In situations where artists themselves have wielded considerable authority within the structure of the art world—either as gatekeepers or as producers of art and art historical discourses—the correlation of interests and power had often been so great that their actions have effectively shaped the art historical narrative to their advantage. To put it in another way, it is undeniable that in the age of art history—a period in which art history has functioned as the value conferring metadiscourse vis-à-vis the art practice—artists have not been passive. They have been actively engaged in the production of their own art historical significance and have been doing so not just by creating "great" works.

In the remainder of this essay I would like to focus on an exceptionally clear case of a coincidence between authority and interests that led to the production of a particular narrative of national art history. In 1897, a group of Polish modernist painters affiliated with the Cracow School of Fine Arts, formed the Association of Polish Artists, "Sztuka" (Towarzystwo Artystów Polskich "Sztuka").[24] The Polish society is interesting both because it typifies the phenomenon of artist-run exhibition societies that emerged throughout Europe at the end of the nineteenth century and because it presents a fascinating study of the power wielded by artists in determining contemporary art's value. Within three years of its founding, Sztuka became the most important arbiter of value within the Cracow art world and within the Polish-speaking art world in general. Much of the society's power came from its close affiliation with the Cracow School of Fine Arts, which was officially recognized as the Academy of Fine Arts in 1900. The idea for creating an exhibition society modeled on the German secessions came from among the younger cadre of the school's professors and was supported by its newly appointed director, Julian Fałat. By 1900, the entire faculty of the Academy of Fine Arts were members of Sztuka. Since the leadership of the organization was invariably drawn from among the ranks of the school's professors, one could say that Sztuka functioned as an extension of the academy, becoming in fact an equivalent of the French academy, while the school itself occupied the position comparable to that of the École des Beaux-Arts.

Sztuka had a number of characteristics that call to mind such an analogy: it promoted itself as the premier national artists association; enjoyed official recognition and support from both the Austrian government and the local Polish authorities; had restrictive membership policies; was committed to promoting a particular form of art practice, that is, modern art, which it dogmatically identified with "Art" as such; was committed ideologically to modernist values, which it used to define quality and historic relevance in narrow and exclusionary terms; and finally, was hyperaware of art history, taking concrete actions to secure for modern art—and consequently its own members—a key location within the developing historic narrative of Polish art.

Although the idea of a "modernist academy" may seem an oxymoron, it does describe extremely well the situation that developed in Cracow. The discomfort with the notion is linked to the standard narrative of modern art, within which the late nineteenth century has been identified as a period of the waning power of all academies and the emergence of market-based avant-gardes, or, to put it another way, of the fall of the external market control and the rise of free market competition. Within this normative model—a model that I would argue is predicated on twentieth-century views concerning the superiority of free market competition rather than on the assessment of actual conditions within many of the nineteenth-century European art markets—the emphasis has been placed on the master, an individual artist-producer of branded art products, rather than on the traditional masterpiece, considered on its own terms outside the specific identity of its maker.[25] Although this normative model may reflect accurately the situation in the French art world—a uniquely developed and configured system unlike any other in Europe and certainly unlike the local art worlds of the European "periphery"—it can not be applied to the analysis of the situation in fin de siècle Poland, nor, I would argue, elsewhere in central Europe. In order to gain any appreciation of the extent to which the conditions in Cracow in 1897 differed from those in the major European art centers one has to consider three major absences that shaped the situation on the ground: the lack of the commercial gallery system, the lack of an authoritative academic tradition prior to 1895, and the lack of statehood, which determined local attitudes toward art and art history.

The Polish art market, or rather the market for art in the three major local art centers of Cracow, Lvov, and Warsaw, was dominated by locally operating exhibition societies modeled on German *Kunstvereins*, which functioned as membership organizations open to various "art lovers" (members of the lay public as well as artists) and ostensibly dedicated to the promotion and support of fine arts in a particular locality.[26] In Warsaw the local exhibition society, the Association for the Encouragement of Fine Arts (Towarzystwo Zachęty Sztuk Pieknych), coexisted with the city's sole commercial gallery, Aleksander Krywult's Art Salon, which tended to show work by the artists who also exhibited at the official venue. In Cracow and Lvov, the local exhibition societies were until the first decades of the twentieth century the only game in town; they held de facto monopoly power on the exhibition of contemporary art and functioned as the primary sites of the "art market" in those cities.

In this context, the founding of Sztuka, the members' decision to operate within the confines of the existing system and the society's self-portrayal as the defender of quality and of "Art" as such assume added significance. Unlike the German secessions, Sztuka artists never "seceded" from anywhere because they had nowhere to secede from. Rather, they banded together, forming an identifiable group that conferred a collective identity on the members' work, created a visible, physical separation (as a rule Sztuka's shows were held in separate rooms), and signaled the superiority of the group's works to everything else concurrently on display within the exhibition space. The Cracow exhibition society, the Society of the Friends of Fine Arts (Towarzystwo Przyjaciół Sztuk Pięknych), while a formidable institutional presence in the city, was not an artists' association. It was a *Kunstverein* and as such it did not promote a particular type of art practice; rather, it operated from an assumption that in order to make a living professional artists had to be able to show their work. Its mission was to provide broad access to exhibition space to all local artists. There were no juries, the society purchased works from its ongoing exhibitions to be distributed via a lottery system among its members, it published annual "premiums," which were usually composed of well-liked works, and it operated a loan program for artists in financial need. From its inception, Sztuka organized its exhibitions in the association's rooms located at the Town Cloth Hall (Sukiennice), which, incidentally, were directly adjacent to the rooms occupied by the National Museum. On one occasion, in 1905, Sztuka organized one of its two annual shows at the museum itself rather than at the society. Whenever Sztuka organized shows in other Polish cities, it also tended to do so at the local art societies.

Because of the decision to exhibit within the existing structures, Sztuka's members took great pains to create a distinction between their work, that is, modern art, and the rest of the work shown at these venues. In fact, according to the society's own published account, the main reason for the society's founding was the artists' desire to distinguish their work in terms of quality from the rest of what was being shown.[27] What was not indicated in the account is as interesting as what was—it did not mention any ideological or aesthetic reasons for the founding of the society. No matter what the Sztuka became later on, its founding and operations within its first years of existence should be seen as a strategic effort by a group of professional artists to achieve visibility and exercise greater control over the valuation of their work. All of Sztuka's activities were aimed at securing those goals and as such could be likened to an effort by a corporation to develop a positive corporate brand identity. While some may consider such a comparison blasphemous, it is difficult not to think of Sztuka in those terms when one considers the whole range of its actions: from its choice of a name, to its staging of exhibitions, to its production of publicity materials such as posters, catalogues, and books, to its "management" of public relations, and, finally, to its close institutional affiliation with all of the major players within the Cracow art world—the federal and local governments, the art school, the city's main exhibition venue, and the art museum.

By 1922, a year in which Sztuka published its twenty-fifth anniversary album, these practical and pragmatic considerations were largely forgotten in keeping with the society's rapidly evolving self-image. In an overview of the society's history that appeared in the album, Franciszek Klein describes the group's first show as a "noble protest" against the low standards prevalent at the Society of the Friends of Fine Arts.[28] In other statements the society was portrayed as the champion of quality and its members were identified, without qualification, as the best Polish artists of the period. Their actions were ascribed in equal measure to the idealistic pursuit of pure art and a deeply felt patriotism. The album suggested that the founding of Sztuka had nothing to do with the members' desire to survive and thrive within a particular sociocultural environment; rather, the members had taken a heroic step to ensure the survival of Polish culture.

Although this rhetoric certainly fits the modernist mythology of rebellion and heroic perseverance, it bears little resemblance to the actual situation. I would like to suggest that the members' decision to ban together was much more likely motivated by positively defined goals—the desires to create a collective identity and visibility, to identify modern art as the only legitimate contemporary practice, and, as a consequence, to establish control over valuation and evaluation. In this context the society's choice of a name—the word *Sztuka* simply means "Art"—should be seen as a major indicator of its commitment to that agenda. The society's name, framed discursively through statements issued by the society itself and by its sympathizers, communicated an uncompromising commitment to quality. It functioned as a guarantee that all of the work shown at the society's exhibits was "Art." Conversely, it also implied that the work of artists who were not invited to join the society or who did not show with it was second rate or perhaps did not even deserve that designation.

The modernist assumptions concerning quality and relevance ultimately defined the distinction between a "work of art" and a mere "painting," the former embodying absolute and transcendent values, the latter designating a particular skill-based practice. A painting recognized as a masterpiece was certainly considered a work of art, but not all paintings deserved such recognition. Many were thought to be nothing more than competently made images. "Art" as a province of genius belonged to art history and as such had little to do with mastery of manual skill. It could not be taught, only encouraged. It was arrived at through personal dedication, experimentation, and continual practice. Innate talent and inspiration were requisite. Since painters who produced academically correct work demonstrated only command of a particular skill, they were viewed by the modernists as competent craftsmen, but they were rarely acknowledged as artists. Conversely, work that was not highly finished or "correct" by academic standards but that fit other expectations could easily qualify as "Art." By this logic, a sketch, a print, or a work of graphic design had potentially more merit than an academic canvas.

The Sztuka cultivated in the public a perception that its name guaranteed the presence of "Art." In order to ensure that the brand Sztuka was synonymous with "quality," the society adopted and maintained a strict review process for membership. The new members could join only by invitation, which had to be approved by a majority vote. In 1899 the society also adopted a jury system under which works submitted for exhibition by members had to be approved first by the membership.[29] Although there is no evidence that this system was ever fully implemented, the fact that it was attempted once again demonstrates the society's self-perception as the guardian of standards, or, as I have argued, as the academy.

More significantly, the shift in art historical discourse that in mid-1890s was increasingly recognizing modern art as the present direction of the Western artistic tradition allowed the members and sympathizers of Sztuka to unambiguously identify modernism as the latest, and from the perspective of those doing the writing, the most glorious chapter in the "History of Polish Art." In 1904, these efforts culminated in the publication of a serial illustrated album simply entitled *Polish Art*, which established the canon of Polish nineteenth-century painting and recognized the founding members of Sztuka as "the foremost masters of Polish painting" (fig. 11.1).[30] The album was the first Polish publication, and one of the first European art publications, to rely extensively on full-color photomechanical reproductions, rather than on descriptions. It included sixty-two color and three black-and-white plates, which illustrated sixty-one works by twenty-five Polish painters. The reproductions were accompanied by essays produced by twenty different contributors. These included, in addition to the two editors, eighteen critics, writers, artists, and art historians with established national reputations.

The album was also the first Polish-language art publication intended for the general public that not only integrated modernism into the historic narrative of national art but also constructed that narrative from a strictly modernist perspective. This is not surprising when one considers that it was edited and produced by two members of Sztuka's inner circle: Feliks Jasieński,

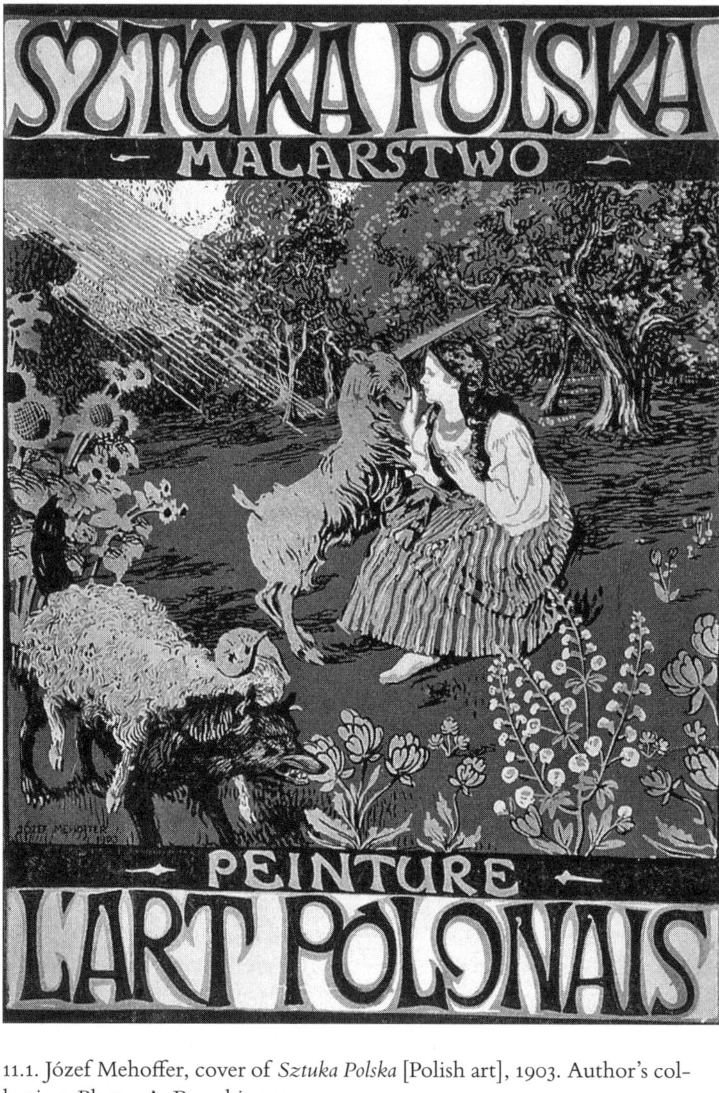

11.1. Józef Mehoffer, cover of *Sztuka Polska* [Polish art], 1903. Author's collection. Photo: A. Brzyski, 2003.

a prominent art critic and collector of modern art, and Adam Łada Cybulski, a young art critic, a future docent of art history at the Cracow Academy of Fine Arts, and the society's recording secretary. The album, which was subtitled *Sixty-Five Reproductions of Works by the Foremost Masters of Polish Painting*, unambiguously identified the key members of Sztuka as the greatest masters of Polish art. Of the twenty-five painters featured, fifteen were still alive when the book went into production—all of them were members of Sztuka. To put it another way, no contemporary artist who was *not* a member of Sztuka made it into the canon and hence into the art historical narrative of the development of Polish painting that the album constructed.[31]

As I have argued elsewhere, the album, which went through two editions, had a profound impact on the perception and production of the history of Polish nineteenth-century art. Although today one can find artists in the collections of Polish museums and accounts of the period who were not featured in the album, they are clearly presented as figures of secondary importance. The most celebrated masters of Polish nineteenth-century painting are still the artists-heroes of Sztuka, identified within Polish art history as Young Poland (Młoda Polska).

There is an interesting subscript to this story. In the late summer of 2004, almost exactly one hundred years after the publication of *Polish Art*, the National Museum in Cracow set up an outdoor "gallery" in Cracow's main city park, the Planty, to announce the opening of its new permanent installation of the Young Poland collection (fig. 11.2). The "Gallery on the Planty" featured reproductions of works in the museum's collection by the canonical painters of the movement. The reproductions, printed on a gray background and fitted into illuminated vitrines, unwittingly recalled the plate pages of *Polish Art*, which presented the reproduced works as color photographs pasted on neutral gray paper. The artists featured in the album were all present in the Planty installation, as were some of the works reproduced in 1904.

I bring up this contemporary example to suggest that institutions, especially if they are invested in particular narratives, easily forget where and how those narratives have been formed. The modernist narrative of Polish nineteenth-century art—presented for the first time in 1904 on the pages of *Polish Art* and celebrated one hundred years later with a remarkable lack of awareness of the precedent by the National Museum in the Planty installation—was shaped in a direct way by the modernist artists who became its heroes. I am not referring here to their work or questioning its quality and value; rather, I would like to draw attention to the impact of their efforts to promote themselves and to frame their practice on contemporary and subse-

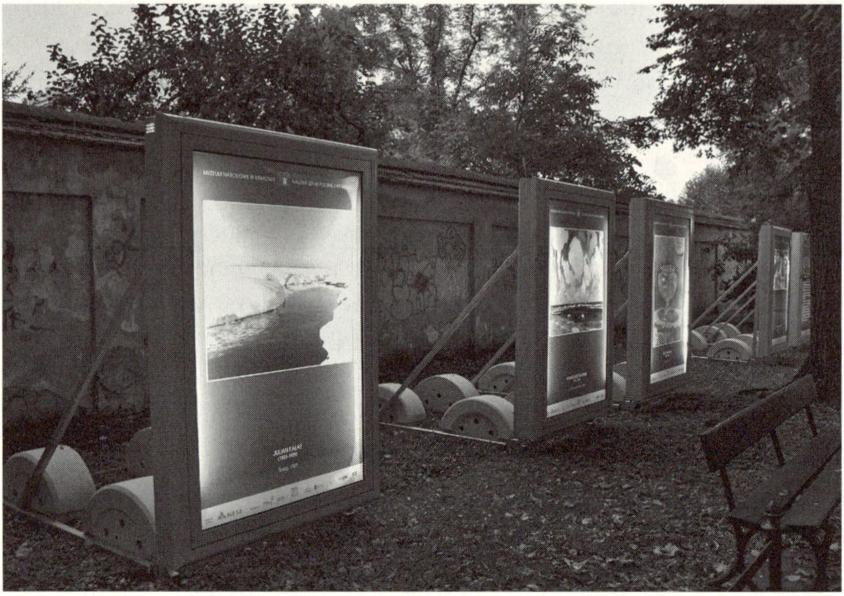

11.2. *Planty Gallery—Young Poland*, Planty Park, Cracow, August 2004. Project of the National Museum in Cracow. Photo: A. Brzyski, 2004.

quent perceptions of their work. The question I would like to ask to end this essay is whether or not such a direct intervention in the production of art historical narratives is still available to artists today—and if so, how? The radically different conditions in existence today within the global network of the art world might suggest that the answer is no. But, is that the case on the local level of a city, a nation, a region? Is there any evidence that suggests that the national art histories and canons produced today are not being shaped by artists' individual and group efforts to breach the threshold of visibility, to draw attention to and discursively frame their practices? One can not compare the system in which museums, private galleries and dealers, powerful collectors, the state, and variously configured artists' groups play major roles in shaping the conditions for the production and reception of art to the situation in fin de siècle Cracow. There, Sztuka's members encountered a discursive and institutional power vacuum, which they exploited masterfully and with weighty consequences. Today, in the major art centers there is no power or discursive vacuum; just the opposite is true. Many voices vie for recognition and many hands hold institutional authority over the production of art discourse and art history. But some of the basic issues remain the same. The value of art is still predicated on its potential to enter art history. The significance is measured by staying power and is reflected in the escalation of prices for works by artists considered to be key figures in artistic movements charted by the field of art history. Consequently, for the artists the problem of achieving visibility and of positioning oneself vis-à-vis the contemporary perception of art historical significance is as much an issue today as it was one hundred years ago. And no doubt it will remain a subject of their interest as long as art history retains its metadiscursive function.

Notes

1 See Preziosi, *Rethinking Art History*, 21–53.
2 See Preziosi, *Rethinking Art History*; and Brzyski, "The Problem of Modernism."
3 Said, *Orientalism*.
4 See, for instance, Fabian, *Time and Other*; and Clifford, *The Predicament of Culture*.
5 On art history as a frame of reference for art practice, see Belting, *Art History after Modernism*, 7–16.
6 Spivak, "Can the Subaltern Speak?" 24–28.
7 Belting makes a similar claim, though unfortunately he does not provide much in terms of specific analysis in *Art History after Modernism*. Writing about the Western art market, he notes that the "historic and art historic position" of a work often matters more than the uncertain issue of quality. Such a position is an effect of what we call art history." Belting, *Art History after Modernism*, 199.
8 See Fitzgerald, *Making Modernism*.
9 See Vande Kopple, "Refining and Applying Views of Metadiscourse," 2; Crismore *Talking with Readers*; Crismore and Farnsworth, "Metadiscourse in Popular and Professional Science Discourse"; Crismore and Vande Kopple, "Hedges and Readers"; and Camiciottoli, "Metadiscourse and ESP Reading Comprehension."
10 Ilie, "Discourse and Metadiscourse in Parliamentary Debates," 71.
11 See Craig, "Metadiscourse, Theory, and Practice"; and Craig, "Theory as Metadiscourse."
12 Moxey, *The Practice of Persuasion*, 62.
13 Ibid., 61.
14 Foucault, *The Order of Things*.
15 For discussion of the impact of Hegel on Baudelaire's art criticism, see Brzyski-Long, "Retracing the Modernist Origins."
16 Kant, *Critique of Judgment*, 150.
17 Ibid., 151–52.
18 Hegel's views on the history of art as articulated in his *Aesthetic Lectures*, far from being uniquely original, should be seen as part of a broader discourse that also encompassed discussions of biological evolution in the natural sciences and of linguistic evolution in philology. See Said, *Orientalism*, 143–45.
19 Hegel, *Aesthetics*, 2:607.
20 Ibid., 2:605. In view of this statement, it may be worth reconsidering the claim of

radical innovation that has been made in recent years in reference to Alois Riegel and the Vienna school of art history, whose practitioners have been credited with severing the causal link between artistic development and the zeitgeist. See for instance Wood, "Introduction"; and Woodfield, ed., *Framing Formalism*. Although Riegel certainly pushed back the autonomy of artistic development to a much earlier period, the basic assumptions behind his notion of Kunstwollen are not dissimilar from those discussed by Hegel.

21 Baudelaire, *Selected Writings on Art and Literature*, 392.

22 Ibid., 75.

23 Ibid., 122.

24 For further discussion of the Sztuka, see Brzyski-Long, "Modern Art and Nationalism," 149–69; Brzyski, "Between the Nation and the World"; and Brzyski, "'Unsere Polen. . . .'" See also Krzysztofowicz-Kozakowska, *Śztuka Kręgu "Sztuki"*; Krzysztofowicz-Kozakowska, *Sztuka Młodej Polski*; Cavanough, *Out Looking In*; and Baranowa, *Stulecie Towarzystwa Artystów Polskich "Sztuka."*

25 See Robert Jensen's essay in this volume. A somewhat different version of this argument is the basis of the distinction drawn by White and White between "canvases" of the salon system and the "careers" of the gallery system in the French art world. See White and White, *Canvases and Careers*.

26 See Lewis, *Art for All*, 124–39.

27 Stanisławski, Axentowicz, and Mehoffer, "Sprawozdanie Wydziału Towarzystwa Artystów Polskich "Sztuka" za rok 1898," 379.

28 *"Sztuka" 1897–1922*, ii.

29 Ibid., viii.

30 For an in-depth discussion of the album, see Brzyski, "Constructing the Canon."

31 Feliks Jasieński and Adam Łada Cybulski were members of the closely knit art community in Cracow. Prior to undertaking work on *Polish Art* both wrote criticism for a broad range of Polish-language periodicals and newspapers, gaining reputations by 1903 as vocal supporters of modernism. Jasieński, in particular, was an important figure in the early history of Polish modernism. A son of a prosperous landowner, he was not just a sympathetic critic but also a passionate collector, popularizer, and promoter of modern art. Adam Łada Cybulski, Jasieński's junior by a decade, was hired in 1906 as the administrative assistant (*sekretarz*) at the Cracow Academy of Fine Arts. The same year he also began to be identified in Sztuka's exhibition catalogues as the society's "recording secretary." In 1908, he was appointed as a docent of art history at the academy, a position he held until 1911. For further discussion of the album *Polish Art* and of Sztuka's involvement in the production of the canon of Polish nineteenth-century painting, see Brzyski, "Constructing the Canon."

12

Kinkade and the Canon: Art History's (Ir)Relevance

MONICA KJELLMAN-CHAPIN

He really is an accomplished painter. He can out-Monet Monet.

—Ken Raasch, quoted by Christina Waters in "Doubting Thomas"

If not necessarily considered a great painter, Thomas Kinkade (fig. 12.1) is recognized as an undisputed master of marketing. He has been billed as the foremost selling artist of all time, a powerhouse of self-promotion and retail savvy.[1] Kinkade has built a multimillion dollar empire on photo-lithographic reproductions marketed through independently owned and operated "Signature Galleries" or peddled by the artist himself on QVC, the home shopping network. In addition to the prints, Kinkadian images are emblazoned on an enormous range of products, from calendars, mugs, and puzzles, to clothing accessories, wallpaper, and a host of collectibles. The assortment of Kinkadiana available for sale is constantly expanding. In 1998, the La-Z-Boy furniture company began producing a line of Thomas Kinkade furniture. A partnership between Kinkade and Sparrow Records, a division of EMI Recorded Music, resulted in a recording of music inspired by Kinkadian imagery that was packaged as a CD-sized book with illustrations by Kinkade. A "deluxe collector's edition" of the CD features a ready-for-framing print.[2] In another artistic crossover, Kinkade co-wrote a novel entitled *Cape Light*, part one of a proposed trilogy about life in a fictional town based on one of his paintings. Kinkade has also lent his name, and the names of his four daughters, to a "cottage-style" housing development near Vallejo, California, called the Village at Hiddenbrooke, which opened in September 2001.[3]

Kinkade's aggressive marketing tactics have earned him a reputation as a huckster, which has served to derail any serious consideration of him as an artist. Certainly there are not many in the art world lining up to praise his artistic skills. Kinkade is, however, a perfectly adequate painter, capable of rendering both figures and landscape with some facility; his handling of the medium is confident and fluid, and he dispenses naturalistic scenes readily. The quintessential Kinkadian image usually conjured up is relentlessly twee, with bulbous cottages, precious stone bridges, and gently winding roads and/or streams, all bathed in his signature glowing light (fig. 12.2). Even when Kinkade renders a more urban setting, his vision of an edenic world is a rigorously homogenous one, in which racial, ethnic, and economic differences are suppressed.[4]

Kinkade's pictures are, however, remarkably varied, marshalling a wide range of pictorial references, influences, and associations; stylistic links can be made to the Hudson River school of American landscape painting, the German romantic landscapes of Caspar David Friedrich, the Barbizon school, and Impressionism, both in its nineteenth-century French form and the slightly later American variants. Kinkadian subjects are likewise quite varied; while dominated by small-town scenes or landscapes, they also include more urban vistas, usually characterized by a temporal mixing peculiar to Kinkade. Consistency across subjects and styles resides both in the focus on and quality of light and in Kinkade's persistent attempt to forge links between his work and "masterpieces" from the Western art canon.

The canon Kinkade references is one constructed and effectively marketed to a wide audience (the same audience to whom Kinkade is pitching

12.1. Thomas Kinkade highlighting a painting. Photograph by George Sakkestad.

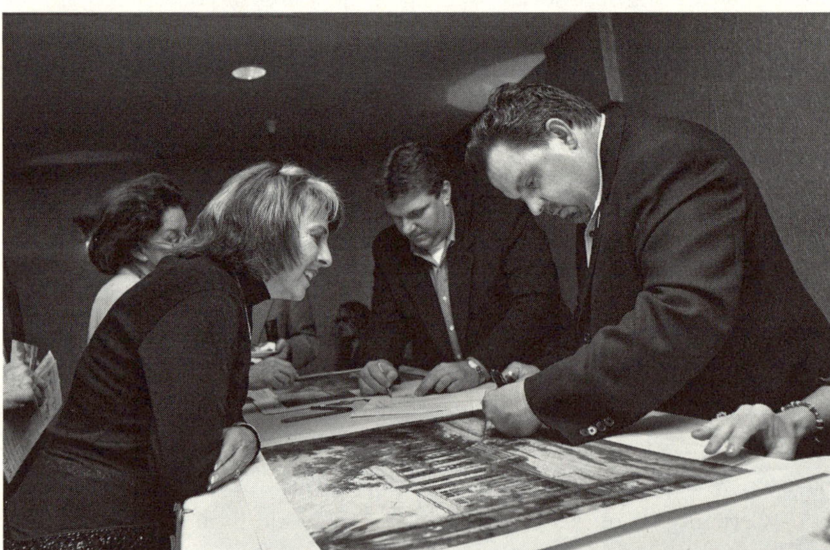

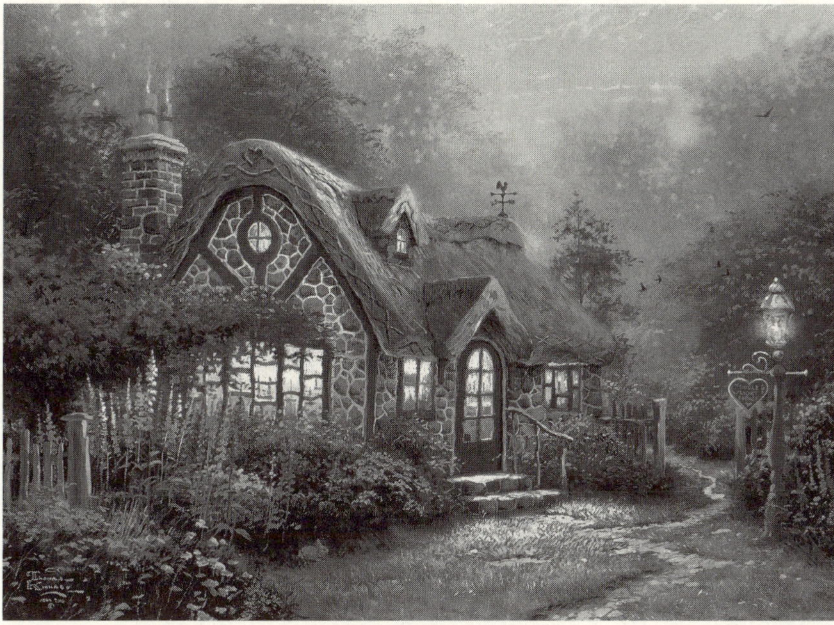

12.2. Thomas Kinkade, *Candlelight Cottage*, 1996. © 2005 Thomas Kinkade, the Thomas Kinkade Company, Morgan Hill, Calif.

his work) through a variety of means such as blockbuster exhibitions, diverse publications, and increasingly through websites and digital archives.[5] The introductory survey texts, such as H. W. Janson's *History of Art* and Marilyn Stokstad's *Art History*, and the courses taught from (or with) them are important disseminators of a particular canonical ideology for a vast majority of college freshmen, as well as a growing number of high school students. Equally potent, if not more so, are populist-oriented recent publications such as Robert Cumming's *Annotated Art*, Thomas Hoving's *Art for Dummies*, and Walter Robinson's *Instant Art History*.[6] Such books promulgate a "pop canon" based on the art historical canon bred and spread by the discipline's institutional and individual practitioners. The intersection and interagency of the populist and the academic is evidenced by the fact that books selling art history to "the masses" are organized like the standard survey texts and promote themselves as pedagogical, as the title of Carol Strickland's 1992 *The Annotated Mona Lisa: A Crash Course in Art History From Prehistoric to Post-Modern* makes clear.

The canon put forth in all such texts is remarkably consistent. The history of Western art is presented chronologically; it begins with Paleolithic cave painting and proceeds smoothly and seamlessly to more or less the present day. All the works included in these texts are presented as inimitable, as are their makers; their only peers are to be found in the pages alongside. Customarily there is a subcategory of the most outstanding artistic specimens, as found in Hoving's *Art for Dummies*, in which the author singles out ten artists as the "Ten Most Interesting," and fifteen works of art as the "Greatest Works of Western Civilization." This hierarchy within a hierarchy appears to be a standard feature, irrespective of whether the books are of the populist or more academic variety. The premise dictates the format of Cumming's *Annotated Art*, wherein fifty artists are singled out for special recognition, and that of his other popular book, *Great Artists*, in which "the world's greatest paintings are explored and explained." Perhaps not surprisingly, all of Hoving's "Big Ten" artists are included in Cumming's list of greats, and there is a similar correlation between the two authors' inventory of great(est) paintings.[7] The same works and authors can be found in every book one might consult; a glance through *Instant Art History* or *The Annotated Mona Lisa* confirms that all the usual suspects are present. An identical match can be made to other populist art history texts, such as *Sister Wendy's 1000 Masterpieces* and *Sister Wendy's Grand Tour: Discovering Europe's Great Art*.[8] The list of canonical artists and artworks included in the pop-art history books is virtually identical, if somewhat pared down, to that embraced by the standard textbooks, which now package and deliver their contents through CD-ROMs and text-specific websites.[9]

In the disciplinary economy of today's post–new art history, an unreflective endorsement of the canon is considered a relic of a bygone era and sensibility, and yet it is abundantly clear that there is a fertile market for exactly such repetition; the public seems to want the art historical equivalent of Who's Who, a desire that may well have been instilled by the publishers of such texts. The qualities that earn an artist or a particular work of art a place in the pantheon of "greats" are often proclaimed to be ineffable, yet every text dedicated to laying out the history of Western art includes some form of justification for its selections that references those presumably ineffable qualities. In its most reductive form, the justifying explanation functions like a formula. Glancing through the opening salvos of the introductory books, the reader is likely to come away with the idea that great artists are exceptional beings in possession of extraordinary gifts of insight, skill, creativity, and imagination, and that great works of art will exhibit those traits in abundance.[10] *Instant Art History*, for instance, defines art as "a special thing with unique qualities, like beauty or craftsmanship."[11] Hoving's *Art for Dummies* instructs its readers on "How to Recognize Good Art" by means of a checklist of questions that is printed at the front of the book on a "Cheat Sheet" and repeated in the first chapter:

✓ Does it express successfully what it's intending to express?
✓ Does it amaze you in a different way each time you look at it?
✓ Does it grow in stature?
✓ Does it continually mature?
✓ Does its visual impact of mysterious, pure power increase every day?
✓ Is it unforgettable?[12]

Not only is the reader now armed with a list of questions, she or he has the mental picture of the map of quality provided by the repetitious reinforcement of the fifty, twenty, or ten greatest works of art from one text to the next. The underlying premise behind such books is that in our culture, it is desirable, expected, and even advantageous to know something about art. The information is packaged in an easily digested form, it is unchallenging, and it is finite. The text's message is invariably this: here is everything you need to know about art throughout history, presented in a paperback of less than three hundred pages written in a user-friendly style.[13]

It is a system that promotes, indeed breeds, standardization and orthodoxy by perpetuating the belief that the history of art is organized into neatly bound period styles and that the viewers' mastery of the style system will give them more secure footing in recognizing which works and artists are "really" great. Hoving is the most programmatic in this respect, stating matter-of-factly that "the secret to knowing the rudiments of art history is to know the styles" and averring that he will steer the reader "through 50 centuries of artistic styles . . . identify[ing] the most typical of each epoch and the best of the best works of art in a particular style."[14] The readers are taught which works and artists are superior, what features are markers of greatness. Certain names are infinitely repeated (for example, Michelangelo, Leonardo, Rembrandt, Monet, and Renoir) and are explicitly associated with the desired values and qualities—inventiveness, originality (slavish dependence does not a great artist make), and a uniqueness of temperament as expressed in the artist's handling of the medium.[15]

While academic art history has increasingly become more theoretically inclined and critical of the canon as a historically produced and contingent entity, the phenomenon and the success of Kinkade, like the popularity of books such as *Art for Dummies*, signals the possibility that such questioning of the canon's assumptions, inclusions, exclusions, and ideological underpinnings is irrelevant to a very large segment of the population. A substantial part of Kinkade's project leans on the canon's success at defining what constitutes art. In fact, one could argue that his popularity depends on his successful co-option of the canonical devices and his ability to base his legitimacy on that prevalent and well-internalized structure.

What the canon entails in this context is less specifically a list of artists and artworks (although that certainly comes into play) than a constellation of attributes and aspects that are used to identify an artist and his work as exemplary of the canonical. Innovation, precocity, originality, and unique authorial identity have been rendered of the utmost importance by the Western canon, and those characteristics, abstract though they might be, are expected to be discernable in any potentially canonical art. Since they can be found in indisputably canonical work, those qualities become necessary traits of canonicity. Any artist aspiring to canonical position must reflect those same traits back. It is not enough to make magisterial pronouncements about one's own importance, as Kinkade and his marketing certainly do; there must be visible evidence present in the artist's work. The necessary characteristics must also operate, however, within an identifiable and appropriate frame of reference; for instance, inventiveness is a desirable quality, but eccentricity is generally not.[16] The requisite qualities are usually demonstrated as inherent in a particular work of art, such as the *Mona Lisa*, and are therefore to be found in its maker, in this case Leonardo, or an entire group, such as the Impressionists. Thus Kinkade aligns himself with a recognizable set of ideas, images, and producers, teasing out venerable associations by drawing upon the art historical equivalent of brand names, such as Rembrandt, Michelangelo, and Impressionism. By self-producing canon-signaling texts that mimic *catalogues raisonnés* and monographs, and establishing a museum dedicated to his work, he further rhetorically effaces the reproducibility, multiplicity, and commercialism on which his work is predicated.

The cornerstone of the Kinkade empire is without a doubt the reproductions sold through the Signature Galleries and formerly on the QVC cable network. Printed on a variety of materials from paper and Masonite to canvas, available in a range of sizes, and priced according to their placement in the hierarchy of editions, these prints are touched up with flecks of paint, either by the self-proclaimed "Master of Light" himself or by specially trained "Master Highlighters." The hand-highlighting with oil paint alters the prints ontologically, rendering them into near-paintings and positioning them as cuspal within an art historical system that is ordered by species. The new ontological identity granted to the reproductions is absolutely vital to Kinkade's enterprise, because it helps conceal the fact of their multiplicity, giving them instead the veneer of uniqueness. Augmenting that sense of specialness and authenticity is the certificate accompanying each print, along with the stamped signature of Kinkade in DNA-coded ink.[17] These almost-paintings are the digitally produced pictorial offspring of rarely glimpsed oil originals painted by Kinkade. Housed in a vault for safekeeping, the originals were displayed on rotation at the Thomas Kinkade Museum and Cultural Center in Monterey, California, which opened in May 2001. The originals are also sent on tour, with a select painting or two exhibited at carefully chosen Signature Galleries across the United States. Additionally, certain oils and sketches could be seen from time to time in the so-called Touring Museum bus.[18]

The purpose of the Thomas Kinkade Museum and Cultural Center is clear enough; his paintings are not acquired for public or private museum collections, and so he built one of his own. Dedicated to promoting the artist's work through repeating thematic exhibitions, such as "The Artist in Nature," the museum's literature proclaims that its permanent collection represents the most comprehensive collection of Kinkade paintings in the world.[19] There are few things that bespeak greatness like having a museum dedicated to one's work; since the fact that it was established by the artist himself is not broadcast in the information it puts forth, the sense given a visitor is that Kinkade is like other artists who have a museum, namely like Vincent van Gogh, Edward Munch, Pablo Picasso, Auguste Rodin, just to name a few. The Kinkade Museum also hosts exhibitions, usually featuring local artists whose focus and style complements that of Kinkade.

The Kinkade Museum has a gift shop, wherein the visitor can purchase books, stationary, calendars, and miniatures, and which is a key element in the carefully orchestrated meeting between the audience and the Kinkadian work. Usually, however, this meeting happens at the Signature Galleries, which are most often located in shopping malls. These spaces are critical sites in the escalating signaling of canonical worthiness and as such make a major contribution to conferring an aura of the "high" artist around Kinkade. Even the distinction Kinkade makes between his mall offerings and that of his neighbors effects this mantle of Art-with-a-capital-A—the Signature Gallery is not a store but a gallery; true art, after all, is not sold in stores. Labeling the place a gallery gives the work's entry into commercial exchange the veneer of respectability and acceptability by partially disguising its status as a commodity under a layer of carefully selected and sealing rhetoric. Perhaps best termed "malleries" to denote their hybrid identity, each Signature Gallery is divided up by movable partitions forming separate rooms where the framed "paintings" are displayed. Painted subdued, deep tones, and with restrained lighting, the mallery (along with the proprietor) encourages the visitor to venture deeper into the space. On display in the first rooms are smaller reproductions on paper and Masonite, some with little or no paint applied to the surface. Brushstrokes, and even the texture and weave of canvas, are nevertheless visible, the result of the digital technology Kinkade utilizes. The larger works, with the most extensive hand-highlighting, are located at the back of the mallery, deepest into the interior, and are carefully hung at eye level on the wall and gently illuminated by "museum" lights suspended above their frames, or propped up on an easel to remind the visitor that this is a very close relative of a painting. Once there, the viewer's immersion in Kinkadia is such that the realities of the mall all but vanish from cognizance; the ambience and organization of the typical Signature Gallery enacts an enormous distance between the mallery and the mall. This space speaks of serious art, not commerce; it suggests the hallowed halls of the museum, an edifice devoted to preserving important cultural artifacts, not the intellectually shallow corridors of the shopping mall, a space bereft of signifiers of high culture.[20]

All the malleries are equipped with an area near the entrance wherein the visitor can purchase souvenirs: plates, mugs, and calendars with Kinkade pictures on them, or reproductions that are packaged and marketed as just that—reproductions, rather than as art. This helps promote the idea that the reproductions hanging in the exhibition portion of the mallery are of a different order—not reproductions at all, but objects close to the unique existence of an original. The items for sale in the "museum shop" portion of the mallery are precisely the kind of thing that one finds in virtually every museum (including Kinkade's own); thus, the layout and experience of a Kinkade mallery replicates that of any such repository of fine art.

One cannot see the framed works hanging on the walls without passing through the "store" part of the mallery, which not only makes the experience similar to that of many major museums, which have their stores located near the entrance, but also follows the logic of a *Dummies*'s dictum. In *Art for Dummies*, the potential art aficionado is encouraged to make the museum shop his or her first stop, which is how the professionals do it the reader is told: "Go first to the postcard shop. There's always one. Even in tiny, out-of-the-way museums . . . there will be a postcard shop. And as you may expect, the pride of the museum's holdings will be sitting there ready for you to purchase. . . . Virtually every museum in the world publishes a color postcard of the hottest material. I buy what I want to see in the galleries."[21] Embedded in such instruction is the near constant repetition of the idea that art is found at museums and galleries, the holdings of which will be reproduced on a range

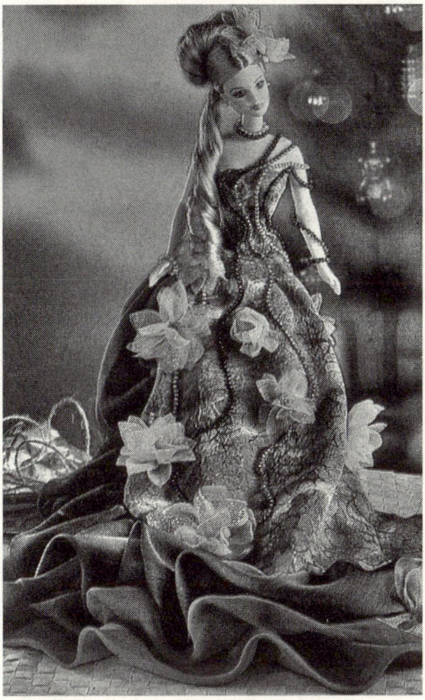

12.3. Water Lily Barbie® Doll, Mattel, Inc. Photo: M. Kjellman-Chapin.

of consumer goods. The logical conclusion, then, given that such establishments—or at least close approximations—are given over to Kinkade, is that what he is offering is indeed "high art."[22] With the "fine art" rhetoric dusting over his production, a Kinkade emblazoned on a La-Z-Boy recliner is less a mercenary commodity and more akin to the licensing agreements that also enable the Water Lily Barbie or a Last Supper lunch box (fig. 12.3).

Because Kinkade's originals are strategically taken out of market circulation, their pictorial progeny offered for sale in the malleries is automatically endowed with increased value; the closer they are to the original—printed on canvas with generous hand-highlighting, preferably by the artist himself—the higher the perceived worth and consequently the price.[23] Second only to the unavailable original painting is the Masters Edition print on canvas, which not only comes with the certificate of authenticity and the DNA-coded signature but also bears Kinkade's thumbprint on the stretcher bar in a layering of authorial markers.[24] Kinkade recognizes that the public purchasing his prints has absorbed the notion that "true art" has the trace of the artist's hand; art must bear the signs of its coming into being, and he supplies that by availing himself of a photolithographic process that is able to reproduce the appearance of canvas regardless of the surface on which the image is printed, and by having actual paint applied over the surface. The print thus looks "hand-painted," because some of it is in fact hand-painted. The paint applied to the surface also helps erase the marks of mass production, because no two prints are strictly speaking exactly alike; thus nonsingularity is compensated for by near-singularity.

In the process of hand-highlighting, Kinkade caters to two other well-entrenched notions: the master/pupil relationship, or the atelier system, and the idea of artistic inventiveness. The "Master Highlighters" are trained by Kinkade himself; they are ancillary to him, lesser luminaries, though still important because they were chosen to be trained by the "master" himself.[25] The idea is prevalent in canonical narratives and the structure works to bestow greatness upon Kinkade: only the best artists have followers and pupils; since he has apprentices in the form of "Master Highlighters," he must be ranked among the best.[26]

Kinkade's production mode, with its multiple workers and "assembly line" quality, brings inevitable comparisons to Andy Warhol and his Factory. One might further compare the two through their relentless self-promotion and the idea of using the artist's name and image as a vital component of the product. Ralph Rugoff, for instance, writes that "the artistic practices of Warhol and Kinkade demonstrate remarkably similar attitudes toward commercial art and marketing," and that a "close kinship" exists between the two artists, despite the obvious differences in subject matter and style.[27] To link Warhol and Kinkade through their participation in mass production, however, is to miss a critical part of Kinkade's project (and likewise Warhol's); while they seem to share a great deal with respect to technology, especially in the use of photolithography, their sense of the role of mass production in art-making is radically different. Warhol's pictures register "accidents" of the mechanical process, thereby intensifying an awareness of their *being* mass produced, whereas Kinkade's pictures suppress traces of multiplicity, if not entirely effacing them, by evidence of an individual hand.[28] Furthermore, Warhol's assistants remain peripheral to the product, if not the production, while Kinkade introduces them as the unnamed "Master Highlighters," training under the maestro in a new, technologically advanced incarnation of the old master atelier.

It is not only who does the highlighting that performs the imperative aggrandizing function; the very paint itself serves a function here. By the criteria set forth in art historical narratives, one of the prerequisites for greatness is innovation; for an artist to be truly worthy of canonical status, he must be inventive—he must "originate" a new technique or style. Kinkade has long broadcast his contribution to the artistic tradition, even trademarking a moniker in its homage, and it is certainly one of the most promoted features of the Kinkadian image: glowing light. Lampposts are a frequent feature, as are sunsets and rays of sunlight breaking through passing storm clouds. Most characteristically, every window in every house, cottage, and homestead is ablaze with a golden orange effulgence. Not content with static preternatural radiance, Kinkade "invented" a technique and a mixture of paint, which, when the lights of the gallery or collector's living room are dimmed, cause the lights of the pictured dwellings to glow exponentially brighter. Most likely the result of phosphorescent paint, Kinkade heralds this "invention," jealously guards the technique and the formula of paint used, and presses this process into service as a canonizing device on par with the "invention" of oil paint to Jan van Eyck.[29] The incandescent gleam of Kinkade's images operates like a signature; it is his unique contribution, immediately recognizable and linkable to him, like the Ben-Day dot of Roy Lichtenstein or the tenebrism of Caravaggio.

The light also enables Kinkade to link his productions more forcefully to one of the most potent signifiers of value in his arsenal of associations: Impressionism. Kinkade is not shy about using art history's roster to augment his own standing, so one might find a "Michelangelo" or "Rembrandt" frame embracing his interpretation of a Casper David Friedrich or Thomas Cole painting.[30] Few art historical precedents are invoked, however, with more frequency and even urgency than Impressionism, which is stripped of much of its historical, geographical, and political specificity in order to serve as a more fluid and effective signifier of artistic merit and worth. Visitors to Kinkadian sites, whether museum, mallery, or on the World Wide Web, are informed about plein-air painting, its historical origins in Impressionism, and Kinkade's contemporary revitalization of it.

Authorship, inventiveness, and Impressionism collide in Kinkade's "Robert Girrard" collection, which makes it a particularly useful and illuminating aperture onto his strategies. In 2003, Kinkade released a new body of work, a previously "unknown" group of paintings, which he produced under the pseudonym Robert Girrard. The Girrard works are perhaps more interesting for their mobilization of certain canonizing tropes than as paintings; they are adequate if undistinguished variations on French Impressionist and Post-Impressionist compositions. *Sunday Afternoon* (fig. 12.4), for instance, is clearly a reworking of Georges Seurat's *Sunday Afternoon on the Island of La Grande Jatte* (1884–86; Chicago Art Institute) minus the exactitude of Seurat's pointillism, the challenge to naturalism in the shifting scale of the figures, and the critique of modernity in the stiffness and isolation of the promenaders.

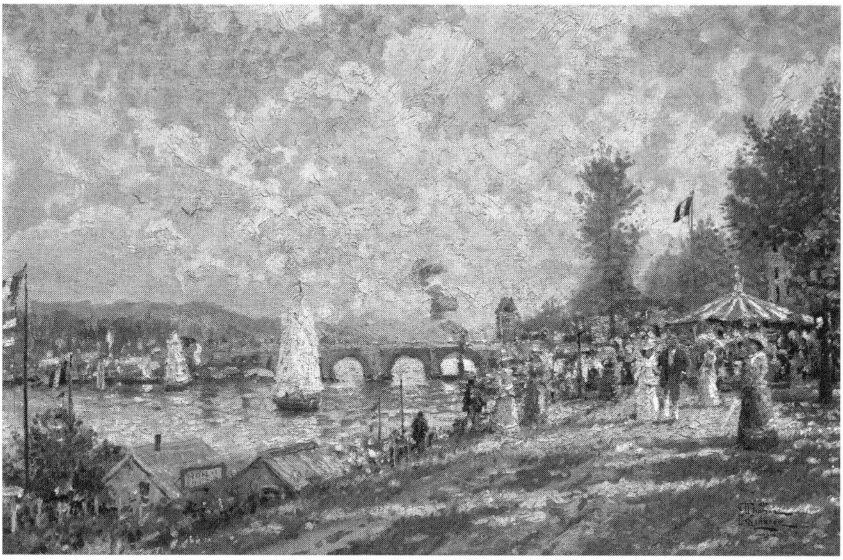

12.4. Thomas Kinkade, *Sunday Afternoon*, 2000. © 2005 Thomas Kinkade, the Thomas Kinkade Company, Morgan Hill, Calif.

Official Kinkade literature explains that Kinkade chose the name Robert Girrard because it had four syllables, but more importantly, because Kinkade "was heavily influenced by the French Impressionists," he thought that "a French-sounding name would be helpful if he were to paint impressionistic works."[31] No further explanation is provided about how a Francophone moniker might aid in painting, but the reader is informed that as Girrard, Kinkade not only mastered Impressionist painting but also improved upon it.[32] Not merely an impressionist, Girrard is a "romantic impressionist [who] applies color with a creative sensitivity few artists, past or present, can match. His sophisticated use of broken color yields a soft atmospheric effect to his canvases."[33] As Girrard, Kinkade produced about sixty paintings between 1984 and 1989.

The Girrard era ended, but Kinkade's involvement with Impressionism continued, resulting in the "French Impressionist Collection," comprised of paintings that were "created by Thomas Kinkade during the Robert Girrard era and later reworked by Thomas Kinkade."[34] This reworking led to the "refinement of the broken color techniques of the French Impressionists," and Kinkade achieved "numerous breakthroughs and advances in . . . artistic techniques and talents."[35] Certainly part of such language owes to the requirements of marketing rhetoric, but it also feeds into certain assumptions and knowledge about art (history) and artists. The equation between Impressionism and light is a compulsive one and is fostered by every text that deals with the group of painters who banded together as the Societé Anonyme in France in the 1870s. In the more populist oriented texts, consideration of Impressionism's relationship to light and color runs the gamut from discussion to mere parity. In his *Annotated Art*, Cumming goes beyond simply stating that Monet "was fascinated by light effects and the challenge of capturing their appearance in paint" by introducing elementary color theory in his discussion of a painting by the artist: "Monet has employed the newly available scientific knowledge about color theory. For example, he has used the optical contrasts between complementary colors that give the maximum optical vibration to the retina of the eye."[36] More often than not, however, the relationship is succinctly broadcast as "Impressionism: Let There Be Color and Light."[37]

Kinkade's reliance on Impressionism has undoubtedly to do with its position in the canon of Western art history. Richard Brettell has argued that French Impressionism is accorded a place of privilege in the organization of most major U.S. and British museums because it attracts more patrons than other holdings in the permanent collections.[38] Its popularity therefore makes it a very attractive candidate for blockbuster shows, which in turn helps further its appeal. Such strategies thus have a reciprocal effect: the more prominence of place, exhibitions, texts, reproductions, and other forms of attention are centered on Impressionism, the more firmly entrenched is its popularity and hence its hegemony, and so the more it will generate shows, writing, and media coverage. Impressionism, Brettell points out, has been effectively and emphatically canonized through such a tautological economy, and it is presented as the very culmination of Western art.

Kinkade's utilization of Impressionism helps perpetuate, reinforce, and enforce this. Morphologically, Kinkade's paintings are located somewhere in the vicinity of the Romantic sublime, American Luminism, Barbizon, or Impressionist styles he carefully references, but that matters less than the efficacy of the association that fosters the illusion of Kinkade's participation in and continuation of these canonical movements and moments. Moreover, Kinkade does not have to compete with individual practitioners; rather, he can get fitted into a much more diffuse understanding of Impressionism, where it is essential that the name and style are known but differences between the individual participants are negated or minimized. *The Annotated Mona Lisa* contains a chart titled "How to Tell Them Apart" for Manet, Monet, Renoir, and Degas, which is divided by subject matter, color usage, style, and advice or aphorisms, suggesting that their work is functionally interchangeable and

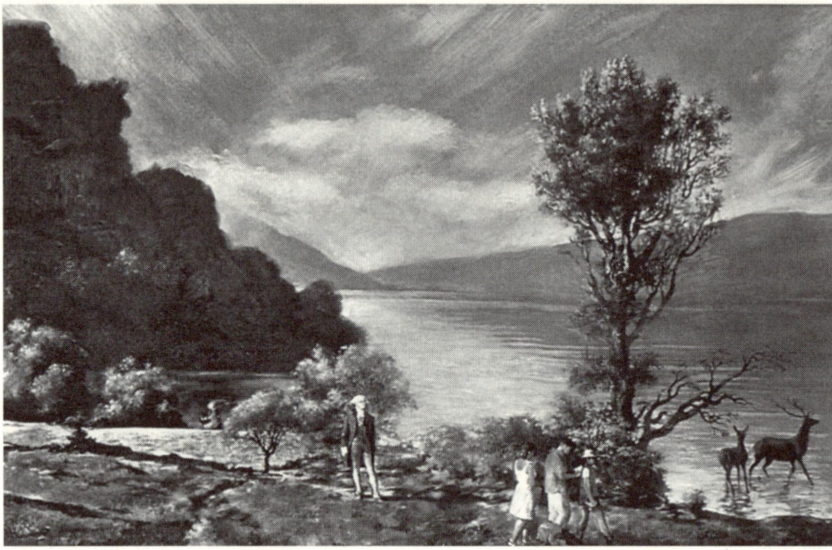

12.5. Vitaly Komar and Alexander Melamid, *America's Most Wanted*, 1994, oil and acrylic on canvas, location unknown.

further that an idiosyncratic style is subservient to the pictorial voice of the group.[39]

Kinkade and his champions claim that part of the current derision of the art world and the resistance to his participation in "high culture" emanates from a snobbish dislike, indeed distrust, of paintings that are not abstruse, impenetrable, arcane, disconcerting, and/or distasteful. Kinkade's paintings reveal themselves too readily to be postmodern. They require neither hermeneutic decoding nor specialized knowledge and they do not appear to be part of a larger, ironical project, as is the case with Vitaly Komar and Alexander Melamid's "Most Wanted" series of paintings, which were based on survey responses.[40]

The result of painting by statistical preference is absurd: *America's Most Wanted* (fig. 12.5) is a landscape with George Washington occupying the middle foreground while a trio of school children wander toward a couple of deer standing in a very blue expanse of water. Nevertheless, its existence, which reflects real, though interpreted, public preferences, demonstrates that Kinkade knows the audience to whom he is catering; he panders to the desire for an untroubled, unchallenging naturalism while at the same time supplying all the requisite features that the public expects of "Art." As Linda Weintraub has written, Kinkade "apparently concurs with the popular assumption that 'pretty' is a component of art, and that definitions of 'pretty' conform to a predictable cluster of visual qualities that include colors that are rich but not garish and compositions that are orderly but not rigid."[41] The qualities Weintraub points to are precisely those on which Komar and Melamid base their tongue-in-cheek *America's Most Wanted*, which highlights the deep division between the art world and the "real" world. The formation of the tastes and desires of the general public, however, is produced by a part of the very same art world that uses them as the fodder for postmodern irony. Naturalism is presented as the highest ideal, once again confirming Impressionism as the zenith of the Western artistic tradition, rather than the beginnings of a modernist teleology that would culminate with the radical reduction of the picture into flattened expanses of color.[42]

It might be easy to conclude that Kinkade indulges so thoroughly in realism because that is what the buying public wants; expressive naturalism sells. While profitability is certainly a powerful motivator, something else seems to drive Kinkade's enterprise and his relentless pursuit of the most illustrious associations capable of being garnered through landscape painting.[43] Saturation of the market with licensed objects and every variety of merchandise is secondary to the desire to pantheonic glory; it is this that fuels Kinkade's incessant repetitions of well-worn artistic and art historical tropes. There are two important intertwined issues considered here. One is that Kinkade draws upon a canon as presented by various mechanisms—books, now CD-ROMs, websites, institutional means, and so on—in order to shed the commercial taint and gain legitimacy as an artist. The carefully scripted performance of evocations, associations, and links is too deliberate and too saturated to be either coincidental or innocent; moreover, Kinkade is too shrewd for either possibility. The immediate result is an ongoing negotiation between Kinkade and the canon's players; Kinkade's audience, trained by the rhetoric of the canon to look for certain features, finds them in ample abundance. They serve to secure his legitimacy as a great "Artist" with a remarkably large percentage of the viewing public.

The second issue that arises out of Kinkade's tactics is that his very reliance on the canon and its favorite sons means that he is actively involved in producing, concretizing, and reifying the canon that includes the Impressionists, Italian Renaissance artists such as Michelangelo and Leonardo, "old masters" such as Rembrandt, and American and German landscape painters of both the sublime and picturesque traditions. Who and what is not included is as equally important as the canonical list. The canon being constructed by and through Kinkade excludes all of the artists of the twentieth and twenty-first centuries; his version of history starts with the quattrocento[44] and ends at the close of the nineteenth century, when Kinkade's historical alter ego, Monet, the "Raphael of the Water," was painting.[45]

Kinkade openly declares his opposition to the majority of modernist and contemporary artistic practice, deliberately marginalizing himself and positioning himself as "controversial." Drawing a comparison between himself and those artists "who use as their medium human urine or shards of broken glass scattered on the floor," Kinkade asserts that "one would think the[y] would be controversial, but the simplicity of what I do generates controversy among the more radical elements in the modernist art scene."[46] In avowing his difference, Kinkade opens up a conceptual terrain in which his (current) exclusion from the canon is temporary and is explained by his controversial status, while simultaneously serving to suggest that canonical status will be assigned to him, as the best artists were misunderstood in their own day. Support for such logic is to be found in a variety of texts, and Kinkade plays to the stereotype. In *The Annotated Mona Lisa*, for instance, the Impressionists are limned as art-altering rebels:

> After Impressionism, painting would never be the same again. Twentieth-century painters either extended their practice or reacted against it. By defying convention, these rebels established the artist's right to experiment with personal style. Most of all, they let the light of nature and modern life blaze through the shadowy traditions of centuries. . . . When urged by a teacher to draw from antique casts, the young rebels dropped formal course work. "Let's get out of here," Monet said. "The place is unhealthy."[47]

In Kinkade's version of the story, it is the art world that is unhealthy, and he has beat a systematic and aggrandizing retreat toward the zenith of canonical cultural achievement, Impressionism.

In his "Coda" to this volume, Terry Smith asks whether there is a way in which canonicity actually shapes contemporary artistic praxis. In the case of Kinkade, the answer would be yes in two ways. Kinkade's entire artistic practice is predicated on the recognizability of the canonical works lurking beneath and behind his "sunset cottages" and "twilight lighthouses," so a traditional art historical trajectory is very much part of his production at a generative level. At the same time, Kinkade's distance from and his (partially self-imposed) "outsider" status relative to the canon enticed Jeffrey Vallance to mount an exhibition of Kinkade's paintings, prints, architecture, furniture, and other Kinkadiana at the Grand Central Art Gallery at California State University, Fullerton, which reinscribes Kinkade in contemporary art practice as someone else's medium.[48]

I have saved discussion of the GCAC exhibition, entitled Thomas Kinkade: Heaven on Earth, until now because it represents a complicated insertion of Kinkade into contemporary artistic discourse. Curated by Vallance, a conceptual artist who uses an object or person around which to built an installation or series of events, Heaven on Earth was not really about Kinkade in the usual sense of an exhibition, but rather about Vallance. There is, of course, a way in which all exhibitions are about their curators, just as all texts are on some fundamental level about their writers as much as their subjects. But Vallance's show of Kinkade intersects with the ideas put forth in his own artworks, such as *Jeffrey Vallance Presents the Nixon Museum*, which began in 1991, or *Cultural Ties*, a project that involved the exchange of neckties with various heads of state. One of his best-known works involved a frozen chicken that Vallance purchased at a grocery store, named Blinky, and provided with an elaborate funeral. As Ralph Rugoff notes, the choice of Vallance as the curator for the exhibition is hardly innocent and he asks whether we should in fact regard it as a "type of appropriation art . . . a meta-artwork of [Vallance's] own."[49]

The details of Heaven on Earth validate Rugoff's caution. Vallance's vision for the show was to create "Kinkadeland," and thus he built environments for the paintings to live in, bringing in furnishings in order to construct a simulacral domestic space. A bridge was erected in one of the galleries so that the experience of walking into Kinkadian bliss would be less an imaginative projection and more a phenomenological experience. Once there, the visitor could have his or her picture taken as if in a Kinkadian pictorial paradise. A mock chapel was also constructed and decorated with examples of Kinkade's overtly Christian images, with sermons about Kinkade's religious work conducted by the Reverend Ethan Acres. Vallance described the show as taking Kinkade's work to "its logical conclusion."[50]

Vallance has created rather more and less than a retrospective exhibition of a particular artist. He has constructed a contemporary art installation and interactive performance piece out of Kinkade's multifaceted contributions to visual culture that partakes of Umberto Eco's notion of "furious hyperreality."[51] Such performativity puts the show on par with things like the Palace of Living Art's three-dimensional *Bedroom at Arles*, complete with a life-size Vincent van Gogh, his face covered with thickly impastoed paint as if he had painted his own visage, or the life-size wax version of Leonardo's *Last Supper*, located in its own chapel and complete with booming voice-over narration about the biblical events leading up to the Passion, attended by a life-size palette-holding Leonardo.[52]

Kinkade lent thirty original paintings to the GCAC exhibition, along with a variety of other Kinkadian objects, and one might well speculate that a "yearning for respect, or at least some acknowledgement from the exclusionary realm of contemporary art . . . led Kinkade to open the vault."[53] Vallance's utilization of Kinkade is mutually beneficial because it can be seen as yet another element in the Painter of Light's arsenal of legitimating strategies, which work to establish him as an Artist-with-a-capital-A as defined by the canon, rather than as a purveyor of kitsch—or worse, as an image-making charlatan, hawking his wares like a modern-day snake oil salesman. Kinkade needs such legitimization in part to justify the steep prices of the reproductions offered for sale at the malleries; any concern the buying public may have had at plunking down a considerable amount of money is alleviated and appeased as the Kinkadian machine smoothly transforms print into painting, reproduction into original, multiplicity into singularity, and customer into collector.

If, however, canonical objects not only police the boundaries of art but in fact work to define what might be considered such, and Kinkade's strategies function as active operatives in that policing, he ends up outside of its boundaries; he effectively writes himself out of the canon he helps to produce. Kinkade is categorically homeless and tangential to contemporary art practices at best, but the Vallance show pries open another possible road to artistic salvation for the Painter of Light. Vallance's show is not about Kinkade in the way that J. Seward Johnson Jr.'s life-size sculptural tableaux of the paintings of Monet, Manet, Caillebotte, and others cannot be considered exhibitions of Impressionist paintings.[54] Instead, Heaven on Earth is fundamentally a conceptual artwork by Vallance that uses Kinkade as its medium. But it does address and problematize the question of where Kinkade might be situated relative to a canonical trajectory and current artistic practice. The GCAC show suggests at least the possibility that Kinkade might be to contemporary artists what the Impressionists are to Johnson, or what Ingres was to John Baldessari; it suggests that he might make it to canonicity yet, even if through a back door.

Notes

1 The numbers are staggering: in 1999, the Media Arts Group, Inc., the company Kinkade founded with the entrepreneur Ken Raasch, posted net sales of $120 million, and in 2000, net sales were in the vicinity of $140 million. The corporation, with its not-so-subtle acronym of MAGI, was publicly traded on the New York Stock Exchange, but it has recently been taken private and renamed the Thomas Kinkade Company. For details, see Hertz, "Darkness Looms for 'Painter of Light'"; and Waters, "Selling the Painter of Light"; and *60 Minutes* (July 4, 2004), transcript available at http://www.CBSNews.com.

2 "Kinkade Art the Focal Point in New 'Music of Light' Label," 18.

3 For a brief mention of the novels, see Hertz, "Darkness Looms for 'Painter of Light.'" On Kinkade's venture into architecture, see Brown, "Ticky-Tacky Houses from 'Painter of Light'"; and Milmo, "Kinkade, King of Kitsch, Coming to a Home Near You," 11. Christopher Pearson has considered how a growing desire for the architecture in Kinkade's paintings necessitated those structures' physical realization; see Pearson "Repetition, Exclusion, and the Urbanism of Nostalgia."

4 Kinkade himself recognizes this; one of his stated reasons for not including more human figures in his works is that the presence of people can be limiting to the viewer's ability to project him- or herself imaginatively into the pictured scene. Conjuring up a Vietnamese American family, Kinkade asks whether they would want to "look at a picture of a dozen white people sitting around a Thanksgiving table." Waters, "Selling the Painter of Light." Kinkade's own examples serve to underscore the stringently Anglo-American racial and ethnic homogeneity of his pictures and perspective on the world, despite his rallying cry of the universality and universal appeal of his imaginary world.

5 On this, see Brzyski's cautionary tale about ARTstor's implications in the introduction to this volume.

6 See also Cumming's *Great Artists*.

7 The only exception is Hoving's inclusion of Lysippos as one of the ten most interesting artists; he does not appear on Cumming's list because the artists on his list all date from the fifteenth century and after.

8 Strickland, *The Annotated Mona Lisa* also provides a section entitled "Landmark Paintings in Art History," which repeats the selections found in other books. See also Beckett, *Sister Wendy's 1,000 Masterpieces*; and *Sister Wendy's Grand Tour*.

9 Pearson Education distributes a CD-ROM entitled *1,000 Images for Study and Presentation* with all Prentice Hall art history survey texts.

10 See Robinson, *Instant Art History*, vii–viii, xi–xiv; Strickland, *The Annotated Mona Lisa*, xi.

11 Robinson, *Instant Art History*, xiv.

12 Hoving, *Art for Dummies*, frontispiece, 12.

13 The authors and publishers of the large universal survey texts seem to have recognized this desire for and the market created by more compact "introduction to art and/or art history" books, as they are now also producing one-volume, briefer, "essential"

histories of art; see, for example, Janson and Janson, *Basic History of Art*; and Stokstad, Oppenheimer, and Addis, *Art*.

14 Hoving, *Art for Dummies*, 4.

15 Hoving writes that "the specific visual language an artist employs to render a certain subject . . . is like your handwriting or your signature—but infinitely more complex, elaborate, and expressive." Hoving, *Art for Dummies*, 4.

16 There are exceptions to this, although they are relatively rare. There is also a difference to be made between eccentricity and madness-cum-genius in the public imaginary; van Gogh's strangeness is seen as of the latter sort.

17 See Kinkade and Barnett, *The Thomas Kinkade Story*, 147; the practice of stamping the prints with Kinkade's DNA-coded signature began in 1997.

18 The Kinkade Museum closed in May 2005. The Touring Bus is no longer operational owing to security concerns, according to Vu Myers, the licensing marketing manager for the Thomas Kinkade Company, in conversation with the author, June 2005. Kinkade lent some thirty paintings to the exhibition at the Grand Central Art Gallery curated by Jeffrey Vallance; the implications of that show will be considered below.

19 See http://www.kinkademuseum.org. The "Artist in Nature" exhibition ran from March to May 2004; an exhibition of the same name had been on view two years earlier, from September to December 2002.

20 There is extensive literature on the strategies retailers use to manipulate shoppers and dictate their experiences; see, for example, Farrell, *One Nation under Goods*.

21 Hoving, *Art for Dummies*, 17–18.

22 In Robinson, *Instant Art History* (xiv), for instance, the reader is told that "art is what you go to a museum to see. Art can also be found in the artist's studio, at art galleries, [and] on collector's walls."

23 The prices range from about $150 to $15,000, depending on size, material, amount of highlighting (and by whom), and edition or collection. The *Thomas Kinkade Company*™ *2004 Limited Edition Comprehensive Catalog*, 211, explains the particular specifications for each subdivision within the "Editions Pyramid." The catalogue is available for purchase at thomaskinkadetoronto.com/collection/gifts/giftitems/books.php.

24 *Thomas Kinkade Company*™ *2004 Limited Edition Comprehensive Catalog*, 211.

25 At least in popular perception; the "Master Highlighters" are sometimes recruited by other "Master Highlighters." Terry Maxwell, a landscapist, was approached by a Kinkade representative at an exhibition of Maxwell's work and asked if he wanted to train to become a "Master Highlighter"; in conversation with the author, September 2004.

26 In Kjellman-Chapin, "Manufacturing 'Masterpieces' for the Market" I consider other canonizing apparatuses Kinkade has pressed into service, including publishing *catalogues raisonnés* dedicated to his work and monographs that detail his development as an artist. In both kinds of publications, one finds an incessant repetition of the myth of the precocious genius and the young artist who inevitably surpassed his teacher. For an analysis of mythmaking in artistic narratives, see Kris and Kurz, *Legend, Myth, and Magic in the Image of the Artist*; on the prevalence of the dynamic between the father and the surpassing son in art histories, see Salomon, "The Art Historical Canon," 344–55.

27 Rugoff, "Kinkade, Warhol, Vallance," 13.

28 David Batchelor has argued that in addition to serial repetition, Warhol's tendency to

alter the amount of ink on the screen during the printing process increases the mass-produced quality of the image; see his "Modernity and Tradition," 132.

29 On the persistence of this particular myth, and the culture of secrecy that has surrounded studio practice from the Renaissance through the nineteenth century, see Gotlieb, "The Painter's Secret." Kinkade's literature tends to play up his inventiveness in other ways as well; his museum website informs the visitor that Kinkade "loves to experiment with other mediums: water color [*sic*], airbrush, charcoal, pencil, and acrylics" (http://www.kinkademuseum.org).

30 For a careful consideration of the motifs Kinkade lifts and tempers from Casper David Friedrich, see Clapper, "Marketing Uplift."

31 The quote is from *Thomas Kinkade, Painter of Light™: 2003 Comprehensive Catalog*, 128, which is no longer available. The *Thomas Kinkade Company™ Limited Edition Comprehensive Catalog* includes a reduced section on Girrard. See also Kinkade and Barnett, *The Thomas Kinkade Story*, 220, which states that "Kinkade was heavily influenced by the French Impressionists early in his career, so he felt using a French-sounding pseudonym would be appropriate when he painted Impressionist works." I have used the 2003 version of the catalogue because it contains an expanded introduction to the Girrard work, since 2003 was the year the work was first publicly released. Girrard is a variation of the name Garrard, which Kinkade found on a record label.

32 *Thomas Kinkade, Painter of Light™: 2003 Comprehensive Catalog*, 128. Kinkade modified his signature for the pictures he signed as "Girrard." His own signature is an adaptation of Norman Rockwell's, which is based on the signature of Albrecht Dürer, so he enacts an artistic lineage; for reference to the Kinkade/Rockwell/Dürer signature, see Waters, "Selling the Painter of Light."

33 *Thomas Kinkade, Painter of Light™: 2003 Comprehensive Catalog*, 128.

34 Ibid., 130.

35 Ibid.

36 Cumming, *Annotated Art*, 84–85.

37 This is the title of Strickland's discussion of Impressionism; see Strickland, *The Annotated Mona Lisa*, 96.

38 Brettell, "Modern French Painting and the Art Museum." See also Mainardi, "Repetition and Novelty." Tinterow, "Blockbuster, Art History, and the Public"; and House, "Possibilities for a Revisionist Blockbuster" are also relevant to the issue of Impressionism's status.

39 Strickland, *The Annotated Mona Lisa*, 97. Strickland further writes that "it doesn't help that Manet's and Monet's names are almost identical or that the whole group often painted the same scenes in virtually indistinguishable canvases." Ibid.

40 Statistically, the American public preferred "realistic-looking" paintings over abstractions; landscapes were the overwhelming favorite, with 88 percent of the vote, and preferably on a "dishwasher-size" canvas. Wypijewski, *Painting by Numbers*, 7.

41 Weintraub, *In the Making*, 20.

42 In part, of course, Impressionism's centrality to aesthetic discourse plays a vital role in affirming naturalism as the ideal.

43 Kinkade claims to be dismayed by artists whose primary motivation is financial; about Picasso, he said that "he is a man of great talent who, to me, used it to create three

Picassos before breakfast because he could get $10,000 each for them" (quoted in a *60 Minutes* segment; http://www.CBSNews.com).

44 Kinkade rarely invokes anyone prior to the sixteenth century.

45 This is what he is called by Robinson, *Instant Art History*, 115.

46 Quoted by Drohojowska-Philp, "Painted into a Corner?"

47 Strickland, *The Annotated Mona Lisa*, 99.

48 The show ran from April 3, 2004 to June 20, 2004.

49 Rugoff, "Kinkade, Warhol, Vallance," 16.

50 Vallance, *Thomas Kinkade*, 10.

51 See Eco, *Travels in Hyperreality*, 3–58.

52 The van Gogh figure and bedroom are now part of the wax population at the Wax Museum at Fisherman's Wharf in San Francisco. The wax *Last Supper* I reference here is located at the Natural Bridge Wax Museum in Virginia; in *Travels in Hyperreality*, Eco mentions a handful of others in California.

53 Drohojowska-Philp, "Painted into a Corner?"

54 See Johnson et al., *Beyond the Frame*.

13

Canons Apart and Apartheid Canons: Interpellations beyond the Colonial in South African Art

JULIE MCGEE

How can African artists be African after Picasso?" asks South African artist Garth Erasmus.[1] For Erasmus, this is neither a rhetorical nor a cynical question, but rather a fundamental inquiry into the canon of art that has defined his profession, delineated the history of African art, and established a system by which his own creative production is judged and valued. For Erasmus, the very word "artist" is suspect in its universal application; it is "a Western construct" with "attendant inadequacies for our [African] context." A deeper understanding of African culture, Erasmus explains, would reveal that "artists" were present long before Western art classification systems arrived in Africa, but they were known by other names, such as shaman.[2] Erasmus is no less critical of art history's entry into South Africa. For him, "The history of art *as received* is the history of colonialism."[3]

The visual arts in South Africa have been and still are to a large degree defined by Western European epistemologies. Western, Eurocentric models provided the foundation for the professionalization of fine arts through education, exhibitions, museums, and degree-granting programs. The effects of this cultural implantation and subjugation are long lasting and, as Ngugi wa Thiong'o has argued, rendered more dangerous through their subtlety.[4] In South Africa, traditional indigenous practices and epistemologies have long coexisted aside professional educational systems of European import and ancestry. But through colonialism and apartheid, through English and Afrikaans, Western canons of knowledge and knowledge production became the preeminent vehicle for writing, documenting, acknowledging, and chronicling South African history. In South Africa today, historical accounts that privilege Western values and epistemologies are openly questioned. At the Fourth Annual Steve Biko Lecture, in a talk entitled "Recovering Our Memory: South Africa and the Black Imagination," Ngugi wa Thiong'o summed up the underlying dangers relevant to colonial histories of Africa:

> Colonialism tried to control the memory of the colonized, or rather . . . it tried to subject the colonized to its memory, to make the colonized see themselves through the hegemonic memory of the colonizing center. Put another way, the colonizing presence wanted to induce a historical amnesia on the colonized by mutilating the memory of the colonized and where that failed, it dismembered it, and then tried to re-member it to the colonizer's memory; his way of defining the world, including his take on the nature of the relations between the colonizer and the colonized.[5]

Today, simplistic divisions between settler and native (colonizer and colonized) can no longer be supported in a contemporary society wherein many South Africans integrate daily traditional and Western habits of mind. Yet what and how indigenous knowledge is constituted and what mechanisms of legitimization are or should be in place to secure its canonization are critical areas of questioning.

With regard to the visual arts and canon formation, the struggle is also over the colonial roots of art history and its relevance and meaning to the present and future South Africa. The Eurocentric epistemological system that is the foundation for art history has not been disrupted in South Africa and often responds poorly to perceived threats from the outside. Of particular concern here is the historical positioning of black artistic practice and black South African voices on the periphery and the development of a "canon" underclass with its own set of meanings, values, and expectations, one that evolved alongside and through the white and Western-dominated South African episteme. Black is used broadly herein to reference artists whose ancestry is not traced primarily to the West. Speaking in terms of art history, there has been little critical success in reconfiguring a new South African canon. Sabine Marschall has suggested that the "reluctance to engage critically with the art produced by Blacks and their relation to Whites is a lack of innovative perspectives or different paradigms that offer new insights and worthwhile avenues of interpretation and contextualisation."[6] Similarly, in her review of the South African National Gallery exhibition, Contemporary South African Art, 1985–1995, the art historian Jacqueline Nolte made the following observation:

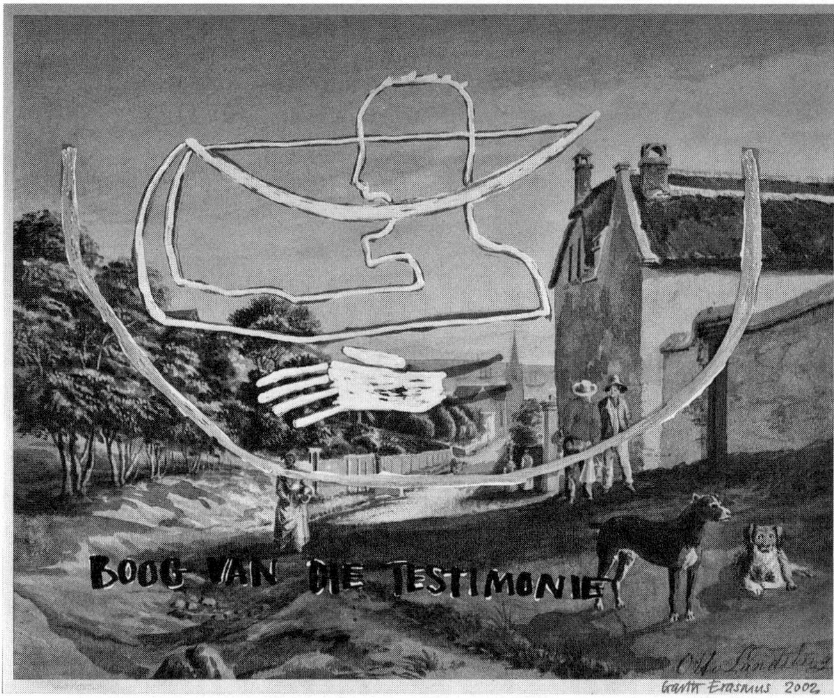

13.1. Garth Erasmus, *Boog van die Testimonie*, from *Boog van die Testimonie* series, 2003, correction fluid and ink over lithographic multiples. Photo: Jurie Senekal. Copyright Garth Erasmus.

> Judging the informing circumstances of cultural production in a country divided by cultural privilege is an unhappy task which leads also to passing judgment on political and moral commitment. Surviving as a privileged citizen in South Africa seems to produce a sort of cultural schizophrenia, benefiting from the system while also struggling for its demise. Some simply dispense with a belief in retrieving an ethical groundplan. The eager embrace of the play of postmodernism is, in certain cases, a release from moral exertion.[7]

Whatever the case may be in the academic or institutional setting, some of the most productive, imaginative, and critical engagements with colonial and African visual arts issues can be found today among contemporary South African artists, such as Garth Erasmus, who are directly affected as producers of art by the system's hierarchies and biases.

In *Boog van die Testimonie* (Arc of the Testimony; fig. 13.1) Erasmus turns lithographic multiples of Otto Landsberg's Cape Town cityscape into a palimpsest. The German-born artist Otto Landsberg settled in the Cape Colony [now Cape Town] as a young boy in 1818. He became one of the earliest exhibitors in the South African Society of Art, which later became the founding body of the South African National Gallery. Landsberg's original watercolor, now in the collection of the South African National Gallery, depicts a view of Kloof Street and Table Bay, in Cape Town, around 1861. Using correction fluid and ink, Erasmus takes possession of Landsberg's view, correcting our reading without erasing the landscape's colonial imprint.[8] Erasmus's "interventions," a word he uses, include a personal iconography of signs and symbols of his own making that reference his interest in the indigenous knowledge, music, and art of the Khoi and San peoples of South Africa, the first inhabitants of the Western Cape and the very people displaced and greatly decimated by European colonization. In *Boog van die Testimonie*, Erasmus's ability to write amid and over the colonial, while resisting the removal of its imprint, offers a welcome antidote to the present critical discourse. Many artists like Erasmus are actively engaged in a restoration project, acts of cultural translation that seek to transform South Africa's art historical canon. I will focus on three Cape Town artists, Garth Erasmus, Thembinkosi Goniwe, and Jane Alexander, whose works have challenged art's colonial vestiges in South Africa.

It is not difficult to sketch the interrelationships of art history, colonialism, and apartheid in South Africa. In political and constitutional terms modern South Africa has been called the lineal descendant of Jan van Riebeeck, a Dutchman who established a revictualing settlement in Cape Town in 1652. The Dutch were followed by the British, who took control of the cape for the first time in 1795, and later an influx of European immigrants (primarily British followed by German and French), who colonized the interior of South Africa. Modern South Africa's cultural heritage institutions, the oldest founded in the nineteenth century, are also lineal descendants of European colonization. For instance, the South African Museum (SAM), largely a museum of social and natural history, was founded in 1825 by Lord Charles Somerset, then the governor of the Cape of Good Hope. Early cultural heritage institutions have followed Eurocentric models in the most fundamental aspects of their work: collecting, preservation, research, education, and ideology. Cultural bias and limited access have been the defining characteristics of these cultural heritage sites. Ideologically speaking, South African culture was settler culture and relevant art history began with settlers' art.

Once considered a canonical if not an encyclopedic document of South African art and its history, Esmé Berman's *Art and Artists of South Africa: An*

Illustrated Biographical Dictionary and Historical Survey of Painters, Sculptors and Graphic Artists since 1875 was published in its first edition in 1970 and enlarged and revised in 1983. Because South Africa was distant from European art centers, Berman noted, "the development of South African art pursued a slow and stumbling course." South African "art" is defined here in reference to the European rather than the indigenous or southern African traditions. The "antecedents" of South African art are laid out in terms of the interests and abilities of early Dutch colonists, European visitors, and later settlers.[9] The assumption is that Western standards of art and its progress have legitimate universal application. Under this rationale, visual material outside normative Western categorizations is excluded from art history, or at best, awkwardly presented. While Berman's text does acknowledge that the "story of painting in South Africa had its beginnings amid a hunter-culture in the distant past" with "artists of the rocks," it asserts that the study of rock art largely interests archaeologists and anthropologists, not artists or art historians.[10] Early rock painting is considered a topic for Afrocentric studies, distinct and apart from South African art. "In recent years, scholars who are aware that South Africa's history has usually been presented from a European viewpoint, have become disposed to adopt a more Afro-centric attitude in examining the legacy of the past," she notes. "Within that legacy, the indigenous contribution of the rock artists is undoubtedly a priceless heritage."[11]

Berman begins her account of South African art in the 1870s, a dating she maintained in her 1993 book *Painting in South Africa*.[12] As Berman insists, "our story begins" in the later third of the nineteenth century, an especially fertile period for the settler artists, when Cape Town saw the establishment of a fine arts school (in 1864) and the South African Fine Arts Association (in 1871).[13] The South African National Gallery (SANG) was a direct outgrowth of the South African Fine Arts Association and the generosity of its members.[14] The current home of the SANG, situated in Cape Town's Company Gardens, opened in 1930.

Tertiary fine arts programs affiliated with national universities began in the 1920s, the first in Cape Town as the Michaelis School of Fine Art of the University of Cape Town (in 1922) and then at the University of Natal, Pietermaritzburg (in 1924).[15] Art history was part of the fine arts curriculum and only later developed as an independent academic subject. By the late 1970s, twelve of South Africa's sixteen "white" universities offered courses in art history with interesting tensions between the English- and Afrikaans- speaking departments, one favoring the art of England and Europe as a whole and the other the art of Germany, the Netherlands, and Western settler artists in South

Africa.[16] In 1970 only one university open to blacks, that of Durban-Westville, had a fine arts department, and by 1971 it had an art history department.[17] Not until the 1980s did the art historical discourse begin to open up, first by bringing the English and Afrikaans art historians together, and second by considering seriously South African material culture and black visual production.[18]

A curious testament to this history is Hans Fransen's textbook, *Three Centuries of South African Art, Fine Art, Architecture, Applied Arts*, which was published in 1982. Fransen, then a senior lecturer in the history of art at the University of Natal, Pietermaritzburg, wrote his text for classroom use, in particular for advanced high school students or introduction level university students. Fransen's three centuries are overlapping categories recognized as a Dutch Period (1652–1820); an English period (ca. 1795–1895); and a South African period (ca. 1885–present day). As Fransen noted, these primary sections consider population groups of Western origin. Three short chapters on "non-western art of South Africa" are included.[19] What is considered indigenous or "non-western" is set apart from primary South African art history even though its significance may be noted.[20]

While Berman wove black artists into her encyclopedic text on South African art and artists, Fransen did not. "Black" and "coloured" artists are not discussed in the South African period, but rather in a separate chapter titled "A South African Art?," in which Fransen investigates the Amadlozi Group and its Africanizing aesthetics, Protest Art and Township Art.[21] To Fransen's credit, he insists there is nothing "particularly coloured" or "typically black" to be found in the black artists' work. Indeed, he notes, "the technical means they employ and their visual responses to their subjects, could equally well be those of white artists."[22] Why then does he separate their work from the main chapter, the South African period ca. 1885 to present day, and why in a chapter whose very title questions nationalist aesthetics? Two reasons surface, both of which suggest that indigenous African artists were expected to produce works with "African" aesthetics. Fransen describes black South African artists as divorced from normative African sculptural traditions and hamstrung by white artistic practice: "The black man of South Africa, unlike those of central Africa (Ife, Benin), does not have a local art tradition that has been handed down through the centuries. This has been ascribed to a shortage of workable wood for sculpture, but it is more likely a result of the break in continuity caused by nineteenth-century upheavals such as the *Mfecane*."[23] Although more than two decades old, Fransen's text is fundamental to understanding the separate consideration black art received, even when its media and forms mirrored that of the settlers. He observes:

> Black art exists almost exclusively by virtue of the white liberals' benign interest. Teachers are white, art administrators are white, the gallery directors are white, and so are the critics and buyers. Our black artists have virtually no black audience. So, can black art really be regarded as black art at all? This black "identity crisis" is further complicated by the fact that the successful black artist seldom remains part of his own community and that if he wants to express the suffering of that community he, too, does so only "by proxy."[24]

Much has transpired since the introduction of European art and art history in South Africa. In 2004 South Africa marked an important anniversary: ten years of post-apartheid democracy. The discourse on art has been slowly undergoing a transformation. It would be misleading to suggest important changes in the arts arena have not been forthcoming.[25] Works by black artists regularly appear in exhibitions, fine art reviews, and critical texts. Recasting cultural heritage and rewriting, reexamining, and recontextualizing aesthetic traditions are not merely theoretical or academic dispositions in South Africa; rather, the gathering of history and the interpreting of culture are significant matters of democratization and nation building. Yet, black artists and black artistic practice remain the most affected by these maneuvers.

On the art historical side, reconciliation and transformation are too often posited as apologia or as a space-making mechanism for those artists and art forms that had been previously ignored. Past cultural narratives reflect and privilege colonial values, and revision requires advancing new narratives and shifting emphases away from Western epistemologies and interpretations. Institutional art discourse is sluggish (sometimes even recalcitrant), bound linguistically and in other intrinsic ways to founder narratives. Some scholars draw a zero-sum game, pitting the "high standards" and "values" of Eurocentrism against a "nationalist," "essentialist" Afrocentrism, as witnessed by the Fransen and Berman texts.[26] There seems little room for complementarities; as white South African art becomes inscribed into the modernist narrative, black Africa's place in that narrative is mediated by Picasso and primitivist modernism. Black South African art is either indigenous or a subset of white South African art laden with socioeconomic interpretations.[27] Absent from these discourses is the notion that the history of South African art can be part of a profound and fundamental restructuring of the art historical canon.[28] Rather than critically examining the established canon for its relevance or using newly incorporated visual culture to shape new epistemologies and praxis, canonical art history continues apace; black and indigenous art are folded into a canon modified principally outside South Africa.[29] In South Africa, indigenous artistic practice—once ignored then reclaimed—has and largely is being "re-membered" into the colonizer's memory.[30] As the art historian Sabine Marschall has noted, "strategies for accommodating the work of black artists into the historically white-dominated canon . . . have been invented and instituted by white agents of the art world—curators, critics, art historians—without the participation or consultation of those who are the subject of their field of interest."[31]

But what are the human scale effects of this for practicing black South African artists, once disenfranchised but now "reclaimed" by the same canon? Beginning in January 2002 and working with Vuyile Voyiya, an artist and then the education officer at the South African National Gallery, I recorded interviews with artists, curators, educators, and gallery directors who were asked to consider the meaning of "black" in so far as it related to or framed their professional lives and practice. We asked for and received frank comments about educational and professional opportunities, art institutions, including the SANG, and the role of art history and criticism. Interviewees expressed their opinions on democratization, transformation, and development in the arts arena post-apartheid, and from these interviews we created an hour-long documentary film titled *The Luggage Is Still Labeled: Blackness in South African Art*.[32]

Garth Erasmus figures prominently in this documentary, wherein he and other artists question the ability of a Eurocentric art historical discourse, maintained and dominated by white South Africans, to address black South African art. Our interviews with black South African artists suggest that little has changed for them in terms of their relationship with and attitudes toward fine arts institutions. A privileged system that once denied black artists equal opportunities, resources, and education still largely controls "the history" of South African art. Black South Africans are not equal partners in the endeavor to collect, curate, write, preserve, and thus construct a history of South African art. When they share the platform they are not equally heard, for they rarely project the same point of view as nonblacks. The pressing need to air and to address these issues surfaces in artists' repetitive calls for a Truth and Reconciliation Commission for the arts.

At the nineteenth annual conference of the South African Association of Art Historians, held at Stellenbosch University in October 2003, discourse failed when a screening of the documentary film and succeeding follow-up papers were dismissed as racist and ill-informed by a few vocal participants. Months of research, ideas, and analyses tracking the experiences, opinions, and beliefs of several practicing black artists were instantly dismissed, as were the presenters.

What prompted such a vehement response? In the documentary film, art history emerges as another form of colonialism, especially as artists question and problematize the dominance of Western art and the relative invisibility of African art in the curriculum to which they were exposed as art students. The marginalization of black art and its practitioners in the history of South African art is also noted and contextualized in the film. Conference papers by the artist Vuyile Voyiya on black curatorship and the artist Pro Sobopha on art competitions provided black, artist-centered perspectives that implicitly critiqued white power dominance in the fine arts profession. But the absence of expected art historical language, documentation, and presentation methods caused some to question the academic integrity of the presentations and the presenters' "credentials." The issues and concerns raised were not entirely new. White domination and control of the art discourse, disparities in perceptions between blacks and whites about transformation in the visual arts, disparate opportunities for white and black artists—these had all been acknowledged before by art historians working in South Africa, most notably by Sabine Marschall.[33]

So what was the fuss really all about? The normalized and validated methods of institutional and epistemological assessment within the art history discipline had been ruptured and this rupture had come from a seemingly "uncredentialed" center. Black South African artists are free to engage politics of domination in their visual work, but when they trespass the boundary between art and art history—mudding the distinction between the object and the subject on which power and cultural authority is predicated—they are accused of racism. This event might have remained a footnote had it not been for the Internet. The rupture at the conference quickly became quite public, focusing attention and debate at various websites, in particular *ArtThrob*, which is known for its focus on the contemporary arts in South Africa.[34]

There are many things to be learned from this, but what is most relevant here is summed up in one of the posted responses by the head of art history at the University of Witwatersrand: "Yes, we need to draw more persons of colour into a discipline that is essentially Western, in a context which is not. But, to start laying out a lot of inaccurate accusations and to do one's accusatory work without the necessary research is pointless. Show us that you can do the Art Historical research properly and you will be taken seriously."[35]

This is clearly a personal response to what are multiple, systemic, methodological and institutional issues. Moreover it conveys problems inherent to colonizing histories of Africa so eloquently noted by Ngugi wa Thiong'o. Clearly the Eurocentric epistemological system that is the foundation for art historical discourse has not been disrupted and, in South Africa, often responds poorly to perceived threats from the outside. Art historical praxis needs decolonization, decanonization, and de-emphasis on the Western episteme, but such must not be seen as loss. What seems most difficult to untangle is who or what is failing most in a necessary transformation process: the discourse of art or those of us who practice it.

What does it mean when an educator positioned in the preeminent art history program in South Africa says: "Yes, we need to draw more persons of colour into a discipline that is essentially Western, in a context which is not"? In 1995, the same scholar documented the ways in which white South Africans have been "staking claim to, and exercising power over, the construction of a national art history"—a construction she described as flawed and overly dependent upon Western parameters. Accordingly she suggested that "less canonical approaches taken in constructing exhibitions and thus histories of 'art' in South Africa need to be explored and indigenous peoples need to be given the opportunities to represent themselves more fully."[36] Despite its promise, such methods seem wedded to essentializing notions of indigenous peoples, and a refiguring of the binary "the Western canon and the rest."

What is indigenous knowledge? What does it mean to "give indigenous peoples opportunities to represent themselves" and "more fully"? Why are indigenous South African artists considered valid informants in terms of beadwork, ritual, and other non-Western expressive forms, but *not* in terms of the realities they face in the largely Westernized arts arena of museums and arts education and history? Is the problem really a "lack of credentials" or "research" or that the subjects are now active agents in retrieval, record making, and value systems, speaking not only about themselves but others as well?[37]

Too few black voices participate in constructing South Africa's art historical narrative and national art collections; and those in power continue to rationalize the situation in the name of Western notions of professionalization. For more than a decade Marilyn Martin, the director of the South African National Gallery, has represented blacks as lacking the ability to participate fully as historians in rewriting South African history. This is repeated, most disappointingly, in the exhibition catalogue for the SANG's 2004 *A Decade of Democracy* exhibition: "So firmly did the apartheid regime place the control of resources and education in the hands of whites that we still lack the black researchers, art historians and curators who can fulfil the task of reclaiming and representing history and art history."[38] Those who achieve recognized professionalism are trained in Western epistemologies, even in South Africa. But what is the value of a credentialing system that replicates disenfranchisements established in the colonial and apartheid eras?

The battle is over ownership of knowledge: what constitutes South African knowledge, who participates in this debate, and who decides.[39] As the artist Thembinkosi Goniwe has asked, "Who and on whose taste or aesthetic habits was and is black culture or art selected and represented? In fact, who is legitimate to negotiate and take charge in selecting and representing or recasting the culture and identity of the 'other' . . . ?"[40] Presently engaged in a process of art historical "legitimization" via a Eurocentric system (studying for his Ph.D. in art history at Cornell University), Goniwe does not shy away from interrogating its relevance and purpose in South Africa. This can be an exhausting undertaking; his place in the establishment is secured, but as a voice of dissension rather than of consent or clear authority. When his voice and others in concord are genuinely centered, and are no longer seen only as oppositional positions, then real change will have taken place.

What methodologies can be used to reimagine past and current practices? What strategies exist to reshape the present and the future? Pitika Ntuli, a South African writer, poet, sculptor, and academic who is notable for promoting an African Renaissance, has suggested the following strategies: a return to first principles, that is guidance from precolonial Africa to create a body of African knowledge systems—both contemporary and indigenous; the restoration of the African as subject of his or her own history; and a detailed analysis of culture as ideology.[41] To find this in the visual arts we must return to the work of Garth Erasmus and other contemporary artists who are creating new spaces for discourse and alternative perspectives on black South African art, engaging, challenging, and rearranging in the process the South African canon.[42] Their work reminds us that art's history cannot be neatly divided into precolonial and postcolonial, settler and native. Through creative juxtapositions of colonial, apartheid, and indigenous interpellations cast in contemporary art language, these artists both question and problematize the processes through which art's history is made and culture becomes ideology.

For the 2003 International Printmaking Conference in Cape Town, Thembinkosi Goniwe curated an exhibition entitled Surface=/≠Print (Surface Equals/Does Not Equal Print), which was held at the Association for Visual Arts. Goniwe's own contribution to the exhibition was an installation of the untitled work seen here in fig. 13.2. Cut into a layer of sand laid out in a rectangular format in the center of the AVA gallery floor were the five capital letters B-L-A-C-K. The rectangular quadrant of sand was "framed" by tape and

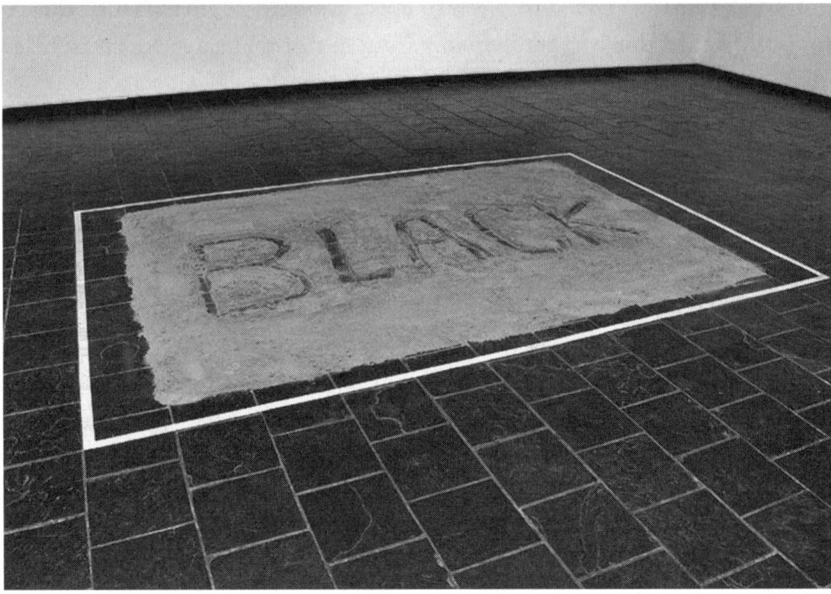

13.2. Thembinkosi Goniwe, *Untitled; Black Print*, 2003, sand, masking tape on black stone floor, installation, the Association for Visual Arts, Cape Town. Copyright Thembinkosi Goniwe.

the space of the work privileged thereby. The surface of the gallery floor was first covered and then exposed by wiping; no surface was primary as both the sand and the floor are codependent for the reading.

In the context of this exhibition, Goniwe's work questioned familiar definitions and assumptions about prints: what defines the "print" medium; is a print dependent upon surface; must the impression be visible as a tangible intervention upon another surface such as paper; must the impression be fixed? If surface equals print, what is Goniwe's surface?—the sand, the gallery floor, or the human sight and cognition that turns absence into letters, then words, then meaning? We are all imprinted in various ways—the word "black" keys into these imprints, which Goniwe knows will be understood politically, historically, and individually with varied readings locally and globally. B L A C K. What is black? Black is what we read though exposure or erasure—it emerges through the sand, through gesture, and through a degraining process. The juxtaposition of color and the texture of the floor and the sand play up the tensions between the surfaces.

Goniwe's work operates on many levels, some conventional and others far less so. Goniwe's questioning of the technical, conceptual, and historical relationships between surface and print is an artistic *and* political gesture understood as coming from an "African" artist whose creative and professional credentials are regulated by Western epistemology and terminology. It engages and critiques formal and historical artistic paradigms. But there is no value for Goniwe in a conceptual discourse that resolidifies these colonial implants; this is no postmodern game. Hence, the real explosiveness of the work is *not* teasing out sacred cows concerning printmaking, *nor* making black visible through erasure's impression—it is the linking of the stability of and reading of *black* to the stability of art's discourse. Here both black and art history are colonial discourses whose impressions we cannot seem to escape.

Let us return now to Garth Erasmus's intervention in Otto Landsberg's view of Kloof Street, Cape Colony, in *Boog van die Testimonie* (Fig 13.1). *Boog* (bow) is both the arc and the line of the Khoisan bow, one of the many instruments Erasmus plays himself. Testimony is also the voice of the bow, literally in that some bows are sounded by using the mouth as resonator, and figuratively in that the bow is as a griot—a storyteller, an oral historian.[43] Erasmus's testimony uses Afrikaans, a colonial language infused with indigenous vocabulary—adding another layer to this palimpsest. Three other works complete what is a four-part series, likewise titled *Boog van die Testimonie*. While Erasmus claims there is no set sequence to the four, he prefers that the series begin with one inscribed "Ek Loop op 'n Voetsek Jy Verkoop My Voetpad." There is no ready English translation of the inscription; "voetsek" is a swear word close to "fuck off"; so roughly translated the inscription means "I leave on a fuck-off; you've sold my footpath."[44] For Erasmus, the inscription voices his disdain for colonial appropriations of South African riches, including land, language, culture, and art's history.

Landsberg's original watercolor, present in reproduction, signifies colonial appropriation of land, history, and discourse. Erasmus's inscriptions interrupt the formal aesthetic and historical colonial gaze. His iconography and style recall but do not imitate San rock painting, thus pulling us back to a noncolonial Africa. The drawings represent the artist and musician himself. The pictographs clarify how certain bowed instruments are played—how the cup-like resonators, or calabashes, of the bows are placed against the mouth, chest, or belly to produce sound. Erasmus's technique anticipates multiple and ambiguous readings.

The tension between Erasmus's marks and Landsberg's composition are both compositional and historical. Landsberg used figures, including a dark-skinned woman in the center, as staffage—elements that occupy his Cape Colony cityscape. Erasmus's figures, however, are primary even in their sketch-like form—and are used to reoccupy the indigenous land. As settlers once marked the African landscape so Erasmus marks the settler's landscape. "My art-making and music *is my testimony*," Erasmus says.[45] "Colonialism grips contemporary us . . . indigenous cultural forms are stolen/appropriated, consumed, and then sold back to us, to the point where we feel even a detachment to what belongs to us. . . . I reclaim this as my heritage . . . my art actions have to do with issue of reclamation."[46]

Boog van die Testimonie is only one example of Erasmus's persistent questioning of "indigenous" and "aboriginal" in their present day configuration, artistically, conceptually, and art historically. Colonialism and the modernist paradigm reduced ethnicity as well as AFRICA to an expedient of Western culture. How can he explore Khoisan culture without being perceived as a post-Picasso appropriator or an African nativist? For Erasmus, colonialism and particularly apartheid were traditions that shaped his life; and his work is a "retrospective condition" that acknowledges this history while simultaneously privileging other traditions.[47] To this end it offers a methodological model for art history.

Both Erasmus and Goniwe acknowledge Western canonicity, but they refuse to find comfort in the status quo; both question established paradigms and their responses are distinct and differing. Erasmus claims that "the history of art *as received* is the history of colonialism." Now, the freedoms to express this fact and find ways to amend it are critical to reshaping the terrain of South African art and its history. It is time to write over, under, and through the operative canon—to amend misrepresentations, transform presentations, and infuse the discourse with other knowledge and alternative languages.

Reshaping the terrain of South African art and its history is not solely a project of black discourse; in addition to centering the African subject it includes the visualization of the messiness, awkwardness, and clumsiness of the Western empire in Africa, a frequent subject of Jane Alexander's work. In her recent project, *African Adventure* (1999–2002; fig. 13.3) the malignant results of the many "scrambles for Africa" are unearthed. *African Adventure* was conceived as an installation for the British Officers' Mess in the Castle of Good Hope, Cape Town. The history of the building and the room is essential to our understanding of the work and its underlying references to colonialism, imperialism, proselytism, war, and racism.[48] The castle is a star-shaped fortress built by the Dutch when the VOC (East India Company) "refreshment station" was established in the 1600s; at that time this room served as a church. In the nineteenth century the castle became the property of the British military and

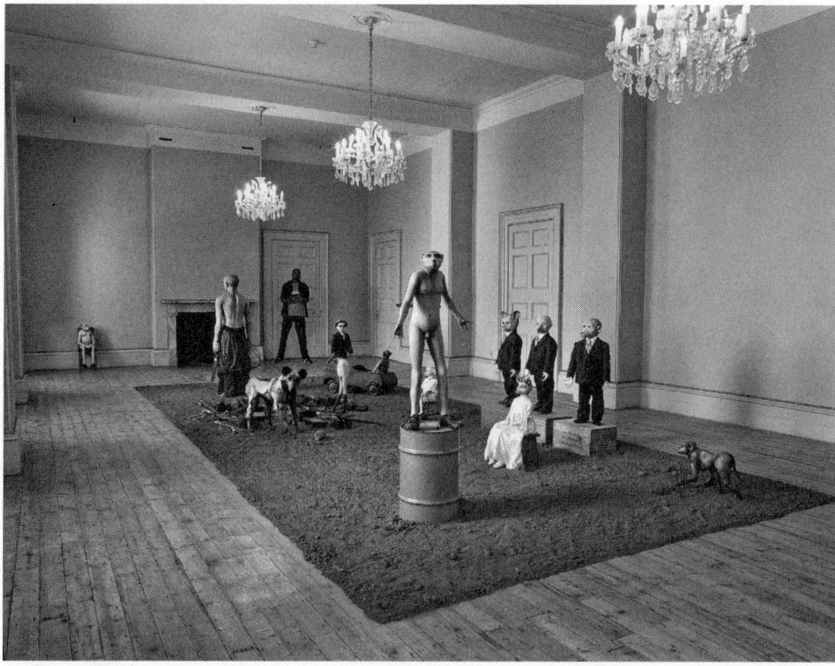

13.3. Jane Alexander, *African Adventure*, mixed media, 1999–2002, as installed in the British Officer's Mess, Castle of Good Hope, Cape Town. Photo: Mark Lewis. Copyright Jane Alexander.

the room became a mess hall. It now belongs to Iziko Museums of Cape Town and is frequently used for art exhibitions.

Alexander's *African Adventure*, a history play of sorts, is staged on a bed of earth collected from the Northern Province, Hantam Karoo (Bushmanland).[49] The characters are animal, human, and admixtures thereof: "Radiance of Faith" are the three figures in black suits who, open handed and unarmed, preach atop boxes of TNT marked as dangerous explosives; seated nearby are "Doll with Industrial-Strength Gloves" and "Girl with Gold and Diamonds." A wild "Dog" and an "Ibis" stand near "Pangaman," the large figure pulling assorted instruments of cultivation and land development. "Pangaman," the sole human laborer in Alexander's play, embodies childish associations of black men with all things evil and threatening.[50] Seated in a car, naked except for work boots is a "Settler." A "Harbinger" stands naked save for shoes on a barrel and is gesturing toward the mise-en-scène; and a "Custodian," another pale "humanimal" is perched on a stand like a pet on display.

Alexander's installation connects the horrors of the past with those of the present; unearthed here are illnesses of colonialism, then and now. We might read the diminutive "Doll with Industrial-Strength Gloves" and "Girl with Gold and Diamonds" as the ghosts of imperialism in Africa; each is adorned with delicate Venetian lace gloves, perhaps a remnant of a refined culture ill suited to African soil. Yet, present-day readings would see the ravages of African wars in the severed limbs of the bejeweled girl, and the physical devastation of AIDS and other infectious diseases in the doll with the blood-red industrial-strength gloves. "Look" the "Harbinger" seems to gesture, "what you sow is what your reap."[51] We find no solace in the diminished "Custodian" of this history, perched and ineffective above the Bushmanland soil.

Alexander's examination is not a re-membering of Khoisan history over and/or amid the colonial but is rather an unearthing and exposing of colonial disfigurements in Africa. In *African Adventure* dubious cultivations arise from the colonized African soil, whereas in Goniwe's untitled "print" BLACK emerges from earth's displacement. As a white artist active in South Africa, Alexander does not release herself from moral and ethical exertion. As with Erasmus and Goniwe, her work expresses the subject of her own history and South Africa's history. The individual works of these artists are not similar but they are complementary; each takes on the presence and imprint of the West in Africa in creative, productive, and dynamic ways. In so doing they offer discerning, South African borne solutions to an art historical canon still wedded to founder narratives and in critical need of revision.

Notes

1 An interview with Garth Erasmus in Voyiya and McGee, *The Luggage Is Still Labeled*.

2 Erasmus, e-mail correspondence to author, October 2003.

3 Ibid.

4 Wa Thiong'o, "Recovering Our Memory." Ngugi wa Thiong'o, a novelist, playwright, and critical thinker, has written extensively about the effects of colonialism on African systems of thought, language, culture, and education. A Kenyan by birth, Ngugi is a distinguished professor and the director of the International Center for Writing and Translation at the University of California, Irvine.

5 Ibid., 7.

6 Marschall, "Who Is in and Who Is Out."

7 Nolte, "Contemporary South African Art 1985–1995," 100.

8 My thanks to Anna Brzyski for noting the relevance here of W .T. J. Mitchell's studies of landscape as works as cultural practice and instruments of cultural power. See Mitchell, *Landscape and Power*.

9 Berman, *Art and Artists of South Africa*, 1–2.

10 Presently, information and samples of work by "artists of the rocks" are in the collection of the South African National Gallery's neighboring institution, the South African Museum (SAM).

11 Berman, *Art and Artists of South Africa*, 366.

12 Berman, *Painting in South Africa*, xviii.

13 William Forster founded the Roeland Street School of Art in Cape Town in 1864. Berman, *Art and Artists of South Africa*, 125–26.

14 An 1871 bequest from the estate of Thomas Butterworth Bayley, one of the society's members, formed the "national collection," which continued to receive gifts thereafter. Twenty-one of the original forty-five works in the Butterworth Bayley Bequest remain in the SANG's collection. Works deemed of low quality were sold during the directorship of Edward Roworth in 1947. In 1895 the collection, then composed of some one hundred works of art, officially came under government control through the South African Art Gallery Act. The collection's current home opened in 1930 in Company Gardens, Government Avenue, and in 1932 the collection became officially the South African National Gallery, a state-aided institution. The history of the SANG is described in various places. See Berman, *Art and Artists of South Africa*, 376–78; Bull, *One Hundred Years Ago*; Martin, *Contemporary South African Art 1985–1995 from the South African National Gallery Permanent Collection*, 17; and Dolby, "A Short History of the South African National Gallery."

15 The history of fine art and art-history training is outlined in Duffey, "Art History in South Africa."

16 Ibid., 113.

17 The Fine Arts Department at the University of Durban-Westville was established in 1962; the Art History Department was established in 1971. Ibid., 113–14.

18 Ibid., 111–16.

19 In less than twenty pages of this four hundred page text, Fransen discusses prehistoric rock art, traditional black African architecture and decoration, and Islamic and Hindu architecture.

20 "We are aware that more justice could have been done to this important area and more subjects touched upon, but we also feel they bear little relation to the rest of the book, where we have tended to stress interrelationship and coherence." Fransen, *Three Centuries of South African Art, Fine Art, Architecture, Applied Arts*, 8.

21 Berman on occasion discussed issues relative to black artists as a group, but she thought it important to "discourage ethnic differentiation of artists, South African or other, at the professional level." Berman, *Art and Artists of South Africa*, 64. Artists who formed the Amadlozi Group, which was active in Johannesburg in the 1960s, were interested in finding and developing a recognizably "African" aesthetic. See Fransen, *Three Centuries of South African Art, Fine Art, Architecture, Applied Arts*, 355–56 and Berman, *Art and Artists of South Africa*, 20.

22 Fransen, *Three Centuries of South African Art, Fine Art, Architecture, Applied Arts*, 360. A similar pairing is found in Berman's text, wherein she writes that "it is almost paradoxical that the Africanist incentive on the part, primarily, of white artists coincided

with the phenomenon of Township Art—a wave of unprecedented productivity by black urban artists, whose own output was characterised by the urge to identify with Western realist tradition." Berman, *Painting in South Africa*, xxi.

23 Fransen, *Three Centuries of South African Art, Fine Art, Architecture, Applied Arts*, 360.

24 Ibid., 359.

25 See especially Marschall, "Strategies of Accommodation"; and Marschall, "The Impact of the Two Johannesburg Biennales (1995 and 1997) and the Formation of a 'New South African Art.'"

26 See Duffey, "Art History in South Africa"; Berman, *Painting in South Africa*; and Nettleton, "'. . . In What degree . . . (They) Are Possessed of Ornamental Taste.'"

27 For a good summary, see Marschall, "Strategies of Accommodation," 50–60.

28 For Pitika Ntuli success depends on how well South Africans position themselves and synthesize the differing worldviews they have inherited. See Ntuli, "The Missing Link between Culture and Education," 199.

29 See the following recent exhibition catalogues: Allara, Martin, and Mtshiza, *CoExistence*; and Bedford, *A Decade of Democracy*. Interesting attempts to subvert this are found in Nettleton and Charlton, *Voice-Overs*; and Nettleton, Charlton, and Rankin-Smith, *Engaging Modernities*.

30 In other words, the very methods and episteme that once denigrated indigenous art had now become its champion and archive. This phrasing is borrowed from wa Thiong'o, "Recovering Our Memory."

31 Marschall, "Strategies of Accommodation," 50–60.

32 We conducted over twenty interviews. Among our interviewees were well-known and established artists such David Koloane, Peter Clarke, Lallitha Jawahirilal, Berni Searle; students and recent graduates of MFA programs (Gabi Ngcobo, Mgcineni Pro Sobopha, Thembinkosi Goniwe); and artists trained outside of the university system (Lundi Mduba, Mandla Vanyaza). Art educators and professionals included Zayd Minty and Graham Falken, the past and present directors of Community Arts Project of Cape Town; Marilyn Martin, the director of the South African National Gallery; Gavin Younge, a professor of fine arts at Michaelis, University of Cape Town; Lloyd Pollak, an art critic; and Estelle Jacobs, a director of a gallery.

33 See Marschall's essays cited above, "Who Is in and Who Is Out?"; "Strategies of Accommodation"; and "The Impact of the Two Johannesburg Biennales (1995 and 1997) and the Formation of a 'New South African Art.'"

34 See http://www.artthrob.co.za/03oct/feedback.html, posted October 6, 2003. Additionally, analysis of the film and the history of its brief reception in South Africa appears in the December 2003 issue of *SA Arts* and the May 2004 issue of *Third Text*.

35 See http://www.artthrob.co.za/03oct/feedback.html, posted October 6, 2003. The full text of the posting follows:

> Do I really want to get into this? Probably not, but there are issues out there, raised in the September issue of this valuable resource that need airing nationally. [Thembinkosi] Goniwe's claim that we (the Art Historians) should be ashamed because there were no black females in our gathering has set the cat amongst the pigeons. I would like to ask—What university department has a large number

> of black female students studying Art History? I have had one who has gone through to MA level and she didn't finish her MA because she got pregnant and decided not to continue with her research report. There is no art taught at the vast majority of South African schools so we have a very small pool from which to draw. Art is anyway, in most parents' minds, a foolish luxury and studying it leads nowhere. Those of us who have made it as Art Historians have studied our proverbials off and have ended up in positions of authority in Universities, and not merely because our skins are white and our gender female (this in response to Pro Sobopha's assertion that white females controlled the art world). What stuck in the gullet of critical viewers of the video and listeners to the papers presented by Goniwe, Sobopha and Voyile [author's spelling] at the Art Historians' conference in September were the wild claims and the lack of intellectual rigour (it was claimed, amongst other gross distortions, by the white art critic in the video that whites were indigenous to South Africa). The fact that Goniwe claimed, on top of all this, to be speaking for 'the Black woman'—essentialised no doubt—put the cherry on a cake which I suppose we were expected to swallow in the spirit of wallowing in our sense of white guilt. This was not going to happen. Yes, we need to draw more persons of colour into a discipline that is essentially Western, in a context which is not. But, to start laying out a lot of inaccurate accusations and to do one's accusatory work without the necessary research is pointless. Show us that you can do the Art Historical research properly and you will be taken seriously.

36 Nettleton, "Collections, Exhibitions and Histories."

37 Ntuli reminds us that "knowledge is not just a collection of dead facts—it is alive and dwells in specific places. . . . Successful knowledge gathering must involve formal and informal education and the way in which these things are brought together to help solve problems." See Ntuli, "The Missing Link between Culture and Education," 197.

38 Martin, "The Horn of the National Art Museum's Dilemma," 64. Martin's text repeats statements made in her essay "Transforming the National Gallery," 146.

39 See Ntuli, "The Missing Link between Culture and Education," 187.

40 Goniwe, "South African Art." See also Nolte's questioning of the criteria used by the SANG for its recasting of categories of craft, popular, folk, community, and fine art in "Contemporary South African Art 1985–1995," 99.

41 Ntuli, "The Missing Link between Culture and Education," 189–90, 198. Ntuli, who lived for over thirty years in exile in England, has published extensively on issues of culture, indigenous knowledge systems, and African Renaissance. The former dean of students and a professor of fine arts at the University of Durban-Westville, he was appointed deputy vice-chancellor of the University of Durban-Westville in 1996–97. Currently he is the executive director of organizational culture and African scholarship at the newly merged University of KwaZulu-Natal.

42 This idea is related to Ntuli's conceptualization of artists as cultural workers in "Fragments from under a Telescope," 71.

43 Erasmus, e-mail correspondence to author, November 2003.

44 Ibid.

45 Erasmus's emphasis. Ibid.

46 Ibid.

47 Garth Erasmus uses the phrase "retrospective condition" to describe his work. Ibid.

48 Jane Alexander listed "tourism, racism, proselytism, aspects of war," as subjects embodied in this work. Njami, "A Turbulent Silence," 18. My thanks to Jane Alexander for the information she supplied about *African Adventure*. Alexander, e-mail correspondence to author, November 2003.

49 Alexander, e-mail correspondence to author, November 2003. *African Adventure* used soil from an area one hundred kilometers north of Calvinia in the Northern Province. Calvinia, named after Johannes Calvin, was originally called Hantam in reference to Hantam Mountain nearby. Hantam is a Khoi word that refers to the red edible bulbs of this mountainous area, also known as Bushmanland and now Hantam Karoo.

50 Alexander, e-mail correspondence to author, November 2003. See also Miki, "Making Invisible Relationships Visible," 27 n. 3.

51 Galatians 6: "Whatsoever a man soweth, that shall he also reap."

14

Coda: Canons and Contemporaneity

TERRY SMITH

In 1953 the reputation of the Abstract Expressionist painter Willem de Kooning was soaring. Soon after he was chosen to represent the United States at the 1950 Venice Biennale, prices for his paintings reached the then extraordinary sum of $10,000. He was about to stage his first retrospective exhibition, and his works were entering major museums—in the case of *Excavation* (1950) the Art Institute of Chicago, where the painting soon became what it remains to this day, the destination work in the room in which that museum's story of modern art culminates in the triumph of American abstract painting. De Kooning, along with Jackson Pollock, had come to be regarded by many of their fellow artists, as the most adventurous and innovative of their company. Artists and critics were beginning to understand that de Kooning was not only the latest in a long line of avant-garde canon breakers; through his startlingly risky compositional methods, he was also the best and most original draftsman among them, and thus he was—as he often said himself—hell-bent on renovating centuries-long traditions of art making. The modern criteria of canonicity were being met, one by one. At this moment, however, de Kooning responded affirmatively to the request of a young colleague for the gift of a drawing to be erased. The result, Robert Rauschenberg's *Erased de Kooning Drawing* (1953; fig. 14.1), now hangs in the San Francisco Museum of Modern Art, where it is one of that institution's key works. It appears in all books on the prodigious output of this artist and in many surveys of recent art, where it is often described as a Neo-Dada anti-art gesture, a turning point in the shift from modern to contemporary art. While these descriptions are true as generalities, there are many more interesting interpretations of the work and of the subtlety of Rauschenberg's motivations in the more specialist literature.[1] For the purposes of this essay, however, his act of erasure raises a pivotal question: what happens to the idea of artistic

14.1. Robert Rauschenberg, *Erased de Kooning Drawing*, 1953, traces of ink and crayon on paper, with mat and label on gold-leaf frame. San Francisco Museum of Modern Art. Purchased through a gift of Phyllis Watts. © Robert Rauschenberg/Licensed by VAGA, New York.

canons in a context when canon busting—including that which generates, in Rauschenberg's own description, a "monochrome no-image"—becomes the starting point, the inspirational ground, and then the norm of art practice?

This question leads straightaway to a number of others, which will shape this essay. What is the status of artistic canons now? How might the idea of such canons be thought in the conditions of contemporaneity? The art world's institutional disseminators and interpreters—including many leading art critics, journal editors, museum curators, grant givers, collectors, auctioneers, and textbook writers—continue to need such structures for their various purposes, and indeed they have arranged them under the loose but powerful framework that they have labeled contemporary art. But official contemporary art does not encompass all current practice, so we may ask: Does canonicity continue to actually shape contemporary art at its most generative points—the studios, the labs, the sites, the net? If contemporary art is the art of contemporaneity, then the answer to this question has to be "no," however qualified. A contradiction between the institutions of art and the deepest conditions of art's emergence is exposed, one with implications for our understanding of how values are formed, sustained, and transformed in contemporary life. I intend to explore the recent history and the currency of this issue from the viewpoints of someone engaged in many of the roles listed above. I will show that there are, indeed, contradictions within the art institutions, and between them and the increasing amount of art being produced outside them. I will also explore the idea that both institutional and counter-institutional art is subject to the double-whammy that batters every other aspect of contemporary life: that the accelerating rupture, disorientation, and disintegration of the everyday, in its public and private forms, occurs in the context of an incessant flow of homogenizing but imperfectly managed information. Both tendencies are the most evident features of contemporaneity. Their conjunction drives the present. Their mark on contemporary art is that it is, at once, the most highly valued commodity in an expanding cultural-entertainment industry and a bit player in the internecine warfare that scars the image economy.

On Contemporaneity

What is contemporaneity? Ordinary usage of the word defines a set of contingent, adventitious, and binding relationships between being and time that have been present in all human societies and are of immediate importance to daily life but of little more general significance. These senses spring into life when contrasted with the meanings of the word "modern." In the ancient world, "modern" meant "the current moment," the "now," that which was "of today"—in another word "contemporary." In the modern world, however, "modern" has become the core of a set of terms that narrate the two hundred year formation of modernity, including its definitive artistic currents, "modernist" art, architecture, and design. The "modern" has, in short, become historical. In ordinary language—in English, and in some but not all other European languages—it has surrendered currency to the term "contemporary" and its cognates. But "contemporary" has always meant more than just "now," more than what "modern" used to mean. The term calibrates a number of distinct but related ways of being "of," or "with," or "in" time. The *Oxford English Dictionary* gives four, three of which are the strong sense of "belonging to the same time, age, or period" (1.a.), the coincidental "having existed or lived from the same date, equal in age, coeval" (2), and the adventitious "occurring at the same moment of time, or during the same period; occupying the same definite period, contemporaneous, simultaneous" (3). In each of these meanings there is a distinctive sense of presentness, of being in the present, of beings who are (that are) present to each other and to the time they happen to be in. Of course, these kinds of relationships have occurred at all times in the historical past, do so now, and will do so in the future. The second and third meanings make this clear, whereas the first points to the phenomenon of two or more people, events, ideas, or things "belonging" to the same historical time. Yet, even here, while the connectedness is stronger, while the phenomena may have some sense of being joined by their contemporaneousness, they may equally well do so, as it were, separately, standing alongside yet apart from each other, existing in simple simultaneity. It is the fourth definition of "contemporary," mentioned above, that brings persons, things, ideas and time together (with, in, of) irrevocably: "Modern; of or characteristic of the present period; especially up-to-date, ultra-modern; specifically designating art of a markedly *avant-garde* quality, or furniture, building, decoration, etc. having modern characteristics."[2] In this definition, the two words have finally exchanged their core meaning: the contemporary has become the new modern. We are, on this logic, out of the modern age, or era, and into that of the contemporary.

But to generalize in this way is to miss an essential quality of contemporaneousness: its immediacy, its presentness, its instanteity, its prioritizing of the moment over the time, the instant over the epoch, of direct experience of multiplicitous complexity over the singular simplicity of distanced reflection. Contemporaneity consists precisely in disjunctures of perception, mismatching ways of seeing the same world, in the coexistence of asynchronous temporalities, in the jostling contingency of various cultural multiplicities, all thrown together in ways that highlight the inequalities within and between them. This is the world as it is now. It is no longer "our time," because "our" cannot stretch to encompass its contrariness. Nor is it a "time," because if the modern was inclined above all to define itself as a period against past periods, any kind of periodization of contemporaneity is impossible.[3]

The crucial point here that the multiple meanings of contemporaneity are not only pervasive in contemporary life but are all we have. Contemporary life is haunted by the absence, and the evident anachronism, of large-scale world pictures capable of accounting for human destiny with any degree of plausibility. These include not only modernity but also postmodernity and their contingent art-world terms, modernism and postmodernism. It is a condition in which both sets of terms have become anachronistic; it is both full of "posts" and past all such posts. It is also marked by the insistence of certain not-modern fundamentalisms on imposing their limited world pictures as if they were universal. The new world (dis)order is shaped, at its base and on its surfaces, by a warring between two paired tendencies: the subtle shifts toward hegemony that drive the forces of globalization and the counterstrategies of persistence within difference, the protection of particularity and the linkage of localities that have arisen within the aftermath of decolonization. In my view, multeity, inequity, and the untimely are emerging as the defining characteristics of all contemporary experience.[4]

The point for us is that while the thirst for order, and specifically the fundamentalist shortfall that underlies the formation of canons, is not only present in contemporaneity but is on a revivalist roll in many parts of the world, *at the same time* it is equally and spectacularly failing to dominate and define these times. While this is the result of the warring between fundamentalisms that takes its current form as both terrorism and the war on terror, it also follows directly from that fact that the definitive energies of contemporaneity, its bottom line, its initiation of heterogeneity, are pitched, perpetually, against closure. Does not the very idea of the canonical presume, at the very least, concentrations of value that have potent effect, intensities that last, standards that set, paradigms that take hold, all of which should lead to practices that echo the exemplary inspiration? Contemporaneity, it would seem, is fundamentally antithetical to the very possibility of this kind of universalizing canon formation. Are the days of canons, finally, over?

On Canonicity

The concept of canon that we have inherited is a blending of a number of earlier usages derived from *kanon*, the Greek word for "rule," and reinforced in Middle English (*canun*) and Old French (*canon*). In antiquity, it meant the lists of prescribed texts that schoolmasters set as essential models for student emulation. During the medieval period in much of the world, its main purposes were ecclesiastical, ranging from rules laid down by clerical councils to the list of books officially regarded as genuinely inspired by divine spirit. Its secular resonance since then, particularly in the arts, metaphorizes these meanings and specifically combines two distinctively modern emphases: in the early seventeenth century the idea of a canon entered the English language as a general standard of judgment or a criterion, and in the late nineteenth century it was joined by the use of the same word for the listing of genuine works by a recognized author, composer, artist, or other creative figure. These new meanings reflect at once the establishment of the professions (in the visual arts, the academies) and the unstoppable spread of public education. Both were accompanied by the felt need of the powerful to contain them within boundaries that would, as far as possible, maintain the current relations of power. This was done by combining the two new meanings and quickly ratcheting them up the quality scale, resulting in the usage that predominated throughout the twentieth century: the canon consists of the great masterworks of those artists, writers, composers, and others recognized to be geniuses. Access to the appreciation of great art is offered to all, but the capacity to produce it is confined to the few.

In humanities disciplines at universities throughout the world courses were built on these principles—in the United States, they began at Columbia University, then were, famously, elaborated as foundational for all students at the University of Chicago in "a list of heavyweight names assembled in chronological order like marble busts in some imaginary pantheon of glory."[5] This kind of canon had been prominent as either the overt or tacit organizing principle of art history survey courses since their inception in the mid-nineteenth century in Berlin—alloyed, of course, with the other imperatives of modern art history: tracing national self-representation, celebrating artists' self-expression, distinguishing between the representational potential of the different mediums, and promoting art's capacity for self-renewal through stylistic refinement and transformation. All of these elements were already present in Vasari's time, as is indicated in the title of his famous set of books, published first in 1550 and then in an enlarged edition in 1568, *Lives of the Most*

Excellent Painters, Sculptors and Architects. One of the most articulate recent defenders of the idea was Ernst Gombrich: using a catchy distinction between "the top ten" list of hit songs and "the first eleven" in a cricket team, he argued that, while the former was merely a popularity contest subject to the vagaries of interest and influence, the outcome of which would dissipate on the winds of fashion, the process of selecting the latter was an exercise of taste and judgment of a higher order. "So I believe . . . that our civilization transmits to us a certain canon of great poets, composers, artists and we are in fact appointed to pass it on to future generations. Not, to be sure, uncritically, but with a certain humility."[6]

Yet there is something too easy in confining ourselves to the absolute—or "canonical"—conception of the canon, in taking it—as Gombrich seems to do in the remark just quoted—as universally valid, as binding on all peoples, as unequivocally the repository of greatness. Such a move fails instantly the test of falsifiability. Any particular set of canons is too readily shown to be selected according to the preferences of the social class, group, culture, or civilization that has constructed it. It is always, in a word, partisan—as Anna Brzyski has shown in her introduction to this volume. Its failure is not that a selection has been made, but that the particular selection is held to be general, to be of universal significance, and, too often, to be binding on future practice. To me, the most profound subversion of the idea lies at the source of its apparent strength: when one reviews those works most often picked out as canonical in art since there has been such a concept, and in most societies with rich visual cultural traditions prior to that time, the favored works are exceptional in character. They tend less toward the confirmation of convention, however brilliantly, than its transformation. The regeneration of tradition, the extension of the canon, is, therefore, precisely what they put at risk.[7]

The cultural economist Steven Connor has usefully drawn attention to the fact that "the structure of value is . . . paradoxical, involving the simultaneous desire to and necessity to affirm unconditional values and the desire and necessity to subject such values to continuous, corrosive scrutiny."[8] He applies this to both economics and culture, noting that the arts—like economics—are embedded in "processes of estimating, ascribing, modifying, affirming and even denying value. . . . We are claimed always and everywhere by the necessity of value in this active, transactional sense."[9] The paradoxical character of both economics and the arts is precisely what enables both of them to negotiate their contradictory drives—those that are distinctive, those that occur between them, and between them and the rest of the world. Definitive of both is a doubling back and forth between a basic thirst for value as such ("unconditional," "pure," even "transcendental") and an irrepressible inclination to render all values conditional, contingent, and material. In ideal situations, this switching mechanism enables differencing and sharedness despite the appearance of fierce battle and grudging reconciliation; it permits one side of the paradoxical double to retreat strategically when the other requires advancement. But actual situations are rarely ideal. Indeed, the switching metaphor presumes a tendency toward equilibrium in all natural, machinic, and human affairs. Yet the starkest, most despairing question posed by contemporaneity is this: Have we not traveled past the point when the balanced resolution of anything will occur as, at best, a temporary figment?

If we have, then Gombrich's understanding of "the real role the canon plays in any culture" tumbles into anachronism. To him, "It offers points of reference, standards of excellence which we cannot level down without losing direction."[10] Writing this in 1973, against the overriding force of commercial and popular culture, and the emergence of the cultural industry, he did not envisage a situation in which canonicity would be threatened, as it were, not from below but from above, from in front, and from the sides. As societies, and entire civilizational blocs, split internally into ever more widely separated haves and have nots, and as they war more strongly against each other, directionality itself is what spins into chaos—at all levels, everywhere.

The Modernist Canon

Within the contemporary visual arts, there is a quite specific recent history of the long-term paradox at the heart of valuing practices, and its arrival at its current, crisis state. During the 1960s, the heyday of high modernism, canons were reduced to a set of formalist formulae through which, it was claimed, direct aesthetic experience could be transmuted into transcendental quality. The main theme of Clement Greenberg's famous essay of 1961, "Modernist Painting," a *locus classicus* of this viewpoint, is that the formal innovations of the modernist masters were at once radical with regard to the degree that they "exhibited and made explicit that which was unique and irreducible not only in art in general, but also in each particular art . . . all that was unique to the nature of its medium," and at the same time "never meant anything like a break with the past." The pursuit of this explicitness by modernist artists was a direct continuity from the ambitions, if not the specific practices, of the old masters.[11] The string of modernist masters nominated by Greenberg and earlier formalists such as Roger Fry became itself canonical. Manet-Monet-Cézanne-Matisse-Picasso-Pollock constituted its vertebrae. This was an acute narrowing of the generality of acceptance of modern masters and movements that had spread throughout the art world by then. It explicitly rejected many other justly celebrated artists, and it excluded entirely most of the major and persistent tendencies of twentieth-century art, especially those that turned on personal, social, or political engagement of some sort: Symbolism, Expressionism, Dadaism, Surrealism, Concrete Abstraction, Social Realism, Socialist Realism, photography, the cinematic, Neo-Dada, and Pop. No thought of art originating elsewhere but in Europe, above all France, entered into the equation. It found value only in a very restricted idea of art's autonomy, its formal "purity." While Greenberg may, perhaps, have been inspired initially by an impulse that parallels Theodor Adorno's famous prescription—"To write poetry after Auschwitz is barbaric"—and the despairing conclusion that, in such circumstances, only an art about art's limits is possible, Greenberg had, by the later 1950s, found a language in which to celebrate the work of his chosen artists as the outcome of a positive, not a negative, dialectic.[12]

Formalist art criticism was a symptom of a much more widespread phenomenon: the canon-busting avant-gardism of the late nineteenth century and the early twentieth—the main narrative line in the dramatic story of modern art, which was so central to the romantic ideals of art's independence and the artist's individualism—had became frozen into official culture. A massive machinery of cultural conformity had, it seemed, settled into place. In the West and in the cultural dependencies of the great metropolitan art centers, adjusting to the modernist mindset continued to be a matter of imitating the prevailing master artist and following the percepts of the master critic. Then, in order to convey a simulation of growth, it also meant finding a slightly distinct, but not deeply challenging, variation on what they defined as the period style. Style following replaced creative innovation, a sure sign of a tradition on the cusp of becalming.

Among artists, however, a wide range of reactions set in. From the late 1950s onward, canon building has received a battering from a number of sources within art practice itself. Experimental artists all over the world have made works that have questioned everything about art's autonomy, art's implication, and art's historicity, including the nature of work itself, of a work, of the object, of making, of the artist, of materials, of nature, and of much else besides. The actions of the Guttai group in Japan or those of the Situationists in France and elsewhere in Europe, the mixed media minimalism of Black Mountain and subsequent Neo-Dada in New York and Fluxus work everywhere, the interrogations of the Neo-Concrétists in Brazil, indeed, the dramatic emergence of performance art, happenings, and environments all over the world, as well as conceptualist interrogation of art in all of its many forms—these are just some instances of the great tide of particularistic art that sought its values everywhere, it seems, but in high art tradition. On top of this internal onslaught, political artists attacked high modernist art's institutional complicity with the military-industry complex, while feminist artists deplored the deep implication in patriarchy of the "masterpiece" and the whole story of modern masters. Postmodern critique soon mocked the very possibility of a singular story of art in an age after the death of the great narratives, after the end of legitimization as such.

During the 1980s a reaction set in, especially in those countries that turned to right-wing governance. The art canon was revived as a citadel to be defended at all costs in the "culture wars" that preoccupied the U.S. cultural polity for a decade. Efforts to modify the list of Dead White European Males were met with stout resistance, indicating the rightward shift of U.S. electorates under Reagan and the general turn in that country toward more conservative and religiously based attitudes. In Britain, largely through the mediation of the collector Charles Saatchi, a generation of "young British artists" found ways to ride the contradictions to glory, or at least to notoriety. On a world scale, however, the irresistible tendency was that deep changes in the nature of the art object, in the practice of spectatorship, and in the mobility of the image counted against the singularity, against the static permanence of canonical work. The present situation, therefore, is one in which fundamentally contradictory currents are in play.

The Canons of Contemporary Art

Musing on the "very strong distinction between 'modern' and 'contemporary'" that became evident in the New York art world in the 1970s and early 1980s, Arthur Danto made the comment that this development had placed the Museum of Modern Art in New York—and, we might add, all other such modern art museums—in an unanticipated bind. Who would have thought that "contemporary art" would cease to be plainly that modern art being made now, that it would change from being simply those current works of art that might (after assessment by MOMA) become modern, indeed, that it would become something different in kind? It was a shock to find that art that "remained under the stylistic imperatives of modernism" was no longer contemporary, except in the trivial sense of being still churned out, anachronistically. "But today," Danto noted, "as we near the end of the century, the Museum of Modern Art has to decide whether it is going to acquire contemporary art that is not modern and thus become a museum of modern art in the strictly temporal sense or whether it will continue to collect only stylistically modern art, the production of which has thinned down to perhaps a trickle, but which is no longer representative of the contemporary world."[13]

In the event, MoMA decided that denial disguised as attack was the best form of defense. In 2000, it made a historic decision to partner with P.S.1, the renovated secondary school building in Long Island City, Queens that had become the successful P.S.1 Contemporary Art Center. The joint mission was collaboration in order "to promote the enjoyment, appreciation, study and understanding of contemporary art to a wide and growing audience." But just in case anyone got the idea that it would be modern art in Manhattan and contemporary art out in Queens, the culminating exhibition before MoMA closed for a five-year long renovation was Open Ends, a survey of the museum's holdings of art made since 1960. In the introduction to the related book, *Modern Contemporary: Art at MoMA since 1980*, the curator Kirk Varnedoe laid down the law:

> There is an argument to be made that the revolutions that originally produced modern art, in the late nineteenth and early twentieth centuries, have not been concluded or superseded—and thus that contemporary art today can be understood as the ongoing extension and revision of those founding innovations and debates. The collection of the Museum of Modern Art is, in a very real sense, that argument. Contemporary art is collected and presented at this Museum as part of modern art—as belonging within, and responding to, and expanding upon the framework of initiatives and challenges established by the earlier history of progressive art since the dawn of the twentieth century.[14]

The main meaning here is crystal clear, as it was when Clement Greenberg had spoken. Continuity, not rupture, is the rule, because we say so, and because we will show you how to see things our way. Contemporary art is repackaged as the new modern art by MoMA as surely as it is by the Guggenheim in Bilbao and in its exhibition venues in New York, Berlin, Las Vegas, and wherever else the franchise might come to extend.[15] After all, the institutions of modern art have, as their first priority, the perpetuation of themselves as the definitive sites of collection and preservation, judgment and interpretation. The practice of art can go its own way, at its own risk. The bet of these institutions—the Mephistophelean lure they hold out to artists—is that art will not go too far away and that it will always find ways to return; that contemporary art will, soon, become modern, just as modern art has, over time, joined art for the ages. At the same time, museums such as MOMA cannot escape the inner logic of art's independence—not, at least, for as long as genuine independence is maintained, recovered, or rediscovered within art practice.

Partisan Strategies: Canons in Contemporaneity

Certain artists have, during the past two decades, developed practices that both respond to the demands of contemporaneity and reveal aspects of what it is to be, and to be different, in its conditions. These practices, because they are rarely, in principle, generalizable, cannot be viewed as canonical in the older sense of the term. Some of them are so closely concerned with the nuances of the multiple temporalities of contemporaneity, are being made so deep into the abyss of scarcity, and are so thoroughly singular that the matter of canonicity becomes, at best, a distraction, at worst, an imposition. This differencing art is, however, both inspiring and highly suggestive as a pointer to value concentrations that are, at once, under threat and in nascent formation. Whether they will, eventually, be absorbed back into the institutions, and canonized, remains to be seen. If so, both institutions and artworks will be profoundly short-changed in the process.

A large body of such work comes from centers, groups, or peoples excluded from the dominant narratives of art's histories, and those opposed to globalizing regimes. A strategic insistence on the canonical status of local initiatives, on the innovative force of particular artists, works, occasions, and actions, can be a successful partisan strategy—partisan in the sense of politically partial, passionate, and resistant. This has been happening, since at least the 1920s in both Europe and its many cultural colonies in the Americas, Africa, Asia, and Australia. The fascinating history of their multiple local, eccentric, national, and regional modernisms has only recently begun to be written. When that mapping has been done, it will go some way toward explaining the powerful presence of critical artists from these backgrounds whose efforts precipitated the shift from modern to contemporary art during the 1960s, one that has carried through to the present.

This approach is more prevalent in the art of countries subject to decolonization. It is a tactic with a long history in Latin America: famously in the interventions of the group Tucumán Arde in the local politics of Rosario, Argentina, during the 1960s and 1970s; more recently in Fabiana de Barro's *Fiteiro Cultural*, a demountable structure used for multiple community-building purposes in Alamar, an outer-lying district of Havana, during the 8th Bienal de La Habana in 2003. The always-open character of such work makes it extremely unlikely that it would become a candidate for canonization. De Barro's work would lose its point in a museum. Subversive strategies—at least at the symbolical level—may also be found in the work of a limited number of artists who work close to the cultural centers, for example, the "poor" art of the Swiss artist Thomas Hirschhorn. Yet when Hirschhorn's installations are shown in orthodox settings—in the Los Angeles Museum of Contemporary Art, for example—they look, at first glance, like leftovers from a school tour "art experience," until, that is, one takes in the irreducible trenchancy of their political challenge. At rare moments, this challenge actually occupies a major site of official art, turning it, for a time into a round of highly political contestation. This occurred at the Documenta 11 exhibition in Kassel, Germany in 2002.[16] The effectiveness of the challenge mounted by that exhibition's curator, Okwui Enwezor, is attested not only in much of the visitor response to the show, but in the international art world's response: vehement rejection followed by callow retreat from engagement with the issues of contemporaneity.

In art and exhibition making such as this, something much more interesting is at stake than whether it will eventually fall subject to the expectant embrace of the canon-conferring art institution, be it a museum or a textbook. Let us look a little more closely at the work of an artist who has attracted much attention from all sides of the art world's divides, and ask where it stands in relation to the issues before us.

In the video *Passage*, made in 2001 by the Iranian artist Shirin Neshat, a group of black-clothed men carrying something, probably a body, move urgently from the seashore across a dry, desert-like terrain (fig. 14.2). They do so for over ten minutes, accompanied by the driving music of the American composer Philip Glass. Lacking symbols, hierarchy, and any evident ritual, the men's purpose is as ambiguous as the state of the white-clothed body they bear. Their progress is constantly contrasted to the actions of a group of hooded women circled closely together, who wail loudly and beat at something unseen in the dusty ground before them. In the penultimate scene, the men deliver their nearly invisible burden into the space cleared by the women. At that moment, a fire breaks out and travels along a triangular stonewall. The camera pans to a young girl who has been hiding there all along, a silent witness to something unfathomable.

This work is typical of the kind of contemporary art that locates itself at the emotional core of a culture that seems to have nothing that is contemporary about it, yet persists in our time. Indeed, in many parts of the world, such cultures are ascendant in our time. The culture in question draws a worldly

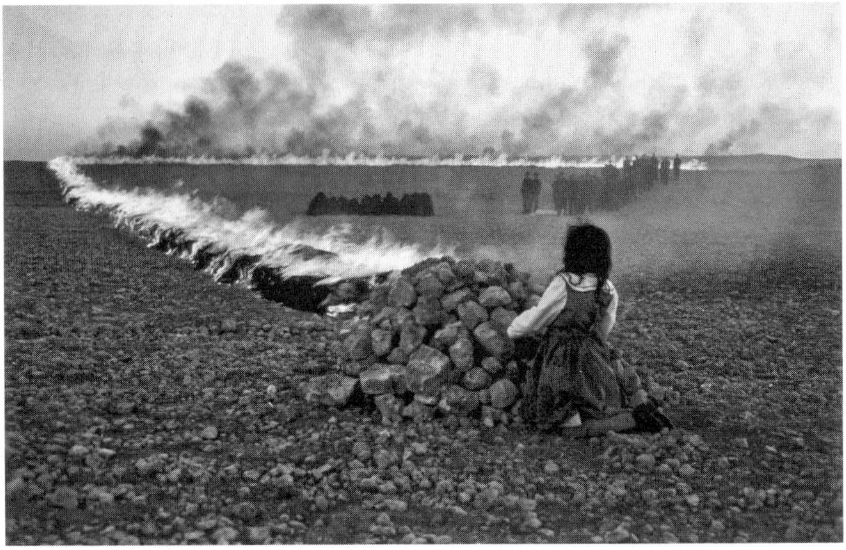

14.2. Shirin Neshat, *Passage*, 2001, production still. Copyright Shirin Neshat 2001. Photo: Larry Barns. Courtesy Barbara Gladstone Gallery, New York.

young feminist artist to it, to its implacable differencing between men and women, as an experience of trauma. In such cases, irony is irrelevant. Anachronism *is* relevant, but here, in Neshat's work, it is questioned. The very idea that one kind of culture, a modernizing one, gets to decide that another is anachronistic is put into doubt. Before September 11, 2001, *Passage* showed us that feudal structures were still so powerful that they shaped the everyday imaginaries of millions and will figure in the future of even more. And it concluded by showing us, in its final image, something even more powerful than that: that death exists beyond gender division, as does the recurrence of life, however marked it may be by death and division.[17]

Official, institutionalized contemporary art is, as I have indicated, devoted above all to finding new, up-to-date, modern ways of re-presenting peculiarly aesthetic beauty. Neshat is drawn to this task and is a celebrated contemporary artist. There are many questions to be asked about the ambiguities of her situation, questions to be put to an artist who makes work about the experience—particularly the experience of women—in a country from which she is an exile. Yet she remains tied to its culture, in a condition of quasi-permanent emigration that she shares with more and more people in the world today. As a mythic enactment of an unspecific ritual, *Passage* shows us something that is, at once, incomprehensibly strange yet hauntingly familiar. The crucial thing is that it does not give us the tools to resolve this tension in favor of one or the other, neither the strange nor the familiar. A work of art that seeks entry into the canons of art—at least those canons tied to a presumed and imposed universality—would do so (however much it might defer that moment). In contrast, a work that is sourced in the complexities of contemporaneity cannot offer closure. It must leave itself open for whatever is to come.

Contemporary Art in the Iconoscape

Neshat's imagery does not exist in art world contexts alone. It draws on, and feeds back into, a much larger circulation of images. In her case, it is the imagery of Muslim women in the modern world, above all the ubiquitous picture of the darkly veiled woman, constrained to invisibility within her own culture, a situation taken as iconic of something essential to the Muslim way of life. To many in the West, this image is one of a string of stereotypical shots that make up the limited repertoire that signifies the Middle East and northern Africa in the global mass media: teeming city streets rising to mosques, romantic profiles of lone camel riders moving across deserts, crowds of protesting Arabs, graphic evidence of sudden famine, and, more recently, reports of suicide bombings and mug shots of suspected terrorists. Working from within Iran, the video artist Ghazel recently showed three works, *Me in 2000*, *Me in 2001*, and *Me in 2002*, which managed to parody both Islamic dress codes and conceptualism by performing a number of nominated actions based on common-sense sentiments while dressed in her bhurka. Muslim women artists all over the world are devising artworks that contrast the harem fantasy, in historical retrospect a primarily Western projection onto the exotic Orient, and contemporary complications of the positioning of women in Islam.[18]

If we consider the entire worldwide economy of images, two operations, at least, seem fundamental, and they seem to tend in opposite directions. The image economy (which we might call the iconomy) continues to generate what we might call iconotypes, that is, images that, however complex and surprising they may initially be, soon become iconic, standing for an entire aspect of human experience—or, in philosophical terms, the entire type of which they are a token. The iconomy as a whole includes a number—limited but potent—of such iconotypes, and it circulates potentially infinite replicas of them throughout its realms. Striking instances of destination architecture (Frank Gehry's Guggenheim Museum in Bilbao is the outstanding recent example) and certain easily read artworks (Monet's water lilies, van Gogh's self-portraits, Picasso's cubist figures, Matisse's odalisques, Pollock's drip paintings,

Warhol's celebrity recycling) regularly appear among the images of place, ideology, leadership, and consumption that dominate this flow.

The German photographer Thomas Struth makes this phenomenon the subject of much of his work—and it is, of course, even more avidly collected by museums for this reason. His large (indeed, history-painting size) photograph of 1999, *National Museum of Art, Tokyo*, records the scene of viewing in the Japanese museum during the loan, by the Louvre, of Eugene Delacroix's *Liberty Leading the People*. An icon of French art, and of the ideals of the French Revolution, the painting can now travel only under the strictest constraints. Struth shows it on display under bullet-proof glass, set back into a large alcove, as if surrounded by a proscenium, and so brilliantly lit that the crowds milling before it are cast into the darkness of indistinct anonymity. The cinematic qualities of the experience are emphasized. The message is one of art as pure spectacle, with the artwork as an iconotype being trafficked within the iconomy through the agency of the museum as a place of entertainment, a venue of attractions. It is no surprise to find this photograph in the collections of the Metropolitan Museum in New York and to see it as part of Struth's one-man show at that museum in 2003, one of the museum's very rare presentations of the work of a contemporary artist. The modern museum (or, in the case of the Met, a treasure-house museum that undertakes incessant but well-disguised modernization) draws contemporary art back into its self-preserving fold yet again.

Yet, at the same time, the qualities most required by the society of the spectacle—repetition, disposability, commodification, and fashion sense—call on canons only in so far as they can be flexible, indeed instantly self-transformatory. Warhol is the most obvious figure of this transition. More recently, it can be seen in the interaction between fashion designers such as Alexander McQueen, music video makers such as Christopher Cunningham, and artists such as Matthew Barney, especially in the latter's extraordinary *Cremaster* cycle of 1994–2003.

Conclusion: there is none. In contemporaneity, the owl of Minerva is always just taking flight, blurring our perceptions with a fluttering grayness, in which we are likely to remain suspended for who knows how long. Contemporary art does meet many of the conditions of canonicity: art museum recognition, avid collecting, high sale prices, inclusion in textbooks, and peer acknowledgment. But certainty, even a degree of confidence, in the widespread valiance of judgment and in the continuity of valuing is gone. As to the fate of canons in these circumstances, we can perhaps guess that, while attempts will continue to be made to affirm them, reconstruct them, and readjust them, these efforts will meet with increasingly diminished, isolated, and futile returns.

Notes

1 See, for example, Kotz, *Rauschenberg/Art and Life*, 82; Hops and Davidson, *Robert Rauschenberg*, 44. On the details of the erasing, see Tomkins, *Off the Wall*, 96. An amusing account may be found in Steinberg, *Encounters with Rauschenberg*, 15–23. It is seen as a gesture within the warring between figuration and abstraction in de Kooning's own art by Butler, "The Woman Problem," 183–84, and as "an evacuation of intentional imagery and individual expression (i.e., 'art') in favor of a receptivity to contingent visual sensations (i.e., 'life')" by B. Taylor, *Random Order*, 63–65.

2 *Oxford English Dictionary Online*, 2002, derived from many earlier print versions, such as that of Simpson and Weiner, *The Complete Oxford English Dictionary*.

3 This may begin to answer the many conundrums posed by Jameson in *A Singular Modernity*, not least presentism, the mistaking of one's current, temporary, and all too familiar position as unprecedented, epochal, and permanent—the risk that is run by any account that acknowledges the power and the persistence of contemporaneity.

4 I develop a fuller account of contemporaneity in the introduction to my book *The Architecture of Aftermath* and relate it specifically to contemporary art in my "Contemporary Art and Contemporaneity." It is debated by a variety of authors in Smith, Enwezor, and Condee, eds., *Antinomies of Art and Culture*.

5 Denby, *Great Books*, 11.

6 Gombrich, *Ideas and Idols*, 171. In the essay in question, "Canons and Values: A Correspondence with Quentin Bell," Gombrich and Bell were debating Gombrich's canonical essay on canons, "Art History and the Social Sciences," which is in the same volume.

7 To be fair to Gombrich, I should draw attention to the fact that he moves, in "Art History and the Social Sciences" at least, toward a view of the canon as not simply a listing of the best poems, paintings, and so forth that are meant to work their magic on subsequent art and taste by exalted example. Rather, he also views the canon as the internal artistic dialogue between those works that have most profoundly addressed matters of the profoundest importance to human nature. He takes these matters to be universal, in the sense of globally spread and continuing, but he is also alive to the ways that works of art may "stand the test of time not as formal exercises but as an embodiment of a value system that they teach us to recognize." See Gombrich, *Ideas and Idols*, 156–59, 162–63.

8 Connor, *Theory and Cultural Value*, 17.

9 Ibid., 8.

10 Gombrich, *Ideas and Idols*, 163.

11 Greenberg, "Modernist Painting," and elsewhere, including Greenberg, *The Collected Essays and Criticism*, 4:85–93.

12 O'Connor, *The Adorno Reader*, 210. For a detailed study of the resonances of Adorno's idea, see Tiedemann, *Theodor W. Adorno*.

13 Danto, *After the End of Art*, 10.

14 Varnedoe, *Modern Contemporary*, 12. For a critique of MOMA's millennial exhibitions, particularly Modernstarts: People, Places, Things, see Moretti, "MoMA2000."

15 On the impact on Bilbao of the Guggenheim franchise, see "Negotiating the Center in Bilbao," a chapter in Holo, *Beyond the Prado*; and Zulaika, *Crónica de una sedducción*.

16 In 2002, Documenta 11 abounded with art that explored the ubiquity of globalization, its overreach, its incomplete reach, its failures, and the counterforces contending against it, not least those following from decolonization. Outstanding among this work was Allan Sekula's *Fish Story*, Chantal Akerman's multiple video installation devoted to U.S.-Mexican border crossing, the Cameroon artist Jean-Marie Teno's video *Trip to the Country*, the installations of Georges Adéagbo and Walid Ra'ad, Ra'ad's quasi-fictive the Atlas Group's various projects documenting contemporary Lebanese history since 1997, and many others. See Enwezor, *Documenta 11_Platform 5*.

17 Further on this and related works by Neshat, see Milani, *Shirin Neshat*.

18 A number of these are reviewed in the exhibition Harem: Fantasies and the New Scheherazades, curated by Fatima Mernissi at the Centre de Cultura Contemporània, Barcelona, 2003.

BIBLIOGRAPHY

Académie des Beaux-Arts. "Protestation respectueuse contre les atteintes qui viennent d'être portées à son caractère, à ses droits, à ces attributions." *Le Moniteur Universel*, January 6, 1864, n.p.

Adams, Carole Elizabeth. *Women Clerks in Wilhelmine Germany: Issues of Class and Gender*. Cambridge: Cambridge University Press, 1988.

Adorno, Theodor. "Art, Culture and Society." In *Prisms*, 17–34. Cambridge, Mass.: MIT Press, 1981.

———. *Can One Live After Auschwitz?* Edited by Rolf Tiedemann. Stanford: Stanford University Press, 2003.

———. *The Culture Industry: Selected Essays on Mass Culture*. Edited by J. M. Bernstein. New York: Routledge, 1991.

Allara, Pamela, Marilyn Martin, and Zola Mtshiza, eds. *CoExistence: Contemporary Cultural Production in South Africa*. Waltham, Mass.: Rose Art Museum, Brandeis University, 2003.

Allen, Harold. "Helen Gardner." In *Notable American Women*, edited by Edward T. James and Janet W. James. Cambridge, Mass.: Harvard University Press, Belknap Press, 1971.

Allen, James Sloan. *The Romance of Commerce and Culture*. Chicago: University of Chicago Press, 1983.

Alpers, Svetlana. *Rembrandt's Enterprise: The Studio and the Market*. Chicago: University of Chicago Press, 1988.

Althusser, Louis. "Ideology and Ideological State Apparatuses (Notes Toward an Investigation)." In *Lenin and Philosophy*, translated by Ben Brewster, 127–86. New York: Monthly Review Press, 1971.

Altmann-Gottheiner, Elisabeth. "Die Frau als Konsumentin." *Die Welt der Frau* 35 (1911): 551.

Amaury-Duval, Eugène-Emmanuel. *Atelier d'Ingres*. Introduced by Daniel Ternois. Paris: Arthena, 1993. First published 1878 by Charpentier (Paris).

Anderson, Benedict. *Imagined Communities: Reflections on the Origins and Spread of Nationalism*. New York: Verso, 1991.

Andrews, Julia F. *Painters and Politics in the People's Republic of China, 1949–1979*. Berkeley: University of California Press, 1994.

Andrews, Julia F., and Kuiyi Shen. *A Century in Crisis: Modernity and Tradition in the Art of Twentieth-Century China*. New York: Guggenheim Museum, 1998.

Anger, Jenny. "Forgotten Ties: The Suppression of the Decorative in German Art and Theory, 1900–1915." In *Not at Home: The Suppression of Domesticity in Modern Art and Architecture*, edited by Christopher Reed, 130–46. London: Thames and Hudson, 1996.

———. "Modernism at Home: The Private Gesamtkunstwerk." In *The Feeling of Seeing: Modernism, Postmodernism, and Beyond; A Festschrift for Kermit Swiler Champa*, edited by David Ogawa and Deborah Johnson, 213–45. New York: Peter Lang, 2004.

———. *Paul Klee and the Decorative in Modern Art*. Cambridge: Cambridge University Press, 2004.

Ash, Russell. *The Top 10 of Everything*. New York: Dorling Kindersley, 2002.

The Asia Foundation: Past, Present and Future. Washington D.C.: Library of Congress, Congressional Research Service, The Foreign Affairs and National Defense Division, 1983.

Assouline, Pierre. *Grâces lui soient rendues: Durand-Ruel le marchand des Impressionistes*. Paris: Plon, 2002.

Atkinson, Brenda, and Candice Breitz, eds. *Grey Areas: Representation, Identity and Politics in Contemporary South African Art*. Johannesburg: Chalkham Hill Press, 1991.

Bal, Mika, and Norman Bryson. "Semiotics and Art History." *Art Bulletin* 73 (1991): 174–208.

Baranowa, Anna, ed. *Stulecie Towarzystwa Artystów Polskich "Sztuka."* Cracow: Universitas, 2001.

Barnhart, Richard, Yang Xin, Nie Chongzheng, James Cahill, Lang Shaojun, and Wu Hung. *Three Thousand Years of Chinese Painting*. New Haven, Conn.: Yale University Press, 1997.

Barr, Alfred H., Jr. *Cubism and Abstract Art*. Cambridge, Mass.: Harvard University Press, 1986. First published 1936 by the Museum of Modern Art (New York).

———. "Is Modern Art Communistic?" *New York Times Magazine*, December 14, 1952, 22–23, 28–30.

Barringer, Tim, and Tom Flynn, eds. *Colonialism and the Object: Empire, Material Culture and the Museum*. London: Routledge, 1998.

Bartning, Otto. "Sollen Damen bauen?" *Die Welt der Frau* 40 (1911): 625–26.

Batchelder, Ernest. *Design in Theory and Practice*. New York: Macmillan, 1910.

Batchelor, David. "Modernity and Tradition: Warhol and Andre." In *Investigating Modern Art*, edited by Liz Dawtrey, Toby Jackson, Mary Masterson, Pam Meecham, and Paul Wood, 129–43. New Haven, Conn.: Yale University Press, 1996.

Bate, W. Jackson. *The Burden of the Past and the English Poet*. New York: Norton, 1970.

Bauch, Kurt. *Rembrandt Gemälde*. Berlin: W. de Gruyter, 1966.

Baudelaire, Charles. *Selected Writings on Art and Literature*. Translated by P. E. Charvet. New York: Penguin, 1993.

Bazin, Germain. *Impressionist Paintings in the Louvre*. Translated by S. Cunliffe-Owen. London: Thames and Hudson, 1958.

Becker, Howard. *Art Worlds*. Berkeley: University of California Press, 1982.

Beckett, Wendy. *Sister Wendy's Grand Tour: Discovering Europe's Great Art*. New York: Stewart, Tabori and Chang, 1994.

———. *Sister Wendy's 1,000 Masterpieces*. London: Dorling Kindersley, 1999.

Beckett, Wendy, and Patricia Wright. *The Story of Painting*. London: Dorling Kindersley, 1994.

Bedford, Emma, ed. *A Decade of Democracy: South African Art 1994–2004*. Cape Town: Double Storey and Iziko Museums of Cape Town, 2004.

Belting, Hans. Afterword to *Entwicklungsgeschichte der modernen Kunst*, by Julius Meier-Graefe, 2:727–60. Munich: Piper, 1987 [reprint].

———. *Art History after Modernism*. Translated by Caroline Saltzwedel, Mitch Cohen, and Kenneth Northcott. Chicago: University of Chicago Press, 2003.

———. *The Invisible Masterpiece*. London: Reaktion Books, 2001.

———. *Likeness and Presence: History of the Image before the Era of Art*. Chicago: University of Chicago Press, 1994.

Benét, William Rose. *The Reader's Encyclopedia*. 2nd ed. New York: Thomas Y. Crowell Company, 1965.

Benhamou, Reed. "Public and Private Art Education in France 1648–1793." In *Studies on Voltaire and the Eighteenth Century*, edited by Jonathan Mallinson, 308:1–184. Oxford: Voltaire Foundation, 1993.

Benjamin, Walter. "The Work of Art in the Age of Mechanical Reproduction." In *Illuminations*, translated by Harry Zohn, 217–51. New York: Schocken Books, 1968.

Bennett, Tony. *The Birth of the Museum: History, Theory, Politics*. London: Routledge, 1996.

Berger, Maurice, ed. *Postmodernism: A Virtual Discussion*. New York: Distributed Art Publishers, 2003.

Bérhaut, Marie. *Gustave Caillebotte: Catalogue raisonné des peintures et pastels*. Paris: La Bibliothèque des Arts, 1994.

Berman, Esmé. *Art and Artists of South Africa: An Illustrated Biographical Dictionary and Historical Survey of Painters, Sculptors and Graphic Artists since 1875*. 2nd ed. Halfway House (Transvaal): Southern Book Publishers, 1983.

———. *Painting in South Africa*. Halfway House (Transvaal): Southern Book Publishers, 1993.

Bie, Oscar. *Das Kunstgewerbe*. Frankfurt am Main: n.p., 1908.

Bloom, Harold. *The Anxiety of Influence: A Theory of Poetry*. Oxford: Oxford University Press, 1973.

Bode, Wilhelm von, and C. Hofstede de Groot. *Rembrandt: beschreibendes Verzeichniss seiner Gemälde*. 8 vols. Paris: C. Sedelmeyer, 1897–1905.

Boime, Albert. *The Academy and French Painting in the Nineteenth Century*. London: Phaidon, 1971.

———. *A Social History of Modern Art*. 3 vols. Chicago: University of Chicago Press, 1987–2004.

———. "The Teaching Reforms of 1863 and the Origins of Modernism in France." *Art Quarterly* 1, no. 1 (1978): 1–39.

Borgmeyer, Charles. *The Master Impressionists*. Chicago: Art Press, 1913.

Bornstein, Robert. "Exposure and Affect: Overview and Meta-analysis of Research, 1968–1987." *Psychological Bulletin* 106 (1989): 265–89.

Bourdieu, Pierre. *The Field of Cultural Production*. New York: Columbia University Press, 1993.

Boyer d'Agen, A. *Ingres d'après une correspondance inedited*. Paris: Crès, 1909.

Bredius, Abraham. *Rembrandt schilderijen, 630 afbeeldingen*. Utrecht: Uitgeversmaatschappy W. De. Haan, n.v., 1935.

Brennan, Marcia. *Modernism's Masculine Subjects: Matisse, the New York School, and Post Painterly Abstraction*. Cambridge, Mass.: MIT Press, 2004.

———. *Painting Gender, Constructing Theory: The Alfred Stieglitz Circle and American Formalist Aesthetics*. Cambridge, Mass.: MIT Press, 2001.

Brettell, Richard. "Modern French Painting and the Art Museum: The Problematics of Collecting and Display, Part 2." *Art Bulletin* 77, no. 2 (June 1995): 166–70.

Breuer, Robert. "Der Einkauf als Kulturelle Funktion." *Deutsche Kunst und Dekoration* 21 (1907–8): 78–82.

———. "Die Frau als Möbelbauerin." *Fachblatt für Holzarbeiter* 10 (1915): 101–4.

Breuilly, John. *Nationalism and the State*. Chicago: University of Chicago Press, 1993.

Brown, Janelle. "Ticky-Tacky Houses from 'Painter of Light.'" *Salon*, March 18, 2002. http://www.salon.com/life.

Bruyn, Josua. "A Descriptive Survey of the Signatures." In *A Corpus of Rembrandt Paintings*, by Josua Bruyn, Bob Haak, Simon H. Levie, Pieter J.J. van Thiel, and Ernst van der Wetering, 1:53–59. Stichting Foundation Rembrandt Research Project. The Hague: M. Nijhoff Publishers, 1982–.

———. "Rembrandt's Workshop: Its Function and Production." In *Rembrandt: The Master and His Workshop—Paintings*, by Christopher Brown, Jan Kelch, and Pieter van Thiel. Exhibition catalogue, 68–89. New Haven, Conn.: Yale University Press in association with National Gallery Publications, 1991.

———. "A Selection of Signatures, 1632–1634." In *A Corpus of Rembrandt Paintings*, by Josua Bruyn, Bob Haak, Simon H. Levie, Pieter J.J. van Thiel, and Ernst van der Wetering, 2:99–106. Stichting Foundation Rembrandt Research Project. The Hague: M. Nijhoff Publishers, 1982–.

———. "A Selection of Signatures, 1635–1642." In *A Corpus of Rembrandt Paintings*, by Josua Bruyn, Bob Haak, Simon H. Levie, Pieter J.J. van Thiel, and Ernst van der Wetering, 3:51–56. Stichting Foundation Rembrandt Research Project. The Hague: M. Nijhoff Publishers, 1982–.

———. "Studio Practice and Studio Production." In *A Corpus of Rembrandt Paintings*, by Josua Bruyn, Bob Haak, Simon H. Levie, Pieter J.J. van Thiel, and Ernst van der

Wetering, 3:12–50. Stichting Foundation Rembrandt Research Project. The Hague: M. Nijhoff Publishers, 1982–.

Bruyn, Josua, Bob Haak, Simon H. Levie, Pieter J.J. van Thiel, and Ernst van der Wetering. *A Corpus of Rembrandt Paintings*. Stichting Foundation Rembrandt Research Project, 4 vols. The Hague: M. Nijhoff Publishers, 1982–.

Bryson, Norman. *Tradition and Desire: From David to Delacroix*. Cambridge: Cambridge University Press, 1984.

Brzyski, Anna. "Between the Nation and the World: Nationalism and Emergence of Polish Modern Art." *Centropa* 1, no. 3 (September 2001): 165–79.

———. "Constructing the Canon: The Album *Polish Art* and the Writing of the Modernist Art History of Polish 19th-Century Painting." *19th-Century Art Worldwide* 3, no. 1 (spring 2004). *http://19thc-artworldwide.org/spring_04/articles/brzy.html.*

———. "The Problem of Modernism: Art Practice under the Gaze of Art History." In *Modernism and Central- and East-European Arts and Culture*, 339–65. Osaka University, the 21st Century COE Program, Research Activities 2004–2006. Osaka: University of Osaka Press, 2007.

———. "'Unsere Polen . . .': Polish Artists and the Vienna Secession." In *Art and National Identity at the Turn of the Century*, edited by Michelle Facos and Sharon Hirsh, 65–89. Cambridge: Cambridge University Press, 2003.

Brzyski-Long, Anna. "Modern Art and Nationalism." PhD diss., University of Chicago, 1999. Ann Arbor, Mich.: UMI, 1999.

———. "Retracing the Modernist Origins: Conceptual Parallels in the Aesthetic Thought of Charles Baudelaire and G. W. F. Hegel." *Art Criticism* 12, no.1 (fall 1997): 95–111. A revised version is available online at *http://www.uky.edu/~abrzy2/Hegel-Baudelaire.htm.*

Bu, Liping. "Educational Exchange and Cultural Diplomacy in the Cold War." *Journal of American Studies* 33, no. 3 (1999): 394–415.

Bull, M. *One Hundred Years Ago: An Exhibition to Commemorate the Opening of the "Cape Town Art Gallery" in New Street*. Cape Town: South African National Gallery, 1975.

Butler, Cornelia H. "The Woman Problem: On the Contemporaneity of de Kooning's Women." In *Willem de Kooning: Tracing the Figure*, by Cornelia H. Butler and Peter Schimmel, 180–91. Princeton, N.J.: Princeton University Press for the Los Angeles Museum of Contemporary Art, 2002.

Butler, Cornelia H., and Peter Schimmel. *Willem de Kooning: Tracing the Figure*. Princeton, N.J.: Princeton University Press for the Los Angeles Museum of Contemporary Art, 2002.

Cahill, James. *Chinese Painting*. Geneva: Skira, 1960.

Calinescu, Matei. *Five Faces of Modernity: Modernism, Avant-Garde, Decadence, Kitsch, Postmodernism*. Rev. ed. Durham, N.C.: Duke University Press, 1987.

Camiciottoli, Belinda Crawford. "Metadiscourse and ESP Reading Comprehension: An Exploratory Study." *Reading in a Foreign Language* 15, no. 1 (April 2003): 28–44.

Camille, Michael. "Rethinking the Canon." *Art Bulletin* 78 (1996): 198–201.

Campbell, Joan. *The German Werkbund: The Politics of Reform in the Applied Arts*. Princeton, N.J.: Princeton University Press, 1978.

Catalogue of Chinese Newspapers and Periodicals, 2002–2003. N.p.: China National Publications Import and Export, 2003.

Catalogue of the International Exhibition of Chinese Art. London: Royal Academy of Arts, 1935–36.

Cavanough, Jan. *Out Looking In: Early Modern Polish Art, 1890–1918*. Berkeley, Calif.: University of California Press, 2000.

Champa, Kermit Swiler. *The Rise of Landscape Painting in France, Corot to Monet*. Manchester, N.H.: Currier Gallery of Art, 1991.

Champaigne, Philippe de. "Contre les copistes de manières." Archives de l'École Nationale Supérieure des Beaux-Arts, Paris, MS 156.

Chave, Anna. "New Encounters with *Les Demoiselles d'Avignon*: Gender, Race, and the Origins of Cubism." *Art Bulletin* 76 (December 1994): 597–611.

Cheetham, Mark A. *Kant, Art, and Art History*. Cambridge: Cambridge University Press, 2002.

Chen Hengke [Chen Hengque or Chen Shizeng]. "Wen ren hua de jiazhi" (The Value of Literati Painting). In *Meishu congshu*, edited by Yen Yiping. Vol. 21, bk 2, 87–99. Taipei: Yiwen yinshuguan, 1975. First published in 1921 in *Huixue zazhi*.

Chiang, Fu-ts'ung. *Zhonghua wenhua fuxing yundong yu gugong bo wu yuan* [The Chinese Culture Renaissance Movement and the Palace Museum]. Taipei: Shangwu Publishing, 1977.

Chinese Art Treasures. Geneva: Skira, 1961.

Chow, Kai-wing, Kevin M. Doak, and Poshek Fu, eds. *Constructing Nationhood in Modern East Asia*. Ann Arbor: University of Michigan Press, 2001.

Chu, Petra ten-Doesschate. *Nineteenth-Century European Art*. New York: Harry N. Abrams, 2003.

Clapper, Michael. "Marketing Uplift: Sources, Strategies, and Purposes of Thomas Kinkade's Work." Paper presented at the annual conference of the College Art Association, Seattle, February 2004.

Clark, T. J. *The Painting of Modern Life*. Princeton, N.J.: Princeton University Press, 1984.

Clarke, Jay A. "Munch, Liebermann, and the Question of Etched 'Reproductions.'" *Visual Resources* 16, no. 1 (2000): 27–63.

Clemen, Paul. *Meisterwerke westdeutscher Malerei und andere hervorragende Gemaälde alter Meister aus Privatbesitz auf der Kunsthistorischen Ausstellung zu Düsseldorf 1904*. Munich: Bruckmann, 1905.

Clifford, James. "Collecting Ourselves." In *Interpreting Objects and Collections*, edited by Susan M. Pearce, 258–68. London: Routledge, 1994.

———. *The Predicament of Culture: Twentieth-Century Ethnography, Literature, and Art*. Cambridge, Mass.: Harvard University Press, 1988.

Clunas, Craig. "China in Britain: The Imperial Collections." In *Colonialism and the*

Object: Empire, Material Culture and the Museum, edited by Tim Barringer and Tom Flynn, 41–51. London: Routledge, 1998.

Cohen, Paul. *Discovering History in China: American Historical Writing on the Recent Chinese Past*. New York: Columbia University Press, 1984.

Cohen, Warren I. *East Asian Art and American Culture: A Study in International Relations*. New York: Columbia University Press, 1992.

Condon, Patricia, Marjorie B. Cohn, Agnes Mongan, and Debra Edelstein. *Ingres, in Pursuit of Perfection: The Art of J.-A.-D. Ingres*. Exhibition catalogue. Louisville, Ky.: J.B. Speed Art Museum, 1983.

Connor, Steven. *Theory and Cultural Value*. Oxford: Blackwell Publishers, 1992.

Cottington, David. *Cubism in the Shadow of War*. New Haven, Conn.: Yale University Press, 1998.

Craig, Robert T. "Metadiscourse, Theory, and Practice." *Research on Language and Social Interaction* 32, no. 1 (1999): 21–29.

———. "Theory as Metadiscourse." Presentation in "Practical Theory in Classroom Contexts," a panel discussion at the annual convention of the National Communication Association, Seattle, Wash., November 2000. Posted at http://spot.colorado.edu/~craigr/theory_as_metadiscourse.htm.

Crane, Susan A., ed. *Museums and Memory*. Stanford, Calif.: Stanford University Press, 2000.

Craven, Thomas. "Art." *The Nation* 139, September 26, 1934, 360.

Crismore, A. *Talking with Readers: Metadiscourse as Rhetorical Act*. New York: Peter Lang Publishers, 1989.

Crismore, A., and R. Farnsworth. "Metadiscourse in Popular and Professional Science Discourse." In *The Writing Scholar*, edited by W. Nash, 119–36. Newbury Park, Calif.: Sage Publications, 1990.

Crismore, A., and W. J. Vande Kopple. "Hedges and Readers: Effects on Attitudes and Learning." In *Hedging and Discourse: Approaches to the Analysis of a Pragmatic Phenomenon in Academic Texts*, edited by S. Markkanen and H. Schroeder, 83–114. Berlin: Walter de Gruyter and Co., 1997.

Croizier, Ralph. *Art and Revolution in Modern China: The Lingnan (Cantonese) School of Painting, 1906–1951*. Berkeley: University of California Press, 1988.

Crosby, Sumner McKay. *See* Gardner, Helen.

Cumings, Bruce. *Parallax Visions: Making Sense of American–East Asian Relations at the End of the Century*. Durham, N.C.: Duke University Press, 1999.

Cumming, Robert. *Annotated Art*. New York: DK Publishing, Inc., 1995.

———. *Great Artists: The Lives of 50 Painters Explored Through Their Work*. New York: DK Publishing, Inc., 1998.

Cutting, James E. "Gustave Caillebotte, French Impressionism, and Mere Exposure." *Psychonomic Bulletin and Review* 10 (2003): 319–43.

———. *Impressionism and Its Canon*. Lanham, Md.: University Press of America, 2006.

Danto, Arthur. *After the End of Art: Contemporary Art and the Pale of History*. Princeton, N.J.: Princeton University Press, 1997.

———. "The Artworld." *The Journal of Philosophy* 61, no. 19 (1964): 571–84.

Dawtrey, Liz, Toby Jackson, Mary Masterson, Pam Meecham, and Paul Wood, eds. *Investigating Modern Art*. New Haven, Conn.: Yale University Press, 1996.

De Corot aux impressionnistes, donations Moreau-Nélaton. Paris: Réunion des musées nationaux, 1991.

de Duve, Thierry. *Pictorial Nominalism: On Marcel Duchamp's Passage from Painting to the Readymade*. Minneapolis: University of Minnesota Press, 1991.

Delaborde, Henri. *Ingres: Sa vie, ses travaux, sa doctrine*. Paris: Plon, 1870.

De la Croix, Horst. *See* Gardner, Helen.

De Landa, Manuel. *A Thousand Years of Nonlinear History*. New York: Zone Books, 2003.

Denby, David. *Great Books*. New York: Touchstone, 1996.

Derrida, Jacques. *Archive Fever: A Freudian Impression*. Chicago: University of Chicago Press, 1996.

———. *The Truth in Painting*. Chicago: University of Chicago Press, 1987.

Dictionnaire de l'Académie des Beaux-Arts. 6 vols. Paris: Firmin-Didot, 1858–87.

"Die Deutsche Werkbund-Ausstellung: Die Architektur." *Kölnische Volkszeitung* 492 (May 31, 1914): 1–2.

Doherty, M. Stephen. "Thomas Kinkade Shares His Light." *American Artist* 65 (October 2001): 20.

Dolby, Joe. "A Short History of the South African National Gallery." *Lantern* (December 1981): 37–50.

Dondero, George A. "Modern Art Shackled to Communism." In *Congressional Record*. House. 81st Congr., 1st sess., August 16, 1949. Vol. 95, pts. 8–9: 11584–87.

Drohojowska-Philp, Hunter. "Painted into a Corner? A Curated Exhibition Asks Whether Thomas Kinkade, the People's Artist, Can Find Respect in Today's Art World." *Los Angeles Times*, April 4, 2004, E48.

Duara, Prasenjit. *Rescuing the Nation from History: Questioning Narratives of Modern China*. Chicago: University of Chicago Press, 1995.

———. "The Regime of Authenticity: Timelessness, Gender, and National History in Modern China." In *Constructing Nationhood in Modern East Asia*, edited by Kai-wing Chow, Kevin M. Doak, and Poshek Fu, 359–85. Ann Arbor: University of Michigan Press, 2001.

du Bos, Charles. "Bibliographie: Histoire du développement de l'art moderne, par J. Meier-Graefe." *Gazette des Beaux-Arts* 35, no. 586 (April 1906): 347.

du Camp, Maxime. *Le Salon de 1861*. Paris: Librairie Nouvelle, 1861.

Duffey, Alexander E. "Art History in South Africa: Past and Present." In *Memory and Oblivion: Proceedings of the XXIXth International Congress of the History of Art, held in Amsterdam, 1–7 September 1996*, edited by Adriaan Wessel Reinink and Jeroen Stumpel, 111–21. Boston: Kluwer Academic Publishers, 1999.

Duffus, R. L. *The American Renaissance*. New York: Alfred A. Knopf, 1928.

Duncan, Carol. *Civilizing Rituals: Inside Public Art Museums*. London: Routledge, 1995.

Dupin, Jacques. *Joan Miró: Catalogue Raisonné; Paintings*. Translated by Cole Swensen and Unity Woodman. 6 vols. Paris: Daniel Lelong, 1999–2004.

Duranty, Edmond. "Le peintre Louis Martin." In *Le Pays des Arts*, 313–50. Paris: Chapentier, 1881.

Duret, Théodore. *Courbet*. Paris: Bernheim Jeune, 1918.

———. *Critique d'avant-garde*. Paris: Charpentier, 1885.

———. *Histoire de J. McN. Whistler et de son oeuvre*. Paris: Floury, 1904.

———. *Whistler*. Translated by Frank Rutter. Philadelphia: Lippincott, 1917.

Eco, Umberto. *Travels in Hyperreality*. Translated by William Weaver. San Diego: Harcourt Brace, 1986.

Eisenman, Stephen, ed. *Nineteenth-Century Art*. London: Thames and Hudson, 2002.

Eitner, Lorenz. *An Outline of 19th-Century Art: A Critical History*. New York: Thames and Hudson, 1994.

Elderfield, John. *The Museum of Modern Art at Mid-Century: At Home and Abroad*. New York: Museum of Modern Art, 1994.

Elkins, James. *Is Art History Global?* The Art Seminar, vol. 3. New York: Routledge, 2006.

———. "Review: David Summers, *Real Spaces*; World Art History and the Rise of Western Modernism." *Art Bulletin* 86, no. 2 (2004): 373–80.

———. *Stories of Art*. New York: Routledge, 2002.

———. *Why Are Our Pictures Puzzles? On the Modern Origins of Pictorial Complexity*. New York: Routledge, 1999.

Enwezor, Okwui, ed. *Documenta 11_Platform 5: Exhibition*. Ostfildern-Ruit: Hatje Cantz Verlag, 2002.

Evans, Dylan. *An Introductory Dictionary of Lacanian Psychoanalysis*. London: Routledge, 1996.

Exposition universelle de 1900: Catalogue illustré official de l'exposition centennale de l'art français de 1800 à 1889. Paris: Imprimeries Lemercier et Cie. and Ludovic Baschet, 1900.

Fabian, Johannes. *Time and Other: How Anthropology Makes Its Object*. Rev. ed. New York: Columbia University Press, 2002.

Fairbank, John King. *Chinabound: A Fifty-Year Memoir*. New York: Harper and Row, 1982.

Farrell, James J. *One Nation under Goods: Malls and the Seductions of American Shopping*. Washington, D.C.: Smithsonian Institution Press, 2003.

Faunce, Sarah, and Linda Nochlin, eds. *Courbet Reconsidered*. Brooklyn: Brooklyn Museum, 1988.

Fb. "Deutsche Werkbund-Ausstellung." *Kölner Tageblatt* 546 (July 25, 1914): [unpaged].

Félibien, André. *Conférences de l'académie royale de peinture et de sculpture pendant l'année 1667*. Paris: Frederic Léonard, 1669.

———. *Entretiens sur les vies et sur les ouvrages des plus excellens peintres*. 4 vols. London: David Mortier, 1705.

Feng, Ming-chu, ed. *Emperor Ch'ienlung's Grand Cultural Enterprise*. Taipei: National Palace Museum, 2002.

Ferguson, Russell. "Can We Still Use the Canon?" *The Art Journal* 58 (1999): 4.

Fernier, Robert. *La vie et l'oeuvre de Gustave Courbet: Catalogue raisonné*. 2 vols. Lausanne: Fondation Wildenstein, 1977.

Feynman, Richard. *"Surely You're Joking, Mr. Feynman": Adventures of a Curious Character*. New York: Norton, 1985.

Files of the Planning Committee for the Exhibition to the United States. Taipei: National Palace Museum, 1960.

Fitzgerald, Michael. *Making Modernism: Picasso and the Creation of the Market for Twentieth-Century Art*. Berkeley: University of California Press, 1996.

Flam, Jack, and Miriam Deutch, eds. *Primitivism and Twentieth-Century Art: A Documentary History*. Berkeley: University of California Press, 2003.

Fong, Wen C. "Why Chinese Painting Is History." *Art Bulletin* 85, no. 2 (June 2003): 258–80.

Foster, Hal. "Archives of Modern Art." *October* 99 (winter 2002): 81–95.

———. "The 'Primitive' Unconscious of Modern Art." *October* 34 (fall 1985): 58–70.

Foster, Hal, Rosalind Krauss, Yve Alain Bois, and Benjamin H. D. Buchloh. *Art since 1900: Modernism, Antimodernism, Postmodernism*. New York: Thames and Hudson, 2005.

Foucart, Bruno. "L'Enseigement des arts et la reforme de 1863, ou fallait-il faire quelque chose?" In *Débats et Polémiques: A propos de l'ensiegnement des arts du dessin*, edited by Louis Vitet and Eugène Viollet-le-Duc, 7–25. Paris: EBA, 1984.

Foucault, Michael. *The Archaeology of Knowledge and the Discourse on Language*. Translated by A. M. Sheridan Smith. New York: Pantheon Books, 1972.

———. *The Order of Things: An Archaeology of the Human Sciences*. New York: Vintage Books, 1994.

Fransen, Hans. *Three Centuries of South African Art, Fine Art, Architecture, Applied Arts*. Johannesburg: Ad Donker, 1982.

Fréart de Chambray, Roland. *An Idea of the Perfection of Painting*. London: Herringmer, 1668.

Freidman, Thomas L. *The Lexus and the Olive Tree: Understanding Globalization*. New York: Anchor Books, 2000.

Frelinghuysen, Alice C., Gary Tinterow, S. Stein, G. Wold, and J. Meech. *Splendid Legacy: The Havemeyer Collection*. Exhibition catalogue. New York: Metropolitan Museum of Art, 1993.

Freud, Sigmund. *Civilization and Its Discontents*. Translated and edited by James Strachey. New York: W. W. Norton and Company, 1961.

———. *Three Essays on the Theory of Sexuality*. Translated and edited by James Strachey. New York: Basic Books, 1962.

Frevert, Ute. *Women in German History: From Bourgeois Emancipation to Sexual Liberation*. Translated by Stuart McKinnon-Evans. Oxford: Berg, 1989.

Fried, Michael. "Courbet's 'Femininity.'" In *Courbet Reconsidered*, edited by Sarah Faunce and Linda Nochlin, 43–54. Brooklyn: Brooklyn Museum, 1988.

———. *Courbet's Realism*. Chicago: University of Chicago Press, 1990.

Friedman, Edward, and Mark Selden, eds. *America's Asia: Dissenting Essays on Asian-American Relations*. New York: Pantheon Books, 1971.

Frieling, Rudolf, ed. *Mapping and Text*. Media/Art/Net. http://www.medienkunstnetz.de/themes/mapping and text/ (accessed March 19, 2005).

Galenson, David. "The New York School versus the School of Paris: Who Really Made the Most Important Art after World War II?" *Historical Methods* 35, no. 4 (October–December 2002): 9–24.

———. *Old Masters and Young Geniuses: The Two Life Cycles of Artistic Creativity*. Princeton, N.J.: Princeton University Press, 2006.

———. *Painting Outside the Lines: Patterns of Creativity in Modern Art*. Cambridge, Mass.: Harvard University Press, 2001.

Galenson, David, and Robert Jensen. "Careers and Canvases: The Rise of the Market for Modern Art in the Nineteenth Century." *Working Papers Series*, no. 9123. National Bureau of Economic Research, September 2002.

Gallatin, A. E., ed. *Museum of Living Art: A. E. Gallatin Collection*. New York: George Grady Press, 1936.

Gallwitz, S. D. "Das Haus der Frau auf der Werkbundausstellung in Köln." *Die Frau* 21, no. 10 (1914): 591–94.

Gálvez, Antonio, Mercedes Maqueda, Manuel Martínez-Bueno, and Eva Valdivia. "Scientific Publication Trends and the Developing World." *American Scientist* 88 (November-December 2000): 526–33.

Gardner, Helen. "The Analytic Method." In *Art Education Today*, 26–38. New York: Columbia University, Teachers College, 1940.

———. *Art through the Ages: An Introduction to Its History and Significance*. 1st ed. New York: Harcourt, Brace, 1926; 2nd ed. New York: Harcourt, Brace, 1936; 3rd ed. New York: Harcourt, Brace, 1948; 4th ed. [and subsequent eds.] published as *Gardner's Art through the Ages*, by Sumner McKay Crosby and the Department of the History of Art at Yale University. New York: Harcourt, Brace, 1959; 5thed., by Horst de la Croix and Richard G. Tansey. New York: Harcourt, Brace, and World, 1970; 6th ed. New York: Harcourt Brace Jovanovich, 1975; 7th ed. New York: Harcourt Brace Jovanovich, 1980; 8th ed. San Diego, Calif.: Harcourt Brace Jovanovich, 1986; 9th ed., by de la Croix, Tansey, and Diane Kirkpatrick. San Diego, Calif.: Harcourt Brace Jovanovich, 1991; 10th ed., by Fred S. Kleiner, Christin J. Mamiya, and Tansey. Fort Worth, Tex.: Harcourt Brace, 1996; 11th ed. Stamford, Conn.: Wadsworth/Thomson, 2001; and 12th ed., by Kleiner and Mamiya. Belmont, Calif.: Wadsworth/Thomson, 2005.

Gates, Henry Louis, Jr. *Loose Canons: Notes on the Culture Wars*. New York: Oxford University Press, 1992.

Genet-Delacroix, Marie-Claude. *Art et Etat sous la IIIe République*. Paris: Publications de la Sorbonne, 1992.

Geoffroy-Schneiter, Bérénice. *Tribal Arts: Africa, Oceania, Southeast Asia*. New York: Vendome Press, 2000.

Gerson, Horst. *Rembrandt Paintings*, edited by Gary Schwartz. London: Weidenfeld and Nicolson, 1968.

Gibbs, Raymond W., Jr. *The Poetics of Mind: Figurative Thought, Language, and Understanding*. Cambridge: Cambridge University Press, 1994.

Gilbert, Dorothy B., ed. *Who's Who in American Art*. New York: R. R. Bowker Company, 1953.

Gillis, John, R., ed. *Commemorations: The Politics of National Identity*. Princeton, N.J.: Princeton University Press, 1994.

Goldman, Gobert, Stephen Papson, and Noah Kersey. *Landscapes of Capital*. A web-based book and database project. http://it.stlawu.edu/~global.

Goldstein, Carl. *Teaching Art: Academies and School from Vasari to Albers*. Cambridge: Cambridge University Press, 1996.

Gombrich, Ernst. *Ideas and Idols: Essays on Values in the History of Art*. Oxford: Phaidon, 1979.

———. *Story of Art*. 16th ed. New York: Phaidon Press, 1995.

Goncourt, Edmond, and Jules de Goncourt. *Manette Salomon*. Paris: Union Générale d'Éditions, 1979.

Goniwe, Thembinkosi. "South African Art: Institutional Control." *BLAC On-Line*, August 4, 2001. http://www.mweb.co.za.blaconline.

Gotlieb, Marc. "The Painter's Secret: Invention and Rivalry from Vasari to Balzac." *Art Bulletin* 84, no. 3 (September 2002): 469–90.

———. "The Pedagogy of Emancipation: Teachers and Students in Nineteenth-Century France." In *Memory and Oblivion: Proceedings of the XXIXth International Congress of the History of Art, held in Amsterdam, 1–7 September 1996*, edited by Adriaan Wessel Reinink and Jeroen Stumpel, 847–53. Boston: Kluwer Academic Publishers, 1999.

Green, Nicholas. "Circuits of Production, Circuits of Consumption: The Case of Mid-Nineteenth-Century French Art Dealing." *Art Journal* 48, no. 1 (spring 1989): 29–34.

Greenberg, Clement. "Avant-Garde and Kitsch." *Partisan Review* 6 (fall 1939): 34–49.

———. *The Collected Essays and Criticism*. Edited by John O'Brian. 4 vols. Chicago: University of Chicago Press, 1986–93.

———. "Modernist Painting." *Arts Yearbook* 4 (1961): 101–8.

Greenblatt, Stephen. "Resonance and Wonder." In *Exhibiting Cultures: The Poetics and Politics of Museum Display*, edited by Ivan Karp and Steven C. Lavine, 42–56. Washington, D.C.: Smithsonian Institution, 1991.

Guide to the Gordon W. Prange Magazine Collection, the University of Maryland Libraries. New York: Norman Ross, 2001.

Guilbaut, Serge. *How New York Stole the Idea of Modern Art: Abstract Expressionism, Freedom, and the Cold War*. Chicago: University of Chicago Press, 1983.

Guillory, John. "Canon." In *Critical Terms for Literary Study*, edited by Frank Lentricchia and Thomas McLaughlin, 233–49. Chicago: University of Chicago Press, 1990.

Haas, Walter. "Die deutsche Werkbundausstellung Köln 1914." *Tägliche Rundschau* 24, no. 174 (July 28, 1914): 693–94.

Harrell, Stevan, and Huang Chun-chieh, eds. *Cultural Change in Postwar Taiwan*. Boulder, Colo.: Westview Press, 1994.

Hartmann, Joan. "The National Palace Museum." *Oriental Art* 14, no. 4 (winter 1968): 305–13.

Haskell, Francis. *Rediscoveries in Art: Some Aspects of Taste, Fashion and Collecting in England and France*. Ithaca, N.Y.: Cornell University Press, 1976.

Haverkamp-Begemann, Egbert. "Rembrandt as Teacher." In *Rembrandt after Three Hundred Years: An Exhibition of Rembrandt and His Followers*, by Egbert Haverkamp-Begemann, J. Richard Judson, and Anne-Marie Logan, 21–30. Chicago: Art Institute of Chicago, 1969.

Haxthausen, Charles W., ed. *The Two Art Histories: The Museum and the University*. Clark Studies in the Visual Arts. New Haven, Conn.: Yale University Press, 2002.

Hay, John. "Toward a Disjunctive Diachronics of Chinese Art History." *Res* 40 (fall 2001): 101–11.

Hegel, G. W. F. *Aesthetics: Lectures on Art*. Translated by T. M. Knox. 2 vols. Oxford: Clarendon Press, 1975.

Heinich, Nathalie. *Du peintre à l'artiste: Artisans and académiques à l'âge classique*. Paris: Éditions de Minuit, 1993.

Herbert, Robert. "Impressionism, Originality, and Laissez-faire." In *From Millet to Léger: Essays in Social Art History*, 90–97. New Haven, Conn.: Yale University Press, 2002.

Hertz, Todd. "Darkness Looms for 'Painter of Light.'" *Christianity Today*, April 15, 2004. http://www.ChristianityToday.com.

Heyl, Hedwig. "Die Ausstellung 'Die Frau in Haus und Beruf.'" *Die Woche* 14, no. 4 (1912): 129–31.

Hirsch, Edward D. *Cultural Literacy: What Every American Needs to Know*. Boston: Houghton Mifflin, 1987.

Hochfield, Sylvia. "What Is a Real Rembrandt?" *Art News* 103, no. 2 (February 2004): 82–93.

Holly, Michael Ann, and Keith Moxey, eds. *Art History, Aesthetics, and Visual Studies*. Clark Studies in the Visual Arts. New Haven, Conn.: Yale University Press, 2002.

Holo, Selma. *Beyond the Prado: Museums and Identity in Democratic Spain*. Washington, D.C.: Smithsonian Institution Press, 1999.

Hops, Walter, and Susan Davidson. *Robert Rauschenberg: A Retrospective*. New York: Guggenheim Museum, 1998.

Horkheimer, Max. *Critical Theory: Selected Essays*. Translated by Matthew J. O'Connell and others. New York: Herder and Herder, 1972.

House, John. *Monet*. New Haven, Conn.: Yale University Press, 1986.

———. "Possibilities for a Revisionist Blockbuster: *Landscapes/Impressions of France*." In *The Two Art Histories: The Museum and the University*, Clark Studies in the Visual Arts, edited by Charles W. Haxthausen, 154–161. New Haven, Conn.: Yale University Press, 2002.

Hoving, Thomas. *Art for Dummies*. Foster City, Calif.: IDG Books Worldwide, Inc., 1999.

Howard, Michael. *Encyclopedia of Impressionism*. London: Carleton Press, 1997.

Huang, Ko-wu, ed. *When Images Speak: Visual Representation and Cultural Mapping in Modern China*. Taipei: Institute of Modern Chinese History, Academica Sinica, 2003.

Huang, Pao-yu. "Zhongshan bo wu yuan zi jian zhu" [The construction of the Zhongshan Museum]. *The National Palace Museum Quarterly* 1, no. 1 (1965): 69–96.

Hughes, Christopher. *Taiwan and Chinese Nationalism: National Identity and Status in International Society*. London: Routledge, 1997.

Ilie, C. "Discourse and Metadiscourse in Parliamentary Debates." *Journal of Language and Politics* 2, no. 1 (2003): 71–92.

Ingres, J.-A.-D. *Réponse au rapport sur l'Ecole impériale des Beaux-Arts adressé au Maréchal Vaillant*. Paris: Didier, 1863.

IRWIN, ed. *East Art Map: Contemporary Art and Eastern Europe*. London: Afterall Books, 2006.

Jacoby, Neil H. *U.S. Aid to Taiwan: A Study of Foreign Aid, Self-Help, and Development*. New York: Praeger Publishers, 1966.

Jaffee, Barbara. "Before the New Bauhaus: From Industrial Drawing to Art and Design Education in Chicago." *Design Issues* 21 (winter 2005): 41–62.

———. *Diagrammatics: Industrialism and the Modernizing of American Art*. Chicago: University of Chicago Press, forthcoming.

Jameson, Fredric. *A Singular Modernity: Essay on the Ontology of the Present*. London: Verso, 2002.

Jane Alexander Daimler Chrysler Award for South African Sculpture 2002. Ostfildern-Ruit: Hatje Cantz Verlag, 2002.

Janson, H. W. *History of Art*. 6th ed. New York: Prentice Hall, 2003.

Janson, H. W., and Anthony F. Janson. *Basic History of Art*. 6th ed. New York: Prentice Hall, 2003.

Jarzombek, Mark. "The Discourses of a Bourgeois Utopia, 1904–1908, and the Founding of the Werkbund." In *Imagining Modern German Culture, 1889–1910*, edited by Françoise Forster-Hahn, 126–45. Studies in the History of Art 53. Washington, D.C.: National Gallery of Art, 1996.

Jatho, Carl Oskar. "Werkbundgedanken III." *Christliche Freiheit* 32 (1914): 512–14.

Jayne, Horace H. F. "How Safe Are the Chinese Treasures in Formosa?" *Art News*, May 1955, 32–35, 60–61.

Jensen, Robert. "Anticipating Artistic Behavior: New Research Tools for Art Historians." *Historical Methods* 37, no. 3 (summer 2004): 137–53.

Jerome, Richard. "Not a Pretty Picture: Ruined Gallery Owners Call Painter Thomas Kinkade a Double-Dealer." *People Weekly*, September 8, 2003, 115.

Jessen, Peter. "Die Deutsche Werkbund-Ausstellung Köln 1914." Deutsche Form im Kriegsjahr: Die Ausstellung Köln 1914. *Jahrbuch des deutschen Werkbundes* 4 (1915): 1–42.

Jewell, Edward Alden. "The Anatomy of Cubism and Abstract Art." *New York Times Book Review*, June 7, 1936, 8.

———. "New Books on the Arts." *New York Times Book Review*, November 25, 1934, 21.

Johnson, J. Seward, David C. Levy, Red Grooms, and Petra ten-Doesschate Chu. *Beyond the Frame: Impressionism Revisited; The Sculptures of J. Seward Johnson, Jr.* Exhibition catalogue. Boston: Bulfinch Press, in association with the Corcoran Gallery of Art, 2003.

Johnson, Marshall. "Making Time: Historic Preservation and the Space of Nationality." *Positions: East Asia Cultures Critique* 2, no. 2 (fall 1884): 177–249.

Joosten, Joop M. *Piet Mondrian: Catalogue Raisonné of the Work of 1911–1944*. 2 vols. New York: Harry N. Abrams, 1998.

Ju, Jane C. "The Palace Museum as Representation of Culture: Exhibitions and Canons of Chinese Art History." In *When Images Speak: Visual Representation and Cultural Mapping in Modern China*, edited by Huang Ko-wu, 477–507. Taipei: Institute of Modern Chinese History, Academica Sinica, 2003.

Junghanns, Kurt. *Der Deutsche Werkbund: Sein erstes Jahrzehnt*. Berlin: Henschelverlag, 1982.

Kallgren, Joyce K., and Denis Fred Simon, eds. *Educational Exchanges: Essays on the Sino-American Experience*. Berkeley: University of California, Institute of East Asia Studies, 1987.

Kambell, Roger. *The Rape of the Masters: How Political Correctness Sabotages Art*. San Francisco: Encounter Books, 2004.

Kant, Immanuel. *Critique of Aesthetic Judgment*. Translated by J. Meredith. Oxford: Oxford University Press, 1952.

———. *Critique of Judgment*. Translated by J. H. Bernard. New York: Hafner Press, 1951.

Kantor, Sybil Gordon. *Alfred H. Barr, Jr. and the Intellectual Origins of the Museum of Modern Art*. Cambridge, Mass.: MIT Press, 2002.

Karp, Ivan, and Steven D. Lavine, eds. *Exhibiting Cultures: The Poetics and Politics of Museum Display*. Washington, D.C.: Smithsonian Institution, 1991.

Kelder, Diane. *The Great Book of French Impressionism*. New York: Abbeville, 1981.

Kessler, Harry Graf. *Harry Graf Kessler: Das Tagebuch, Dritter Band 1897–1905*. Edited by Carina Schäfer and Gabriele Biedermann. Stuttgart: Cotta, 2004.

———. "Whistler." *Kunst und Künstler* 3, no. 2 (August 1905): 445–66.

"Kinkade Art the Focal Point in New 'Music of Light' Label." *Art Business News* 27 (December 2000): 18.

Kinkade, Thomas, and Rick Barnett. *The Thomas Kinkade Story: A 20-Year Chronology of the Artist*. Boston: Bulfinch Press, 2003.

Kjellman-Chapin, Monica. "Manufacturing 'Masterpieces' for the Market: Thomas Kinkade, the Rhetoric of 'High Art.'" Paper presented at the annual conference of the College Art Association, Seattle, February 2004.

Klein, Christina. *Cold War Orientalism: Asia in the Middlebrow Imagination, 1945–1961*. Berkeley: University of California Press, 2003.

Kleiner, Fred S. *See* Gardner, Helen.

Klopfer, Paul. "Die Frau und das Kunstgewerbe." *Kunstwart* 24, no. 15 (1911): 215–18.

Koch, Hugo. "Die Deutsche Werkbund-Ausstellung Cöln 1914." *Bau-Rundschau* 11 (1914): 93–98.

Kotz, Mary Lynn. *Rauschenberg/Art and Life*. New York: Abrams, 1990.

Krahmer, Catherine. *Julius Meier-Graefe: Kunst ist nicht für Kunstgeshichte da, Briefe und Dokumente*. Göttingen: Wallstein, 2001.

———. "Meier-Graefes Weg zur Kunst." *Hofmannsthal, Jahrbuch zur europäischen Moderne* 4 (1996): 168–226.

———. "Tschudi and Meier-Graefe: Museumsmann und der Kunstschriftsteller." In *Manet bis van Gogh: Hugo von Tschudi und der Kampf um die Moderne*, edited by Johann Georg Prinz von Hohenzollern and Peter-Klaus Schuster, 371–76. Munich: Prestel, 1996.

Krauss, Rosalind E. *The Originality of the Avant-Garde and Other Modernist Myths*. Cambridge, Mass.: MIT Press, 1985.

Krichwey, Freda. "One World or None." *The Nation*, August 18, 1945, n.p.

Kris, Ernst, and Otto Kurz. *Legend, Myth, and Magic in the Image of the Artist: A Historical Experiment*. New Haven, Conn.: Yale University Press, 1979.

Kristeller, Paul Oscar. "The Modern System of the Arts: A Study in the History of Aesthetics." *Journal of the History of Ideas* 12, no. 4 (October 1951): 496–527.

Krzysztofowicz-Kozakowska, Stefania. *Sztuka Kręgu "Sztuki."* Cracow: Muzeum Narodowe, 1995.

———. *Sztuka Młodej Polski*. Cracow: Wydawnictwo Kluszczyński, 1999.

Kubler, George. *The Shape of Time: Remarks on the History of Things*. New Haven, Conn.: Yale University Press, 1962.

Kuo, Chi-sheng, ed. *Dang dai Taiwan hui hua wen xuan 1945–1990* [Writings on contemporary Taiwan painting 1945–1990]. Taipei: Xiongshi Publishing, 1991.

Kuo, Jason C. *Discovering Chinese Painting: Dialogues with American Art Historians*. Dubuque, Iowa: Kendall/Hunt Publishing Co., 2000.

———. *Innovation within Tradition: The Painting of Huang Binhong*. Williamston, Mass.: Williams College Museum of Art, 1989.

LaCapra, Dominick. *Representing the Holocaust: History, Theory, Trauma*. Ithaca, N.Y.: Cornell University Press, 1994.

Lakoff, George, and Mark Johnson. *Metaphors We Live By*. 2nd ed. Chicago: University of Chicago Press, 2003.

Lapauze, Henri. *Histoire de l'Académie de France à Rome*. 2 vols. Paris: Plon, 1924.

Laurent, Jeanne. *Arts et pouvoirs en France de 1793 à 1981: Histoire d'une démission artistique*. Saint Etienne: CIEREC, 1982.

Lewis, Beth Irwin. *Art for All: The Collision of Modern Art and the Public in Late Nineteenth-Century Germany*. Princeton, N.J.: Princeton University Press, 2003.

Li, Chu-tsing, and Thomas Lawton. *The New Chinese Landscape*. New York: American Federation of Arts, 1966.

Li, Lin-ts'an. *Guo bao fu mei zhanlan riji* [Diary about the National Treasures Exhibition in America]. Taipei: Shangwu, 1972.

Lichtwark, Alfred. *Briefe an die Kommission für die Verwaltung der Kunsthalle in Auswahl*. Edited by Gustav Pauli. Hamburg: Westermann, 1923.

Liedtke, Walter, Carolyn Logan, Nadine M. Orenstein, and Stephanie S. Dickey. *Rembrandt/Not Rembrandt in the Metropolitan Museum of Art*. Vol. 2, *Paintings, Drawings and Prints: Art-Historical Perspectives*. Exhibition catalogue. New York: Metropolitan Museum of Art, 1995.

Lippe, Aschwin. "Art Journey to Formosa." *Archives of the Chinese Art Society of America* 9 (1955): 9–19.

Liu, Lydia. *Translingual Practice: Literature, National Culture, and Translated Modernity—China, 1900–1937*. Stanford, Calif.: Stanford University Press, 1995.

Longman, Lester. "On the Uses of Art History." *Parnassus* 12 (December 1940): n.p.

Löttgen, Joseph. "Von der deutschen Werkbundausstellung in Köln: Das Haus der Frau." *Deutsche Bauhütte* 18, no. 29 (1914): 355.

L[ux], [Joseph August]. "Erziehung zur Sentimentalität." *Die Hohe Warte* 3 (1906–7): 25.

Mäcen. "Bric-à-brac in der Sezession." *Die Standarte* 49 (1907): 1497–1501.

Mainardi, Patricia. "Editor's Statement: Nineteenth-Century French Art Institutions." *Art Journal* 48, no. 1 (spring 1989): 7–8.

———. "Repetition and Novelty: Exhibitions Telling Tales." In *The Two Art Histories: The Museum and the University*, edited by Charles W. Haxthausen, 81–86. Clark Studies in the Visual Arts. New Haven, Conn.: Yale University Press, 2002.

Makgoba, Malegapuru William, ed. *African Renaissance: The New Struggle*. Cape Town: Tafelberg, 1999.

Mancall, Mark, ed. *Formosa Today*. New York: Frederick A. Praeger, 1964.

Mansfield, Elizabeth. *Art History and Its Institutions: Foundations of a Discipline*. London: Routledge, 2002.

Marrinan, Michael. "Caillebotte as Professional Painter: From Studio to the Public Eye." In *Gustave Caillebotte and the Fashioning of Identity in Impressionist Paris*, edited by Norma Broude, 21–65. New Brunswick, N.J.: Rutgers University Press, 2002.

Marquis, Alice Goldfarb. *Alfred H. Barr Jr.: Missionary for the Modern*. Chicago: Contemporary Books, 1989.

Marschall, Sabine. "The Impact of the Two Johannesburg Biennials (1995 and 1997) and the Formation of a 'New South African Art.'" *Social Dynamics* 25, no. 2 (1999): 119–37.

———. "Strategies of Accommodation: Toward an Inclusive Canon of South African Art." *Art Journal* 60, no. 1 (spring 2001): 50–60.

———. "Who Is in and Who Is Out? The Process of Re-Writing South African Art History in the 1990s." *Mot Pluriels* 12 (December 1999). http://www.arts.uwa.edu.au/MotsPluriels/MP1299sm.html.

Martin, Marilyn. *Contemporary South African Art 1985–1995 from the South African National Gallery Permanent Collection*. Cape Town: South African National Gallery, 1997.

———. "The Horn of the National Art Museum's Dilemma." In *A Decade of Democracy: South African Art 1994–2004*, edited by Emma Bedford, 54–64. Cape Town: Double Storey and Iziko Museums of Cape Town, 2004.

———. "Transforming the National Gallery." In *Grey Areas: Representation, Identity and Politics in Contemporary South African Art*, edited by Brenda Atkinson and Candice Breitz, 145–52. Johannesburg: Chalkham Hill Press, 1991.

Mather, Frank Jewett, Jr. "The New Books." *Saturday Review of Literature*, May 11, 1935, 25.

McClellan, Andrew. *Inventing the Louvre: Art, Politics, and the Origins of the Modern Museum in Eighteenth-Century Paris*. Berkeley: University of California Press, 1994.

Meier-Graefe, Julius. *Cézanne und sein Kreis*. Munich: Piper, 1918.

———. *Corot und Courbet: Ein Beitrag zur Entwicklungsgeschichte der modernen Kunst*. Leipzig: Insel, 1905.

———. *Entwickelungsgeschichte der modernen Kunst: Vergleichende Betrachtung der bildenden Künste, als Beitrag zu einer neuen Aesthetik*. 3 vols. Stuttgart: Hoffmann, 1904.

———. *Entwicklungsgeschichte der modernen Kunst: Vergleichende Betrachtung der bildenden Künste, als Beitrag zu einer neuen Aesthetik*. 2nd ed. Munich: Piper, 1914–24.

———. *Entwicklungsgeschichte der modernen Kunst*. Edited by Benno Reifenberg and Annemarie Meier-Graefe-Broch. Reprint of 3rd ed. with introduction by Reifenberg. Munich: Piper, 1966.

———. *Félix Vallotton: Biographie*. Berlin: Stargardt, 1898.

———. *Modern Art: Being a Contribution to a New System of Aesthetics*. Translated by Florence Simmonds and George W. Chrystal. London: Heinemann; and New York: Putnam's, 1908.

———. *Papers*. Deutsches Literaturarchiv, Marbach am Neckar.

Migeon, G., P. Jamot, R. Vitry, and C. Dreyfus. *La Collection Isaac de Camondo au Musée du Louvre*. Paris: Gazette des Beaux-Arts, 1914.

Miki, Akiko. "Making Invisible Relationships Visible: Jane Alexander and the Act of Sculpting." In *Jane Alexander Daimler Chrysler Award for South African Sculpture 2002*, 21–27. Ostfildern-Ruit: Hatje Cantz Verlag, 2002.

Milani, Farzaneh. *Shirin Neshat*. Milan: Charta, 2001.

Mileaf, Janine. "Body to Politics: Surrealist Exhibition of the Tribal and the Modern at the Anti-Imperialist Exhibition and the Galerie Charles Ratton." *Res* (fall 2001): 239–54.

Milmo, Cahal. "Kinkade, King of Kitsch, Coming to a Home Near You." *The Independent*, May 5, 2001, 11.

Milner, John. *The Studios of Paris: The Capital of Art in the Late Nineteenth Century*. New Haven, Conn.: Yale University Press, 1988.

Mitchell, W. J. T. *Picture Theory*. Chicago: University of Chicago Press, 1994.

———. "Ut Pictura Theoria: Abstract Painting and the Repression of Language." *Critical Inquiry* 15 (winter 1989): 347–71.

———, ed. *Landscape and Power*. Chicago: University of Chicago Press, 1994.

"Modern 'Redirections.'" *New York Times*, August 26, 1934, 6x.

Moffett, Charles S. *The New Painting: Impressionism 1874–1886*. Oxford: Phaidon, 1986.

Moffett, Kenworth. *Meier-Graefe as Art Critic*. Munich: Prestel, 1973.

Moretti, Franco. "MoMA2000: The Capitulation." *New Left Review*, 2nd ser., 4 (July-August 2000): 98–102.

Moxey, Keith. *The Practice of Persuasion: Paradox and Power in Art History*. Ithaca, N.Y.: Cornell University Press, 2001.

———. *The Practice of Theory: Poststructuralism, Cultural Politics, and Art History*. Ithaca, N.Y.: Cornell University Press, 1994.

Muller, Jeffrey M. "Rubens's Theory and Practice of the Imitation of Art." *Art Bulletin* 64, no. 2 (1982): 229–47.

Murdock, John. *The Courtauld Gallery at Somerset House*. London: Thames and Hudson, 1998.

Muthesius, Anna. "Die Ausstellung künstlerischer Frauen-Kleider im Waren-Haus Wertheim-Berlin." *Deutsche Kunst und Dekoration* 14 (1904): 441–56.

Nelson, Robert S. "The Map of Art History." *Art Bulletin* 79, no. 1 (March 1997): 28–40.

Nelson, Robert S., and Richard Shiff, eds. *Critical Terms for Art History*. 1st ed. Chicago: University of Chicago Press, 1996; 2nd ed. Chicago: University of Chicago Press, 2003.

Nettleton, Anitra. "Collections, Exhibitions and Histories: Constructing a New South African Art History." In *Africus 95*, 65–73. Johannesburg: Johannesburg Transitional Metropolitan Council, 1995.

———. "'. . . In what degree . . . (They) Are Possessed of Ornamental Taste': The History of the Writing on Black Art in South Africa." In *African Art in Southern Africa: From Tradition to Township*, edited by Anitra Nettleton and David Hammond-Tooke, 22–29. Johannesburg: Ad Donker, 1989.

Nettleton, Anitra, and Julia Charlton, eds. *Voice-Overs: Wits Writings Exploring African Artworks*. Johannesburg: University of the Witwatersrand Art Galleries, Standard Bank African Art Collection, 2004.

Nettleton, Anitra, Julia Charlton, and Fiona Rankin-Smith, eds. *Engaging Modernities: Transformations of the Commonplace*. Johannesburg: University of the Witwatersrand Art Galleries, Standard Bank African Art Collection, 2003.

Nietzsche, Friedrich. *The Birth of Tragedy*. Translated by Francis Golffing. New York: Doubleday, 1956.

Nisbett, Richard E., and Lee Ross. *Human Inference: Strategies and Shortcomings of Social Judgments*. Englewood Cliffs, N.J.: Prentice Hall, 1980.

Njami, Simon. "A Turbulent Silence." In *Jane Alexander Daimler Chrysler Award for South African Sculpture 2002*, 11–19. Ostfildern-Ruit: Hatje Cantz Verlag, 2002.

Nochlin, Linda. "Courbet's Real Allegory: Rereading *The Painter's Studio*." In *Courbet Reconsidered*, edited by Sarah Faunce and Linda Nochlin, 17–41. Brooklyn: Brooklyn Museum, 1988.

Nolte, Jacqueline. "Contemporary South African Art 1985–1995." *Third Text* 39 (summer 1997): 95–103.

Nord, Philip. *Impressionists and Politics: Art and Democracy in the Nineteenth Century*. London: Routledge, 2000.

Ntuli, Pitika. "Fragments from under a Telescope: A Response to Albie Sachs." *Third Text* 23 (summer 1993): 69–77.

———. "The Missing Link between Culture and Education: Are We Still Chasing Gods That Are Not Our Own?" In *African Renaissance: The New Struggle*, edited by Malegapuru William Makgoba, 184–99. Cape Town: Tafelberg, 1999.

Nylan, Michael. *The Five Confucian Classics*. New Haven, Conn.: Yale University Press, 2001.

O'Brian, John. *Ruthless Hedonism: The American Reception of Matisse*. Chicago: University of Chicago Press, 1999.

O'Connor, Brian, ed. *The Adorno Reader*. Oxford: Blackwell, 2000.

O'Doherty, Brian. *Inside the White Cube*. Santa Monica, Calif.: Lapis Press, 1986.

Offizieller Katalog der Deutschen Werkbund-Ausstellung Cöln 1914. 1st ed. Berlin: Rudolf Mosse, 1914; 2nd ed. Berlin: Rudolf Mosse, 1914.

Ogawa, David. "Alfred Robaut, Étienne Moreau-Nélaton, and Writing Corot." *Word and Image* 22, no. 4 (October-December 2006): 327–39.

Oppler-Legband, Else. "Das Haus der Frau auf der Werkbundausstellung." *Illustrirte Zeitung* 142, no. 3699 (1914): 18.

Ortony, Andrew, ed. *Metaphor and Thought*. 2nd ed. Cambridge: Cambridge University Press, 1993.

Owens, Craig. "The Allegorical Impulse: Towards a Theory of Postmodernism." *October* 12 (1980): 67–86.

Painting and Calligraphy of Taiwan during the Ming and Ch'ing Dynasties. Taipei: Council for Cultural Planning and Development, 1983.

Panofsky, Erwin. "Book Comment." *The Bulletin of the Museum of Modern Art* 2 (November 1934): 3.

———. *Meaning in the Visual Arts*. Woodstock, N.Y.: Overlook Press, 1974.

Paul, Barbara. *Hugo von Tschudi und die moderne französische Kunst im deutschen Kaiserreich*. Mainz: von Zabern, 1993.

Pauli, Gustav, ed. *Briefe an die Kommission für die Verwaltung der Kunsthalle in Auswahl*. 2 vols. Hamburg: Westermann, 1923.

Pearce, Susan M., ed. *Interpreting Objects and Collections*. London: Routledge, 1994.

Pearlman, Allison. "Landscapes in a Clustered World." In *Joel Feldman: Annotated Landscapes*. Exhibition catalogue, 38–46. Mt. Vernon, Ill.: Cedarhurst Center for the Arts, 2004.

Pearson, Christopher. "Repetition, Exclusion, and the Urbanism of Nostalgia: The Architecture of Thomas Kinkade." Paper presented at the annual conference of the College Art Association, Seattle, February 2004.

Perry, Gill, and Collin Cunningham, eds. *Academies, Museums, and Canons of Art*. Art and Its Histories. New Haven, Conn.: Yale University Press, in association with the Open University, 1999.

Piper, Reinhard. *Mein Leben als Verleger: Vormittag, Nachmittag*. Munich: Piper, 1964.

Pirsig, Robert. *Zen and the Art of Motorcycle Maintenance*. New York: Morrow, 1974.

Podro, Michael. *The Critical Historians of Art*. New Haven, Conn.: Yale University Press, 1982.

Pollock, Griselda. *Differencing the Canon: Feminist Desire and the Writing of Art's Histories*. London: Routledge, 1999.

———. *Vision and Difference: Femininity, Feminism, and the Histories of Art*. London: Routledge, 1988.

Prendergast, Christopher. *The Order of Mimesis: Balzac, Stendhal, Nerval, Flaubert*. Cambridge: Cambridge University Press, 1986.

Preziosi, Donald. *The Art of Art History: A Critical Anthology*. Oxford: Oxford University Press, 1998.

———. *Brain of the Earth's Body: Art Museums and the Phantasms of Modernity*. Minneapolis: University of Minnesota Press, 2003.

———. *Rethinking Art History: Meditations on a Coy Science*. New Haven, Conn.: Yale University Press, 1989.

Proceedings of the International Symposium on Chinese Painting. Taipei: National Palace Museum, 1970.

Procès verbaux de l'Académie des Beaux-Arts. Edited by Marcel Bonnaire. 2 vols. Paris: Armand Colin, 1940.

Property from the Estate of the Late James Johnson Sweeney. New York: Sotheby's Auction Catalogue for November 18, 1986.

Quatremère de Quincy. *An Essay on the Nature, the End, and the Means of Imitation in the Fine Arts*. Translated by J. C. Kent. London: Smith, Elder, 1837.

Rapport sur les ouvrages des élèves pensionnaires à l'Académie royale de France à Rome pour l'année 1825. Paris: Imprimerie Royale, 1825.

Rapport sur les ouvrages envoyés de Rome par les pensionnaires à l'Académie royale de France à Rome pour l'année 1838. Paris: Institut de France, 1838.

Read, Herbert. *Art and Industry*. New York: Harcourt, Brace, 1935.

Registre des procès-verbaux. Archives de l'Institut de France (Beaux-Arts), Paris, 2 E 6.

Rehorst, Carl. "Lage und Plan der Werkbundausstellung." *Illustrirte Zeitung* 142, no. 3699 (1914): 8–13.

Reifenberg, Benno. "Einleitung." In *Entwicklungsgeschichte der modernen Kunst*, by Julius Meier-Graefe. Vol. 1. Munich: Piper, 1966.

Rewald, John. *The History of Impressionism*. New York: Museum of Modern Art, 1946.

Rich, Daniel Catton. "The Freedom of the Brush." *Atlantic Monthly* 181 (February 1948): 47–51.

Robaut, Alfred, and Etienne Moreau-Nélaton. *L'oeuvre de Corot: Catalogue raisonné et illustré, précédé de l'histoire de Corot et de ses oeuvres*. Paris: Floury, 1905.

Robb, Marilyn. "New Chicago Outlook." *Art News* 45 (December 1947): 48.

Robinson, Walter. *Instant Art History: From Cave Art to Pop Art*. New York: Byron Preiss Visual Publications, Inc., 1995.

Roos, Jane Mayo. *Early Impressionism and the French State, 1866–1874*. New York: Cambridge University Press, 1996.

Rosenberg, Adolf. *Rembrandt, des Meisters Gemälde in 565 Abbildungen*. Klassiker der Kunst in Gesamtausgaben, 2.Bd. Stuttgart and Leipzig: Deutsche Verlagsanstalt, 1906.

———. *Rembrandt; des Meisters Gemälde in 643 Abbildungen, mit einer biographischen Einleitung*. Edited by Wilhelm Reinhold Valentiner. 3rd ed. Stuttgart, Leipzig: Deutsche Verlags-Anstalt, 1909.

Rosenberg, Jakob. *On Quality in Art: Criteria of Excellence, Past and Present*. Princeton, N.J.: Princeton University Press, 1967.

Rosenblum, Robert. Foreword to *Cubism and Abstract Art*, by Alfred H. Barr Jr. Cambridge, Mass.: Harvard University Press, 1986. First published 1936 by the Museum of Modern Art (New York).

Rosenblum, Robert, and H. W. Janson. *Art of the Nineteenth Century*. London: Thames and Hudson, 1984.

Rubin, James. *Impressionism*. London: Phaidon, 1999.

Rubin, William, ed. *"Primitivism" in 20th-Century Art: Affinity of the Tribal and the Modern*. 2 vols. New York: Museum of Modern Art, 1984.

Rugoff, Ralph, "Kinkade, Warhol, Vallance." In *Thomas Kinkade: Heaven on Earth*, edited by Jeffrey Vallance, 13–17. San Francisco: Last Gasp, 2004.

Runciman, Walter G., ed. *Max Weber: Selections in Translation*. Translated by E. Matthews. Cambridge: Cambridge University Press, 1978.

Said, Edward W. *Orientalism*. 25th anniversary ed. New York: Random House, 2003.

Salomon, Nanette. "The Art Historical Canon: Sins of Omission." In *The Art of Art History: A Critical Anthology*, edited by Donald Preziosi, 344–55. Oxford: Oxford University Press, 1998.

Sandler, Irving. *The Triumph of American Painting: A History of Abstract Expressionism*. New York: Praeger Publishers, 1970.

Sandler, Irving, and Amy Newman, eds. *Defining Modern Art: Selected Writings of Alfred H. Barr, Jr*. New York: Harry N. Abrams, 1986.

Sargent, Walter. *Instruction in Art in the United States*. Advance sheets from Biennial Survey of Education in the United States, 1916–1918, 29–30. Washington, D.C.: Government Printing Office, 1919.

Sarna, Nahum M., Roger T. Beckwith, and Andrie B. du Toit. "Canon." In *The Oxford Companion to the Bible*, edited by Bruce M. Metzger and Michael D. Coogan, 98–104. New York: Oxford University Press, 1993.

Schäfer, Wilhelm. "Die Baukunst der Deutschen Werkbund-Ausstellung in Köln." *Die Rheinlande* 14, nos. 8–9 (1914): 263–302.

Schapiro, Meyer. *Modern Art, 19th and 20th Centuries: Selected Papers*. New York: George Braziller, 1982.

Scheffler, Karl. *Die Frau und die Kunst*. Berlin: J. Bard, 1908.

———. "Gute und schlechte Arbeiten im Schnellbahngewerbe." *Der Verkehr: Jahrbuch des deutschen Werkbundes* 3 (1914): 42–47.

———. "Meier-Graefe." *Die Zukunft* 49 (1904): 324–30.

Schneider, Andrea Kupfer. *Creating the Musée d'Orsay: The Politics of Culture in France*. University Park, Penn.: Pennsylvania State University Press, 1998.

Schneider-Schönfeld, Irma. "Eine moderne Kunstgewerblerin." *Die Welt der Frau* 25, no. 4 (1906): 51–54.

Schulz-Weidner, Willy. "Shamanism." In *Encyclopedia of World Art*, 13:1–6. New York: McGraw-Hill, 1967.

Schütze, E. W. *A Selection of Works by Twentieth-Century Artists*. Chicago: Renaissance Society of the University of Chicago, 1934.

Schwartz, Frederic J. *The Werkbund: Design Theory and Mass Culture before the First World War*. New Haven, Conn.: Yale University Press, 1996.

Schwartz, Gary. "Connoisseurship: The Penalty of Ahistoricism." *Artibus et Historiae, an Art Anthology* 9, no. 18 (1988): 201–6.

———. The Schwartzlist, February 2, 2003, and listserv e-mail exchange, March 13–21, 2003. *www.garyschwartzarthistorian.nl*.

Sheffy, Rakefet. "The Concept of Canonicity in Polysystem Theory." *Poetics Today* 11, no. 3 (fall 1990): 511–22.

Shiff, Richard. *Cézanne and the End of Impressionism: A Study in the Theory, Technique, and Critical Evaluation of Modern Art*. Reprint ed. Chicago: University of Chicago Press, 1996.

———. "The Original, the Imitation, and the Spontaneous Classic: Theory and Painting in Nineteenth-Century France." *Yale French Studies* 66 (1984): 27–54.

Shiner, Larry. *The Invention of Art: A Cultural History*. Chicago: University of Chicago Press, 2001.

Simpson, J. A., and E. S. C. Weiner. *The Complete Oxford English Dictionary*. 2nd ed. 20 vols. Oxford: Clarendon Press, 1989.

Singerman, Howard. *Art Subjects: Making Artists in the American University*. Berkeley: University of California Press, 1999.

Sitterson, Joseph C., Jr. "Canon." In *The New Princeton Encyclopedia of Poetry and Poetics*, edited by Alex Preminger and T. V. F. Brogan, 166–67. Princeton, N.J.: Princeton University Press, 1993.

Smith, Barbara Herrnstein. "Contingencies of Value." In *Canons*, edited by Robert von Hallberg, 5–39. Chicago: University of Chicago Press, 1984.

Smith, Terry. *The Architecture of Aftermath*. Chicago: University of Chicago Press, 2006.

———. "Contemporary Art and Contemporaneity." *Critical Inquiry* 32, no. 4 (summer 2006): 681–707.

———. *What Is Contemporary Art?* Chicago: University of Chicago Press, forthcoming.

Smith, Terry, Okwui Enwezor, and Nancy Condee, eds. *Antinomies of Art and Culture: Modernity, Postmodernity and Contemporaneity*. Durham, N.C.: Duke University Press, forthcoming.

Song, Chao-lin, ed. *Gugong kua shiji da shi lu yao* [Major events of the Palace Museum across the centuries]. Taipei: National Palace Museum, 2000.

Special issue. *Program Bulletin* (Asia Foundation) 40 (August 1966).

Speyer, A. James. "Art News from Chicago." *Art News* 54 (September 1955), 11.

Spivak, Gayatri Chakravorty. "Can the Subaltern Speak?" In *The Post-Colonial Studies Reader*, edited by Bill Ashcroft, Gareth Griffiths, and Helen Tiffin, 24–28. London: Routledge, 1995.

Stafford, Barbara Maria. *Visual Analogy: Consciousness as the Art of Connecting*. Cambridge: MIT Press, 1999.

Stahl, Fritz. "Der Werkbund, seine Idee und seine Ausstellung." *Berliner Tageblatt* 306 (June 19, 1914): [unpaged].

Stanisławski, Jan, Teodor Axentowicz, and Józef Mehoffer. "Sprawozdanie Wydziału Towarzystwa Artystów Polskich "Sztuka" za rok 1898." *Tygodnik Ilustrowany* 19 (1899): 379.

Stankiewicz, Mary Ann. "Virtue and Good Manners: Toward a History of Art History Instruction." In *The Early Years of Art History in the United States: Notes and Essays on Departments, Teaching, and Scholars*, edited by Craig Hugh Smyth and Peter M. Lukehart, 183–93. Princeton, N.J.: Princeton University, Department of Art and Archeology, 1993.

Steinberg, Leo. *Encounters with Rauschenberg*. Chicago: University of Chicago Press, 2000.

Steiner, Wendy. *Venus in Exile: The Rejection of Beauty in Twentieth-Century Art*. Chicago: University of Chicago Press, 2001.

Stokstad, Marilyn, Margaret Oppenheimer, and Stephen Addis. *Art: A Brief History*. New York: Prentice Hall, 2003.

Stokstad, Marilyn, Marion Spears Grayson, Stephen Addis, Bradford R. Collins, Chu-tsing Li, Marylin M. Rhie, and Christopher D. Roy. *Art History*. Upper Saddle River, N.J.: Prentice Hall, 1995; Rev. 2nd ed., by Marilyn Stokstad, David Cateforis, Stephen Addiss, Chu-tsing Li, Marylin M. Rhie, and Christopher D. Roy. New York: Prentice Hall, 2004.

Stratigakos, Despina. "Architects in Skirts: The Public Image of Women Architects in Wilhelmine Germany." *Journal of Architectural Education* 55, no. 2 (2001): 90–100.

———. "Skirts and Scaffolding: Women Architects, Gender, and Design in Wilhelmine Germany." PhD diss., Bryn Mawr College, 1999. Ann Arbor, Mich.: UMI, 1999.

———. "Women and the Werkbund: Gender Politics and German Design Reform, 1907–14." *Journal of the Society of Architectural Historians* 62, no. 4 (2003): 490–511.

Strickland, Carol. *The Annotated Mona Lisa: A Crash Course in Art History from Prehistoric to Post-Modern*. Kansas City: Andrews and McNeel, 1992.

Summers, David. "Real Spaces: World Art History and the Rise of Western Modernism." *The Art Bulletin* 86, no. 2 (2004): 373–80.

Sweeney, James Johnson. *African Negro Art*. New York: Museum of Modern Art, 1935.

———. "African Negro Art." *The New Republic* 82 (April 10, 1935): 244.

———. "A Note on Super-Realist Painting." *The Arts* 16 (May 1930): 611–13.

———. "Painting." In *Museum of Living Art: A. E. Gallatin Collection*. New York: George Grady Press, 1936.

———. *Plastic Redirections in 20th-Century Painting*. Chicago: University of Chicago Press, 1934.

Symposium on the Chinese Art Treasures Exhibition, October 4, 1962. New York: Asia House Gallery, 1962.

Szpunar, Karl K., E. Glenn Schellenberg, and Patricia Plinar. "Liking and Memory for Musical Stimuli as a Function of Exposure." *Journal of Experimental Psychology: Learning, Memory, and Cognition* 30 (2004): 370–81.

"Sztuka" 1897–1922. Cracow: Drukarnia Narodowa, 1922.

Taylor, Brandon. *Random Order: Robert Rauschenberg and the Neo-Avant-Garde*. Cambridge, Mass.: MIT Press, 2003.

Taylor, Charles. *Sources of the Self: The Making of the Modern Identity*. Cambridge, Mass.: Harvard University Press, 1989.

Testelin, Henri. *Mémoires pour servir à l'histoire de l'Académie royale de peinture et de sculpture depuis 1648 jusqu'en 1664*. Edited by Anatole de Montaiglon. 2 vols. Paris: P. Jannet, 1853.

Thomas Kinkade Company™ 2004 Limited Edition Comprehensive Catalog. thomaskinkade toronto.com/collection/gifts/giftitems/books.php.

Thomas Kinkade, Painter of Light™: Thomas Kinkade Company 2003 Comprehensive Catalog. http://www.thomaskinkade.com.

Thomson, Ellen Mazur. "Thorstein Veblen at the University of Chicago and the Socialization of Aesthetics." *Design Issues* 15, no. 1 (spring 1999): 3–15.

Thoré-Bürger. *Salons de T. Thoré 1844, 1845, 1846, 1847, 1848*. Paris: Librairie internationale, 1868.

Thuillier, Jacques. "Académie et classicisme en France: Les débuts de l'Académie royale de peinture et de sculpture (1648–1663)." In *Il Mito del Classicismo nel Seicento*, edited by Stefano Bottari, 181–209. Messina: Casa Editrice G. d'Anna, 1964.

Tiedemann, Rolf, ed. *Theodor W. Adorno: Can One Live After Auschwitz?* Stanford, Calif.: Stanford University Press, 2003.

Tinterow, Gary. "Blockbuster, Art History, and the Public: The Case of *Origins of Impressionism*." In *The Two Art Histories: The Museum and the University*, edited by Charles W. Haxthausen, 143–53. Clark Studies in the Visual Arts. New Haven, Conn.: Yale University Press, 2002.

Tomkins, Calvin. *Off the Wall: Robert Rauschenberg and the Art World of Our Time*. New York: Penguin Books, 1981.

Trier, Marilyn Robb. "New Chicago Outlook." *Art News* 45 (December 1947): 48.

Troy, Nancy. *Modernism and the Decorative Arts in France: Art Nouveau to Le Corbusier*. New Haven, Conn.: Yale University Press, 1991.

Tu, Cheng-sheng. "A Message from the Director." *The National Palace Museum Newsletter* 33, no. 1 (January-March, 2001).

Tucker, Nancy B. *Taiwan, Hong Kong, and the United States, 1945–1992: Uncertain Friendships*. New York: Twayne Publishers, 1994.

U.S. Department of State. Bureau of Educational and Cultural Affairs. *Educational and Cultural Diplomacy*. Washington, D.C.: U.S. Government Printing Office, 1960.

Vaisse, Pierre. *La Troisième République et les peintres*. Paris: Flammarion, 1995.

Valentiner, Wilhelm Reinhold. *Rembrandt; widergefundene gemälde (1910–1920) in 120 Abbildungen*. Klassiker der Kunst in Gesamtausgaben; 27.bd. Stuttgart, Berlin: Deutsche verlags-anstalt, 1921.

Vallance, Jeffrey, ed. *Thomas Kinkade: Heaven on Earth*. San Francisco: Last Gasp, 2004.

Vande Kopple, William J. "Refining and Applying Views of Metadiscourse." Paper presented at the 48th Annual Meeting of the Conference on College Composition and Communication, Phoenix, Ariz., March 1997. ERIC Document Reproduction Service No. ED411529.

van de Wetering, Ernst. "The Invisible Rembrandt: The Results of Technical and Scientific Examinations." In *Rembrandt: The Master and His Workshop—Paintings*, by Christopher Brown, Jan Kelch, and Pieter van Thiel. Exhibition catalogue, 90–105. New Haven, Conn.: Yale University Press in association with National Gallery Publications, 1991.

———. "Painting Materials and Working Methods." In *A Corpus of Rembrandt Paintings*, by Josua Bruyn, Bob Haak, Simon H. Levie, Pieter J.J. van Thiel, and Ernst van der Wetering. 1:11–33. Stichting Foundation Rembrandt Research Project. Boston: M. Nijhoff Publishers, 1982–.

———. "Problems of Apprenticeship and Studio Collaboration." In *A Corpus of Rembrandt Paintings*, by Josua Bruyn, Bob Haak, Simon H. Levie, Pieter J.J. van Thiel, and Ernst van der Wetering. 2:45–90. Stichting Foundation Rembrandt Research Project. Boston: M. Nijhoff Publishers, 1982–.

———. *Rembrandt, the Painter at Work*. Berkeley: University of California Press, 2000.

———. "Rembrandt's Manner: Technique in the Service of Illusion." In *Rembrandt: The Master and His Workshop—Paintings*, by Christopher Brown, Jan Kelch, and Pieter van Thiel. Exhibition catalogue, 12–39. New Haven, Conn.: Yale University Press in association with National Gallery Publications, 1991.

Varnedoe, Kirk. *Gustave Caillebotte*. New Haven, Conn.: Yale University Press, 1987.

———. *Modern Contemporary: Art at MOMA since 1980*. New York: Museum of Modern Art, 2000.

Vasari, Giorgio. *The Lives of the Artists*. Translated by Julia Conaway Bondanella and Peter Bondanella. Oxford: Oxford University Press, 1998. First published 1550 as *Lives of the Most Excellent Painters, Sculptors and Architects*.

Vitet, Louis. *Académie royale de peinture et de sculpture: Etude historique*. Paris: Calman Lévy, 1880.

———. "Les arts du dessin en France." *Revue des Deux-Mondes*, November 1, 1864, 74–107.

Vitet, Louis, and Eugène Viollet-le-Duc. *Débats et Polémiques: A propos de l'ensiegnement des arts du dessin*. Paris: EBA, 1984.

von Hallberg, Robert, ed. *Canons*. Chicago: University of Chicago Press, 1984.

von Sonnenburg, Hubert. *Rembrandt/Not Rembrandt in the Metropolitan Museum of Art*. Vol. 1, *Paintings: Problems and Issues*. New York: Metropolitan Museum of Art, 1995.

Voyiya, Vuyile C., and Julie L. McGee, producers. *The Luggage Is Still Labeled: Blackness in South African Art*. DVD 2003.

Wang, Chen-ho. *Rose, Rose I Love You*. Translated by Howard Goldblatt. New York: Columbia University Press, 1998.

Wang, Cheng-hua. "Chen xian 'zhongguo': Wan qing can yu 1904 nian meiguo sheng lu yi wan guo bo lan hui zi yen jiu" [Representing "China": A study of late Qing participation in the 1904 St. Louis World Exposition]. In *When Images Speak: Visual Representation and Cultural Mapping in Modern China*, edited by Huang Ko-wu, 421–75. Taipei: Institute of Modern Chinese History, Academica Sinica, 2003.

Ward, Martha. *Pissarro, Neo-Impressionism, and the Spaces of the Avant-Garde*. Chicago: University of Chicago Press, 1996.

Warlich, Else. "Der Deutsche Werkbund und die Frau." *Das Werk* (1909): 103–4, 109–10.

Waters, Christina. "Doubting Thomas." *Metro Weekly* (San José), September 6–12, 2001.

———."Selling the Painter of Light." *Metro Santa Cruz*, October 16, 2001. http://www.alternet.org/story/11730/.

wa Thiong'o, Ngugi. "Recovering Our Memory: South Africa and the Black Imagination." Fourth Annual Steve Biko Lecture, University of Cape Town, Cape Town, South Africa, September 12, 2003, 7–8. http://www.sbf.org.za/lectures.php?lecture=2003.

Weber, Berndt. "Der Werkbund in Köln: Von Bauten und Ausstellungssorgen." *Hamburger Nachrichten* 320 (July 11, 1914): [unpaged].

Webster's New World Dictionary of the American Language. College ed. New York: World Publishing Co., 1959.

Weintraub, Cynthia. *In the Making: Creative Options for Contemporary Art*. New York: Distributed Art Publishers, Inc., 2003.

Wellington, Hubert, ed. *The Journal of Eugène Delacroix*. Translated by Lucy Norton. London: Phaidon, 1995.

Westheim, Paul. "Die Frauenausstellung." *Kunst und Handwerk* 9 (1912): 268–75.

White, Harrison C., and Cynthia A. White. *Canvases and Careers: Institutional Change in the French Painting World*. 2nd ed. Chicago: University of Chicago Press, 1993.

White, Hayden. *The Content of the Form: Narrative Discourse and Historical Representation*. Baltimore: Johns Hopkins University Press, 1987.

———. "The Fiction of Factual Representation." In *Grasping the World: The Idea of the Museum*, edited by Donald Preziosi and Claire Farago, 22–34. Burlington, Vt.: Ashgate, 2004.

Widmer, Karl. "Die Gebildete Frau im Kunstgewerbehandel." *Deutsche Kunst und Dekoration* 25 (1909–10): 63–69.

Wigley, Mark. *White Walls, Designer Dresses: The Fashioning of Modern Architecture*. Cambridge, Mass.: MIT Press, 1995.

Wille, Fia. "Das Schaufenster als Erzieher." *Die Welt der Frau* 26, no. 16 (1907): 251–53.

Williams, Raymond. *Keywords: A Vocabulary of Culture and Society*. Rev. ed. New York: Oxford University Press, 1983.

Wirz, Wilhelm. "Frau und Qualität." *Wohlfahrt und Wirtschaft* 1, no. 4 (1914): 196–200.

Wolff, Irma. "Die Frau als Konsumentin." *Archiv für Sozialwissenschaft und Sozialpolitik* 34, no. 3 (1912): 893–904.

———. "Die Frau als Kunstgewerblerin." *Neue Bahnen* 49, no. 7 (1914): 51–54.

Wolff, Janet. *The Social Production of Art*. New York: New York University Press, 1981.

Wong, Aida Yuen. *Parting the Mists: Discovering Japan and the Rise of National-style Painting in Modern China*. Honolulu: University of Hawaii Press, 2006.

Wood, Christoper. "Introduction." In *The Vienna School Reader. Politics and Art Historical Method in the 1930s*, edited by Christopher Wood, 9–81. New York: Zone Books, 2000.

Woodfield, Richard, ed. *Framing Formalism: Riegel's Work*. Critical Voices in Art, Theory and Culture, edited by Saul Ostrow. Amsterdam: G+B Arts International, 2001.

Woodford, Susan. *Looking at Pictures*. Cambridge: Cambridge University Press, 1983.

Wypijewski, JoAnn, ed. *Painting by Numbers: Komar and Melamid's Scientific Guide to Art*. Berkeley: University of California Press, 1999.

Zajonc, Robert. "Attitudinal Effects of Mere Exposure." *Journal of Personality and Social Psychology* 9 (1968): 1–27.

Zimmermann, Michael, ed. *The Art Historian: National Traditions and Institutional Practices*. Clark Studies in the Visual Arts. New Haven, Conn.: Yale University Press, 2003.

Zulaika, Joseba. *Crónica de una sedducción: El museo Guggenheim Bilbao*. Madrid: Edítorial Nevea, 1997.

CONTRIBUTORS

JENNY ANGER is an associate professor of art at Grinnell College, where she teaches twentieth-century European art history and theory. She is the author of *Paul Klee and the Decorative in Modern Art* (Cambridge University Press, 2004). Her research focuses on modernism and its legacy in contemporary art, especially in terms of gender.

MARCIA BRENNAN is an associate professor of art history at Rice University. She is the author of *Painting Gender, Constructing Theory: The Alfred Stieglitz Circle and American Formalist Aesthetics* (MIT Press, 2001), and *Modernism's Masculine Subjects: Matisse, the New York School, and Post Painterly Abstraction* (MIT Press, 2004).

ANNA BRZYSKI is an assistant professor of art history at the University of Kentucky. Her research focuses on East-Central Europe, in particular, Poland, and the impact of nationalism and historicism on reception and practice of art in the region. Her work has appeared in *Art Criticism*; *Centropa*; *19th Century Art Worldwide*; *Art and National Identity at the Turn of the Century*, edited by Michelle Facos and Sharon Hirsh (Cambridge University Press, 2003); and *Local Strategies-International Ambitions. Modern Art and Central Europe, 1918–1968*, edited by Vojtech Lahoda (Prague: Artefactum, 2006). In 2001, she co-edited the issue "Modernism and Nationalism, Postmodernism and Postnationalism?" of the journal *Centropa* and is currently co-editing another *Centropa* issue, "Parallel Narratives," which explores parallel and alternative narrations of art history in Central Europe.

JAMES CUTTING is a professor of psychology at Cornell University, the author of *Impressionism and Its Canon* (University Press of America, 2006), the editor of *Psychological Science*, and the author of more than one hundred scientific articles, mostly in the field of vision and the psychology of perception. Among other things, he is interested in the relations among painting, photographs, cinema, and the natural world around us.

PAUL DURO is a professor in and the chair of the Department of Art and Art History at the University of Rochester. He is the author of *The Academy and the Limits of Painting in Seventeenth-Century France* (Cambridge University Press, 1997) and co-editor of *The*

Rhetoric of the Frame: Essays on the Boundaries of the Artwork (Cambridge University Press, 1996).

JAMES ELKINS is a professor in the Department of Visual and Critical Studies and the Department of Art History, Theory, and Criticism at the School of the Art Institute of Chicago. He is the author of numerous books and articles, including *Our Beautiful, Dry, and Distant Texts: Art History as Writing* (Penn State University Press, 1997), *The Domain of Images* (Cornell University Press, 1999), *Stories of Art* (Routledge, 2002), *Visual Studies: A Skeptical Introduction* (Routledge, 2003), *Art History versus Aesthetics* (Routledge, 2005), *Master Narratives and Their Discontents* (Routledge, 2005), and *Is Art History Global?* (Routledge, 2006).

BARBARA JAFFEE is an associate professor of art history at Northern Illinois University, DeKalb. Her work on American modernism and design has appeared in *Art Criticism, Design Issues, Art Journal, Art in Chicago: 1945–1995*, an exhibition catalogue edited by Lynne Warren (Chicago Museum of Contemporary Art, 1996), and *REAL TEXT: Reflections on the Periphery of the Subject*, an anthology edited by G. Schöllhammer and Christian Kravagna (Verlag Ritter Klagenfurt, 1993). Her essay on Helen Gardner is part of a larger project exploring the use of diagramming as a tool of art pedagogy and the popularizing of modernist aesthetics in the United States in the early twentieth century.

ROBERT JENSEN is an associate professor of art history at the University of Kentucky and the author of *Marketing Modernism in Fin-de-Siècle Europe* (Princeton University Press, 1994) and other studies on the economics of art. He has also published on photography, most recently, "The Photographic Grotesque" in *Exposure* (spring 2003). His current work concerns the study of artistic behavior in response to changing markets. This includes the essay "Anticipating Artistic Behavior: New Research Tools for Art Historians" in *Historical Methods* (fall 2004).

JANE C. JU is an associate professor in the Department of History at the National Chengchi University in Taipei, Taiwan. She spent 2003–4 as a visiting fellow in the East Asian Studies Department of Princeton University, where she worked on a project dealing with museums as cultural representation.

MONICA KJELLMAN-CHAPIN is an assistant professor of art history at Emporia State University. Her research and teaching interests focus on Western European and American art of the late nineteenth century and the early twentieth. She is especially interested in the border crossings between high and low forms of visual culture, art history and kitsch, strategies of self-promotion and self-canonization, and the ways in which the art historical discipline operates. She has published on J. M. Whistler's reliance on Ingres (in the February 2004 issue of *Art History*). Recent projects include a consideration of the discursive and tactical intersections between collage and pastiche, and she is currently working on a book-length manuscript about Whistler's female nudes.

JULIE L. MCGEE is a visiting assistant professor of art history and Africana studies at Bowdoin College in Brunswick, Maine. Her primary fields of research and teaching include modern and contemporary African, African American, and African diaspora art. Recent relevant publications include the documentary film *The Luggage Is Still Labeled: Blackness in South African Art*, co-produced with Vuyile C. Voyiya, and an essay on institutional transformation with regard to the South African National Gallery, in *New Museum Theory and Practice*, edited by Janet Marstine (Blackwell Press, 2005).

TERRY SMITH is the Andrew W. Mellon Professor of Contemporary Art History and Theory in the Department of the History of Art and Architecture at the University of Pittsburgh. He is the author of a number of books, notably *Making the Modern: Industry, Art and Design in America* (University of Chicago Press, 1993) and *Transformations in Australian Art*, vol. 1, *The Nineteenth Century: Landscape, Colony and Nation*, and vol. 2, *The Twentieth Century: Modernism and Aboriginality* (Craftsman House, Sydney, 2002). He is the editor of many others, including *In Visible Touch: Modernism and Masculinity* (Power Publications and the University of Chicago Press, 1997), *First People, Second Chance: The Humanities and Aboriginal Australia* (Australian Academy of the Humanities, 1999), *Impossible Presence: Surface and Screen in the Photogenic Era* (Power Publications and the University of Chicago Press, 2001), and with Paul Patton, *Jacques Derrida, Deconstruction Engaged: The Sydney Seminars* (Power Publications, 2001). His recent projects include *The Architecture of Aftermath* (University of Chicago Press, 2006) and the anthology *Antinomies of Art and Culture: Modernity, Postmodernity, and Contemporaneity* (Duke University Press, forthcoming), edited with Okwui Entwezor and Nancy Condee. He was a member of the Art & Language Group, a founder of Union Media Services, a founding director of the Museum of Contemporary Art in Sydney, and he is currently a board member of the Warhol Museum in Pittsburgh.

LINDA STONE-FERRIER is a professor in and the chair of the History of Art Department at the University of Kansas. Her research focuses on socioeconomic aspects of seventeenth-century Dutch art, in particular, genre, landscapes, and the art of Rembrandt and Gabriel Metsu. She is the author of *Images of Textiles: The Weave of Seventeenth-Century Dutch Art and Society* (UMI Research Press Art, 1985). Her work has appeared in the journals *Art Bulletin*, *Art History*, and *Artibus et Historiae*, as well as the books *Saints, Sinners and Sisters: Women and the Pictorial Arts of Northern Europe in Medieval and Early Modern Culture*, edited by Alison G. Stewart and Jane L. Carroll (Ashgate Publishing Ltd., 2003), and *The Public and the Private in Dutch Culture of the Golden Age*, edited by Arthur K. Wheelock Jr. and Adele Seeff (University of Delaware Press, 2000).

DESPINA STRATIGAKOS is a lecturer on women's studies at Harvard University and an architectural historian with an overarching interest in gender and modernity in European cities. Her essays have been published in journals and edited volumes, most recently in the *Journal of the Society of Architectural Historians* and the *Journal of Architectural Education*, as well as in *Embodied Utopias: Gender, Social Change, and the Modern Metropolis*, edited by Amy L. Bingaman et al. (Routledge, 2002), and *Negotiating Domesticity: Spatial Productions of Gender in Modern Architecture*, edited by Hilde Heynen and Gülsüm Baydar (Routledge, 2005). Her book, *A Women's Berlin* (University of Minnesota Press, forthcoming), investigates the conception of a city built by and for women, a place that was imagined and partially realized in the years before the First World War.

INDEX